HARD EVIDENCE
CASE STUDIES
IN FORENSIC ANTHROPOLOGY

EDITED BY

DAWNIE WOLFE STEADMAN
BINGHAMTON UNIVERSITY, STATE UNIVERSITY OF NEW YORK

UPPER SADDLE RIVER, NEW JERSEY 07458

Library of Congress Cataloging-in-Publication Data

Hard evidence: case studies in forensic anthropology/edited by Dawnie Wolfe Steadman.
    p. cm.
Includes bibliographical references.
ISBN 0-13-030567-7
    1. Forensic anthropology—Case studies.   2. Forensic osteology—Case studies.
I. Steadman, Dawnie Wolfe.

GN69.8 .H37 2003
599.9—dc21   2002012660

AVP, Publisher: Nancy Roberts
Editorial assistant: Lee Peterson
Senior marketing manager: Amy Speckman
Marketing assistant: Anne Marie Fritzky
Editorial/production supervision: Kari Callaghan Mazzola
Prepress and manufacturing buyer: Ben Smith
Electronic page makeup: Kari Callaghan Mazzola and John P. Mazzola
Interior design: John P. Mazzola
Cover director: Jayne Conte
Cover design: Kiwi Design
Cover photo: Peter Dazeley/Getty Images, Inc.

This book was set in 10/12 Palatino by Big Sky Composition
and was printed and bound by RR Donnelley & Sons Company.
The cover was printed by Phoenix Color Corp.

© 2003 by Pearson Education, Inc.
Upper Saddle River, New Jersey 07458

Printed in the United States of America
10 9 8 7 6 5 4 3 2

ISBN 0-13-030567-7

Pearson Education LTD., London
Pearson Education Australia PTY, Limited, Sydney
Pearson Education Singapore, Pte. Ltd
Pearson Education North Asia Ltd, Hong Kong
Pearson Education Canada, Ltd., Toronto
Pearson Educación de Mexico, S.A. de C.V.
Pearson Education—Japan, Tokyo
Pearson Education Malaysia, Pte. Ltd
Pearson Education, Upper Saddle River, New Jersey

To my grandparents, who have taught me
the value of education,
the merit of service,
and the importance of family

CONTENTS

PREFACE

Nearly twenty years ago, Ted Rathbun and Jane Buikstra published a seminal book, *Human Identification: Case Studies in Forensic Anthropology*, with the notion that forensic anthropologists learn best by sharing case studies. The volume was oriented to their professional colleagues, as the field was little known within the general population. However, case studies made the science easily understandable and the book was therefore attractive to college students and lay people alike. Over the past decade, this accessibility, as well as tremendous media interest in the forensic sciences, has catapulted forensic anthropology out of relative obscurity. In addition to prime time programming, cable television currently offers a daily dose of "forensic detective" programs that frequently highlight forensic anthropology. The popularity of fictional books—including novels by Patricia Cornwell, who often features anthropology, and novels by Kathleen Reichs, a practicing forensic anthropologist whose female protagonist shares her chosen career path—has further thrust the discipline into the public light. Eminent professional forensic anthropologists have also written tomes about their most interesting cases in a manner accessible to scientists and nonscientists alike. The net result is that forensic anthropology is now much more visible on the popular landscape and, most important, in college curricula.

Though two decades have passed since *Human Identification* was published, case studies remain at the core of information dissemination among forensic scientists. Not only do case studies demonstrate how formal procedures are implemented and followed, but they also give authors the opportunity to discuss technical and interpretive difficulties they have encountered in the investigative process. The purpose of *Hard Evidence: Case Studies in Forensic Anthropology* is to supplement formal forensic anthropology and osteology texts and manuals with high-quality case studies that demonstrate practical experiences and innovations in the field. While textbooks provide specific methodological and theoretical information imperative to a basic understanding of the subject matter, there is often little opportunity to present a satisfactory number of pertinent case studies that illustrate important points. This book will give introductory and advanced biological anthropology students a strong sense of the scope of forensic anthropological casework in the United States, the professional and ethical responsibilities inherent in forensics, the scientific rigor required, and the multidisciplinary nature of forensic science.

Personal identification is the cornerstone of forensic anthropology, and the importance of case reports that include appropriate, well-documented identification methods cannot be overemphasized. However, numerous methodological and technical advances have allowed forensic anthropologists to expand their knowledge beyond traditional roles to make a greater contribution to the forensic sciences. Many forensic anthropologists are well-versed in archaeology, histology, radiology, biomechanics, or odontology, while others have gained significant experience in medicolegal and international policy and procedures. Consequently, forensic anthropologists are now regular members of local search and recovery teams, federal mass disaster response units, and international human rights missions. Forensic anthropologists also facilitate teamwork with other forensic specialists, particularly forensic entomologists, geologists, and botanists, and have strengthened their time-honored partnership with forensic pathologists. Thus, the cases herein capture the spirit of traditional forensic anthropology cases and highlight some of the new skills and opportunities that have helped steer the discipline in new directions.

This book is divided into sections that demonstrate the broad scope of modern forensic anthropology as well as its scientific foundations. The five sections cover personal identification and legal considerations, search and recovery, interpretation of trauma and taphonomy, analytical techniques, and applications of forensic anthropology. Each section starts with an overview that places the case studies within a larger context of forensic science, emphasizes multidisciplinary relationships, and introduces new concepts or technologies. The chapters in this book are independent of each other and are written in a nontechnical prose suitable for undergraduate students. However, it is assumed that the reader has, or will be gaining, a basic background in human skeletal biology. While several authors take a narrative approach and follow a case from recovery through final resolution, others display the technical writing, sophisticated anatomical terminology, and level of quantification and detail required for professional forensic reports and publications. Several chapters underscore the importance of court testimony and caution that the most effective forensic techniques mean little if the scientific components cannot be communicated proficiently to a judge and jury.

All of us who have contributed to this text hope that students will not only find the cases scientifically informative and interesting, but also will gain insight into the human aspect of forensic anthropology. Forensic anthropology provides an important service to the community. It is founded upon the desire to help the living by identifying the remains of loved ones while giving the dead an opportunity to tell their story. To understand the dead, we must be able to interpret the hard evidence they left behind—the history of their life and death recorded in the bones.

ACKNOWLEDGMENTS

Editing this book has been a distinct pleasure because it has allowed me to work with distinguished individuals who maintain diverse interests in the forensic sciences. I want to thank all of the contributors to this volume for their dedication, perseverance, and professionalism.

A number of people have assisted me in writing portions of this book. Robert Mann offered information concerning the history and operations of the Central Identification Laboratory, Hawaii (CILHI). Thomas Anderson and Thomas H. Miller of the Iowa State Attorney General's Office imparted considerable knowledge about the rules of evidence and generously contributed to the preparation of Section I. Lyle Konigsberg assisted me in preparing the FORDISC discussion in Chapter 1. Paul Sledzik provided background information for DMORT, presented in Section V. Terry Melton and Anne Stone gave important insight into the forensic applications of nuclear and mitochondrial DNA in Section IV. Ann Webster Bunch and Norman Sauer offered suggestions on early drafts of this book. I am grateful to Carol Raemsch, Jane Gerber, and Jennifer Bauder for reading drafts and offering constructive feedback in a very limited amount of time. John Dorn provided the excellent anatomical drawings in Chapter 1 and Section IV, and Gary Steadman produced photographs for Chapter 1 and Section II.

Three distinguished forensic anthropologists reviewed the manuscript and provided insightful comments that greatly improved the quality of the text: John A. Williams, University of North Dakota; Richard L. Jantz, University of Tennessee; and Jane E. Buikstra, University of New Mexico. I also want to thank my graduate and undergraduate students who constantly prodded me to finish the book (and give them free copies) before they graduated. I am sure it is not easy to work with a novice textbook editor, but Nancy Roberts at Prentice Hall had the patience and expertise to make the process relatively painless for me. The events of September 11 created a serious obstacle to completing the book, as several authors and I spent many weeks and months involved in the identification of the victims. Nancy understood my priorities and worked with me to pull it all together in a timely manner.

I would like to acknowledge the hard work of all of the men and women in the Iowa forensic community, including the Division of Criminal Investigation, Polk County Medical Examiner's Office, the Iowa Office of the State Medical Examiner, and numerous county sheriff's offices with whom I have worked. Many of them will recognize their efforts amidst these pages.

My parents deserve much recognition for their support and enthusiasm over the years, even if they were not exactly sure what I was doing or why I was doing it. I hope this book can shed some light on my professional passions. Elements of this book impact me deeply because of the influence of my grandparents, a veteran of World War II and the woman who proposed to him when he returned from the Pacific. My grandparents taught me the value of human life and liberty, so I think they will enjoy learning about the forensic anthropological efforts to identify service persons who died on foreign soil, as well as the victims of the terrorist attacks within our own borders.

The human rights work discussed in this book is also close to my heart. I would like to acknowledge, on both personal and professional levels, the contributions of Dr. Clyde C. Snow. The impact that Dr. Snow has made on the direction of forensic anthropology in the past two decades cannot be overstated. Dr. Snow is accurately credited as the first to apply forensic anthropological methods and techniques to human rights investigations. He has traveled the world countless times, with Camel cigarettes and fedora in tow, to respond to those who have nowhere else to turn in their quest to locate loved ones or to obtain justice. Perhaps Dr. Snow's most tangible legacy will be the Argentine Forensic Anthropology Team and the other investigative groups that followed. I have had opportunities to work with Dr. Snow and the Argentine Team, and I feel strongly that anthropology is enriched by their dedicated application of scientific principles to modern sociopolitical problems. I am thrilled to include a chapter by Dr. Snow and Mercedes Doretti of the Argentine Forensic Anthropology Team, for my experiences working with them early in my career have shaped my professional path and passions ever since. I hope current students will find their efforts just as inspirational.

Over the years, writing dedications to my husband, Gary, has become increasingly difficult, for how does one use limited space to thank another for making a sometimes difficult, and certainly unconventional, life so enjoyable? His patience and encouragement is unparalleled. In the past year alone, my absences have far outnumbered my home "visits," and my attention is rarely undivided. I owe him many things, but especially time. For over a decade he has supported my endeavors, even though we have missed date nights, vacations, family events, and even holidays. I would tell him it will not happen again, but he knows better.

Dawnie Wolfe Steadman

ABOUT THE CONTRIBUTORS

BRUCE E. ANDERSON, PH.D.
Office of the Medical Examiner
Forensic Science Center
2825 E. District Street
Tucson, AZ 85714

Department of Anthropology
University of Arizona
Tucson, AZ 85721

Dr. Anderson received his M.A. and Ph.D. degrees from the University of Arizona, where he currently teaches a course in forensic anthropology. He worked as a physical anthropologist for the U.S. Army Central Identification Laboratory in Hawaii beginning in 1992 and departing in 1996 as Senior Anthropologist. Dr. Anderson currently holds a position as a medical investigator for the Office of the Medical Examiner, Pima County, as well as serving as a forensic anthropologist. His academic interests include forensic anthropology, human anatomy, and human evolution.

MARK E. BLUMER
Office of the Michigan Department of the Attorney General
Criminal Division
P.O. Box 30218
Lansing, MI 48909

Mark Blumer is a First Assistant Attorney General in the Criminal Division, Michigan Department of the Attorney General. He joined the Attorney General's Criminal Division in 1976 and became the Chief Trial Attorney in 1985 and the First Assistant in 1990. His primary responsibility is the trial of high visibility, complex felony cases, with some specialization in cold file homicides.

ANN WEBSTER BUNCH, PH.D., D.A.B.F.A.
Department of Anthropology
State University of New York at Oswego
Oswego, NY 13126

Dr. Bunch received her Ph.D. from the University of Chicago in 1993. She is currently an Assistant Professor of Anthropology at SUNY Oswego. Dr. Bunch was previously employed as a forensic anthropologist for the U.S. Army, where she performed fourteen missions for the Central Identification Laboratory, Hawaii. Her research interests include forensic science in general, human anatomy and osteology, and archaeology.

KAREN RAMEY BURNS, PH.D.
Anthropology Department
Baldwin Hall
University of Georgia
Athens, GA 30602-1619

Dr. Burns received her M.A. and Ph.D. in Forensic Anthropology under the direction of the late Dr. William R. Maples at the University of Florida. She is an adjunct professor at the University of Georgia and maintains an active consulting practice in forensic anthropology and human rights. She worked as a crime lab scientist in Toxicology and Forensic Anthropology for the Georgia Bureau of Investigation, Division of Forensic Sciences (1988–1991). Dr. Burns has devoted much of her professional career to excavation and identification of human remains in international genocide cases. She has also conducted bioarchaeological research and training in the United States and abroad. Her research interests include the microstructure of mineralized tissues and effects of burning and cremation.

MERCEDES DORETTI, LIC.
Argentine Forensic Anthropology Team
140 West 22nd Street, Suite 303
New York, NY 10011

Mercedes Doretti received her degree as a *licenciada en Ciencias Antropologicas* at the National University at Buenos Aires, Argentina, in 1987. She is a co-founder and a full-time member of the Argentina Forensic Anthropology Team (EAAF). As such, she works as an expert witness for judiciary, special commissions of inquiry, and international tribunals, applying forensic anthropology and archaeology to the investigation of human rights cases. She has worked in Argentina and other Latin American countries, the Balkans, Ethiopia, South Africa, Zimbabwe, the Ivory Coast, and Congo (DRC), the Philippines, East Timor, and Iraq. Since 1992, she has coordinated the New York office of the EAAF.

JENNIFER FILLION, M.A.
Department of Anthropology
354 Baker Hall
Michigan State University
East Lansing, MI 48824

Jennifer Fillion is a Ph.D. student in the Department of Anthropology at Michigan State University. She received her B.A. from the University of Michigan and M.A. from the University of Alabama. Her interests include forensic anthropology, skeletal biology, and facial reconstruction. Her most recent project (featured in the *Washington Post*) involved the facial reconstruction of two Egyptian mummies at the Van Andel Public Museum of Grand Rapids, Michigan.

H. GILL-KING, PH.D., D.A.B.F.A.
Biological Sciences
University of North Texas
P.O. Box 3055220
Denton, TX 76203-5220

Dr. Gill-King received a Ph.D. in Anthropology from Southern Methodist University and completed postdoctoral studies in hard tissue pathology at the University of Texas Southwestern Institute of Forensic Sciences. He is Director of the Laboratory of Forensic Anthropology and Human Identification in the Department of Biological Sciences at the University of North Texas, where he also holds joint appointments in Criminal Justice and Anthropology, and in the Department of Pathology at the University of North Texas Health Science Center. His current research interests are in the areas of skeletal endocrinology and the dietary adaptations of New World colonials. He consults regularly with local, state, and federal agencies in the United States as well as the Servicio Periciale and the Judicial Federal Police in Mexico.

DAVID M. GLASSMAN, PH.D., D.A.B.F.A.
Department of Anthropology
Southwest Texas State University
601 University Drive
San Marcos, TX 78666-4616

Dr. Glassman is Chairman of the Department of Anthropology at Southwest Texas State University. He received his doctorate from the University of Tennessee. Dr. Glassman is a past Chairman of the Physical Anthropology section of the American Academy of Forensic Sciences. He has twenty-two years of experience in forensic anthropology and skeletal biology, and has an active record of scholarly publication and presented papers. Dr. Glassman has consulted in more than 250 cases of skeletal identification.

WILLIAM E. GRANT, M.A.
Holland Community Hospital
602 Michigan Avenue
Holland, MI 49423

William Grant received a Master of Arts degree in Anthropology from the University of Tennessee. He is currently a research assistant at Holland Community Hospital in Holland, Michigan. His academic interests include taphonomy (to include time since death research), trauma, and sexual dimorphism among past and present human populations.

THOMAS D. HOLLAND, PH.D., D.A.B.F.A.
U.S. Army Central Identification Laboratory, Hawaii
310 Worchester Avenue
Hickam AFB, HI 96853

Dr. Holland received his Ph.D. from the University of Missouri, Columbia, where he was the Associate Curator for the Museum of Anthropology prior to becoming the Scientific Director of the U.S. Army Central Identification Laboratory in Hawaii. He is on the board of directors for the American Board of Forensic Anthropology. Dr. Holland has published in *American Journal of Physical Anthropology*, *American Antiquity*, *Journal of Forensic Sciences*, *Current Anthropology*, *Studies in Archaeological Method and Theory*, *Quaternary Research*, and *Plains Anthropologist*, among others. His research interests include forensic anthropology, bioarchaeology, and evolutionary theory.

MARY JUMBELIC, M.D.
Center for Forensic Sciences
100 Elizabeth Blackwell Street
Syracuse, NY 13210

Dr. Jumbelic is the Chief Medical Examiner for the County of Onondaga in Syracuse, New York. In addition, she holds the position of Clinical Associate Professor in the Department of Pathology for Upstate Medical University and is director of their Autopsy Service. Dr. Jumbelic is the primary instructor for pathology residents during their autopsy rotations, and teaches second-year medical students forensic pathology and death certification. Her areas of interest include the prevention of injuries in children, mass disasters, and collaboration with forensic anthropology.

KENNETH A. R. KENNEDY, PH.D., D.A.B.F.A.
Professor of Ecology and Evolutionary Biology, Anthropology, Asian Studies
Department of Ecology and Evolutionary Biology
Corson Hall, Cornell University
Ithaca, NY 14853

Dr. Kennedy is a biological anthropologist and a Professor in the Department of Ecology and Evolutionary Biology at Cornell University. He has affiliations with the Department of Anthropology, the Department of Asian Studies (South Asia Program), and the Archaeology Program at Cornell University. His major research interests include forensic anthropology, paleoanthropology of the South Asian countries of India, Pakistan, Sri Lanka, and their bordering nations, and the history of biological anthropology. Dr. Kennedy is a recipient of the T. Dale Stewart Award for Distinguished Service in Forensic Anthropology. He currently serves as the Secretary for the American Board of Forensic Anthropology.

LYLE W. KONIGSBERG, PH.D.
Department of Anthropology
250 South Stadium Hall
The University of Tennessee
Knoxville, TN 37996

Dr. Konigsberg is a Professor of Anthropology at the University of Tennessee, Knoxville. He received his B.A. in Anthropology and Biology from Indiana University, and his M.A. and Ph.D. in Anthropology from Northwestern University. Following a postdoctoral position in the Department of Genetics at the Southwest Foundation for Biomedical Research in San Antonio, Texas, he moved to the University of Tennessee. His research interests include osteological and statistical analysis, with a particular emphasis on the bases for estimation and presentation of statistical evidence from the skeleton.

PAULETTE LEACH, M.A.
Department of Anthropology
California State University, Chico
Chico, CA 95929-0400

Paulette Leach received her Master's Degree in Anthropology from California State University, Chico. She currently resides in Phoenix, Arizona.

E. MARK LEVINSOHN, M.D., F.A.C.R.
Department of Medical Imaging
Crouse Radiology Associates
410 S. Crouse Avenue
Syracuse, NY 13210

Dr. Levinsohn is a Clinical Professor of Radiology at SUNY Upstate Medical University in Syracuse, New York. He is head of the Musculoskeletal Radiology Section at Crouse Hospital, Syracuse. He is also the radiologic consultant to the Onondaga County Medical Examiner.

JENNIFER C. LOVE, PH.D.
Regional Forensic Center
1060 Madison Avenue
Memphis, TN 38104-2106

Jennifer Love received her B.A. in Anthropology from Pennsylvania State University. She received her M.A. and Ph.D. in Anthropology from the University of Tennessee. She is currently an assistant anthropologist at the Regional Forensic Center at the University of Tennessee, Memphis. Her research interests include forensic anthropology, taphonomy, and rates of decomposition.

WILLIAM A. LOVIS, PH.D.
354 Baker Hall
Department of Anthropology
Michigan State University
East Lansing, MI 48824

William Lovis has been on the faculty at Michigan State University since 1973. He holds a joint appointment at Michigan State University as Curator of Anthropology at the Michigan State University Museum and Professor in the Department of Anthropology. His primary research interests are in hunter/gatherer adaptations, particularly in terms of paleoenvironmental change as it relates to subsistence, settlement, and mobility, as well as in the application of field and analytic methods. While he conducts bioarchaeological fieldwork in the Great Lakes and Northern England, he also regularly works with forensic anthropologists in the training of students and law enforcement personnel in human remains recovery, and has been directly involved in a number of forensic cases in Michigan.

ROBERT W. MANN, PH.D.
U.S. Army Central Identification Laboratory, Hawaii
310 Worchester Avenue
Hickam AFB, HI 96853

Dr. Mann is the Supervisory Senior Anthropologist, U.S. Army Central Identification Laboratory, Hawaii (CILHI). He received his Ph.D. from the University of Hawaii in 2001. Prior to joining the CILHI, Dr. Mann worked as an anthropologist at the Smithsonian Institution for nearly five years. He has worked at the CILHI for nearly ten years and has worked in Vietnam, Laos, Cambodia, Japan, Okinawa, Latvia, North Korea South Korea, and Russia. His research interests include paleopathology, trauma, and human skeletal variation.

ANTHONY MANOUKIAN, M.D.
Pan Pacific Pathologists
Maui Memorial Medical Center
221 Mahalani Street
Wailuku, HI 96793

University of Hawaii
Pathology Residency Program
1960 East-West Road D209E
Honolulu, HI 96822

Dr. Manoukian is a forensic pathologist in Hawaii who covers the "Neighbor Islands," including Maui, Kauai, and Hawaii Counties, as well as many Islands of the South Pacific. He studied pathology at the University of Hawaii and at the Office of the Chief Medical Examiner in Baltimore, Maryland. He considers the anthropologists he has met to be an interesting and unusual assortment of characters and feels fortunate for the expert consultation he has received over the years, especially from the Forensic Anthropologists and Dentists at the U.S. Army's Central Identification Laboratory at Hickam Air Force Base in Honolulu, Hawaii.

MURRAY K. MARKS, PH.D., D.A.B.F.A.
Associate Professor
Department of Anthropology
250 South Stadium Hall
The University of Tennessee
Knoxville, TN 37996

MURRAY K. MARKS, PH.D., D.A.B.F.A.
Associate Professor
Department of Pathology
Regional Forensic Center
The University of Tennessee Medical Center
Knoxville, TN 37920

Dr. Marks received his M.A. from the University of Arkansas and Ph.D. from the University of Tennessee. He is Associate Director of the Forensic Anthropology Center, a consultant to the Tennessee Bureau of Investigation, and director of the Human Remains Recovery School for the Federal Bureau of Investigation Evidence Response Teams. He is a dental anthropologist and skeletal biologist with research interests in time since death, computer graphic facial approximation, mineralized tissue histology, and bioarchaeology.

TERRY MELTON, PH.D.
Mitotyping Technologies, LLC
1981 Pine Hall Drive
State College, PA 16801

Dr. Melton is President and CEO of Mitotyping Technologies, a company that performs mitochondrial DNA (mtDNA) analyses for law enforcement, attorneys, and private individuals. She received a B.S. from Wake Forest University and both M.S. and Ph.D. degrees in Genetics from Penn State University. She has a research background in the study of mtDNA as a forensic typing locus. Research topics include an evaluation of the diversity and subpopulation heterogeneity present in the mtDNA of approximately forty populations from Europe, North America, Africa, and Asia, studies of mtDNA and nuclear DNA variation in indigenous aboriginal populations from Kenya and Taiwan, and research into the mtDNA variation associated with Southeast Asian and Polynesian prehistory. She is currently serving on the editorial board of the *Journal of Forensic Sciences* and is an affiliate researcher with the Department of Anthropology at Penn State University.

AMY ZELSON MUNDORFF, M.A.
Office of Chief Medical Examiner
520 1st Avenue
New York, NY 10016

Amy Zelson Mundorff is the Anthropologist for the Office of Chief Medical Examiner, the City of New York. She is a clinical instructor in the Department of Forensic Medicine for the New York University School of Medicine and an adjunct lecturer at Hunter College. Prior to receiving her Master's degree from California State University, Chico, she was a field archaeologist in California, Hawaii, Jamaica, and New York, excavating prehistoric and historic sites as well as performing osteological analyses.

ELAYNE J. POPE, M.A.
252 South Stadium Hall
University of Tennessee
Knoxville, TN 37996

After completing a Master's degree from the University of Arkansas, Elayne Pope is now pursuing her Ph.D. at the University of Tennessee. Her dissertation research focuses on prehistoric mortuary patterns in vertical and horizontal karst systems of middle Tennessee and burned bone research of forensic skeletal remains.

DAVID R. RANKIN, M.A.
U.S. Army Central Identification Laboratory, Hawaii
310 Worchester Avenue
Hickam AFB, HI 96853

David Rankin received his B.A. and M.A. from the University of Arizona and joined the U.S. Army Central Identification Laboratory in Hawaii (CILHI) in 1995. David has worked at the CILHI since 1995 and has led numerous recovery and investigation missions in Vietnam, Lao P.D.R., Burma, Guadalcanal, China, Turkey, Germany, and the United States. He also participates in Joint Forensic Reviews in Hanoi, where he examines the remains of suspected American MIAs. He aided in the analysis and identification of individuals aboard Korean Airlines Flight 801, which crashed in Guam in August of 1997. In addition, David participated in the exhumation, mtDNA sample preparation, and skeletal analysis of the remains from the Tomb of the Unknowns, Vietnam War, at Arlington National Cemetery and the Armed Forces Institute of Pathology in May of 1998.

NORMAN J. SAUER, PH.D., D.A.B.F.A.
Department of Anthropology
354 Baker Hall
Michigan State University
East Lansing, MI 48824

Dr. Sauer is a Professor of Anthropology, Adjunct Professor of Criminal Justice, and Director of the Forensic Anthropology Laboratory at Michigan State University. He has been assisting the medicolegal community on human remains cases since the 1970s and has trained medicolegal personnel from throughout the United States, Europe, and China. A past Chair and Secretary of the Physical Anthropology Section of the American Academy of Forensic Sciences, he teaches graduate and undergraduate classes in forensic anthropology and regularly directs a five-week Summer Study Abroad Program in Forensic Anthropology in England. His research interests include bioarchaeology in the Great Lakes area, the concept of race in anthropology, and the skeletal effects of trauma.

FRANK P. SAUL, PH.D, D.A.B.F.A.
USPHS DMORT V
2595 Arlington Avenue
Toledo, OH 43614-2674

Dr. Saul is the Regional Commander of DMORT Region V as well as Professor Emeritus of Anatomy and Associate Dean Emeritus of the Medical College of Ohio, Toledo, Ohio. He is a member of the NTSB Forensic Team and a Forensic Anthropology consultant to the Lucas County Coroner's Office (Toledo, Ohio), the Wayne County Medical Examiner's Office (Detroit, Michigan), the FBI Evidence Response Team (Cleveland, Ohio), and other agencies.

JULIE MATHER SAUL, B.A.
USPHS DMORT V
2595 Arlington Avenue
Toledo, OH 43614-2674

Julie Saul is the Director of the Forensic Anthropology Laboratory at the Lucas County Coroner's Office and a Research Associate of Anatomy at the Medical College of Ohio in Toledo, Ohio. She is a member of the NTSB Forensic Team and a Forensic Anthropology Consultant to the Wayne County Medical Examiner's Office (Detroit, Michigan), the FBI Evidence Response Team (Cleveland, Ohio), and other agencies. She is a Fellow of the American Academy of Forensic Sciences.

COLLEEN CARNEY SHINE, B.S.
Frauenlobstrasse 28 80337
Munich, Germany

After earning her B.S. in Psychology from Wellesley College in 1986, Colleen Carney Shine served as Director of Public Relations for the National League of POW/MIA Families, a Washington, D.C.-based nonprofit organization dedicated to the fullest possible accounting for Americans who are still prisoner or missing as a result of the Vietnam War. A staunch advocate for veterans' issues, Ms. Shine responds to media interest, and frequently addresses student, civic, military, and veterans organizations. She has served on the Board of Directors of the National League of POW/MIA Families, Sons and Daughters in Touch, Inc., and The Friends of the Vietnam Veterans Memorial. Ms. Shine is married and lives in Munich, Germany, where she works as a writer and marketing consultant.

PAUL S. SLEDZIK, M.S.
Curator, Anatomical Collections
National Museum of Health and Medicine
Armed Forces Institute of Pathology
Washington, D.C. 20306-6000

Paul Sledzik received his M.S. in Biological Anthropology from the University of Connecticut and has been curator of the anatomical collections at the National Museum of Health and Medicine, Armed Forces Institute of Pathology, since 1990. In 1998, he was the first forensic scientist to be appointed as a Disaster Mortuary Operational Response Team (DMORT) regional commander. He has worked in different capacities in several major disasters, but always seeks to incorporate forensic anthropological methods to the disaster response. He also conducts research in historic period skeletal biology, particularly on the remains of U.S. military personnel.

JOHN E. SMIALEK, M.D.
Division of Forensic Pathology
Department of Pathology
University of Maryland School of Medicine
111 Penn Street
Baltimore, MD 21201

The late Dr. John Smialek graduated from the University of Toronto, School of Medicine. Dr. Smialek worked in forensic medicine with the Province of Ontario, Thunder Bay, Canada, and Office of the Medical Examiner of Wayne County in Detroit before becoming Chief Medical Examiner for the State of New Mexico and subsequently for the State of Maryland. He also held positions with Medical Schools at the University of Maryland and Johns Hopkins. He was active in teaching and research initiatives in forensic medicine with special emphasis on sudden infant death.

O. C. SMITH, M.D.
Department of Pathology
University of Tennessee
Regional Forensic Center
1060 Madison Avenue
Memphis, TN 38104-2106

Dr. Smith received his M.D. from the Medical College of Wisconsin in 1978. He received training in Anatomic, Clinical, and Forensic Pathology at the University of Tennessee, Memphis, followed by board certification in these three areas in 1983. Dr. Smith received training in forensic firearms examination in 1985 and is a full-time faculty member of the University of Tennessee and medical examiner for Shelby County, Tennessee. His focus in forensic pathology in civilian life and the Naval Reserve involves the biomechanics of skeletal, ballistic, and blast injury, burns, and aircraft mishap investigation.

CLYDE C. SNOW, PH.D., D.A.B.F.A.
Norman, OK

Dr. Snow received his Ph.D. from the University of Arizona. Since 1979, after retiring from the Federal Aviation Administration, he has served as an independent consultant for over 3,000 cases in forensic anthropology. His cases include the 1979 American Airlines DC-10 crash in Chicago, the John Wayne Gacy serial murders, and the Green River murders. In 1985, he headed a team of U.S. forensic scientists who went to Brazil to aid in the identification of the skeleton of the notorious Nazi war criminal, Dr. Josef Mengele. In 1995, he directed the anthropological phase of the identification of the 168 victims of Murrah Building bombing in Oklahoma City. In 1984, Dr. Snow began his human rights work when he traveled to Argentina to assist in determining the fate of thousands of Argentines who were abducted, tortured, and murdered by military "Death Squads" between 1976 and 1983. He has served on similar missions in over 20 countries, including UN-sponsored missions to the former Yugoslavia to collect forensic evidence to be used in war crimes trials.

DAWNIE WOLFE STEADMAN, PH.D.
Department of Anthropology
Binghamton University, SUNY
P.O. Box 6000
Binghamton, NY 13902-6000

Dr. Steadman received her M.A. and Ph.D. from the University of Chicago. She is currently an Assistant Professor at Binghamton University, SUNY, following three years as an Assistant Professor at Iowa State University. Dr. Steadman serves as a forensic anthropology consultant to the Iowa Office of the State Medical Examiner and several New York agencies. Her research interests are in bioarchaeology and forensic anthropology. She has conducted excavations and skeletal analyses of several historic and prehistoric archaeological sites in Illinois, Iowa, and New York. Dr. Steadman is particularly interested in paleopathology, population genetic modeling of past populations, and the application of forensic anthropology to human rights investigations.

SAM D. STOUT, PH.D.
Department of Anthropology
124 W. 17th Avenue
244 Lord Hall
Ohio State University
Columbus, OH 43210-1364

Dr. Stout received his Ph.D. in biological anthropology from Washington University in St. Louis, Missouri, in 1976. He is currently Professor Emeritus at the University of Missouri and Professor at Ohio State University. His general research interests are in skeletal biology. Specifically, his research involves the microstructural analysis of bone (histomorphometry) and its applications in forensic anthropology, bioarchaeology, and paleontology.

STEVEN A. SYMES, PH.D., D.A.B.F.A.
Department of Pathology
University of Tennessee
Regional Forensic Center
1060 Madison Avenue
Memphis, TN 38104-2106

Dr. Symes is an Assistant Professor in the Department of Pathology at the University of Tennessee, Memphis, and consulting forensic anthropologist for the Department of Forensic Pathology and Medical Examiner's Office at the Regional Forensic Center for Shelby County, Tennessee. He received his M.A. and his Ph.D. in Anthropology from the University of Tennessee, Knoxville. His interests and research involve human skeletal biology with an emphasis on forensic tool mark and fracture pattern interpretation. His special expertise is in sharp trauma (i.e., saw and knife marks on bone and cartilage in instances of dismemberment and mutilation). Other interests include taphonomical influences of recent, historic, and prehistoric skeletons, healing bone trauma in cases of child abuse, bloodstain pattern analysis, and 35 mm and digital laboratory and crime scene photography.

DOUGLAS H. UBELAKER, PH.D., D.A.B.F.A.
Department of Anthropology
National Museum of Natural History, MRC 112
Smithsonian Institution
Washington, D.C. 20560

Dr. Ubelaker is a Curator of Physical Anthropology at the Smithsonian Institution's National Museum of Natural History in Washington, D.C., and Professorial Lecturer in the Departments of Anthropology and Anatomy at the George Washington University in Washington, D.C. His research interests focus on human skeletal biology and its forensic applications. Since 1977 he has served as the primary consulting forensic anthropologist for FBI Headquarters in Washington, D.C., and has reported on over 700 cases for the FBI and other law enforcement agencies.

JOHNIE E. WEBB, JR., B.A.
Deputy Commander
U.S. Army Central Identification Laboratory, Hawaii
310 Worchester Avenue
Hickam AFB, HI 96853

Johnie Webb assumed the duties as the Deputy to the Commander, U.S. Army Central Identification Laboratory (CILHI) in August 1994. He received a Bachelor of Arts degree in Business Administration from Benedictine College, in Atchison, Kansas. Prior to entering Federal Government Civil Service he completed twenty-six years of service as an Army officer in the Quartermaster Corps, retiring in 1994 with the rank of Lieutenant Colonel. He is a Vietnam veteran and has multiple personal awards and decorations. As an Army officer, Mr. Webb had extensive duty with the Central Identification Laboratory. He was fortunate enough to lead the first joint recovery operation into Vietnam in 1985 to recover the remains of missing Americans.

ALLISON WEBB WILLCOX, M.A.
Research Collaborator
National Museum of Natural History
Smithsonian Institution
Department of Anthropology
10th Street & Constitution Avenue, NW
Washington, D.C. 20560-0112

Allison Webb Willcox is a doctoral candidate in human skeletal biology at the University of Pennsylvania. She has been on the faculty of the annual Armed Forces Institute of Pathology Forensic Anthropology Course for over ten years, and has been a member of the Disaster Mortuary Operational Response Team (DMORT) since its inception in 1993. In addition to forensic anthropology, her research interests include health and nutritional status in ancient Egypt and the application of modern laboratory methods to skeletal remains.

P. WILLEY, PH.D., D.A.B.F.A.
Department of Anthropology
California State University, Chico
Chico, CA 95929-0400

Dr. Willey is a Professor of Anthropology at Chico State. He has served on the board of directors for the American Board of Forensic Anthropology. His research interests include historic skeletal series, and in recent years he has examined remains of Seventh Cavalry troopers from the Little Bighorn and bones from the Donner Party.

MARK WILSON, M.A.
Supervisory Special Agent, FBI
Research Scientist
Forensic Science Research Unit
FBI Academy
Quantico, VA 22135

Mark Wilson is currently a research scientist in DNA analysis methods at the FBI Academy in Quantico, Virginia. He previously served as the mitochondrial DNA Program Manager in DNA Analysis Unit II, FBI Laboratory, Washington, D.C. He earned an M.A. degree in Biology from California State University, Fullerton, in 1983. Mr. Wilson was instrumental in developing mtDNA analysis for forensic use, and testified in the first mitochondrial DNA case in the United States, *State of Tennessee vs. Ware*, in 1996.

CHAPTER

1

INTRODUCING FORENSIC ANTHROPOLOGY

Dawnie Wolfe Steadman

The Case Study Approach

In the summer of 1990, four male friends entered an abandoned farmhouse in Iowa, but only three emerged alive. Two of the men shot their friend multiple times and threw his body into a well behind the farmhouse where it remained until it was recovered nearly a decade later. Could the last moments of his life be interpreted from his mangled bones? In another part of the Midwest, an incomplete, disarticulated female skeleton was found scattered along a riverbank. Two women of the same age, height, and ancestry were missing from the area. How could experts determine whether the handful of bones belonged to one woman or the other? Could this also be a case of foul play?

No matter in what morose scenario unknown human remains are recovered, every jurisdiction in the United States has statutes requiring a medicolegal investigation of the identity of the individual and the circumstances of his or her death. By virtue of their expertise in skeletal biology, forensic anthropologists may be called upon by law enforcement agencies, coroners, medical examiners, and forensic pathologists to assist in the recovery of human remains, conduct skeletal analyses for the purposes of identification, describe the nature and extent of skeletal trauma, and potentially provide expert testimony in a court of law. Forensic anthropological services are typically requested when human remains are decomposed, burnt, fragmentary, cremated, dismembered, fully skeletonized, or otherwise unidentifiable by visual means. Scenarios in which a forensic anthropologist may consult include burials, structural fires, explosions such as the Oklahoma City bombing, mass graves, commercial and clandestine cremations, and mass fatality incidents. The most recent example of large-scale forensic anthropological involvement is the identification of victims killed in the terrorist attacks of September 11, 2001. Increasingly, forensic anthropologists are also expanding their purview beyond the local landscape and working around the globe to identify the victims of wars, human rights atrocities, mass disasters, and soldiers missing in action.

Forensic anthropology is best defined as the application of anthropological and skeletal biological principles to medicolegal issues. The term *medicolegal* refers to the capability of medical science to shed light on legal matters, such as the identity of the deceased and circumstances of death (Fisher 1993). Skeletal biology is the study of the human skeleton and encompasses several subdisciplines, including forensic anthropology and bioarchaeology, the study of past population behavior, health, and disease. Bioarchaeology adopts a population-oriented approach and typically involves the examination of human remains and artifacts from an entire historic or prehistoric cemetery. While forensic anthropologists typically analyze only one or a few individuals at a time, they must also be knowledgeable about the entire range of human variation. In fact, by virtue of their casework, forensic anthropologists contribute directly to our understanding of skeletal diversity among contemporary populations (Ubelaker 2000; Ousley and Jantz 1998). Although the fundamental methods of skeletal analyses are identical, there is a profound difference between forensics and other fields of skeletal biology, in that forensic anthropologists have the potential to limit personal freedoms. Thus, the methods and interpretations of a forensic anthropological skeletal analysis are subject to the rules and regulations of evidence in a court of law and come under intense scrutiny. In court-related procedures, forensic anthropologists are required to discuss their choice of methods, explain the theoretical underpinnings of those techniques, and defend their opinions, often under fierce cross-examination, in language that a judge and jury can comprehend.

Forensic anthropological involvement in the medicolegal community begins with, and is based upon, an exhaustive case report including, as appropriate, documentation of the methods of identification, an accurate reconstruction of trauma that occurs at or around the time of death (perimortem trauma) as well as after death (postmortem trauma), and an estimate of the postmortem interval, or time since death. If a case goes to trial, this report becomes the central core of the forensic anthropologist's testimony. Once there is legal resolution, forensic anthropologists can publish a case study in order to share important new information or techniques with students and colleagues. With this in mind, the purpose of this volume is to utilize case studies to demonstrate the appropriate techniques, ethical responsibilities, and training involved in the practice of forensic anthropology in the United States today. The contributing authors provide comprehensive coverage of one or more cases, demonstrate the forensic methods utilized to resolve the case, and, when appropriate, offer personal insight about mistakes, pitfalls, and ethical issues related to their experiences. Ultimately, the case studies in this volume illustrate three principal themes—the roles and methods of modern forensic anthropology in local and international casework, the well-developed scientific methodology upon which forensic anthropological techniques are founded, and the multidisciplinary nature of forensic science.

The goal of this chapter is to provide a brief synopsis of the basic theoretical and methodological principles of forensic anthropology that produce high-caliber case studies. As this is only a summary, more comprehensive osteology texts should be consulted, including, but not limited to, *Human Osteology* (White 2000), *Anatomy and Biology of the Human Skeleton* (Steele and Bramblett 1988), *Skeleton Keys* (Schwartz 1995), *Data Collection Procedures for Forensic Skeletal Materials* (Moore-Jansen et al. 1994), *A Field Guide for Human Skeletal Identification* (Bennett 1993), and *Human Osteology: A Laboratory and Field Manual* (Bass 1995). For a bioarchaeological perspective, see also *Standards for Data Collection from Human Skeletal*

Remains (Buikstra and Ubelaker 1994) and *Human Skeletal Remains: Excavation, Analysis, Interpretation* (Ubelaker 1999).

A Foundation in Skeletal Biology

Despite the far-reaching applications of modern forensic anthropology, all of the underlying methods and theories in the field are well-grounded in the principles of skeletal biology—the study of the development, anatomy, physiology, histology, and biomechanics of bone tissue. The human skeleton is typically divided into the axial skeleton, comprising the head, thorax, and pelvis; and the appendicular skeleton, which includes the limb bones. Bones articulate or connect with each other at joints. Forensic anthropologists study the anatomy of the 200-plus bones of the adult and subadult skeletons in order to glean as much information as possible from extremely small fragments. In addition, they must be familiar with the morphological variation of the skeleton among individuals and populations. Figure 1.1 is a labeled diagram of the bones of the normal adult skeleton.

Bone is a visco-elastic material, meaning it has both rigid and flexible properties. Approximately 75 percent of bone is inorganic, consisting primarily of minerals such as calcium and phosphorous, that give bone its rigid strength. However, bone cannot be too rigid or it will become brittle and break upon impact, much like glass. Thus, nearly 90 percent of the organic component of bone is composed of collagen, which provides some flexibility. Further, bone consists of two structural components, compact bone and spongy bone. Compact bone is very hard, dense bone that withstands stress and provides strength, resistance, and protection. Spongy bone is porous and consists of bony spicules, or trabeculae, that form a latticework to absorb and distribute stress. The histological structure of bone is discussed in Section IV.

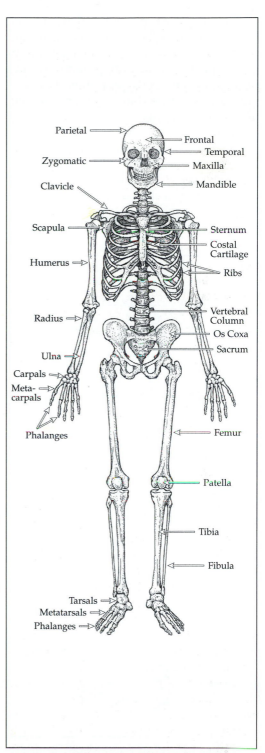

FIGURE 1.1 BONES OF THE ADULT SKELETON

A basic rule of anatomy is that form follows function. Indeed, the structure and morphology of bones are well-adapted for their functions, including support and movement of the body, protection of vital organs, hemopoiesis (blood cell production), and mineral storage. A closer examination of bone architecture will help demonstrate the relationship between the form and function of cortical and spongy bone (Figure 1.2). A long bone is divided into three sections—the diaphysis, or shaft, two or more epiphyses located at the ends of the long bone, and the metaphysis, a section of bone between the epiphysis and diaphysis. A layer of tough connective tissue, known as the periosteum, envelops the outer cortex of the diaphysis, while the medullary cavity is lined by the endosteum. Long bones function to produce blood cells inside the medullary cavity, provide structure to the body, and act as levers for movement. Accordingly, the outer cortex of the long bone consists of very thick cortical bone to protect the medullary cavity and support the body, while spongy bone is concentrated in the metaphyses and epiphyses, as most stress occurs at the joints. In contrast, short bones, such as those of the wrist (carpals) and ankle (tarsals), function to distribute stress and hence have a relatively thin cortex and a considerable amount of spongy bone. The flat bones of the skull consist of outer and inner tables of compact bone (consider the protective function this provides for the brain), and a layer of spongy bone in between, called diploe.

By applying the principles of skeletal biology, forensic anthropologists have the skills to interpret the story bones tell for the purposes of identification. The identification process begins with an inventory of the available skeletal elements and other evidence present. The next step is to construct a biological profile of the individual that can be compared to that of missing individuals. Finally, a description of any perimortem and postmortem traumatic injuries is required.

Forensic Anthropological Procedures

Inventory

The forensic anthropologist must know how to properly process and sort bones and bone fragments received in a forensic context. The first phase in an osteological analysis is to determine if the bones are human. Typically, the forensic analysis will be terminated if the bones are those of animals. Next, individual

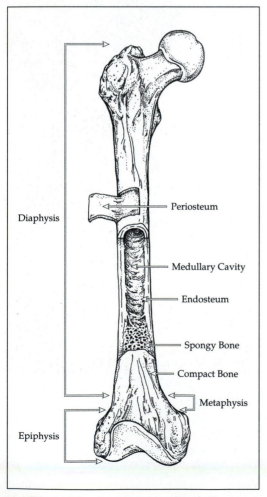

Diaphysis

Periosteum

Medullary Cavity

Endosteum

Spongy Bone

Compact Bone

Metaphysis

Epiphysis

FIGURE 1.2   ANATOMY OF A LONG BONE

bones are identified. If a bone or bone fragment cannot be readily identified, one can attempt to specify the part of the skeleton to which it belongs by assessing the bone type—a long bone (e.g., femur or humerus), flat bone (e.g., bones of the vault), short bone (bones of the wrist or ankle) or irregular bone (e.g., the vertebrae). Once the bone is identified, the forensic anthropologist determines whether it is from the left or right side of the body in the case of bilateral bones. This procedure is known as "siding."

When all of the available bones or bone fragments are sorted and sided properly, they should be laid out on a table in anatomical position (Figure 1.3). Standardized forms are used to record the number and identity of the bones present, document their condition, and describe the presence of soft tissue and any associated evidence (Moore-Jansen et al. 1994). Following a complete inventory, a biological profile of the individual can be constructed.

Skeletal Biology and the Biological Profile

The underlying principle of skeletal biology is that certain aspects of an individual's life history are recorded in his or her skeleton. Bone is a dynamic tissue that adapts to changes in height, weight, age, and activity levels, as well as to certain diseases and traumatic events. Further, aspects of an individual's population history, or ancestry, are also recorded in the skeleton, as is his or her sex. What story might your skeleton tell about your life history? What is your current height? Are you fairly muscular? Are you right-handed or a southpaw? Are you male or female? Have you ever broken a bone? What other characteristics might make your skeleton unique? How might your skeleton change over the next twenty, thirty, or fifty years? When a person's death is set within a forensic context, it is the forensic anthropologist's responsibility to

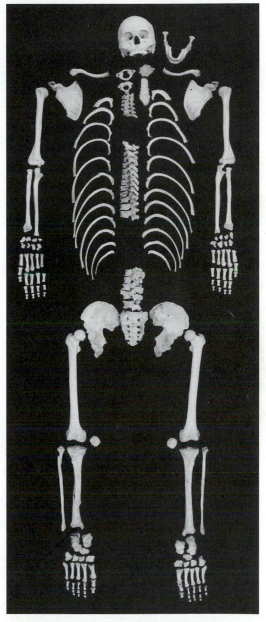

FIGURE 1.3 ANATOMICAL DISPLAY OF A SKELETON FOR INVENTORY AND ANALYSIS

interpret the "evidence" recorded in the bones to determine identity and the circumstances of his or her demise. To accomplish this, forensic anthropologists begin by establishing a biological profile of the skeleton—the sex, age, ancestry, and stature, as well as any skeletal anomalies or pathologies that make an individual unique.

Sex   The pelvis is considered the most sexually dimorphic skeletal element in humans because the female pelvis must accommodate the relatively large head of an infant during childbirth—a function obviously not shared by males. Thus, the female pelvis is typically wider in every dimension than the male pelvis (Figures 1.4 and 1.5). Particular features to examine include the presence of a ventral arc, ischiopubic ridge, and preauricular sulcus, as well as the breadth of the sciatic notch and subpubic concavity (Phenice 1969; Sutherland and Suchey 1991; Bennett 1993). Table 1.1 lists some of the more useful sex discriminating skeletal traits of the pelvis.

Though the pelvis is considered to be the most reliable skeletal indicator of sex, the cranium is also sexually dimorphic in many populations. Because the function of the skull does not vary between males and females, only general differences are observed in the size of the muscle attachments and the shape of certain features. Males tend to have larger neck muscles than females, which means that the bony areas where those muscles attach must be correspondingly robust. For example, one of the muscles on the side of the neck, the sternocleidomastoid muscle, originates on the clavicle and sternum and inserts on the mastoid process of the temporal bone, just behind the ear. When both the left and right muscles contract, they pull the mastoid process (and hence the head) forward and down towards the chest. Unilateral

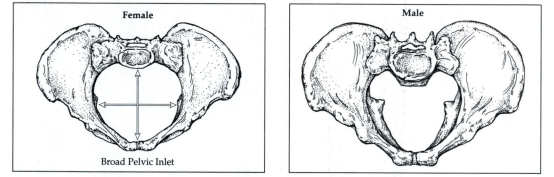

FIGURE 1.4   SEX-RELATED DIFFERENCES IN THE PELVIS (SUPERIOR VIEW)

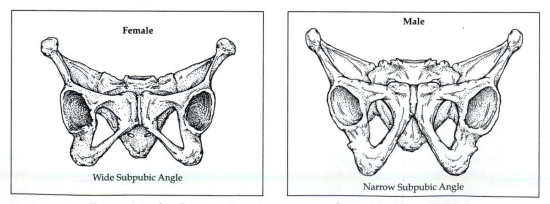

FIGURE 1.5   SEX-RELATED DIFFERENCES IN THE PELVIS (ANTERIOR VIEW)

TABLE 1.1   COMMONLY USED MORPHOLOGICAL INDICATORS OF SEX IN THE PELVIS

SKELETAL INDICATOR	MALE	FEMALE
Subpubic Angle	Narrow, V-shaped	Wider, U-shaped
Ventral Arc	Absent or not well defined	Present, well defined
Greater Sciatic Notch	Narrow, less than 68°	Wider, greater than 68°
Preauricular Sulcus	Absent or thin and shallow	Present, deep and wide
Obturator Foramen	Oval, larger	Triangular, smaller
Pubic Bone	Short, triangular	Longer, rectangular
Ishiopubic Ramus	Broad and flat	Thin and sharp

contraction moves the head to one side. Adhering to the rule that form follows function, an individual with a large stern-ocleidomastoid muscle will have a larger mastoid process than an individual with a relatively smaller muscle mass. Thus, the mastoid processes of males tend to be wider and longer than those of females (Figure 1.6). The same general rule applies to the muscles on the back of the neck (nuchal muscles) that attach to the nuchal crest of the occipital (Figure 1.7).

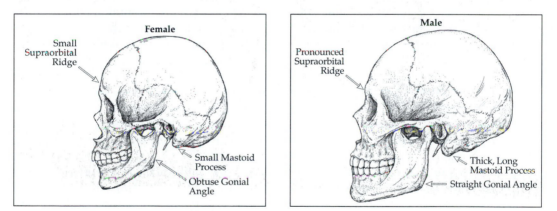

FIGURE 1.6   SEX-RELATED DIFFERENCES IN THE CRANIUM (LATERAL VIEW)

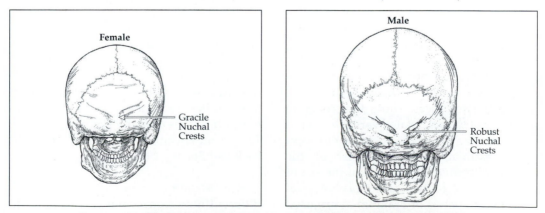

FIGURE 1.7   SEX-RELATED DIFFERENCES IN THE CRANIUM (POSTERIOR VIEW)

TABLE 1.2   COMMONLY USED MORPHOLOGICAL INDICATORS OF SEX IN THE CRANIUM

SKELETAL INDICATOR	MALE	FEMALE
Nuchal Crest	Well developed, robust	Less developed, gracile
External Occipital Protuberance	Well developed	Weak, smooth
Mastoid Process	Large, wide and robust	Thinner, narrow and gracile
Glabella and Supraorbital Ridges	More pronounced	Less pronounced
Supraorbital Margins	Thick, blunt	Thin, sharp
Forehead	Sloping, less rounded	Vertical, more rounded
Gonial Angle	Vertical (approaches 90°)	Angled (less than 90°)
Chin	Square, U-shaped	Pointed, V-shaped

There are other important sex-related differences of the cranium (Table 1.2). For instance, the superior margins of the orbit, called the supraorbital margins, tend to be thin and sharp in females and thick and blunt in males. The jaw line (gonial angle) and chin of males are often more square and pronounced, while the gonial angle of females is more obtuse and their chins are generally more pointed than square. Skeletal biologists cannot offer good explanations as to why such variation exists but they are nonetheless useful for discriminating between the sexes in skeletal material.

Note that most of the differences between the traits listed in Tables 1.1 and 1.2 are relative. For instance, the greater sciatic notch is "wider" in females than in males while the glabella is "more pronounced" in males than in females. There is a great deal of overlap between the sexes in all of these traits, including those of the pelvis, and some populations are more sexually dimorphic than others. Thus, it is crucial to understand the sex-related variability within and among populations in order to accurately estimate this parameter of the biological profile. Estimation of the sex of children based on the same morphological traits of the pelvis or cranium as are used for adults is unreliable because the female pelvis does not widen, or deviate from the male form, until after puberty. However, sex can be estimated in subadult skeletons using genetic and dental attributes (see Saunders 2000 for a review).

Measurements of the skull and postcranial skeleton are also useful for assessing sex. Bennett (1993) and France (1998) present a synthesis of measurements and statistical sectioning points useful for sex estimation. Summary data can also be found in Krogman and Iscan (1986) and Stewart (1979). Notably, Giles and Elliot (1962, 1963) developed discriminant functions for cranial data from the nineteenth-century Terry collection, though changes in the size and shape of crania over time (secular changes) have limited their utility. Cranial metric data from the Forensic Data Bank (Ousley and Jantz 1998) currently offer the best comparative standards for modern forensic cases. Measurements of the humerus, femur, and tibia can outperform those of the cranium in discriminating between the sexes of many populations (e.g., Thieme and Schull 1957; Bennett 1993; Dittrick and Suchey 1986).

Age SUBADULT Your skeleton appears different now from when you were born, and it will certainly look very different in fifty years. The estimation of age at death from skeletal materials is based on morphological changes in the skeleton over time. The development of the skeleton and teeth is useful for estimating the age of subadults (infants, children, and teenagers). Longitudinal growth occurs at the epiphyseal growth plate, a section of hyaline cartilage between the epiphysis and metaphysis of long bones (Figure 1.8). Cartilage cells, called chondrocytes, proliferate and eventually die, thereby forming a cartilaginous matrix upon which osteoblasts (bone-forming cells) lay down bone. The bone lengthens at both ends as this process continues. Longitudinal growth cannot continue indefinitely, however, or we would all be giants. A hormone secreted from the pituitary gland, called the growth hormone, determines the rate and duration of bone growth. When the growth hormone is "turned off,"

the growth plate ossifies, the epiphysis fuses to the metaphysis, and longitudinal growth ceases. Fortunately for anthropologists, the growth plates of each bone turn off at different times, yet the timing of epiphyseal fusion for any one growth plate is relatively constant across populations. Therefore, anthropologists can compare the observed pattern of epiphyseal fusion of an unknown skeleton to modern growth standards. A general chart is presented in Figure 1.9 on page 10, though more specific information can be found in Scheuer and Black (2000). Female skeletons will typically mature faster than those of males. There may be some population differences as well, and childhood malnutrition may negatively impact skeletal growth and development.

The formation and eruption of teeth are also useful for estimating the age of subadult skeletons. Humans are diphodont,

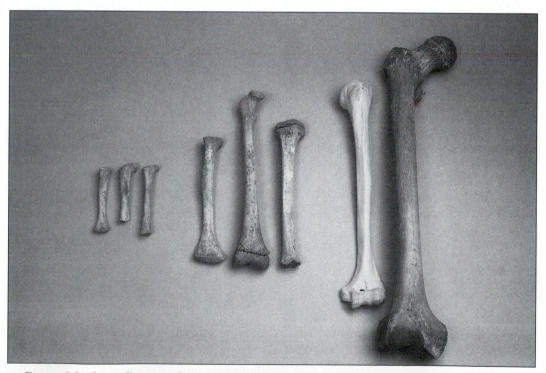

FIGURE 1.8 LONG BONES OF INDIVIDUALS AT DIFFERENT AGES (INFANT, SUBADULT, AND ADULT)

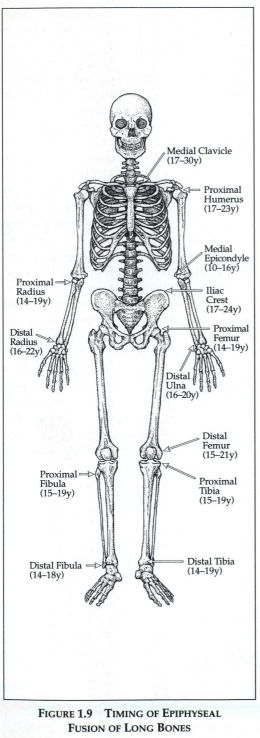

**FIGURE 1.9   TIMING OF EPIPHYSEAL
FUSION OF LONG BONES**

Source: Adapted from White (2000); Ubelaker (1999); and
Buikstra and Ubelaker (1994).

meaning they have two sets of teeth. The deciduous, or "baby," teeth begin to erupt in late infancy while eruption of adult, "permanent," teeth commences during middle childhood, typically around the age of seven years. Dental development terminates in the late teens or early twenties with the eruption (and/or extraction) of the third molars, or "wisdom teeth." The timing of third molar eruption is highly variable, and some individuals do not have them at all (agenesis). Thus, skeletal biologists can accurately estimate subadult age from the dentition between infancy and approximately fifteen years, when the second molars erupt and their roots complete their development. Schour and Massler (1941, 1944) have developed a chart of dental eruption patterns at different ages that is commonly used by forensic anthropologists.

Dental formation is considered more accurate than eruption patterns for chronological age estimation (Ubelaker 1989). Here, observations of crown and root development are used to estimate chronological age from prenatal to late teens (Moorrees, Fanning, and Hunt 1963a, b). Dental histological aging techniques are also available, and Fitzgerald and Rose (2000) provide an excellent review of these techniques. Because there is relatively little variability in dental development and epiphyseal fusion among populations, age ranges of two to five years may be estimated for subadult remains. However, age-related variability increases among adults and the age range must increase accordingly.

ADULT   A skeleton is considered to be an adult once all of the epiphyses have fused. The last epiphysis to fuse is the medial clavicle, which occurs between approximately seventeen and thirty years of age—earlier in females, later in males (Webb and Suchey 1985). At this point, the bones are no longer developing and growing but instead slowly begin to break down. Anthropologists have identified features of the skeleton that undergo regular age-associated changes and are not generally affected by other stresses, such as locomotion, weight, or muscularity. The most commonly used adult age indicator is the pubic symphysis.

The pubic symphysis is the joint at which the two pubic bones meet at the front of the pelvis. In life, the faces of the pubic bones are separated by fibrocartilage. The pubic symphysis is not directly weight bearing and, in the absence of trauma, experiences relatively standard change over time. There are differences between the sexes, however, and it is imperative to estimate the sex of the individual prior to assessing age based on the pubic symphysis. There are also some differences among populations in the United States (Katz and Suchey 1989).

In general, the symphyseal face of a youthful individual has a number of ridges and furrows with no distinct rim (Figure 1.10). Over time, the ridges and furrows level out, a ventral rampart develops, and a complete rim forms around the face. Later, both the face and the rim begin to break down. Since it is difficult to create discrete

age ranges from a continual process of change, anthropologists must settle for broad, statistically derived age ranges. Three techniques of pubic symphyseal aging are frequently used today: Suchey-Brooks (Katz and Suchey 1986; Suchey and Katz 1998), McKern and Stewart (1957), and Todd (1921a, b). The latter techniques were developed from the study of war dead (a sample dominated by males, though see Gilbert and McKern 1973 for female standards) and late nineteenth-century medical-school cadavers, respectively. In contrast, the six-phase Suchey-Brooks technique is based upon the study of over 1,200 modern individuals of both sexes, all ages, and multiple ancestral affiliations from the L.A. County Coroners Office. For purposes of standardization, it is recommended that case reports include the Suchey-Brooks observations, when available.

Another aspect of the pelvis, the auricular surface of the ilium, is also useful for estimating adult age (Lovejoy et al. 1985). Important features of the aging process of the face include a decrease in the number of striations, an increase in porosity and degree of apical lipping, and changes in bone

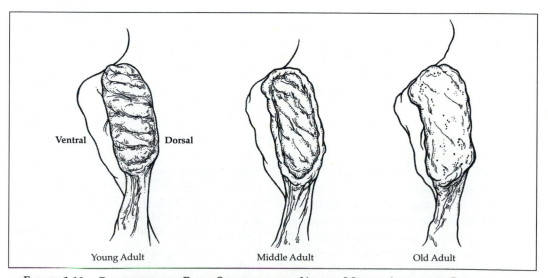

Ventral Dorsal

Young Adult Middle Adult Old Adult

FIGURE 1.10 COMPARISON OF PUBIC SYMPHYSIS OF A YOUNG, MIDDLE AGED, AND OLDER ADULT

texture. In addition, changes also occur on the ilium immediately posterior to (behind) the auricular surface. Again, a broad age range is the best we can expect from this technique given the variability of age-related changes in adults.

Other aging techniques employed by forensic anthropologists include the examination of the sternal end of the fourth rib (Iscan and Loth 1986a, b) and cranial suture closure (Meindl and Lovejoy 1985). The sternal rib ends can yield quite reliable age estimations (Saunders et al. 1992), and adjacent ribs can be used without losing information. However, debate continues concerning the utility of cranial suture closure as an accurate age indicator (Singer 1953; Meindl and Lovejoy 1985; Nawrocki 1998; Robling and Stout 2000), and most agree that the best it can render is a fifteen-year age range. Nonetheless, a forensic anthropologist has little choice but to use cranial sutures when only the skull is present. Histological aging methods are also available and are very useful for aging burnt and extremely fragmentary materials (Stout 1992; Ericksen 1991; Kerley and Ubelaker 1978; Ubelaker 1986; see Chapter 18).

In casework, forensic anthropologists use as many aging techniques as are available and then reconcile the results of each method into an appropriate age range, which may be quite broad (e.g., ten years or more). While a wide range may frustrate police investigators, it is the responsibility of the anthropologist to explain to law enforcement agents that excessively narrow age ranges may result in the inappropriate exclusion of missing persons from consideration.

Forensic anthropologists must be able to communicate to the court a sense of the accuracy of skeletal age and sex estimations. Most authors include an estimate of accuracy and reliability in the seminal articles that describe their techniques. For instance, Phenice (1969) reports an accuracy of 96 percent when the ventral arc, ischiopubic ramus, and subpubic concavity are analyzed together to estimate sex. However, it is important to be familiar with "blind" studies designed to test the accuracy and reliability of the methods (Saunders et al. 1992). Lovell (1989) and others (e.g., Ubelaker and Volk 2002) applied the Phenice technique to skeletal samples of known age and sex but obtained an accuracy below 90 percent. Ubelaker and Volk (2002) further found that the accuracy of sex estimation increased substantially (from 88.4 percent to 96.5 percent) when additional pelvic morphological indicators (e.g., sciatic notch and preauricular sulcus) were incorporated with Phenice's traits. Further, they argue that observer experience is also a key factor in accurate sex estimation. Thus, forensic anthropologists should test and quantify their own proficiency for various methods using unfamiliar skeletons of known age and sex.

Ancestry Biological anthropology is historically rooted in raciology, a typological approach to human variation in which individuals are segregated into discrete groups based on the relative frequency of particular physical traits. However, the approach today is no longer typological in nature and biological anthropologists are now interested in understanding the range of variation within and between groups without necessarily creating artificial boundaries between them. In general, anthropologists argue that race (white, black, Hispanic, Chinese, etc.), is a social construct that has no biological basis (Montagu 1964; Marks 1995; Brace 1995; Lewontin 1972). The term *ancestry*, on the other hand, takes into account the population origins and history of an individual, which does have a biological foundation. According to Ousley and Jantz (1996), biological differences "reflect the different origins and separate histories of each [population], which can be highly correlated with many social, geographic, temporal, historical, or linguistic groupings of populations. These correlations form the basis of the study of human variation and of forensic anthropology."

Forensic anthropologists have been criticized by other anthropologists for upholding the race concept whenever they estimate the "race" of a skeleton (e.g., Belcher et al. 2002). Sauer (1992) counters this point by arguing that race must be discussed in forensic reports since the goal of the analysis is identification. "To be of value the race categories used by forensic anthropologists must reflect the everyday usage of the society with which they interact" (Sauer 1992, 109). That is, anthropologists must report how this individual may have classified himself or herself in life, or was classified by society at large.

When personal identification is an issue, forensic anthropologists look first to the cranium to assess ancestry. Forensic anthropologists examine morphological features of the skull and collect cranial measurements, which are then statistically compared to skulls of known ancestry. Morphological features typically examined include the overall shape of the skull vault, orbits, palate, and nasal aperture, as well as the presence or absence of certain characteristics, including Wormian bones (or ossicles, bones within the sutures) and a nasal sill. Many other morphological features are listed in various anthropology papers and books (e.g., Gill 1998; Gill and Rhine 1990; Stewart 1979).

Forensic anthropologists rely on metric data from the Forensic Data Bank (FDB) for a comparative sample of modern individuals of known sex, ancestry, and stature. Since 1983, forensic anthropologists from around the country have contributed metric information from their cases when positive identifications are made. The Data Bank is maintained at the University of Tennessee (Ousley and Jantz 1996, 1998) and, as of early 2002, contains data on 1,800 individuals, most of known sex and ancestry (Jantz, personal communication). The FDB is often consulted to estimate the ancestry of an unknown individual using a program called FORDISC 2.0, written by Ousley and Jantz (1996). FORDISC works by treating the documented forensic cases in the FDB as a comparative sample that can be used to classify unknown individuals from forensic cases. The unknown is then classified by finding the group to which the individual in question is most similar. In discriminant function analysis, the statistical method used in FORDISC, posterior probabilities of group membership can be calculated for each group. These are called posterior probabilities because they are calculated after (posterior to) analysis of the bone measurements. Before evaluating the measurements, there are prior probabilities of group membership, which FORDISC assumes are equal. In other words, if four groups are under consideration, then the prior probability that the case belongs to each group is 0.25. Following the analysis, the metric information from the case presumably modifies these priors so that (ideally) all but one of the probabilities will become very small. These modified probabilities are the posterior probabilities of group membership; the higher the posterior probability, the more likely the unknown case belongs to that group.

Even when the posterior probabilities seem to clearly and unambiguously assign an individual to a single group, it is possible that the individual is not "typical" of that group. For example, if an unknown cranium from a group not represented in the data base (e.g., a Biaka Pygmy) was analyzed using FORDISC, the program will still assign the cranium to a particular group, but the skull will probably not be typical of that group. The probability of getting a cranium that is similar to others in that group is called a "typicality probability" or "typicality index" (McLachlan 1992; van Vark and Schaafsma 1992). FORDISC uses the same statistical methods and theories to estimate sex from cranial and postcranial measurements.

Stature   An individual's standing height is also part of his or her biological profile. Since average height differs between the sexes and among populations, forensic anthropologists estimate living stature by measuring the long bones and applying sex- and population-specific regression equations. Formulae are available for a number of different populations, including World War II and Korean War dead (Trotter and Gleser 1952; Trotter 1970) as well as modern forensic samples (Ousley 1995) which can be found in *FORDISC 2.0*. In addition, the appropriate measurement techniques are found in several sources (e.g., Bass 1995; Moore-Jansen et al. 1994). Typically, measurements of the leg bones tend to be more reliable than those of the arms (Trotter and Gleser 1958), but the forensic anthropologist must pay particular attention to the measurement protocol for the tibia. Jantz and colleagues (1994, 1995) describe how Trotter's measurements of maximum tibial length do not correspond to the measurement descriptions she provided and results in the underestimation of living stature. All stature estimates should be reported as a range by including appropriate confidence intervals (Giles and Klepinger 1988; Konigsberg et al. 1998; Ousley 1995).

To establish a personal identification, stature estimates derived from long bone measurements are compared to statures recorded in medical records and/or driver's licenses of potential matches. However, self-reported height may not always be accurate. For instance, Willey and Falsetti (1991) have found that many people, especially men, tend to overstate their true stature on their driver's licenses. Further, Galloway (1988) reports that significant stature loss in elderly individuals is often not recorded in medical records or on driver's licenses. In other words, older adults tend to report their more youthful stature. The errors of self-reporting emphasize the need for forensic anthropologists to report appropriate statistical ranges so that a missing individual is not falsely excluded from consideration.

Antemortem Pathology   For any particular case, a biological profile consisting of age, sex, ancestry, and stature may not significantly reduce the number of missing individuals, especially in urban areas where the missing persons list is often quite lengthy. Thus, the forensic anthropologist must examine the bones carefully and note any unique characteristics that will help exclude one or more individuals from a pool of potential identifications. Pathological conditions that occur before death are called antemortem pathologies. However, for a pathology or anomaly to be forensically important, an antemortem record must exist in the form of radiographs (x-rays), dental records, or medical records. Individuals close to the missing person may also convey information about his or her medical history, even if records are not available. Ideally, information gathered from non-medical sources should be consistent across multiple family members or friends.

The most common skeletal pathology encountered in forensic anthropology cases is bone fractures. These are especially useful since most people seek medical care when a bone is broken and radiographs are routinely ordered to diagnose and treat the fractures. Anthropologists can compare the location and morphology of the fracture, including the amount of healing present, to the specific site and date of fracture as recorded in the medical records (e.g., Maples 1984; Klepinger 1999).

Bone infections also leave diagnostic markers on the bone. Osteomyelitis is an infection of the bone marrow and is characterized by exuberant bone proliferation and may include one or more cloacae—defects in the bone that allow infection byproducts to drain from the medullary cavity. Osteomyelitis can occur as a complication of a

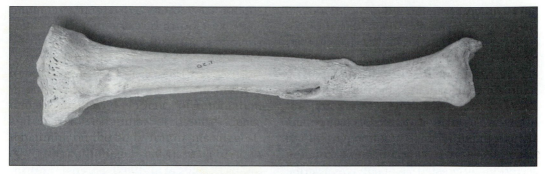

FIGURE 1.11   HEALED FRACTURE OF THE TIBIA WITH OSTEOMYELITIS

bone fracture (Figure 1.11) or via the spread of bacteria to bone through the bloodstream (Ortner and Putschar 1981). Periostitis, on the other hand, is an inflammation of the periosteum, which will stimulate osteoblastic activity such that new bone is laid down on top of the original cortex (Figure 1.12). It may not be possible to determine the cause of osteomyelitis or a periosteal lesion, though the location and age of such "non-specific" lesions can still be useful for identification.

Other more subtle bone disorders or unique characteristics observed on radiographs are also forensically important, such as the location and extent of osteoarthritis, particular trabecular patterns within a bone, and frontal sinus morphology. Comparisons of antemortem and postmortem radiographs may require the

assistance of a radiologist, especially if the anthropologist does not have extensive experience in radiograph interpretation. The time elapsed between when a radiograph was taken and the death of the individual is also an important consideration since significant bone remodeling may modify or obscure lesions. Medical prosthetics and surgical devices with serial numbers are also useful for identification (Ubelaker and Jacobs 1995). Similarly, dental pathologies and restorations, particularly fillings and crowns, can be used to identify human remains (e.g., Stimson and Mertz 1997).

Certain habitual tasks will alter the biomechanical stresses placed on bone and provide the anthropologist with clues as to the types of activities the individual might have performed in life (Wilczak and Kennedy 1998; Kennedy 1989; Saul and

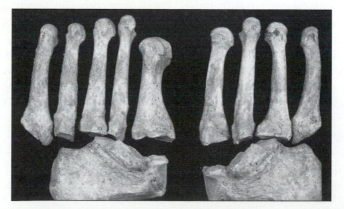

FIGURE 1.12   ACTIVE AND HEALED (SCLEROTIC) PERIOSTITIS ON METATARSALS AND CALCANEI BILATERALLY

Saul 1999). For instance, in certain cultures females spend a great deal of time kneeling or squatting while processing food. This habitual activity alters the way the tibia and femur and the tibia and talus articulate, leaving distinct accessory or modified facets on these bones—so called "squatting facets" (Kennedy 1989; Kostick 1963). Kennedy et al. (1986) determined that an Egyptian mummy, whose burial case inscriptions suggested he or she was a scribe in life, indeed exhibited bony changes on one of the fingers of the right hand that was consistent with routinely holding a stylus and writing. When a forensic anthropologist observes accessory facets, unilateral muscle development, or other unique markers of stress on bone, he or she may be able to include a description of general activities that may have contributed to these traits, such as pitching, carrying heavy loads on the shoulder, or even writing. Though an occupational marker may not lead directly to an identification, attention to subtle bony details may be helpful if several missing individuals share otherwise similar biological profiles.

The Process of Identification

As mentioned above, forensic anthropologists compare the postmortem biological profile to that of missing persons provided by law enforcement. Some missing individuals may be excluded by their sex, age, ancestry, height, and/or the presence or absence of a particular skeletal pathology. Antemortem dental and medical records of potential matches still remaining from the list are then obtained and compared to the remains.

Presumptive anthropological and dental identifications may be confirmed by genetic analyses. Alternatively, DNA may be the only mode of identification if the remains are too fragmentary or incomplete for a conclusive identification. Two types of DNA analyses are possible. While nuclear (or genomic) DNA can be obtained from bone tissue or the marrow (if present), the amount of nuclear DNA is often too small to obtain reliable results. Mitochondrial DNA (mtDNA), on the other hand, is present in greater quantities within cells and can be recovered from bone in forensic, historic, and prehistoric skeletons, and even fossils (Krings et al. 1997). Forensic anthropologists often work closely with DNA laboratories to select and procure appropriate bone samples for genetic analysis.

Perimortem Trauma and Postmortem Alterations

In addition to identification of skeletal remains, a forensic anthropologist may be called upon to describe wounds on the skeleton that occurred at or near the time of death (perimortem wounds). Wounds from knives, saws, blunt objects, or guns leave diagnostic markers in bones. However, taphonomic processes may blur the distinction between perimortem and postmortem wounds. Taphonomic processes are those that affect the body after death, including rodent and scavenger damage, weathering, or burning. There are clues to help distinguish peri- and postmortem trauma. For instance, perimortem wounds will undergo the same decompositional processes as the rest of the skeleton, including color changes. Therefore, the wound margins will exhibit the same color as the surrounding, undamaged bone. Conversely, trauma to bones that have already decomposed and changed color (due to sun exposure, contact with soil, etc.) will demonstrate margins that are lighter than the surrounding bone. Fresh bone will also respond differently to blunt and sharp trauma than dry bone (Galloway 1999; Maples 1986; Sauer 1984, 1998). For example, fresh bone will bend before breaking and bone spurs may result. However, dry bone is more brittle and will snap without leaving any deformed spurs of bone.

The forensic anthropological report must include clear descriptions of which wounds are perimortem and postmortem, and which are inconclusive. Because of their skills in interpreting skeletal trauma and identifying potentially confounding taphonomic processes, forensic anthropologists are often consulted by forensic pathologists to examine bone trauma even when the remains are fleshed or the identity of the individual is not an issue. Further, the anthropologist can study the postmortem changes and associated evidence (e.g., insects) to help estimate the postmortem interval, or time since death.

Introduction to the Cases

This text is divided into five thematic sections representing the most common areas of casework and research in forensic anthropology. A section overview introduces the chapters and provides contextual information about the applications of forensic anthropology and specific forensic techniques and approaches. As mentioned above, an essential difference between forensic anthropology and other subdisciplines of biological anthropology is that forensic anthropologists must prepare scientifically valid legal records in the form of case reports, and competently present their results in judicial proceedings. Thus, their methods and reports undergo critical review by their peers as well as nonscientific parties in a court of law. The chapters in Section I examine the fundamental principles of identification, the multidisciplinary relationships among experts, and the roles and responsibilities of the forensic anthropologist in the courtroom.

Section II explores the methods utilized to detect and recover human remains. Since humans have devised a number of peculiar methods to dispose of a body, it is difficult to predict just when and where human remains might be found. Forensic anthropologists should have archaeological training, which allows them to assist law enforcement with the recovery of human remains from a number of different contexts. Basic outdoor search strategies are discussed in the section overview, while the chapters provide specific examples of recovery techniques for a variety of locales.

The chapters in Section III collectively provide an overview of how forensic anthropologists interpret perimortem trauma and major taphonomic processes from skeletal remains. Two chapters provide an excellent overview of the three types of trauma forensic anthropologists most often encounter—gunshot wounds, sharp force trauma, and blunt trauma. These chapters also illustrate how anthropologists and pathologists work together to interpret trauma in both soft tissue and bone when human remains are decomposed. Other cases illustrate how taphonomic principles can be utilized to estimate the postmortem interval (PMI) and establish the context of human bones found in unusual locations.

Section IV on Analytical Techniques demonstrates how forensic anthropologists use sophisticated equipment and techniques to address special problems. For instance, when only small fragments of bone are available, certain parameters of the biological profile can be determined from the microstructure of bone (histomorphology), or identity may be established through genetic and anthropological analysis. Experiments can be conducted to replicate tool mark characteristics in bone in order to reconstruct peri- or postmortem trauma or answer questions about the antiquity of an individual. Techniques presented in the case studies include histomorphology, mitochondrial DNA analysis, cut mark analysis, and mass spectrometry.

Finally, Section V provides some insight into the broad applications and current directions of forensic anthropology. Three different applications are presented—international human rights investigations, recovery and identification of war dead, and mass fatality incidents. The U.S. Public Health Service Disaster and Mortuary Operational Response Teams (DMORT) activate forensic anthropologists in mass casualty situations, such as transportation disasters, bombings, and floods. In addition, the Central Identification Laboratory in Hawaii (CILHI) is revisited with an additional perspective—that of a daughter of an MIA from the Vietnam War. Finally, the excavation of mass graves for the purposes of identification and evidence collection is key to the investigation of past human rights atrocities. The *Equipo Argentino de Antropología Forense* (EAAF), or Argentine Forensic Anthropology Team, was the first group to apply forensic anthropology methods to investigate human rights abuses. All of these applications provide exceptional examples of the importance of multidisciplinary collaboration among forensic scientists.

References

Bass, William M. 1995. *Human Osteology: A Laboratory and Field Manual*. Columbia, MO: Missouri Archaeological Society.

Belcher, R., F. Williams, and George J. Armelagos. 2002. Misidentification of meroitic Nubians using *FORDISC 2.0*. Paper presented at the American Association of Physical Anthropology. Buffalo, NY.

Bennett, Kenneth A. 1993. *A Field Guide For Human Skeletal Identification*. 2nd ed. Springfield, IL: Charles C. Thomas.

Brace, C. Loring. 1995. Region does not mean "Race"—Reality versus convention in forensic anthropology. *Journal of Forensic Sciences* 40(2):171–175.

Buikstra, Jane E., and Douglas H. Ubelaker. 1994. *Standards for Data Collection from Human Skeletal Remains*. Fayetteville, AR: Arkansas Archeological Survey Research Series No. 44.

Dittrick, Jean, and Judy M. Suchey. 1986. Sex determination of prehistoric central California skeletal remains using discriminant analysis of the femur and humerus. *American Journal of Physical Anthropology* 70:3–9.

Ericksen, M. F. 1991. Histological estimation of age at death using the anterior cortex of the femur. *American Journal of Physical Anthropology* 84:171–179.

Fisher, Russell S. 1993. History of forensic pathology and related laboratory sciences. Pp. 3–13 in *Spitz and Fisher's Medicolegal Investigation of Death: Guidelines to the Application of Pathology to Crime Investigation*, ed. Werner U. Spitz. Springfield, IL: Charles C. Thomas.

Fitzgerald, Charles M., and Jerome C. Rose. 2000. Reading between the lines: Dental development and subadult age assessment using the microstructural growth markers of teeth. Pp. 163–186 in *Biological Anthropology of the Human Skeleton*, ed. M. Anne Katzenberg and Shelley R. Saunders. New York: Wiley-Liss.

France, Diane L. 1998. Observational and metric analysis of sex in the skeleton. Pp. 163–186 in *Forensic Osteology: Advances in the Identification of Human Remains*, ed. Kathleen J. Reichs. 2nd ed. Springfield, IL: Charles C. Thomas.

Galloway, Alison. 1988. Estimating actual height in the older individual. *Journal of Forensic Sciences* 33(1):126–136.

Galloway, Alison, ed. 1999. *Broken Bones*. Springfield, IL: Charles C. Thomas.

Gilbert, B. M., and T. W. McKern. 1973. A method for aging the female *Os pubis*. *American Journal of Physical Anthropology* 38:31–38.

Giles, Eugene, and Linda L. Klepinger. 1988. Confidence intervals for estimates based on linear regression in forensic anthropology. *Journal of Forensic Sciences* 33:1,218–1,222.

Giles, Eugene, and Orville Elliot. 1962. Race identification from cranial measurements. *Journal of Forensic Sciences* 7(2):147–157.

Giles, Eugene, and Orville Elliot. 1963. Sex determination by discriminant function analysis of crania. *American Journal of Physical Anthropology* 21:53–68.

Gill, George W. 1998. Craniofacial criteria in the skeletal attribution of race. Pp. 293–317 in *Forensic Osteology: Advances in the Identification of Human Remains*, ed. Kathleen J. Reichs. 2nd ed. Springfield, IL: Charles C. Thomas.

Gill, George W., and Stanley Rhine, eds. 1990. *Skeletal Attribution of Race*. Anthropology Papers No. 4, Maxwell Museum of Anthropology.

Iscan, Mehmet Yasar, and Susan Loth. 1986a. Determination of age from the sternal rib in white males: A test of the Phase Method. *Journal of Forensic Sciences* 31:122–132.

Iscan, Mehmet Yasar, and Susan Loth. 1986b. Determination of age from the sternal rib in white females: A test of the Phase Method. *Journal of Forensic Sciences* 31:990–999.

Jantz, Richard L., David R. Hunt, and Lee Meadows. 1994. Maximum length of the tibia: How did Trotter measure it? *American Journal of Physical Anthropology* 93:525–528.

Jantz, Richard L., David R. Hunt, and Lee Meadows. 1995. The measure and mismeasure of the tibia: Implications for stature estimation. *Journal of Forensic Sciences* 40:758–761.

Katz, Darryl, and Judy M. Suchey. 1986. Age determination of the male *os pubis*. *American Journal of Physical Anthropology* 69:427–435.

Katz, Darryl, and Judy M. Suchey. 1989. Race differences in pubic symphyseal aging patterns in the male. *American Journal of Physical Anthropology* 80:167–172.

Kennedy, Kenneth A. R. 1989. Skeletal markers of occupational stress. Pp. 129–160 in *Reconstruction of Life from the Skeleton*, ed. Mehmet Yasar Iscan and Kenneth A. R. Kennedy. New York: Alan R. Liss.

Kennedy, Kenneth A. R., Thomas Plummer, and John Chiment. 1986. Identification of the eminent dead: Penpi, a scribe of ancient Egypt. Pp. 290–307 in *Forensic Osteology: The Recovery and Analysis of Unknown Skeletal Remains*, ed. Kathleen J. Reichs. Springfield, IL: Charles C. Thomas.

Kerley, Ellis R., and Douglas H. Ubelaker. 1978. Revisions in the microscopic method of estimating age at death on human cortical bone. *American Journal of Physical Anthropology* 49:545–546.

Klepinger, Linda L. 1999. Unusual skeletal anomalies and pathologies in forensic casework. Pp. 226–236 in *Forensic Osteological Analysis: A Book of Case Studies*, ed. Scott I. Fairgrieve. Springfield, IL: Charles C. Thomas.

Konigsberg, Lyle W., Samantha M. Hens, Lee Meadows Jantz, and William L. Jungers. 1998. Stature estimation and calibration: Bayesian and maximum likelihood perspec-

tives in physical anthropology. *Yearbook of Physical Anthropology* Suppl 27(41):65–92.

Kostick, E. L. 1963. Facets and imprints on the upper and lower extremities of femora from a western Nigerian population. *Journal of Anatomy* 97:393–402.

Krings, Matthias, Anne Stone, R. W. Schmitz, H. Krainitzki, Mark Stoneking, and Svante Pääbo. 1997. Neandertal DNA sequences and the origin of modern humans. *Cell* 90:19–30.

Krogman, Wilton Marion, and Mehmet Yasar Iscan. 1986. *The Human Skeleton in Forensic Medicine*. 2nd ed. Springfield, IL: Charles C. Thomas.

Lewontin, R. C. 1972. The apportionment of human diversity. Pp. 381–398 in *Evolutionary Biology*, ed. M. K. Hecht and W. S. Steere. Vol. 6. New York: Plenum Press.

Lovejoy, C. Owen, Richard Meindl, Thomas R. Pryzbeck, and Robert P. Mensforth. 1985. Chronological metamorphosis of the auricular surface of the ilium: A new method for the determination of age at death. *American Journal of Physical Anthropology* 68:15–28.

Lovell, Nancy C. 1989. Test of Phenice's visual sexing technique for determining sex from the *os pubis*. *American Journal of Physical Anthropology* 79:117–120.

Maples, William R. 1984. The identifying pathology. Pp. 363–356 in *Human Identification: Case Studies in Forensic Anthropology*, ed. Ted A. Rathbun and Jane E. Buikstra. Springfield, IL: Charles C. Thomas.

Maples, William R. 1986. Trauma analysis by the forensic anthropologist. Pp. 218–228 in *Forensic Osteology: Advances in the Identification of Human Remains*, ed. Kathleen J. Reichs. Springfield, IL: Charles C. Thomas.

Marks, Jonathon. 1995. *Human Biodiversity: Genes, Race and History*. New York: Aldine De Gruyter.

McKern, Thomas, and T. Dale Stewart. 1957. *Skeletal Age Changes in Young American Males*. Technical Report EP-45, Natick, MA: U.S. Army Quartermaster Research and Development Center, Environmental Protection Research Division.

McLachlan, Geoffrey J. 1992. *Discriminant Analysis and Statistical Pattern Recognition*. New York: Wiley & Sons.

Meindl, Richard, and C. Owen Lovejoy. 1985. Ectocranial suture closure: A revised method for the determination of skeletal age at death based on the lateral-anterior sutures. *American Journal of Physical Anthropology* 68:57–66.

Montagu, Ashley, ed. 1964. *Man's Most Dangerous Myth: The Fallacy of Race*. 4th ed. Cleveland, OH: World Press.

Moore-Jansen, Peer M., Stephen D. Ousley, and Richard L. Jantz. 1994. *Data Collection Procedures for Forensic Skeletal Material*. Reports of Investigations No. 48. Department of Anthropology. Knoxville, TN: University of Tennessee.

Moorrees, C. F. A., E. A. Fanning, and E. E. Hunt. 1963a. Formation and resorption of three deciduous teeth in children. *American Journal of Physical Anthropology* 21:205–213.

Moorrees, C. F. A., E. A. Fanning, and E. E. Hunt. 1963b. Age variation of formation stages for 10 permanent teeth. *Journal of Dental Research* 42:1,490–1,502.

Nawrocki, Stephen. 1998. Regression formulae for estimating age at death from cranial suture closure. Pp. 276–292 in *Forensic Osteology: Advances in the Identification of Human Remains*, ed. Kathleen J. Reichs. 2nd ed. Springfield, IL: Charles C. Thomas.

Ortner, Donald J., and Walter G. J. Putschar. 1981. *Identification of Pathological Conditions in Human Skeletal Remains*. Washington, D.C.: Smithsonian Institution Press.

Ousley, Stephen. 1995. Should we estimate "biological" or forensic stature? *Journal of Forensic Sciences* 40:768–773.

Ousley, Stephen, and Richard Jantz. 1996. *FORDISC 2.0*. Department of Anthropology, University of Tennessee, Knoxville.

Ousley, Stephen, and Richard Jantz. 1998. The Forensic Data Bank: Documenting skeletal trends in the United States. Pp. 441–457 in *Forensic Osteology: Advances in the Identification of Human Remains*, ed. Kathleen J. Reichs. 2nd ed. Springfield, IL: Charles C. Thomas.

Phenice, T. W. 1969. A newly developed visual method of sexing the *os pubis*. *American Journal of Physical Anthropology* 30:297–302.

Robling, Alexander G., and Sam D. Stout. 2000. Histomorphometry of human cortical bone: Applications to age estimation. Pp. 187–213 in *Biological Anthropology of the Human Skeleton*, ed. M. Anne Katzenberg and Shelley R. Saunders. New York: Wiley-Liss.

Sauer, Norman J. 1984. Manner of death: Skeletal evidence of blunt and sharp instrument wounds. Pp. 176–184 in *Human Identification: Case Studies in Forensic Anthropology*, ed. Ted A. Rathbun and Jane E. Buikstra. Springfield, IL: Charles C. Thomas.

Sauer, Norman J. 1992. Forensic anthropology and the concept of race: If races don't exist, why are forensic anthropologists so good at identifying them? *Social Science and Medicine* 34(2):107–111.

Sauer, Norman J. 1998. The timing of injuries and manner of death: Distinguishing among antemortem, perimortem, and postmortem trauma. Pp. 321–332 in *Forensic Osteology: Advances in the Identification of Human Remains*, ed. Kathleen J. Reichs. 2nd ed. Springfield, IL: Charles C. Thomas.

Saul, Julie Mather, and Frank P. Saul. 1999. Biker's bones: An avocational syndrome. Pp. 237–250 in *Forensic Osteological Analysis: A Book of Case Studies*, ed. Scott I. Fairgrieve. Springfield, IL: Charles C. Thomas.

Saunders, Shelley R. 2000. Subadult skeletons and growth-related studies. Pp. 135–161 in *Biological Anthropology of the Human Skeleton*, ed. M. Anne Katzenberg and Shelley R. Saunders. New York: Wiley-Liss.

Saunders, Shelley R., C. Fitzgerald, T. Rogers, C. Dudar, and H. McKillop. 1992. A test of several methods of skeletal age estimation using a documented archaeological sample. *Canadian Society of Forensic Sciences Journal* 25(2):97–118.

Scheuer, Louise, and Sue Black. 2000. *Developmental Juvenile Osteology*. San Diego, CA: Academic Press.

Schour, I., and M. Massler. 1941. The development of the human dentition. *Journal of the American Dental Association* 28:1,153–1,160.

Schour, I., and M. Massler. 1944. Development of the human dentition. Chart, 2nd ed. Chicago, IL: American Dental Association.

Schwartz, Jeffrey H. 1995. *Skeleton Keys: An Introduction to Human Skeletal Morphology, Development, and Analysis*. New York: Oxford Press.

Singer, Ronald. 1953. Estimation of age from cranial suture closure: A report on its unreliability. *Journal of Forensic Medicine* 1:52–59.

Steele, D. Gentry, and Claud A. Bramblett. 1988. *Anatomy and Biology of the Human Skeleton*. College Station, TX: Texas A&M University Press.

Stewart, T. Dale. 1979. *Essentials of Forensic Anthropology*. Springfield, IL: Charles C. Thomas.

Stimson, Paul G., and Curtis A. Mertz. 1997. *Forensic Dentistry*. Boca Raton, FL: CRC Press.

Stout, Sam D. 1992. Methods of determining age at death using bone microstructure. Pp. 21–35 in *Skeletal Biology of Past Peoples: Research Methods*, ed. Shelley R. Saunders and M. Anne Katzenberg. New York: Wiley-Liss.

Suchey, Judy Myers, and Darryl Katz. 1998. Applications of pubic age determination in a forensic setting. Pp. 204–236 in *Forensic Osteology: Advances in the Identification of Human Remains*, ed. Kathleen J. Reichs. 2nd ed. Springfield, IL: Charles C. Thomas.

Sutherland, Leslie D., and Judy M. Suchey. 1991. Use of the ventral arc in pubic sex determination. *Journal of Forensic Sciences* 36(2):501–511.

Thieme, Frederick P., and W. J. Schull. 1957. Sex discrimination from the skeleton. *Human Biology* 29(3):242–273.

Todd, T. Wingate. 1921a. Age changes in the pubic bone I: The white male pubis. *American Journal of Physical Anthropology* 3:285–334.

Todd, T. Wingate. 1921b. Age changes in the pubic bone III: The pubis of the white female, IV: The pubis of the female White-Negro hybrid. *American Journal of Physical Anthropology* 4:1–70.

Trotter, Mildred. 1970. Estimation of stature from intact long bones. Pp. 71–83 in *Personal Identification in Mass Disasters*, ed. T. Dale Stewart. Washington, D.C.: Smithsonian Institution Press.

Trotter, Mildred, and Goldine C. Gleser. 1952. Estimation of stature from long bones of American Whites and Negroes. *American Journal of Physical Anthropology* 10:463–514.

Trotter, Mildred, and Goldine C. Gleser. 1958. A re-evaluation of estimation of stature based on measurements of stature taken during life and of long bones after death. *American Journal of Physical Anthropology* 16:79–123.

Ubelaker, Douglas H. 1986. Estimation of age at death from histology of human bone. Pp. 240–247 in *Dating and Age Determination of Biological Materials*, ed. M. R. Zimmerman and J. Lawrence Angel. London: Croom Helm.

Ubelaker, Douglas H. 1989. The estimation of age at death from immature human bone. Pp. 55–70 in *Age Markers in the Human Skeleton*, ed. Mehmet Yasar Iscan. Springfield, IL: Charles C. Thomas.

Ubelaker, Douglas H. 1999. *Human Skeletal Remains: Excavation, Analysis, Interpretation.* 3rd ed. Washington, D.C.: Taraxacum.

Ubelaker, Douglas H. 2000. Methodological considerations in the forensic applications of human skeletal biology. Pp. 41–67 in *Biological Anthropology of the Human Skeleton*, ed. M. Anne Katzenberg and Shelley R. Saunders. New York: Willey-Liss.

Ubelaker, Douglas H., and Carl H. Jacobs. 1995. Identification of orthopedic device manufacturer. *Journal of Forensic Sciences* 40(2):168–170.

Ubelaker, Douglas H., and Crystal G. Volk. 2002. A test of the Phenice method for the estimation of sex. *Journal of Forensic Sciences* 47(1):19–24.

VanVark, G. N. and W. Schaafsma. 1992. Advances in the quantitative analysis of skeletal morphology. Pp. 225–257 in *Skeletal Biology of Past Peoples: Research Methods*, ed. Shelley R. Saunders. New York: Wiley-Liss.

Webb, Patricia A. O., and Judy M. Suchey. 1985. Epiphyseal union of the anterior iliac crest and medial clavicle in a modern multiracial sample of American males and females. *American Journal of Physical Anthropology* 68:457–466.

White, Tim D. 2000. *Human Osteology.* 2nd ed. San Diego, CA: Academic Press.

Wilczak, Cynthia A., and Kenneth A. R. Kennedy. 1998. Mostly MOS: Technical aspects of identification of skeletal markers of occupational stress. Pp. 461–490 in *Forensic Osteology: Advances in the Identification of Human Remains*, ed. Kathleen J. Reichs. 2nd ed. Springfield, IL: Charles C. Thomas.

Willey, P., and Anthony Falsetti. 1991. Inaccuracy of height information on driver's licenses. *Journal of Forensic Sciences* 36(3):813–819.

Further Reading

Burns, Karen R. 1999. *Forensic Anthropology Training Manual.* Upper Saddle River, NJ: Prentice Hall.

Fairgrieve, Scott I., ed. 1999. *Forensic Osteological Analysis: A Book of Case Studies.* Springfield, IL: Charles C. Thomas.

Iscan, Mehmet Yasar, and Kenneth A. R. Kennedy, eds. 1989. *Reconstruction of Life from the Skeleton.* New York: Wiley-Liss.

Joyce, Christopher, and Eric Stover. 1991. *Witnesses from the Grave: The Stories Bones Tell.* Boston, MA: Little, Brown & Company.

Maples, William R., and Michael Browning. 1994. *Dead Men Do Tell Tales: The Strange and Fascinating Cases of a Forensic Anthropologist.* New York: Doubleday.

Pickering, Robert B., and David C. Bachman. 1997. *The Use of Forensic Anthropology*. Boca Raton, FL: CRC Press.

Rathbun, Ted A., and Jane E. Buikstra. 1984. *Human Identification: Case Studies in Forensic Anthropology*. Springfield, IL: Charles C. Thomas.

Rhine, Stanley. 1998. *Bone Voyage: A Journey in Forensic Anthropology*. Albuquerque, NM: University of New Mexico Press.

Schwartz, Jeffrey H. 1993. *What the Bones Tell Us*. Tucson, AZ: University of Arizona Press.

Ubelaker, Douglas H., and Henry Scammell. 1992. *Bones: A Forensic Detective's Casebook*. New York: Edward Burlingame Books.

PERSONAL IDENTIFICATION AND LEGAL CONSIDERATIONS OF FORENSIC ANTHROPOLOGY CASEWORK IN THE UNITED STATES

The hallmark of forensic anthropology is the identification of the dead through the analysis of skeletal remains. The cases presented in this section illustrate the forensic approaches and methods utilized in the identification process as well as the legal responsibilities of forensic anthropologists. These chapters also keenly demonstrate the nature of multidisciplinary work among forensic experts. While Chapter 1 discusses the parameters of skeletal identification, this overview provides some background information concerning the professionalization of the discipline and the important legal rulings that impact the forensic anthropologist's role in the courtroom. Since forensic anthropologists can be called to testify in both civil and criminal cases, it is imperative that they are familiar with the rules of evidence and proceedings of our current legal system and stay abreast of relevant changes.

PROFESSIONALISM AND TRAINING IN FORENSIC ANTHROPOLOGY

Although prominent anthropologists have practiced forensic anthropology since the 1920s and 1930s (see Ubelaker 1990, 1999, 2000; Kerley 1978; and Stewart 1979 for historical reviews), the profession was formalized in the United States in 1972 with the formation of the Physical Anthropology Section of the American Academy of Forensic Sciences (AAFS). The AAFS is the primary professional organization of forensic science in the United States and currently consists of ten professional sections, listed below. As of this writing, there are over 250 members of the Physical Anthropology section.

Criminalistics
Odontology
Questioned Documents
Toxicology
Jurisprudence
Engineering
Pathology/Biology
Physical Anthropology
Psychiatry and Behavioral Sciences
General

Over the past few decades, many anthropologists have received specialized training in forensic methods in addition to their general anthropological education. This trend continues today as more and more institutions are developing formal graduate programs or programmatic emphases in forensic anthropology. However, since relatively few anthropologists find full-time employment practicing forensic anthropology exclusively, it is imperative that students maintain broad anthropological training. That is, specializations that are unique to forensic anthropology, such as gunshot trauma analysis or facial reproduction, should enhance, not replace, an extensive education in the four fields of anthropology—linguistics, cultural anthropology, physical anthropology, and archaeology (Ubelaker 2000). Archaeological methods are especially important in forensic anthropology, as is cultural anthropological theory, particularly in international work. A robust education in the social and biological sciences is also valuable, and should include genetics, biochemistry, anatomy, evolutionary biology, criminal justice, and statistics.

A well-grounded foundation in physical anthropology underlies the success of any professional forensic anthropology position, whether it is within or apart from academia. While most professional forensic anthropologists work in a university setting, nonacademic positions also offer many opportunities for those who are broadly educated. For instance, anthropologists at the Smithsonian Institution accomplish a considerable amount of forensic work (Grisbaum and Ubelaker 2001) and also conduct research in paleopathology, bioarchaeology, and population genetics (e.g., Verano and Ubelaker 1992; Owsley and Jantz 1994). Similarly, anthropologists from the Central Identification Laboratory in Hawaii (CILHI) apply their forensic anthropological and archaeological expertise to recover and identify U.S. soldiers and civilians lost in past conflicts. A growing number of anthropologists are also involved in international human rights investigations (Steadman and Haglund 2001). Finally, some forensic anthropologists holding either master's or doctoral degrees now maintain full-time anthropological positions in medical examiners' offices or crime labs. Clearly, broad-based experiences and education gained in both the natural and social sciences are important as the discipline continues to expand in new directions.

Multidisciplinary Interactions in Forensic Science

Forensic anthropology forms an integral component of an investigative team in the field, laboratory, and courtroom. For example, during the identification process, forensic anthropologists may work with police investigators, crime scene technicians, forensic pathologists, odontologists (dentists), molecular geneticists, radiologists, and fingerprint experts. New members are added to the team if a case goes to trial, including the attorneys and a variable number of additional forensic specialists, such as ballistics experts, trace evidence examiners, and document examiners, each of whom testifies as to his or her scientific or technical findings. But how does forensic anthropological evidence become integrated into a web of other physical, trace, and circumstantial evidence to make a legally compelling case?

In most criminal cases, the initial responsibility falls upon the lead law enforcement investigator(s) to decide which consultants will have access to certain evidence, how much information to share with each specialist, and when. If a suspect is apprehended and charged, the attorneys join the investigations to weave all available evidence and expert opinions into a complex web of facts that may ultimately be presented in court. Thus, each forensic discipline represents but one thread in the web, and each thread must function together or the entire superstructure will fail. The bones are the hard evidence with which a forensic anthropologist works, but not the only evidence. Communication between experts, strict adherence to scientific methods, and high ethical standards are at the forefront of forensic science, and forensic anthropologists are partners in this process.

THE SCIENTIST/EXPERT IN THE COURTROOM

The adversarial nature of the U.S. justice system holds a number of surprises for the scientific expert witness. The rules for the admissibility of expert testimony vary from state to state and have undergone sweeping and dramatic changes in the federal courts during the last decade. The forensic anthropology expert must be familiar with the basic process of the legal system and the standards of admissibility of evidence in both state and federal courts, for if an expert cannot meet the gatekeeping requirements now applied to expert testimony, his or her opinions will never make it past the threshold reliability requirements imposed by most courts. There are very specific rules as to what constitutes admissible expert evidence, and additional rules as to how expert interpretations of that evidence can be presented in court. In particular, the anthropologist must know whether his or her testimony will be evaluated by *Frye* or *Daubert* standards.

The traditional *Frye* standard (*Frye v. United States*, 293 F. 1013 [D.C. Cir. 1923]) allowed scientific evidence to be presented in court if it had gained "general acceptance" within the scientific discipline. The *Frye* rule stated that the underlying principles and methods of presented testimony must be accepted as scientifically valid by the discipline. Under *Frye*, the judge did not rule directly on the admissibility of evidence. Instead, opposing experts openly debated the issue of general acceptance in the courtroom. This often pitted one expert relying on older scientific standards against another who was attempting to incorporate new scientific methods. While theoretically *Frye* should have limited the amount of "junk science" and "pseudoscience" allowed in court, it also restricted the ability to assert new scientific evidence or principles, such as DNA evidence in the 1980s and 1990s.

Concerns by the federal courts about perceived "junk science" expert opinion testimony in high-profile products liability cases, including Agent Orange, breast implants, and asbestos led the U.S. Supreme Court to sharply curtail the admissibility of expert testimony in federal courts. In 1993, the U.S. Supreme Court case of *Daubert v. Merrill Dow Pharmaceuticals* established a four-factor "gatekeeping" test to be applied by judges to determine the reliability and admissibility of proposed scientific testimony. These four factors focus on peer review, determination of error rates, testing, and acceptability within the discipline. In the 1999 case of *Kumho Tire*, the U.S. Supreme Court announced that this test would be applied to the admissibility of all expert testimony, not just that of scientific experts (*Fed. R. Evid. 702* advisory committee's note). The revised *Federal Rule of Evidence 702* became effective in 2001, and was intended to incorporate the *Daubert* and *Kumho* standards:

> If scientific, technical, or other specialized knowledge will assist the trier of fact to understand the evidence or to determine a fact in issue, a witness qualified as an expert by knowledge, skill, experience, training, or education, may testify thereto in the form of an opinion or otherwise, *if (1) the testimony is based upon sufficient facts or data, (2) the testimony is the product of reliable principles and methods, and (3) the witness has applied the principles and methods reliably to the facts of the case.* (Fed. R. Evid. 702 [2001])

In other words, the judge, not the scientific community, determines whether acceptable scientific standards have been met. These issues are typically raised in pre-trial motions and argued before a judge well before a jury has been seated. At issue is whether a particular scientist is deemed an expert by the court and/or if a certain aspect of the testimony in which the scientist is prepared to present is admissible. The judge must make a ruling based on whether the evidence or scientific method is "reliable and relevant" to the case at hand. Thus, *Daubert* addresses the question of whether a method or technique is good science. For instance, what is the error rate of the method? Are the methods reliable and replicable? Has the method or technique been subjected to peer review? If the judge rules that the methods or underlying principles do not achieve a threshold of scientific reliability or are irrelevant to the case, the expert will not be allowed to testify in court.

The number of state and federal cases utilizing forensic anthropology increases each year. It is likely that most courts will deem standard identification methods admissible given the demonstrated reliability of these techniques. So how does the forensic anthropologist prepare to be evaluated by the courts? A court will assess the forensic anthropologist's testimony and opinions by reviewing the case report and considering whether the methods and opinions are admissible under the appropriate rules of evidence. Thus, the first step is to submit an accurate, unambiguous forensic anthropology case report. The report should clearly demonstrate the scientific foundations of the methods and interpretations, and include a bibliography of relevant and updated sources. The anthropologist should also justify his or her final opinions. In other words, it should be apparent from the methods and results how the anthropologist arrived at the stated conclusions.

Perhaps the most important points to keep in mind are that the expert must openly state the scientific limitations of his or her interpretations and never offer opinions that stray beyond the evidence at hand. For instance, forensic anthropologists should not testify as to the motive of the crime, the perpetrator's or victim's state of mind at the time of the murder, if the victim suffered, or how long it took him or her to die. Such questions are best addressed by criminal profilers, psychologists, medical doctors, and forensic pathologists. Any attempt to answer questions beyond the purview of the discipline greatly diminishes the anthropologist's standing as an expert witness in the eyes of the judge and jury, as well as among his or her scientific peers.

The demeanor and professionalism of the expert witness may be as crucial as the evidence presented. The adversarial system is just that, and many attorneys try to weaken the opposing council's case by undermining their expert witnesses. Any behavior or answers that appear unprofessional can hurt the credibility of the witness and the evidence he or she is presenting. Attempts at humor by the expert in court or in depositions are never appropriate and will inevitably be misconstrued.

To prepare for their involvement in the U.S. medicolegal system, forensic anthropologists consult topical books that provide a good overview of the judicial process, from scene analysis to case report preparation and trial testimony (e.g., Geberth 1996; Fisher 2000). Anthropologists should also learn directly from their anthropology peers (Stewart 1979; Galloway et al. 1990; Skinner 1999). In addition, the *Reference Manual on Scientific Evidence*, 2nd ed. (NIJ 2000), a publication prepared for and by the federal courts, will prove helpful, especially the chapter entitled "Reference Guide on DNA Evidence." Perhaps the best source of guidance as to what factors a given court will likely apply to the admissibility of forensic anthropological expert testimony is the attorney who seeks to utilize his or her expertise. The attorney can help prepare the anthropological witness for presenting evidence and opinions at an appropriate level of difficulty and tone without compromising any scientific aspects of the case. Further, by this point in the process, the attorney will be aware of the operating theory and strategy of the opposing side and will be able to more adequately prepare the expert witness for cross-examination.

Some Ethical Issues in Forensic Anthropology

Forensic anthropologists must remember that their reports, testimony, and conduct can have immediate and long-term ramifications for defendants, families, and the judicial process as a whole. Thus, in addition to strict adherence to scientific principles and professional protocols, it is imperative that forensic anthropologists also demonstrate a strong ethical commitment to their work.

Ethical issues underlie all professional actions, many of which go well beyond normal scientific issues. For instance, forensic anthropologists are obligated to report all of their findings, even if they seem contradictory to other lines of evidence or muddy a good timeline or investigative theory (but see Gill-King's poignant story in Chapter 17). Forensic anthropologists are required to keep their cases confidential and not present cases in public or even private settings until they have been legally resolved. They also have a responsibility to protect the identity of the victims and their families when their cases are presented for educational purposes. That said, it should be stated that all of the cases presented in this book have been legally resolved. Further, most authors in this volume have changed or omitted the names of the victims. However, real names are used in a few chapters because the cases have been presented elsewhere, including nationally televised programs, or permission has been granted by appropriate parties.

It may be useful here to distinguish between *evidence* and the *individual*, as these terms are used throughout the text of this book. Evidence can be defined as any object or statement by a witness that has bearing in a court of law. According to Fisher (2000), evidence can take two forms: testimonial and physical (real) evidence. "Testimonial evidence is evidence given in the form of statements made under oath, usually in response to questioning. Physical evidence is any type of evidence having an objective existence, that is, anything with size, shape, and dimension" (Fisher 2000, 1). Further, physical evidence is used to "reconstruct the crime, identify participants, or confirm or discredit an alibi" (Geberth 1996, 169). Thus, a lesion on a humerus that was used to determine the identity of an individual or a cut mark on a rib suggestive of the circumstances of death constitutes "evidence." However, forensic anthropologists never lose sight of the fact that an individual skeleton with which they work is just that, an individual. The evidence gleaned from the bones of an individual can be presented as such in court, but this application does not detract from the fact that the person was once a living human being who had a history, family, and unique identity. The very fact that forensic anthropologists interpret the life history of a person from their bones argues that they are extraordinarily cognizant of the relationship between "bones" and "individuals."

THE CHAPTERS

The cases presented by the authors in this section demonstrate a variety of difficult challenges, particularly related to the identification process, and the importance of multidisciplinary teamwork is emphasized. In Chapter 2, Karen Burns presents a case in which communication among forensic experts broke down, turning a relatively straightforward identification into a lengthy and nearly disastrous predicament. The process of identification is also detailed in this chapter, including the description of antemortem pathologies and anomalies within the skeleton that rendered an accurate description of a biological profile nearly impossible. Burns provides some perspectives as to why interdisciplinary cooperation in this case failed and some suggestions for how to avoid such situations in the future.

This chapter is followed by an excellent example of how multidisciplinary collaboration can and should work. Presented by Douglas Ubelaker and colleagues, this case concerns the identification of the dismembered remains of a young female that were found in several different contexts. Scientific investigators were confronted with the task of constructing an accurate biological profile and determining how she died when only incomplete and fragmentary remains were available. The authors, including a forensic anthropologist, a pathologist, a radiologist, and a molecular geneticist, each report on the important contributions they made to the identification process. If any of these specialists had not been involved in the investigation, the case might not have been resolved in such a timely manner.

In Chapter 4, Amy Zelson Mundorff provides a shining example of how a forensic anthropologist can become integrated into a large-scale urban Medical Examiner's Office in New York City. She demonstrates how the multicultural nature of the city, the high murder rate, and the creative modes of disposal of human remains necessitated by crowded city life provide an endless list of anthropological investigations. The Office of the Chief Medical Examiner in Manhattan is responsible for the identification of the victims of the World Trade Center disaster, and Mundorff discusses the anthropological role in this unprecedented incident.

The process of developing and statistically evaluating a presumptive identification is the focus of Chapter 5 by Steadman and Konigsberg. In this case, several consistencies were observed between the antemortem medical records and postmortem skeletal remains, but the authors find that it is unclear just how many points of similarity are required for a positive identification in the eyes of the law. Other forensic scientists, including fingerprint analysts, have struggled with this issue of "positive identification." In light of this problem, the authors present some probability statements that may be useful for similar cases.

Kenneth Kennedy skillfully discusses the caveats of courtroom testimony in Chapter 6. Based on thirty years of experience in the field, Dr. Kennedy offers some advice and philosophical perspectives on the role of the anthropologist in the courtroom. He describes three cases for which he has served as an expert witness, each involving very different testimonial subjects and outcomes. In one case, he was not asked to give an opinion about physical evidence, but rather the current anthropological view of "race." This underscores the importance of forensic anthropologists being recognized as well-rounded biological anthropologists, not only the so-called bone experts.

REFERENCES

Daubert v. Merrill Dow Pharmaceuticals, 113 S.Ct. 2786; 1993 U.S. LEXIS 4408 (1993).

Federal Judicial Center, National Institute of Justice. 2001. *Reference Manual on Scientific Evidence*. <http://air.fjc.gov/public/pdf.nsf/lookup/sciman00.pdf/$file/sciman00.pdf>

Federal Rules of Evidence 702, Advisory Committee Note. 2001.

Fisher, Barry A. J. 2000. *Techniques of Crime Scene Investigation*. 6th ed. Boca Raton, FL: CRC Press.

Frye v. United States, 293 F. 1013 (D.C. Cir. 1923).

Galloway, Alison, Walter H. Birkby, T. Kahana, and Laura Fulginiti. 1990. Physical anthropology and the law: Legal responsibilities of forensic anthropologists. *Yearbook of Physical Anthropology* 33:39–57.

Geberth, Vernon J. 1996. *Practical Homicide Investigation: Tactics, Procedures, and Forensic Techniques*. 3rd ed. Boca Raton, FL: CRC Press.

Grisbaum, Gretchen A., and Douglas H. Ubelaker. 2001. *An Analysis of Forensic Anthropology Cases Submitted to the Smithsonian Institution by the Federal Bureau of Investigation from 1962 to 1994*. Washington, D.C.: Smithsonian Institution Press.

Kerley, Ellis R. 1978. Recent developments in forensic anthropology. *Yearbook of Physical Anthropology* 21:160–173.

Owsley, Douglas W., and Richard L. Jantz, eds. 1994. *Skeletal Biology in the Great Plains: Migration, Warfare, Health, and Subsistence*. Washington, D.C.: Smithsonian Institution Press.

Skinner, Mark. 1999. Cremated remains and expert testimony in a homicide case. Pp. 151–172 in *Forensic Osteological Analysis: A Book of Case Studies*, ed. Scott I. Fairgrieve. Springfield, IL: Charles C. Thomas.

Steadman, Dawnie W., and William D. Haglund. 2001. The scope of anthropological contributions to human rights investigations. Paper presented at the American Academy of Forensic Sciences. Seattle, WA. February 2001.

Stewart, T. Dale. 1979. *Essentials of Forensic Anthropology*. Springfield, IL: Charles C. Thomas.

Ubelaker, Douglas H. 1990. J. Lawrence Angel and the development of forensic anthropology in the United States. Pp. 191–200 in *A Life in Science: Papers in Honor of J. Lawrence Angel*, ed. Jane E. Buikstra. Center for American Archaeology, Scientific Papers 6.

Ubelaker, Douglas H. 1999. Ales Hrdlicka's role in the history of forensic anthropology. *Journal of Forensic Sciences* 44:724–730.

Ubelaker, Douglas H. 2000. Methodological considerations in the forensic applications of human skeletal biology. Pp. 41–67 in *Biological Anthropology of the Human Skeleton*, ed. M. Anne Katzenberg and Shelley R. Saunders. New York: Wiley-Liss.

Verano, John W., and Douglas H. Ubelaker, eds. 1992. *Disease and Demography in the Americas*. Washington, D.C.: Smithsonian Institution Press.

FURTHER READING

Brogdon, B. G., ed. 1998. *Forensic Radiology*. Boca Raton, FL: CRC Press.

DiMaio, Vincent J., and Dominick DiMaio. 2001. *Forensic Pathology*. 2nd ed. Boca Raton, FL: CRC Press.

Dix, Jay, and Robert Calaluce. 1998. *Guide to Forensic Pathology*. Boca Raton, FL: CRC Press.

Katzenberg, Anne M., and Shelley R. Saunders, eds. 2000. *Biological Anthropology of the Human Skeleton*. New York: Wiley-Liss.

Siegel, Jay, Pekka J. Saukko, and Geoffrey C. Knupfer, eds. 2000. *Encyclopedia of Forensic Sciences*. Orlando, FL: Academic Press.

Spencer, Frank, ed. 1997. *History of Physical Anthropology*. 2nd ed. New York and London: Garland Publishing, Inc.

Spitz, Werner U., ed. 1993. *Spitz and Fisher's Medicolegal Investigation of Death*. 3rd ed. Springfield, IL: Charles C. Thomas.

Stimson, Paul G., and Curtis A. Mertz, eds. 1997. *Forensic Dentistry*. Boca Raton, FL: CRC Press.

CHAPTER

2

THE HERRING CASE—AN OUTLIER

Karen Ramey Burns

People working in the field of human identification soon realize that each case is an education. Some cases contain even more lessons than others. The Herring case is an example. It is replete with contradictions and provides the opportunity to rethink each old "rule of thumb." This case is presented in a step-by-step fashion by working through the recovery, description, analysis, and identification. The reader can follow the case as it unfolds and test assumptions.

There are a few basic operating principles to keep in mind. Two distinct phases exist in the process of human identification—osteological description and human identification. Osteological description is the basic part, but obviously it is going to differ from the description in a missing person report. Eye color, hair color, and weight are not on the list. Instead, osteological description begins with general characteristics such as age, sex, ancestry, stature, and handedness. These are followed by more specific characteristics, including evidence of muscularity, physical anomalies, disease, and trauma. With each characteristic, the field of possibilities

slowly narrows—unless, of course, a mistake occurs along the way.

The human identification phase begins with a comparison of the osteological description with basic information about missing persons. When the missing person information is found to be consistent with the osteological description, a tentative identification is formed, and the identification process progresses to the next stage. From this point on, specific data is needed from the most likely missing person(s). Radiographs, dental charts, and/or smiling photographs are compared with data from the unidentified remains, and, hopefully, a positive identification is accomplished.

An experienced forensic anthropologist usually finds that the skeletal description is fairly routine while the actual identification requires greater effort. This is not so with the Herring case. On first glance, it appears to be nothing more than a typical forensic anthropology case—a box of bones recovered from a vacant lot. Human remains were reported by passersby, collected by police, sealed in a cardboard box, and turned over to the state crime lab without much

31

hope for identification. But this case was not typical. Instead of being easy to describe and moderately difficult to identify, it was difficult to describe and extremely easy to identify. From the beginning, it was an example of the errors that can be committed by crime labs and anthropologists. The Herring case teaches the necessity of flexibility and thoroughness. It also highlights the need for greater communication and cooperation between forensic disciplines.

The Recovery

The following account is quoted from the police reports with permission of the investigating authorities. The police handled the case expeditiously.

> At approximately 0900 hours, Sunday, 090990, Officer A. V. Escartin reports answering a call to the Pump House, at Goodrich Street Extension. Upon arrival (he) spoke with the complainant who stated that at approximately 0850 hours, this date, and while he was walking with the witness . . . they observed several parts of a human body lying down in the ground. (Head, ribs, hip, etc.) Richmond County Coroner was called to the scene, investigation continues by unit 609 (Det. Sgt. Christenson) and unit 613 (Det. Harris) who were called to the scene for assistance. It is unknown at this time any identification at all of the deceased person, too included [sic] race, sex and age. The remains of the body were skeletal only.
> September 9, 1990/1110 hours, Det. Sgt. D. Christenson: Received a call to Goodrich Street Ext. Upon arrival, Det. Sgt. D. Christenson spoke with the Coroner and Det. Harris. Human remains had been reported found in the woods. The scene is described as an area approx. 90 yards north of Goodrich Street Ext., approx. 1.8 miles from the canal locks, approx. 2/10's of a mile west of the I-20 crossing. Examination of the area revealed human remains scattered through an approx. 30 yard diameter area. Victim was apparently clothed at the time of deposit into the area. All human remains were recovered. All

> clothing was recovered from the site and transported to headquarters with the concurrance [sic] of the Deputy Coroner. This is to allow for preliminary processing prior to submission to the Dept. of Forensic Sciences. The scene was photographed and these photographs will be on file with 609. A sketch of the area was prepared and this will also be on file with 609.
> On September 10, 1990 at 0935 hours, Det. Sgt. Christenson reports that one (1) box containing the skeletal remains and artifacts of an unknown subject previously recovered, were turned into Dept. of Forensic Sciences at this time and date on their number. . . .

The Years Between

The cardboard box was taken into custody by a crime lab pathologist and placed in the morgue facilities. The pathologist called me in briefly to give an opinion on ancestry. I said that the individual was unusual in many ways and a thorough examination would be necessary before conclusions could be attempted. The case was not transferred to my custody, so I did nothing more.

Three years passed. A long line of other cases demanded everyone's attention. Meanwhile, the dusty cardboard box of dirty bones, mummified flesh, old clothes, and shaggy hair was forgotten. These things happen. The squeaky wheel gets the oil; the silent bones are ignored.

In 1993, a flurry of morgue clean-up activities brought the box to light once again. This time, the remains and associated artifacts were transferred to my custody. The tentative identification was made within the day, and the positive identification was completed within the week. However, the "simple osteological description" turned out to be both confusing and humbling.

The Osteological Description

The following section is taken from the state anthropological report, 30 April 1993.

The skeleton is almost complete. Only small bones, particularly those of the hands and feet, are missing. The bones are in reasonably good condition with the exception of the left hip (iliac crest) and left lower leg (both tibia and fibula). It appears that the left foot was gnawed off at the ankle. The ragged edges and occasional small puncture marks are consistent with scavenging by dogs.

Mummified tendons and ligaments are present. The mummified flesh was removed only from the pelvis and left leg in order to visualize bony detail.

There is nothing to suggest that the skeleton was moved in any way other than by scavengers. The bones and mummified flesh were stained the same color as the surrounding soil and numerous small bones and loose teeth were found in the area with the larger bones.

Dental Remains

Only eleven of the original thirty-two adult teeth are present in the maxilla and mandible. Thirteen teeth were lost before death and eight teeth fell out after death but were not recovered from the scene.

The chart at the bottom of the page uses the universal numbering system and provides a quick way to visualize the teeth and recognize which teeth were lost before and after death. Take time to imagine the chart superimposed on the mouth of the smiling subject (or dental patient) before you read it. The right part of the subject's mouth is on your left; therefore, his upper right third molar, #1, is in the upper left corner of the chart. The lower right third molar (#32) is in the lower left corner. Likewise, tooth #16 is above #17 on the other side of the mouth. In other words, the chart is read from left to right on the upper row and from right to left on the lower row. This chart mimics the image of a panoramic dental radiograph. Use the abbreviated dental key for the codes in the chart, but note that there are no dental restorations or carious lesions present.

Associated Objects

Several other items are found in the box with the human bones. These include hair, clothing, and three hospital identification bracelets. The hair is medium gray-brown and slightly wavy. It is 3–4 inches long. The hair form and color is consistent with hair of older persons of European ancestry. The brownish color in the hair may be an artifact of the soil color. Georgia soil deposits strong metallic stains. The clothing is typical women's clothing, including a dress and a wool coat. The clothing appears very well worn and appropriate for winter weather in Georgia. The hospital identification bracelets are orange plastic with paper labels. They appear to have been exposed to water and/or other fluids, and the writing is not visible to the naked eye.

O	#2	#3	#4	#5	#6	O	X	X	O	O	#12	#13	#14	O	XA
X	X	X	X	X	#27	O	X	X	O	O	X	X	X	#18	#17

Abbreviated Dental Key

Universal tooth number (e.g., #17) means that the tooth is present.

"X" means that the socket is healed (antemortem loss).

"O" means that the socket is open (postmortem loss).

"A" means that there is evidence of abscess. In other words, the alveolar bone appears "hollowed out" around the root tip.

Analysis of Skeletal Remains

The analysis is divided into sections that represent objectives: determination or recognition of sex, age, ancestry, stature, antemortem disease and trauma, perimortem trauma, postmortem trauma, and number of individuals. The contributions of specific bones are discussed in subsections.

Sex

It is important to use as many indicators as possible in skeletal analysis. For sex determination, the pelvis and skull are used most frequently, and each has several useful components, though the components of the pelvis are considered to be more reliable. Other bones, such as the femur and humerus, can also be informative. After everything is evaluated, the anthropologist takes into account the relative merit of each component.

Pelvic Features   The sciatic notch is wide, but not extremely so (Figure 2.1). It is interesting to note that most textbooks point to the sciatic notch as a standard indicator of sex, but McLaughlin and Bruce reported from their research that, "sciatic notch width alone proved to be a poor sex discriminator" (MacLaughlin and Bruce 1986, 1389). The sciatic notch is undoubtedly a good indicator at the extremes (very wide or very narrow), but like so many skeletal discriminators, it is ambiguous in the mid-range of variation.

A slight preauricular sulcus exists. This is a groove between the sciatic notch and the auricular surface and is most often encountered in females (Bass 1995). The preauricular sulcus is generally thought to be related to the trauma of childbearing. Nevertheless, it is sometimes found in a reduced form in men. I wonder what other types of trauma to the sacroiliac region result in the same phenomenon. For example, would a study of jockeys or cowboys show

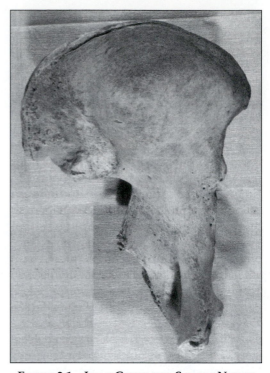

FIGURE 2.1   Iliac Crest and Sciatic Notch
The epiphysis of the iliac crest is not completely fused and the angle of the sciatic notch is intermediate in width.

consistent preauricular sulci? The auricular surface is elevated, but it is not extended posteriorly. The elevation indicates female, but the lack of extension lessens the certainty. The pubic portion of the os coxa is not elongated. The ventral arc and subpubic concavity are slight. The medial aspect of the ischiopubic ramus is not sharp. The subpubic angle seems more typical of a male, but not absolutely male.

Cranial Features   The supraorbital border is rounded and a moderate supraorbital ridge is present. A typical female skull has a sharp supraorbital border and no supraorbital ridge. The typical male skull has a rounded border and an enlarged supraorbital ridge. But a closer look at the literature shows statements like, "males range from moderate to excessive development, the females from a mere trace to moderate" (Krogman 1962, 116). Both statements include "moderate" development.

The frontal bone is clearly double-bossed. That is, it has two prominences ("bumps"), laterally placed. This form is typical of a masculine forehead (El-Najjar and McWilliams 1978). A smoothly rounded forehead is more typical of a female. The mastoid process is robust and within typical male parameters. Since a major muscle of the neck attaches at the mastoid, the larger mastoid process is an indication of a larger neck, thus, it is characteristic of a male. The cranial base is rugged in appearance. There is an identifiable nuchal ridge, but it is definitely not a nuchal crest. The morphology is more characteristic of females. The major part of the mandible is feminine. The chin is pointed, not squared. The gonial angle, however, is flared and more masculine looking. It is possible that this skull is an example of age-related masculinization of a female skull. Walker (1995) reports age-related changes in all of the cranial features osteologists use for sex determination and emphasizes heavier supraorbital ridges in females forty-five and older.

Cranial Measurements Cranial measurements were taken and the computer software program *FORDISC 2.0* was utilized to estimate sex. Ousley and Jantz (1998) give a thorough discussion of *FORDISC* and the Forensic Anthropology Data Bank that provides comparative data. For this case, the *FORDISC* results are less ambiguous. The posterior probability is .985 (or 98 percent) that the cranial measurements are from a male skull. It is important to note, however, that this does not preclude the possibility that this is a female skull. It is unlikely that the skull is female, but not impossible. The typicality probability is .019, which means that the skull may be male but is not very typical of males in the Forensic Data Bank.

Postcranial Measurements The femoral head measures 43 mm. This is within the questionable female range, and very close to the male/female intersection of 43.5–46.5 mm (Pearson 1917/19; Thieme 1957; Oliver 1969). In other words, it is not very useful in this case. The humerus is known to be a poor indicator of sex (Bass 1995, 156), but the measurements are included here as a point of curiosity. The vertical diameter is 49.5 mm, which is within the male range of 47 mm (Stewart 1979, 100).

In summation, I was not sufficiently confident about the sex of this individual to make a statement. This is not something to regret. In urban cases, I have seen the remains of three transvestites and listened to officer's frustrations after long searches for missing persons when the unidentified person was reported as the wrong sex. Sex is not as clear-cut as Western culture would have us believe. A wide overlap exists in the physical characteristics of the sexes (as well as sexual identities!). It is far better to state uncertainty honestly and encourage a broader search. As it turned out, the identity (and the sex) became known through other means.

Age

The age of an individual is determined by observing both developmental and degenerative age-related changes. The various stages of change are then compared with those in persons of known age. Under normal conditions, developmental changes are completed by the mid-twenties (e.g., clavicular epiphyses are completely fused). By the late teens, degenerative changes have already begun to appear (e.g., pubic symphysis changes). There is a decade of mixed information—both developmental and degenerative changes in the same individual. However, after thirty years of age, changes are usually all categorized as degenerative.

This does not mean that they are negative, just that they indicate an aging body rather than a developing body.

In the Herring Case, the age information is mixed. Developmental changes are combined in the same body with advanced degenerative changes, but the stages of change are not typical of the late teens and twenties. The following is a description of age-related information from this skeleton.

The medial epiphysis of the clavicle is fused. A line is visible on the inferior border of the epiphyseal plate, but the other edges are obliterated. Fusion occurs between 18 and 25 years. The last site of union is the fissure along the inferior border, which is reportedly obliterated by age 31 in males (McKern and Stewart 1957) or age 33 in females (Webb and Suchey 1985). Fusion of the iliac crest is incomplete (see Figure 2.1 on page 34). Partial fusion of the iliac crest is usually consistent with an age of 14–22 years. Normally the iliac crest is completely fused by 23 years. Scheuer gives a thorough discussion of the literature on this topic (Scheuer and Black 2000).

The pubic symphyses are confusing, whether they are compared to male or female standards. Following the Suchey-Brooks technique, the right symphysis is similar to male Phase 5 (Katz and Suchey 1986). The symphyseal face has lost the ridged surface of younger phases; there is no ventral rampart; the oval outline is almost complete; there is a symphyseal rim, but ossified nodules are also present and the symphyseal face is not flat. Phase 5 indicates an age range of 28 to 78 years. The left pubic symphysis is more typical of male Phase 6. It is eroded with very erratic ossification, irregular lipping, and degenerating borders. The central symphyseal face has large pores. Phase 6 indicates an age range of 36 to 87 years. There is always the possibility that an injury caused the discrepancy between sides. The right leg had sustained several fractures during life. Either the incident(s) themselves or the poor healing results may have caused undue stress to the pelvis.

The auricular surface of the ilium is porous and lacking in ridge detail. This condition makes standard aging analysis impossible. The ribs are difficult to age because of postmortem damage, but ossified projections exist on the floors of some of the sternal rib ends. These projections are consistent with Phases 7 and 8 of rib phase analysis for white females over 59.2 years of age (Iscan et al. 1985). The cranial sutures are open but the margins of the cranial bones are rounded due to thickening on either side of the sutures. Cranial sutures are inconsistent indicators of age, but completely open cranial sutures usually indicate a youthful person. The sutures in this case, however, are more characteristic of a condition known as "lapsed union" (Cobb 1952; Krogman 1962). Bone tends to "pile up" at the edges of the suture rather than cover the suture. In such cases, standard aging data do not apply.

In sum, important age standards are sex-specific, so I computed age using sex standards for both males and females, then broadened the age range for the final estimate. Again, this is better than throwing the investigators completely off the trail. I was convinced, however, that this individual was more than fifty years of age. The characteristics associated with advancing age are much more convincing than the smattering of youthful characteristics.

Ancestry

Overall observation leads me to conclude that the remains are consistent with European ancestry. The nasal aperture is not narrow, but this is probably an artifact of the nasal fracture(s). A nasal spine is present, there is no nasal gutter, and the maxilla is not prognathic (Figure 2.2). Slightly wavy gray-brown hair was present with the remains.

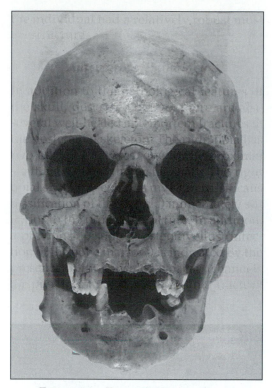

FIGURE 2.2 FRONTAL VIEW OF SKULL

FORDISC 2.0 was again used, this time to analyze cranial measurements for ancestry. Analysis was carried out for both males and females. The results fell neatly within the white male group, with a posterior probability of 0.993 and a typicality of 0.047. I see no reason not to accept the ancestry analysis when compared with the gross anatomical observations. The sex placement, however, is still uncertain.

Stature

Assuming that the ancestry placement is accurate, the undamaged long bones were measured to estimate stature. The results indicate a height of approximately 5'4" for a white female (95 percent confidence interval [C.I.] = 64.5 ± 2.7 inches), and approximately 5'6" for a white male (95 percent C.I. = 65.7 ± 3.4 inches). The full range of the estimate, including both males and females, is 5'2"–5'9" (stature information can be found in Trotter and Gleser 1952; Giles and Klepinger 1988; Ousley 1995; Klepinger and Giles 1998; Ousley and Jantz 1998). Stature decreases after the age of 30, but it is common for people to continue to report their height as measured in their youth (Galloway 1988). The actual stature of this unidentified person is probably even less than a standard age-corrected estimate because of the collapsed vertebral bodies, spinal scoliosis, and poorly healed leg fractures.

Antemortem Disease and Trauma

A wide variety of information is available about life and health from the mouth. The teeth remaining in the maxilla (molars and premolars) display very little abrasion. In fact, the cusps are completely intact. This could be an indicator of youth. However, some of the molar crowns are covered with calculus (calcified plaque), and the teeth are supererupted. With or without the mandible to study, occlusal calculus suggests a lack of opportunity for abrasion. This means that the person could not grind one tooth against another tooth to chew. This usually happens when there is no tooth in the other dental arch (i.e., no lower molar to place against the upper molar). It can also happen when the mouth is immobilized. For instance, a fractured jaw is typically wired shut to allow it to heal. When the jaw is released, calculus must be scraped from all of the dental surfaces. The same thing happens with invalids on life support systems. In the present case, the mandibular molars and premolars are absent and were probably extracted during the person's youth, before the teeth had time to wear.

Malocclusion can also affect the temporomandibular joint. This mandible shows advanced bilateral degenerative joint disease. This could be associated with bruxism (grinding the teeth) or arthritic changes. There is no sign of bruxism on the remaining teeth. Many teeth were lost long before death and resorption of the alveolar ridge is advanced. Periodontal disease is rampant. The overall oral condition may indicate advanced age or low socioeconomic condition.

The skeleton is severely osteoporotic. Sex hormone deficiency is a common cause of this condition. Osteoporosis occurs mainly in postmenopausal women. Men are also affected, but to a lesser degree. Hyperparathyroidism is another major cause. Other causes include starvation, anorexia nervosa, scurvy, disuse, and several rare diseases (Murray and Jacobson 1977). Here, several of the vertebral bodies are collapsed, scoliosis is obvious, and a "dowager's hump" is present. This is the result of severe osteoporosis. It allows us to draw some conclusions about the appearance of the unidentified person. He or she carried the head forward with the back rounded and the shoulders somewhat hunched. The stature just before death would be significantly less than that reported earlier in life.

A number of antemortem fractures were observed in the skull and postcranial bones. The distal halves of both nasals and the frontal process of the right maxilla were broken during life (Figure 2.3). None of the fractured bones reunited during the healing process, and the edges of the remaining bone were remodeled. The result was a slight inclination of the nose to the right. In other words, the nose was crooked. According to personal communication with orthopedic surgeons, women tend to have broken noses repaired immediately. Men are more likely to allow the nose to heal without intervention, resulting in more long-term consequences.

The left radius had been fractured and healed with a decided curvature (see Figure 2.6 on page 41). It is not unusual for an osteoporotic elderly woman to sustain a wrist fracture in a simple fall. The right femur had been fractured and healed in a sigmoid shape with a projecting "keel" of bone on

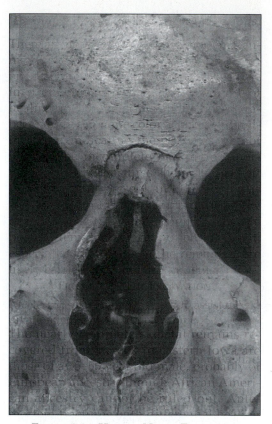

FIGURE 2.3   HEALED NASAL FRACTURES

the mesiodistal midshaft (see Figure 2.8 on page 42). This is unusual in the United States where broken bones are typically set properly. The right distal tibia and fibula had also been fractured and healed with slight displacement.

The fractures of the right femur, tibia, and fibula resulted in a shortened leg and a limping walk. The pelvic morphology should be re-evaluated in light of these fractures. Following trauma to the leg, the pelvis was under unusual stress. Over time the pubic symphysis was affected, possibly creating the discrepancy in age information from the left and right symphyseal faces. Given this, the pubic symphysis should not be trusted for age estimation.

Some of a person's life history is written in their broken bones, particularly when there are many fractures, as in this case. But the interpretation varies according to the age, health, and activity level of the person as well as the extent of healing and remodeling of the fractured bones. If all of the fractures are estimated to be at the same stage of healing, a major accident may be the cause. If the fractures are at different stages of healing, the person may be the victim of serious illness, physical abuse, or an unusually high activity level related to work or athletics. Age figures in when considering the amount of stress required to actually break the bones. In general, a young person can endure more stress than an older person. Putting age aside, an active, healthy person can generally endure more stress than an inactive person or someone in poor health.

In the skeleton at hand, the fractures are in different stages of healing, so they did not all occur in the same incident. Any further interpretation, however, depends on age and health analysis. If the person is young, a rigorous or dangerous lifestyle may be the cause of the fractures. If the person is elderly and suffering with osteoporosis, common events, such as falling down steps, may be causal.

Perimortem Trauma

None of the skeletal trauma can be correlated with the time of death. There are no bullet wounds, knife wounds, blunt force trauma, or unhealed fractures. There is no skeletal evidence other than poor health to suggest the circumstances of death.

Postmortem Trauma

As quoted at the beginning of the osteological description, several areas of the skeleton appear to have been gnawed by dogs. The left iliac crest, the medial condyle of the right femur, and the left distal tibia and fibula all show ragged edges together with puncture marks typical of large canine teeth.

Number of Individuals

As Table 2.1 (on page 40) demonstrates, there is so much inconsistency in this case that an important question hangs in the air, "Are these the remains of more than one person?" If so, the set of bones has been very cleverly constructed. They are consistent in size, color, condition, and state of decomposition. The bones articulate well at each joint or suture. A near-complete skeleton is present, and there are no duplicate bones. In short, there is nothing to indicate more than one individual.

The Identification

Methods of Identification

The hospital bracelets found with the remains provided the first line of action to determine identity, but they were illegible (see Figure 2.4 on page 40). Anything that may have once been written on the paper inserts appeared to have been completely washed off or obscured by other fluids. It seemed likely, however, that the bracelets once carried the name of the victim, and the ink residue should still be visible by other means. They were sent to a questioned documents examiner who used an alternate light source to examine the bracelets (Leaver and Smith 1999). The name, "June Herring," was visible on two of the three bracelets (see Figure 2.5 on page 40).

On the basis of this tentative identification, I called the detective responsible for the case. He immediately recognized the name and asked, "Where is she? I haven't seen her in ages." I requested the antemortem records.

On March 26, 1993, I received two large folders of hospital radiographs covering the time period, May 5, 1983 to March 26, 1990. Positive identification was made on the basis of the radiographs of antemortem fractures (see Figures 2.6 and 2.7 on page 41, and Figures 2.8 and 2.9 on page 42), which shows that the fracture locations are consistent with those of the unidentified bones.

TABLE 2.1   REVIEW OF SKELETAL EVIDENCE

AGE

EVIDENCE FOR YOUTH	EVIDENCE FOR ADVANCED AGE
unfused iliac crest open cranial sutures molars without wear	osteophytic vertebra deterioration of pubic symphysis osteoporosis "dowager's hump" worn auricular surface numerous extracted teeth

SEX

EVIDENCE FOR MALE	EVIDENCE FOR FEMALE
short pubis large mastoid double-bossed frontal computer analysis of cranial measurements	preauricular sulcus pointed chin advanced osteoporosis female clothing

ANCESTRY

EVIDENCE FOR WHITE (EUROPEAN) ANCESTRY	EVIDENCE FOR BLACK (AFRICAN) ANCESTRY
white cranial measurements according to FORDISC 2.0 nasal spine	wide nasal aperture

Special attention was also given to the frontal sinus pattern. Note in Figures 2.10 and 2.11 on page 43 that despite the difference in radiographic quality, the antemortem skull radiograph is consistent in detail with the postmortem film. Note the frontal sinus pattern, the nasal aperture, infraorbital area, and the dental condition.

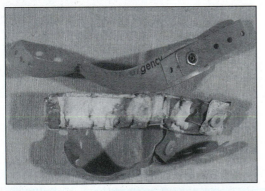

FIGURE 2.4   HOSPITAL BRACELETS

Three hospital bracelets were found with the remains. None are legible with the naked eye.

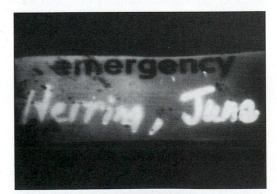

FIGURE 2.5   HOSPITAL BRACELETS

The name could be seen clearly with the use of an alternate light source.

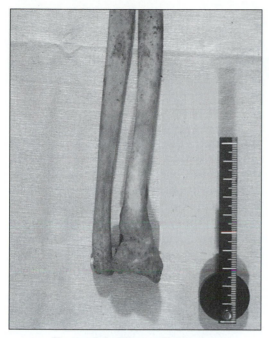

**FIGURE 2.6 HEALED FRACTURE
OF DISTAL RADIUS**
Note the malalignment.

Case Resolution

The police recognized June Herring's name because they knew her well. June Herring was a 68- or 69-year-old "bag lady" who had been arrested for drunkenness, disorderly conduct, robbery, and several variations of disturbing the peace. Herring was also listed as a victim in several incidents, such as purse theft and assault. The stolen items were worth very little, but the complaints reflect her economic condition and her vulnerability. Herring was given assistance by the police numerous times for sickness and injury. Usually, she was transported to the hospital. Occasionally, she was taken to jail first to sober up. As a street person, she was constantly exposed to conditions that led to ill health and injury. The police may have been her only source of aid. The behaviors cited are interrelated with her deteriorated life. The

indigent status and evidence of alcoholism explain the skeletal evidence of poor nutrition and health care. It may also explain why no one seemed to be looking for her, as there was no missing person report.

In conclusion, the police reports provide an approximate date of death. The dates of arrest or aid are almost monthly for several years. The final incident was "general assistance" on March 25, 1990. The remains were collected on September 9, 1990. Thus, the reports provided a tentative identification, a recent history of the deceased, and an approximate date of death. The mug shot was also very useful. Several characteristics

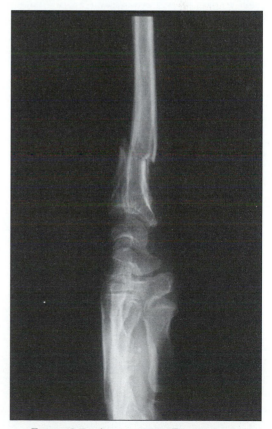

**FIGURE 2.7 ANTEMORTEM RADIOGRAPH
OF FRACTURED RADIUS CLEARLY
DEMONSTRATING THE LOCATION
OF THE FRACTURE**

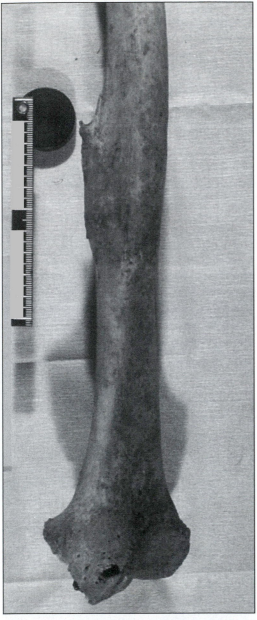

FIGURE 2.8   HEALED FRACTURE OF RIGHT FEMUR
Note a "keel" of projecting bone on the mesiodistal midshaft.

the broken nose on the skull. The head is lowered on the shoulders and jutting forward—consistent with the "dowager's hump" apparent in the vertebrae. The brow is rounded and consistent with the supraorbital curvature on the skull. The hair is wavy and dark gray.

The dates of the hospital records are consistent with the dates of police assistance for "injury." The healed fractures in the skeleton correspond to the fractures visible in the hospital radiographs. Also, her breasts are visible on the chest radiographs. This provides a final piece of evidence regarding the actual sexual identity. The skeleton may appear somewhat masculine, but there was no deception during

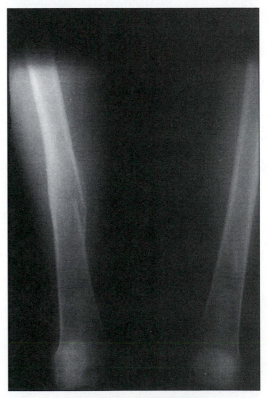

FIGURE 2.9   ANTEMORTEM RADIOGRAPH OF RIGHT FEMUR
The plane of the photograph is not identical to the plane of the radiograph, but the fracture can be seen.

noted in the skeletal analysis can be seen in this photo (see Figure 2.12 on page 44). The nose is slightly deviated—consistent with

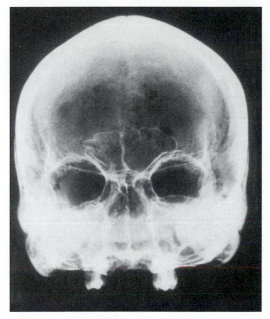

FIGURE 2.10   POSTMORTEM FRONTAL SINUS PATTERN

life. This is important, because there is always the possibility that an individual identifies with the opposite sex and dresses accordingly, thereby confusing investigators after death.

Complete Description of June Herring at the Time of Death

June Herring was a white female, 68 or 69 years old, depending on the month of death. She measured 5'3" to 5'5" according to measurements taken in the police station. She would have been taller in her youth, before the injuries to her leg and back. Herring had dark gray hair that was slightly wavy and about three to four inches long. She was well known by the local police because she was an alcoholic who frequently lived on the streets. She was in poor health and had many medical complaints. The local hospital admitted her numerous times to treat broken bones, including the femur, ankle, wrist, and nose.

What If . . . ?

Was the Herring case a disaster or a success? The answer depends on your perspective. One thing is clear, though. Three years is too long to wait for an identification that takes one day to accomplish. In this particular case, there was no grieving family. What if there had been? There was no evidence of homicide. What if there had been? June Herring was identified, but not in a timely way that served the community as expected.

There are many more "What-if . . . ?" questions. Of course these questions cannot be answered, but each leads in a direction that may provide strategies for the future. For instance, what if the crime scene investigator approached the crime

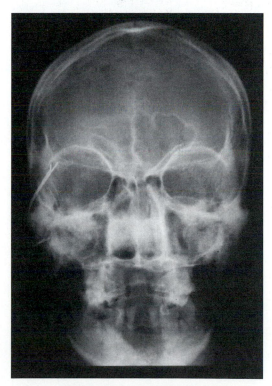

FIGURE 2.11   ANTEMORTEM FRONTAL SINUS PATTERN

Note the frontal sinus pattern, the nasal aperture, intraorbital area, and the dental condition.

FIGURE 2.12   MUG SHOT OF JUNE HERRING

lab differently? If the remains had been recent, the investigator *would* have approached the case differently. Specific work would have been requested of appropriate specialists. The body would go to the pathologist, suspected drugs to the drug analyst, bodily fluids to the toxicologist or the serologist, hair and fiber to the criminologist, suspicious papers to the documents examiner, latent prints to the fingerprint examiner, and so on. As it was, the investigator turned over the entire box to the pathologist simply because it contained human remains. Fewer protocols exist for skeletonized remains so the investigator made no distinction between recent and skeletonized remains. As it was, neither the investigator nor the pathologist expected results. If the investigator were to approach the crime lab with more knowledge about each and every forensic science discipline, including forensic anthropology, more cases would be solved.

The investigator was not the only person to drop the ball in this investigation. What if the pathologist had thought of the case as a crime lab case or a forensic case rather than only a pathology case? He might have immediately distributed parts of the case to other forensic scientists, including the documents examiner. The hospital bracelets would have been examined, and the documents examiner would have made a tentative identification. The pathologist could have made a positive identification from a radiographic comparison, and the anthropologist would not have been needed. The case would have been "neater" from the very beginning. Another possibility is earlier transfer of custody to the anthropologist who could have functioned as a facilitator a few years earlier. In fact, anthropologists often search out new approaches to cases. The multidisciplinary nature of anthropological work encourages contact with a wide variety of specialists. Of course, if the anthropologist had focused only on the bones and ignored all other evidence, this case would probably still be in storage.

References

Bass, William M. 1995. *Human Osteology, A Laboratory and Field Manual*. Columbia, MO: Missouri Archaeological Society.

Cobb, W. Montague. 1952. Cowdry's problems of aging; biological and medical aspects. Pp. 791–856 in *Skeleton*, ed. A. I. Lansing. Baltimore, MD: Williams & Wilkins.

El-Najjar, Mahmoud Y., and K. Richard McWilliams. 1978. *Forensic Anthropology*. Springfield, IL: Charles C. Thomas.

Galloway, Alison. 1988. Estimating actual height in the older individual. *Journal of Forensic Sciences* 33:126–136.

Giles, Eugene, and Linda L. Klepinger. 1988. Confidence intervals for estimates based on linear regression in forensic anthropology. *Journal of Forensic Sciences* 33:1,218–1,222.

Iscan, Mehmet Yasar, Susan R. Loth, and Ronald K. Wright. 1985. Age estimation from the rib by phase analysis: White females. *Journal of Forensic Sciences* 30:853–863.

Katz, Darryl, and Judy Myers Suchey. 1986. Age determination of the male *Os pubis*. *American Journal of Physical Anthropology* 69:427–435.

Klepinger, Linda L., and Eugene Giles. 1998. Clarification or confusion in forensic osteology. Pp. 427–440 in *Forensic Osteology, Advances in the Identification of Human Remains*, ed. Kathleen J. Reichs. Springfield, IL: Charles C. Thomas.

Krogman, Wilton M. 1962. *The Human Skeleton in Forensic Medicine*. Springfield, IL: Charles C. Thomas.

Leaver, W., and J. Smith. 1999. Using an alternate light source to restore writing. *Journal of Forensic Sciences* 44(3):653–655.

MacLaughlin, Susan M., and Margaret F. Bruce. 1986. The sciatic notch/acetabular index as a discriminator of sex in European skeletal remains. *Journal of Forensic Sciences* 31(4): 1,380–1,390.

McKern, Thomas W., and T. Dale Stewart. 1957. *Skeletal age changes in young American males*. U. W. Army Quartermaster Research and Development Command.

Murray, Ronald O., and Harold G. Jacobson. 1977. *The Radiology of Skeletal Disorders*. Edinburgh, Scotland: Churchill Livingstone.

Oliver, G. 1969. *Practical Anthropology*. Springfield, IL: Charles C. Thomas.

Ousley, Stephen D. 1995. Should we estimate biological or forensic stature? *Journal of Forensic Sciences* 40:768–773.

Ousley, Stephen D., and Richard L. Jantz. 1998. The Forensic Data Bank: Documenting skeletal trends in the United States. Pp. 441–457 in *Forensic Osteology, Advances in the Identification of Human Remains*, ed. Kathleen J. Reichs. Springfield, IL: Charles C. Thomas.

Pearson, Karl. 1917/19. A study of the long bones of the English skeleton. I. The femur. University of London, *University College, Department of Applied Statistics, Company Research, Memoirs*, Biometric Series X, Chapters 1–4.

Scheuer, Louise, and Sue Black. 2000. *Developmental Juvenile Osteology*. San Diego, CA: Academic Press.

Stewart, T. Dale. 1979. *Essentials of Forensic Anthropology*. Springfield, IL: Charles C. Thomas.

Thieme, Frederick P. 1957. Sex in Negro skeletons. *Journal of Forensic Medicine* 4:72–81.

Trotter, Mildred, and Goldine C. Gleser. 1952. Estimation of stature from long bones of American whites and Negroes. *American Journal of Physical Anthropology* 10:463–514.

Walker, Phillip L. 1995. Problems of preservation and sexism in sexing: some lessons from historical collections for palaeodemographers. Pp. 31–47 in *Grave Reflections, Portraying the Past through Cemetery Studies*, ed. Shelley R. Saunders and Ann Herring. Toronto: Canadian Scholars' Press.

Webb, Patricia A. O., and Judy M. Suchey. 1985. Epiphyseal union of the anterior iliac crest and medial clavicle in a modern multiracial sample of American males and females. *American Journal of Physical Anthropology* 68:457–466.

CHAPTER

3

MULTIDISCIPLINARY APPROACH TO HUMAN IDENTIFICATION IN HOMICIDE INVESTIGATION

A CASE STUDY FROM NEW YORK

Douglas H. Ubelaker, Mary Jumbelic, Mark Wilson, and E. Mark Levinsohn

Investigative approaches to human identification are increasingly multidisciplinary in nature. By providing specific information about the individual or individuals represented by decomposed or skeletal remains, forensic anthropologists supplement information supplied by other disciplines and can help construct a biological profile of the individual, exclude individuals not represented by the remains, and provide a positive identification. Increasingly, identification in fragmentary, incomplete, or other difficult cases is established through molecular analysis. However, even in these investigations, anthropology can play a significant role.

The case reported here exemplifies how forensic anthropology can be incorporated into the broader investigation of death and help establish identification. It also demonstrates how specialists in forensic pathology, radiology, molecular biology, and anthropology can work together to achieve a personal identification. While the remains were ultimately identified using both nuclear and mitochondrial DNA technology, forensic anthropology

and radiology provided corroborative information that was instrumental in solving the case.

Interdisciplinary Collaboration

In February 1996, some local youths in Syracuse, New York, discovered incomplete, partially decomposed human remains in the front seat of a pickup truck. Additional well-wrapped body parts were recovered from within and outside of the vehicle owner's residence. While being detained at the police station for questioning, the suspect and owner of the vehicle committed suicide but had not confessed or revealed any details about the crime.

Forensic Pathological Analysis

The central forensic problem was the identification of the victim. Examination by the forensic pathologist in Syracuse provided a description of both the recovered remains and associated materials, including clothes, linens, and plastic bags that were used to wrap different body parts. The human remains recovered from all locations consisted of left and right upper extremities, a left leg, a segment from the pelvic area (separated at the lumbar spine and upper femur area), and one thigh (from area of upper femur to lower femur). All of these remains displayed evidence of amputation and sharp force trauma. Soft tissue evidence remaining on the body fragments suggested to the pathologist that they were of an African American female teenager, and that they had been previously buried. Evidence for burial consisted of the presence of soil within the wrappings on the body parts. Some alterations also were noted on the skin surfaces that were probably related to bacterial/fungal growth that would have been promoted underground.

Radiological Analysis

The remains were submitted to a musculoskeletal radiologist in the Department of Medical Imaging of Crouse in Syracuse. A radiological analysis, including CT scans of the remains, revealed considerable detail. The radiologist noted the following very significant findings: spina bifida occulta of the first sacral vertebra; unfused epiphyses on the greater and lesser trochanters, femoral head, distal femur, proximal tibia, and some bones of the wrist; sesamoid bones within both hands, and evidence of a healed fracture of the right radius. The radiologist noted grooves on the outer cortical surfaces of the right femur and left humerus, suggesting that a saw had been used to amputate those parts.

By matching the biological profile composed thus far against the data from the missing persons' list, three potential victims were identified. The radiologist then compared radiographs of the recovered body parts to the clinical radiographs taken of three local missing individuals that fit the biological profile. The radiologist readily

excluded two of the potential victims. One of those patients displayed a fracture of a phalanx of the hand and a pattern of sesamoid bones not apparent on the recovered remains, as well as general size differences. The other patient displayed fusion of the proximal femoral epiphysis and anatomical details of the first sacral vertebra that were not present in the recovered remains. For these reasons, the two individuals were excluded as possibly representing the recovered remains.

Examination of anterior-posterior and lateral radiographs of the right forearm and wrist of the third patient revealed numerous areas of consistency and no major inconsistencies. A CT scan through the middle of the right forearm showed a subtle change interpreted as a healed fracture at the midshaft of the radius. The changes were sufficiently subtle so as not to be visible on standard radiographs. It was known that the third potential victim had sustained a right forearm fracture at age eight. Although this finding did not result in positive identification, it supported the possibility that the third patient was represented by the recovered remains because the location of the fracture closely matched that found on the victim.

On the basis of investigative evidence and the findings of the pathologist and radiologist, samples of the remains were submitted for further testing to the Federal Bureau of Investigation in Washington D.C. The FBI Laboratory is the only public forensic laboratory in the United States currently conducting mitochondrial DNA (mtDNA) analysis free of charge. The Onondaga County Medical Examiner's Office contacted the FBI Laboratory in 1996 upon learning that mtDNA analysis might assist in the identification of the victim in this case. The FBI Laboratory agreed to accept the evidence for mtDNA analysis. Samples were also submitted to another DNA laboratory for independent analysis. In addition, a dried blood specimen was obtained from the third patient's mother for comparison.

Anthropological Analysis

In March 1997, following established protocols, a representative of the FBI brought the remains to Ubelaker's laboratory at the Department of Anthropology in the Smithsonian Institution's National Museum of Natural History for anthropological analysis. The FBI protocol for the examination of human remains requires a thorough anthropological examination prior to DNA analysis. If an anthropological examination has not been conducted prior to the submission of the evidence to the FBI Laboratory, the remains are submitted to Ubelaker.

At the Smithsonian, a detailed inventory documented the anatomical parts present and their condition. Although some soft tissue and odor were present, many skeletal details were visible. All surface and other alterations were described and documented (Figure 3.1). Radiographic analysis revealed a pattern of cortical bone variation in the right radius suggestive of a well-remodeled antemortem fracture, thus corroborating the findings of the radiologist. Comparison of the morphology of the ends of the three separate left femur

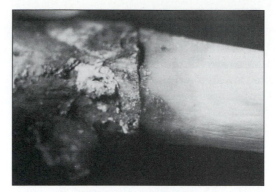

FIGURE 3.2   ARTICULATION OF PROXIMAL SEGMENT OF LEFT FEMUR TO LEFT FEMUR DIAPHYSIS

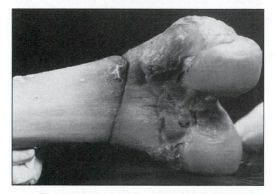

FIGURE 3.3   ARTICULATION OF DISTAL SEGMENT OF LEFT FEMUR TO LEFT FEMUR DIAPHYSIS

segments revealed evidence of articulation, suggesting that they originated from one femur of the same individual (Figures 3.2 and 3.3). No evidence for multiple individuals was found.

Anthropological analysis suggested the remains originated from a female, likely between the ages of thirteen and nineteen years (Figure 3.4). The determination of female sex was based primarily upon the morphology of the pelvis. Features especially indicative of female sex were a relatively wide pubis, wide subpubic angle, wide sciatic notch, elevated auricular area, and general pubis morphology. The age

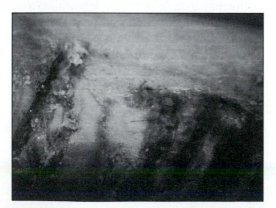

FIGURE 3.1   CUTS ON LEFT HUMERUS

FIGURE 3.4   SYMPHYSEAL FACE OF PUBIS
Prominent ridges and furrows indicate a younger individual.

range was suggested based upon the extent of bone development, including observations on the extent of epiphyseal union and the probability of female sex. Since female bones mature earlier than those of males, knowledge of the sex helped to narrow the age range suggested for this individual. No anthropological analysis of ancestry was attempted since the skull was absent and the skeleton was otherwise incomplete.

DNA Analysis

Within the DNA II unit of the FBI, a mitochondrial DNA (mtDNA) sequence was obtained from the submitted blood sample from the mother of the possible victim as well as from a submitted bone sample of the deceased. Mitochondria are small structures found in the cytoplasm of many living cells, including cells from human beings (Figure 3.5). They produce the majority of the energy a cell requires in order to function. Mitochondria contain their own small piece of DNA, called mitochondrial DNA (mtDNA). Mitochondria are passed from generation to generation through the cytoplasm of the egg cell. Therefore, a mother contributes her mtDNA to her offspring, while the father does not. The small mtDNA is known to have a high rate of mutation.

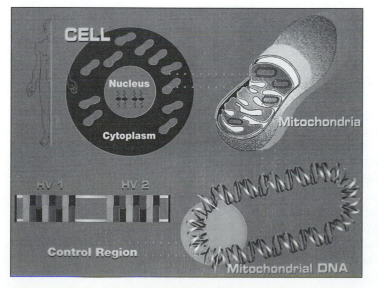

FIGURE 3.5   MITOCHONDRIA
Mitochondria are small structures found within cells. These structures contain their own DNA, called mitochondrial DNA (mtDNA). The control region of mtDNA is most often used for identification purposes, because this region contains the most differences between unrelated individuals. Two hypervariable regions, abbreviated as HV 1 and HV 2, are typically examined in a forensic identification case.

This results in many changes in the mtDNA over time, so there are many different types of mtDNA in the human population.

Because there are many more copies of mtDNA in a cell than nuclear (or chromosomal) DNA, mtDNA is often chosen in cases where old or degraded material is present. Also, due to the maternal nature of mtDNA transmission, it is the marker of choice when known maternal samples are available for typing. The mtDNA from siblings is the same as the mtDNA of their mother, and hence direct comparisons are possible when maternal reference material is present for typing.

When there is a match between a sample and a maternal reference, a database is queried in order to estimate the rarity of the particular mtDNA type in question. While it is currently not known how many different mtDNA types exist in the human species, the forensic mtDNA database is growing rapidly. Statistical estimates of the population frequency of specific mtDNA profiles can be conducted in order to provide a weighted assessment of a profile in a specific case.

In this case, direct mtDNA comparisons revealed that the mtDNA sequences obtained from the mother of the victim and the bone from the crime scene were the same. Because mtDNA is inherited maternally, a daughter of the person represented by the submitted blood specimen could not be eliminated as the source of the submitted sample from the crime scene.

Some sense of the probabilities involved in the DNA comparison is provided through utilizing the mtDNA population database available to the FBI laboratory. This database has been assembled by the Scientific Working Group in DNA Analysis and Methods (SWGDAM), comprised of specialists throughout the profession. The particular mtDNA sequence obtained from the submitted specimens had not been observed in 349 individuals of African descent, consisting of 118 African-Americans, 116 Afro-Caribbeans, and 115 Africans; 887 individuals of European descent; 99 individuals of Hispanic descent; nor in 221 individuals of Asian descent, consisting of 58 Asian-Americans and 163 individuals of Japanese descent. Similar results were reported for both mitochondrial DNA and nuclear DNA by an independent laboratory.

Resolution

The exhaustive investigative and forensic effort outlined above ultimately convinced authorities that the recovered remains all belonged to one individual and that individual, who had been missing since the age of thirteen, was indeed the suspected missing person. The victim and the suspect knew each other and resided in the same neighborhood. The time interval between the girl's disappearance and the discovery of the remains was approximately five years. Cause of death was listed as "trauma of undetermined etiology" and the manner of death as homicide. In August 1997, the family buried the remains and, since the only suspect committed suicide, the case is officially closed.

Summary

The case presented here documents how specialists from different disciplines contribute to the identification process. The investigators and medical examiner played central, key roles, but specialists in forensic anthropology, radiology, and molecular biology also made significant contributions. In this case, radiological examination was able to exclude two possible victims, greatly facilitating the investigation. Radiological and anthropological analysis helped pinpoint the age at death and sex of the individual, as well as call attention to the healed fracture and other unique anatomical features to aid identification. In addition, the anthropologist was able to articulate three of the segments showing they originated from one individual. The last word came from the molecular analysis, which increased the probability that the particular missing person was the individual represented by the remains. With increasing specialization, forensic science has become quite complex. Anthropology can make significant contributions to forensic investigation and complements those of other disciplines.

CHAPTER

4

URBAN ANTHROPOLOGY

CASE STUDIES FROM THE NEW YORK CITY
MEDICAL EXAMINER'S OFFICE

Amy Zelson Mundorff

An Urban Setting

New York City has a population of over 8 million. In 1999, approximately 62,000 people died within the 5 boroughs; 23,600 of those deaths came under the jurisdiction of the medical examiner (Summary of Vital Statistics, City of New York 1999). Such large numbers guarantee that the city has its share of most postmortem phenomena, including skeletal remains. Most people's images of skeletons are limited to those found in rural, isolated places. Although far from rural, with isolation a scarce commodity, the city contains a large number of nooks and crannies in which to hide bodies that subsequently are reduced to bones.

The Office of Chief Medical Examiner (OCME), New York City, has always received skeletal remains, which until November 1999 were examined by a part-time anthropology consultant on a case-by-case basis. At that time, the OCME decided to employ a full-time anthropologist, which is when I joined the office. The anthropology laboratory is located in the morgue at the main office in Manhattan, but my jurisdiction includes all

five boroughs: Manhattan, Brooklyn, Bronx, Queens, and Staten Island. My duties are not restricted to the laboratory, and I frequently journey to the outermost corners of the city to excavate and recover human remains.

The goal of this chapter is to provide an overview of the responsibilities of a forensic anthropologist in one of the most populous urban environments, New York City, by discussing cases processed during the year 2000. Of the sixty-two cases I investigated, forty-eight were anthropological cases and thirteen were medical examiner cases in which an anthropologist's expertise was requested. The addition of a full-time anthropologist brought a dramatic increase in the number of requests for anthropological consultation, expanding the traditional role from examining bones to include the examination of bodies that had been dismembered, putrefied, burned, mummified, or otherwise sufficiently altered to render visual recognition unreliable. As a resource for the OCME, I teach the forensic pathology fellows, pathology residents, and medical students who rotate through the office. The fellows are particularly inquisitive

52

about a week or so before they take the forensic boards. This is when they all want to know, among other things, "What is the last bone in the body to fuse?"

The Medical Examiner's Office in New York City has a wide variety of in-house resources ranging from toxicology and histology labs, photographers and x-ray technicians, a full DNA lab, a crime scene reconstruction unit (MESATT), and a unit of NYPD missing-person detectives. There are thirty full-time medical examiners who, due to their large caseloads, are lucky to have a specially qualified team of medicolegal investigators (MLIs). The MLIs are all certified physician assistants who do the scene investigations. This multidisciplinary arrangement makes it very easy for an anthropologist to fit in and meld well with the investigative unit.

Forensic Anthropology Protocols at the OCME

An anthropologist should be present at scenes where bones are discovered, especially if they are to be disinterred. This ensures that contextual information is properly collected, which may later prove critical in solving an investigative puzzle by assessing how the remains were recovered, documenting their original position *in situ*, and identifying any associated artifacts (Haglund 1998; Haglund and Sorg 1997). To someone who is not familiar with bone morphology, carpals can look just like pebbles. The thorough and correct recovery of human remains is essential to any homicide investigation.

As a staff anthropologist, I quickly and seamlessly became a part of the medical examiner's routine. When bones are discovered, it always creates quite a stir. Any delay in the determination of whether remains are human causes inevitable complications, such as shutting down a construction site,

unnecessarily activating the NYPD Crime Scene Unit, or gaining media attention, not to mention the extra paperwork. This is especially frustrating if the bones turn out to be nonhuman. During the year 2000, twenty-four cases, or 50 percent of the total anthropological caseload, were nonhuman bones. It became apparent that an anthropologist could save many people a lot of work. Eventually, the MLIs began taking me to their scenes when bones were discovered, a procedure everyone welcomed. One advantage of this protocol, which saves the city a great deal of money, is that now the NYPD Crime Scene Unit does not respond to a bone scene until I have determined that the bones are human. Then everyone willingly hands over his or her shovels to qualified personnel who properly excavate the scene.

The combination of laboratory and field-work has enabled me to develop relationships with seasoned professionals from a variety of agencies: the cold case unit, canine unit, crime scene unit, homicide task force, and the city's missing person squad. I have even worked alongside the transit police when a skeleton turned up near the railroad tracks in the Bronx. That man had been missing for over eleven years.

I have worked with the pathologists to develop a formal forensic anthropological protocol for the office. Skeletal cases brought into the medical examiner's office initially are assigned to a pathologist, with whom I consult. Most of the pertinent scene information is provided by the MLI report. First, I determine whether the items are bones. So far, only two cases have turned out not to be bone; one was a glob of melted plastic with a tee-shirt wrapped around it, and the other case was a handful of burned rocks and slag from inside an old furnace. Then it is determined whether the bones are human. This usually is accomplished by looking at the articular surfaces, comparing the bone size to developmental age, the teeth (herbivores have very different teeth than carnivores), and the overall bone morphology. The most common non-human bones encountered in New York City are associated with food, such as chicken, leg of lamb, shanks, and ribs. Occasionally someone inadvertently disturbs the graves of buried pets, mostly cats and dogs. I also determine whether the bones are of recent origin, historic, or prehistoric in nature. The condition of the bones, the occlusal surface of the teeth, the presence of dental restorations, the context in which they were discovered, and associated artifacts all help with this determination. Finally, after it is decided conclusively that the remains are human bones, the forensic analysis begins. Everything is photographed and cleaned, if necessary. Many times there are small amounts of putrefied or mummified soft tissue still adherent to the bones. If soft tissue is present, a sample is usually submitted to toxicology by the medical examiner. The bones will also be radiographed as a potential means of personal identification and to help document previous or recent fractures, highlight the presence of metal fragments (bullets), identify other artifacts such as prostheses or bone pins, and evaluate dental development.

The analysis of the remains focuses on gathering information that will help determine the individual's sex, stature, ancestry, age at the time of death, the postmortem interval, any individualizing pathologies, and trauma that may have been inflicted at or around the time of death. If teeth are present, a consulting forensic odontologist will complete a dental chart as well. Based on this information, a report is compiled that the medical examiner and missing person detectives use to focus their search for personal identification. Finally, a small sample of bone is submitted to the DNA lab for later analysis.

Urban Anthropology Cases

There are no typical anthropology cases in New York City. The breakdown of skeletal cases in the year 2000 is as follows: twenty-four nonhuman, ten skulls, eight complete skeletons, three mummified remains, two postcranial only, one burned case, and thirteen varying consultations. This latter category ranges from determining the developmental age of fetuses and floaters (bodies recovered from water) to looking at tool marks on bone removed during autopsy, aiding in a dismemberment case, and examining fractures to help determine their age. Sometimes a consultation is simple, such as assisting a medical examiner in the autopsy room to describe the location of radiating fractures across multiple bones of the skull. Here are a few examples of urban anthropology cases from New York City examined in the year 2000.

Skulls and Isolated Bones

Not all of the bones that come to the attention of the OCME are as sinister as they might at first seem. One Sunday a man had been reported missing by his fellow church members. When the police went to look for him at his home, they found bones under his porch and in his backyard, probably those of children, the detectives hypothesized. A police cruiser picked me up and brought me to the scene. During the ride over, the "missing" man had returned to his home. When I reached his home, the poor man was trembling, and in a barely audible voice said he was sorry, he would not feed the local cats his leftovers anymore. A quick glance at the bones indicated that they were indeed pig and chicken, and his brief brush with being branded a serial killer ended as abruptly as it had started.

The boundaries between the normal and bizarre are often blurred, and what once seemed strange is now commonplace. For instance, a surprising number of New Yorkers are in possession of human remains, especially skulls. The skull owners fall into two discrete groups: those using the skulls as decoration, and those using them for religious purposes. However, the real question is, where are all of these skulls coming from? Though this may never be determined, the discovery of skulls in private residences is often shocking.

When a local dominatrix passed away, it fell upon her landlord to clean out her apartment. He found a human skull displayed on her bookcase and quickly took it to the closest police precinct. The skull, that of an adult male, was covered in dust with candle wax dripped on top. Upon further examination, it was determined that the skull was actually archaeological; this was determined in part by the condition of the teeth. Ancient American Indians processed their food with stone mortar and pestles, which added a healthy dose of sand to their food and, in turn, ground the occlusal surface of their teeth so flat that often there is almost no visible crown remaining (Figure 4.1). In addition, *FORDISC* confirmed the ancestry as American Indian with a posterior probability of .980 and the sex as male with a posterior probability of 1.0. *FORDISC 2.0* (Ousley and Jantz 1996) is a computer program that uses multidiscriminant functions to assist anthropologists in determining sex and ancestry from cranial measurements. Although this case was still forensically important, it could be ruled out as a recent homicide.

Another case began when a police officer saw gunshots being fired in the air. The officer did not hesitate to pursue the individual firing the weapon and followed the shooter into his apartment. Here he was confronted by three human skulls sitting in an open suitcase on the floor. They were collected and brought to the office for answers:

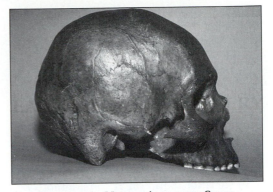

FIGURE 4.1   NATIVE AMERICAN SKULL
SHOWING EXTREME OCCLUSAL ATTRITION

Did we have another Jeffrey Dahmer on our hands, or was this something a little less sinister? The latter turned out to be true, luckily, since the discovery had already reached the newspapers. All three of the skulls were old, with considerable surface flaking and exfoliation. In addition, soil was still present within the orifices and cranium, indicative of previous burial (Ubelaker 1997). The combination of soil adhesion and erosion indicated that they had most likely been buried a long time ago. Sometimes the demand for human skulls is so high that unscrupulous people go to cemeteries and exhume remains to sell them. These three individuals, a white male, a black male, and a white female, whose sex and ancestry were corroborated by *FORDISC*, probably had death certificates issued decades ago.

Santeria

Human remains are also valued by persons involved in certain religious cults for use in ceremonies. Santeria, a religious cult of African origin, was introduced into the United States by Caribbean immigrants. The practice blends Christianity with a West African religious system from Yoruba, Nigeria (Gregory 1999). Santeria flourishes in areas where there are large populations of

Cuban immigrants, such as South Florida and New York City. Since there are no Bibles or written documents, the traditions are passed down orally from one practitioner to another. Because of the large Santeria following, there are many "botanicas" in New York City. A botanica is a specialty shop where practitioners can purchase their religious items and ingredients used for rituals and ceremonies (Curry 1997).

Although some of the rituals include animal sacrifice, Santeria is considered a benign religion. However, there is a "black magic sect of Santeria, derived from the Congo region of Africa, known as *palo mayombe*" (Wetli and Martinez 1981, 507). For a fee, these practitioners will perform rituals to inflict harm or worse on others. Items often included in the rituals used by this subgroup are chicken feathers, blood, sacred dirt, iron caldrons, coins, and human bones. These practices routinely go undetected, except when authorities stumble across them. Then the medical examiner's office is called to explicate.

This is exactly what happened in mid-July of 2000, after a woman was struck and killed by an 18-wheel tractor-trailer. That evening, the police arrived at the decedent's apartment to notify the next of kin. Her son, who lived with her, refused to allow the police to enter. He barricaded the door and exhibited very bizarre behavior, yelling and cursing. When police finally gained access, they were greeted by religious shrines everywhere—above the door, down the length of the hallway, and even filling an entire bedroom. When they discovered a human skull, the OCME was notified and the MLI on duty took me to the scene.

The apartment was musty and dimly lit but the familiar scent of decomposition was prevalent. All of the religious shrines had statues and candles covering almost every surface. There were plates with burned items and ashes, a decomposing pig head on a plate, no fewer than four severed chicken heads, a goat skull, iron cauldrons filled with dirt, coins, paper money, jars of unidentified liquid (some with solids floating in them), and much, much more. Religious idols, animal cages, crosses, and portraits of Jesus and saints decorated the apartment from wall to wall.

The human skull, found on a plate in the closet, created the most initial interest and precipitated our involvement, though there was much more to come. A cord was wrapped around the skull, thereby securing a candle to the forehead, and fake paper money was shoved into the left orbit. Blood and chicken feathers covered the skull as well (Figures 4.2 and 4.3). The bone was greasy to the touch, not dry and clean like an anatomical supply house specimen. Another shrine was behind the bedroom door as well. Among the swords, hair, and array of other items, an iron cauldron in the corner held two human humeri, a fibula, and a sacrum. Further, a large plastic container on

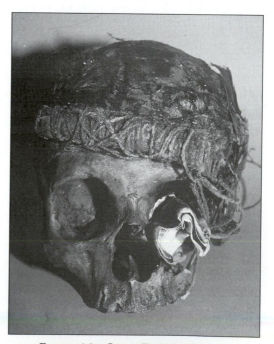

FIGURE 4.2   SKULL FOUND ON PLATE
AT SCENE WITH SANTERIAN SHRINES

FIGURE 4.3   A SECOND EXAMPLE
OF A SKULL FOUND ASSOCIATED
WITH A DIFFERENT SANTERIAN SHRINE

the floor of the closet held a newborn human infant preserved in some kind of fluid. A small plastic clamp was in the umbilical region and there was black ink on the soles of the feet. This indicates that the infant had been documented either by a hospital or a midwife.

The Crime Scene Unit was notified and the next day all of the items were brought to the medical examiner's office. The baby in the container was assigned to a medical examiner and the bones became an anthropology case. All of the bones were human. Though free of any soft tissue, they were still greasy. The sacrum appeared to have been burned postmortem and a portion of the lateral epicondyle of one humerus had been severed, allegedly a common finding in long bones associated with Santeria, although the purpose of this characteristic is unclear (Wetli and Martinez 1981).

Both humeri were from the right side and therefore could not have come from the same individual. Measurements of the vertical diameter of the heads of the humeri and their gracile morphology indicated that they were both from females (Stewart 1979). In addition, the gracile morphology of the fibula and the size and curvature of the sacrum also indicated female. So, minimally, there were two females: one likely older

than the other because one humerus was osteoporotic and much lighter in density than the other. The sacrum exhibited arthritic lipping and could have been from the same individual as the older appearing humerus. The skull had no soft tissue and the mandible was missing. There were no signs of trauma, though the zygomatics, the left petrous portion of the temporal bone and some teeth were all lost postmortem. The central and lateral incisors were missing and showed complete alveolar resorption, indicating that they had been missing before death. The skull had the same greasy surface as the long bones but also had drips of dried blood and chicken feathers adherent to its surface. The skull also had been burned postmortem, primarily on the inferior surface and within the cranial cavity, most likely from a candle being placed inside the foramen magnum.

The morphological attributes of the cranium, including small mastoids, sharp superior orbital margins, frontal and parietal bossing, a small occipital bun, and generally gracile features, indicate that this skull was from a female (Bass 1987). *FORDISC* was again employed, which gave a posterior probability of .768 and typicality probability of .163 that the individual was female. The *FORDISC* assessment is consistent with the morphological estimate of sex, but the low probabilities are likely a function of the small number of measurements available. The age of the skull was consistent with an adult, as the spheno-occipital synchondrosis was fused and, although the third molars were missing postmortem, they had fully erupted. Although mostly obscured by the blood and feathers, it was obvious that the sagittal suture was almost completely obliterated.

Ancestry is often the most difficult aspect to assess in a skeleton. This is made even more complicated in large cities such as New York, in which all popul ions and cultures mix (Rathbun and Buil a 1984).

Unfortunately, in this instance, diagnostic portions of the mid-face and cranium were fragmented or missing and any attempt to assess ancestry would be tentative at best.

The remains from these shrines and altars thus represented a minimum of two females, possibly more. One individual was substantially older than the other and likely suffered from osteoarthritis. Where these remains originated will probably never be determined since the woman, who was the practitioner using these items for religious purposes, is deceased. Ironically, had she not been killed by a truck, these bones probably would never have been discovered.

A Matter of Murder

Not all cases are so benign. In mid-March, an individual was walking along a trail in the woods of Queens County when he saw a large blue Tupperware container with a bungee cord around it down in a ravine. Upon opening the container, he found dismembered human remains and immediately called 911. The remains were transferred to the Queens mortuary of the Office of the Chief Medical Examiner. Because parts of the remains were skeletonized, the medical examiner needed anthropological assistance.

This case consisted of human remains in various stages of decomposition. A left foot, covered with decomposing soft tissue and active maggots, was amputated approximately 1.5 inches superior to the distal articulation of the tibia and fibula (Figure 4.4). The smooth, sharply cut margin with straight parallel striae indicated a power saw was used (Symes et al. 1998). The left os coxa and sacrum were present and articulated with each other cleanly. These were free of all soft tissue but still greasy. Also present was a skull and mandible, though the skull was fractured into many small fragments and missing a significant portion

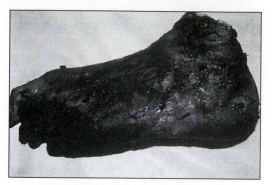

FIGURE 4.4   AMPUTATED FOOT COVERED IN SOFT TISSUE

of the facial bones. The condition of the skull and mandible were very curious, compared to the other remains present. The bones were clean of soft tissue and not at all greasy, unlike the foot or pelvic bones. Additionally, they were much whiter than the os coxa and sacrum. The immediate question at hand was whether the remains represented more than one individual since they were all in such different stages of decomposition.

The consistency of the skull bone was very porous and degraded, while the teeth were totally stripped of all of their enamel and were blunted (Figure 4.5). It appeared that these bones had been processed in some type of strong chemical. Written in black marker on the left parietal bone were derogatory racial and anti-gay slurs as well as what appeared to be a social security number that ended in 666. The 666 was underlined and followed by "#1," which conjured up many different and wild scenarios among the detectives. Could this be a hate crime because of the slurs written on the skull? Or was it cult-related because of the underline of the 666? The #1 evoked questions of whether there were more parts to be found or whether more than one individual had been mutilated.

No skeletal elements were duplicated, the os coxa and sacrum had a clean articulation,

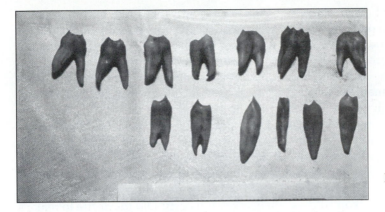

FIGURE 4.5   BLUNTED TEETH
Note the absence of enamel.

and the age estimation of the skull and os coxa were consistent with each other. The conclusion that all of the bones came from one person was later confirmed by DNA testing. The difference in their condition was due to the fact that some elements had been chemically processed and others had not.

Since the skull and os coxa were present, it was easy to determine the individual's sex and age at the time of death. The os coxa had a broad medial aspect of the ishiopubic ramus, a short pubic bone, narrow sciatic notch, and virtually no subpubic concavity. The skull exhibited a well-developed brow ridge, a distinct occipital protuberance, and well-developed mandibular rami, all traits associated with males. The skull was too fragmentary and incomplete to accurately conduct measurements for *FORDISC* to confirm sex or determine ancestry.

Although all of the bones were consistent with adult status, the mandibular third molars were not fully erupted, yielding an age range of 17–21 (Moorrees et al. 1963). The morphological characteristics of the pubic symphysis were consistent with Suchey-Brooks phase I, which yielded an age range of 15–23 for males, with a mean of 18.5 years (Katz and Suchey 1986). Ultimately, age was estimated between 17 and 21 years.

There was a semicircular defect on the right portion of the occipital bone directly posterior to the mastoid process. However, because of the fragmented condition of the skull, it was not clear if this was related to the other skull fractures. After reconstruction, however, it became clear that the defect was a gunshot entrance wound that measured approximately 5/8" in diameter and was internally beveled. Radiating fractures traveled along the squamosal suture, across the parietal and temporal bones, and anteriorly across the frontal bone, terminating approximately one inch above the right supraorbital foramen (Figure 4.6).

While the medical examiner's office was working on a profile of whom this individual

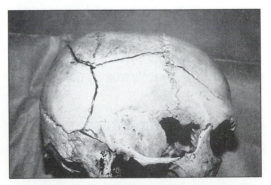

FIGURE 4.6   RECONSTRUCTED SKULL
WITH GUNSHOT WOUND
AND RADIATING FRACTURES

might be, the police tracked down the social security number written on the skull. It turned out to belong to a young man who had been missing for approximately six months. The condition of the foot could be consistent with an approximate six-month postmortem interval through winter. However, the defleshed and processed remains made an accurate estimate more challenging. When the police informed the stepfather that his stepson's remains had been recovered, the stepfather made a comment to a news agency that his stepson's "dismembered" remains were found. Unfortunately for him, that information had not been mentioned to him by the police or released to the media, and he had implicated himself. When confronted with this, he went to the roof of his house with a gun. He held the police at bay on the street for several hours, then took his own life. The case is now closed with exceptional clearance, meaning that the police know who committed the crime but cannot arrest him because he is dead.

The decedent was nineteen years old when he disappeared, which is within the age range estimated from the skeletal remains, and of mixed ancestry—one parent was white and the other black. Why this man murdered his stepson will never be known. The nature of the chemical processing remains undetermined, but the stepfather was a roofer and had access to many caustic chemicals. Documentation of this case is important since the rest of the remains may still surface and could be equally obscure in terms of postmortem processing.

Bizarre Places, Identified Cases

Skeletons are discovered in an amazing variety of locations and circumstances. Plastic garbage bags and duct tape are the packaging materials of choice for those wishing to dispose of a body in New York City. Four cases came into the office in this manner, and a fifth case was rolled up in a carpet. Another skeleton was discovered under a basement floor during renovations in a building that had been vacant for ten years. So far, two skeletons have been unearthed during the construction of a new mall in Brooklyn. In August 2000, a bargain hunter, who purchased an impounded car from a police auction, got more than he bargained for. When he opened the trunk, he discovered a badly decomposed and partially skeletonized body. Did his desire to make a good deal mask his olfactory senses?

Clearly, there is a wide variety of skeletal material submitted to the medical examiner's office, including isolated bones, full skeletons, nonhuman remains, and obvious homicides. They are all interesting in their own way. During the year 2000, three skeletal identifications were confirmed. The first was made by dental comparison after the police took the anthropological profile of sex, age, ancestry, and stature and matched it to a woman missing for sixteen months. The second anthropological identification was confirmed by mitochondrial DNA (mtDNA). This nineteen-year-old black man had been missing for eleven years. When the remains were discovered, there was no skull associated with the postcranial bones. Since there could be no dental comparison and there were no antemortem radiographs, a positive match could not initially be made. The sex, age, stature, and postmortem interval were consistent with the missing man, and mtDNA extracted from the bones compared positively with his mother. The third identification is still tentative. While the information discerned from the remains matches the sex, ancestry, stature, and place of discovery with the missing individual, there are no antemortem records or access to familial DNA to confirm the presumptive identification. The police are presently seeking a photograph of the missing individual for facial superimposition. This technique cannot legally confirm identification, but it can be used for the purposes of exclusion.

There are many exciting prospects for the future of forensic anthropology, especially when enhanced by the powerful tools of molecular biology. The office is in the process of creating an unidentified persons database. A bone sample is taken from every anthropological case and submitted for mitochondrial or nuclear DNA typing. This sequence is then entered into the database. The plan is to collect missing person exemplars (DNA sources) as soon as possible following the filing of a police report. Exemplars include personal items such as a toothbrush, hairbrush, or an unlaundered undergarment. This will establish a missing persons profile, which in the future can be cross-referenced with the unidentified persons profile to provide matches.

Epilogue

Subsequent to the initial completion of this chapter, the city of New York fell prey to the worst act of terrorism in the history of the United States. Two fully fueled airliners were flown into the World Trade Center buildings, instantly killing hundreds. The two 110-story buildings then collapsed, killing thousands more. These two large commercial buildings, plus five more, were totally destroyed, covering an area of approximately sixteen acres in downtown Manhattan. The Office of Chief Medical Examiner and other New York City authorities had a well-defined disaster management program in place, but the scope of the World Trade Center disaster was beyond our imagination.

Every person in the office, no matter their specialty, had a role in the implementation and processing of this disaster, not to mention the added support and assistance from multiple outside agencies. The role of the anthropologist became apparent from the beginning. The human remains were brought into the office in every condition and state

of decomposition imaginable—burned, calcined, mummified, and putrefied—and ranged from whole bodies to small bone fragments. Anthropologists took on the role of triage, and solved some of the initial problems by discerning human from nonhuman remains. Many restaurants were located within the area of destruction and therefore it was expected that nonhuman remains would be collected during the excavation process. Each bag brought from the site was labeled with a grid number. However, these bags potentially contained the remains of multiple individuals. Due to the number of victims and the force of the destruction, many of the remains were commingled. In order to ensure that DNA was properly collected from every individual, it was imperative to sort out commingled remains. During triage, the anthropologist separated remains that were not attached or failed to articulate with each other. Nonhuman remains were discarded, and fragmented human remains that could be articulated were bagged together. Commingled burned remains were sorted for minimum number of individuals as well. Assistance also was provided with regard to more typical anthropological roles such as the examination of healed fractures and prostheses that could be used to aid identification.

The traditional role of the anthropologist was partially obsolete in these circumstances. Due to the thousands of victims, the tens of thousands of fragments, and a recovery process measured in months, most identifications will be made by DNA. Therefore, determining the age and stature ranges of fragmentary bones was not necessary. Had the number of individuals been smaller, this would have been useful; however, with a population this large, knowing that a femur was from a 5'10"–12" male does not narrow down the identification process. DNA will be used to confirm the identity of the individuals and to match and correlate parts that are received separately. This by no means suggests that an anthropologist was not necessary, just that the role in a mass disaster of this magnitude was different from traditional expectations. Triaging, separating human from nonhuman bones, and analyzing commingled, burned, and fragmented remains assisted medical examiners in their tasks and enabled appropriate samples of DNA to be obtained.

Conclusions

Working at the medical examiner's office has been a broadening experience. The importance of having a full-time anthropologist in a large medical examiner facility has become very clear. It seems that my participation on hand at scenes has been the most important contribution to the city. However, the paramount lesson is the importance of teamwork between the anthropologist, medicolegal investigator, police, medical examiner, dentist, radiologist, and molecular biologist. In this regard, a major urban office such as the New York City medical examiner enjoys the advantage of having the entire team under one roof.

References

Bass, William M. 1987. *Human Osteology: A Laboratory and Field Manual.* Columbia, MO: Missouri Archaeological Society.

Curry, M. C. 1997. *Making the Gods in New York City.* New York: Garland Publishing.

Gregory, Steven. 1999. *Santeria in New York City: A Study in Cultural Resistance.* New York: Garland Publishing.

Haglund, William D. 1998. The scene and context: Contributions of the forensic anthropologist. Pp. 41–56 in *Forensic Osteology: Advances in the Identification of Human Remains,* ed. Kathleen J. Reichs. Springfield, IL: Charles C. Thomas.

Haglund, William D., and Marcella H. Sorg. 1997. Method and theory of forensic taphonomic research. Pp. 13–26 in *Forensic Taphonomy: The Postmortem Fate of Human Remains,* ed. William D. Haglund and Marcella H. Sorg. Boca Raton, FL: CRC Press.

Katz, Darryl, and Judy M. Suchey. 1986. Age determination of the male *os pubis. American Journal of Physical Anthropology* 69:427–435.

Moorrees, C. F. A., E. A. Fanning, and E. E. Hunt. 1963. Age variation of formation stages for ten permanent teeth. *Journal of Dental Research* 42:1,490–1,502.

New York City Department of Health. 1999. *Summary of Vital Statistics 1999.* The City of New York. Office of Vital Statistics, New York City Department of Health, New York.

Ousley, Stephen, and Richard Jantz. 1996. *FORDISC 2.0.* Department of Anthropology, University of Tennessee, Knoxville.

Rathbun, Ted A., and Jane E. Buikstra. 1984. *Human Identification: Case Studies in Forensic Anthropology.* Springfield, IL: Charles C. Thomas.

Stewart, T. Dale. 1979. *Essentials of Forensic Anthropology.* Springfield, IL: Charles C. Thomas.

Symes, Steven A., Hugh E. Berryman, and O'Brien C. Smith. 1998. Saw marks in bone: Introduction and examination of residual kerf contour. Pp. 389–409 in *Forensic Osteology: Advances in the Identification of Human Remains,* ed. Kathleen J. Reichs. Springfield, IL: Charles C. Thomas.

Ubelaker, Douglas H. 1997. Taphonomic applications in forensic anthropology. Pp. 77–90 in *Forensic Taphonomy: The Postmortem Fate of Human Remains,* ed. William D. Haglund and Marcella H. Sorg. Boca Raton, FL: CRC Press.

Wetli, Charles V., and R. Martinez. 1981. Forensic sciences aspects of Santeria, a religious cult of African origin. *Journal of Forensic Sciences* 26(3):506–514.

CHAPTER 5

MULTIPLE POINTS OF SIMILARITY

Dawnie Wolfe Steadman and Lyle W. Konigsberg

Alas, poor Yorick! I knew him, Horatio: a fellow of infinite jest, of most excellent fancy: he hath borne me on his back a thousand times; and now, how abhorred in my imagination it is! my gorge rises at it. Here hung those lips that I have kissed I know not how oft. Where be your gibes now? your gambols? your songs? your flashes of merriment, that were wont to set the table on a roar? Not one now, to mock your own grinning?

—Hamlet Act 5, scene 1

Through his able protagonist Hamlet, Shakespeare recognized that the naked skull still bears a physical resemblance to a person so well known and loved in life. Gaps between the teeth, a terribly disfigured nose, or a wide, toothy grin are natural features or results of past transgressions that make a skeleton unique in life and in death. Forensic anthropologists, radiologists, odontologists, and pathologists use these characteristics to render a personal identification. But how many points of similarity are sufficient to identify a skeleton?

This is not an easy question for anthropologists to answer, and other forensic scientists face similar dilemmas. For instance, fingerprint examiners do not always agree upon the minimum number of characteristics required to establish a match between evidentiary (unknown) and exemplar (known) prints. While some texts on friction ridge prints suggest a minimum of only three points, other standards suggest that upwards of seventeen characteristics are required for a positive identification (Cowger 1993). This lack of standardization has frustrated the courts and forensic scientists, yet the experience of the examiner is considered a stronger key element in the identification process than a certain number of matching "points." According to Cowger ". . . an 'identification' is made when, *in the judgment of the examiner*, the degree of similarity between two prints is sufficient to warrant that conclusion" (1993, 146, emphasis original). The International Association of Identification (IAI) agrees. The IAI is a professional organization of fingerprint examiners and other forensic scientists who examine physical evidence. Over twenty years ago they attempted to establish a set of minimum standards of

63

identification but ultimately determined that "each identification represents a unique set of circumstances, and the number of required matching characteristics is dependent upon a variety of conditions which automatically rule out the practicality of mandating a pre-determined minimum" (1973 IAI Resolution). In 1995, the IAI reviewed the 1973 Resolution and found little had changed. "No scientific basis exists for requiring that a pre-determined minimum number of friction ridge features must be present in two impressions in order to establish a positive identification" (1995 IAI Ne'urim, Israel Symposium). Thus, the quality of the print, proper selection of unique traits, and experience of the examiner are crucial.

The less formalized "standards" in forensic anthropology are somewhat similar. If a characteristic is highly unique, then a putative identification can be established with just one trait *if* the skeletal analyst has sufficient experience to distinguish between features that are truly unique and those that reflect normal variation. However, like other forensic scientists, forensic anthropologists prefer to observe multiple points of similarity. Depending on the nature of the data, probability statements can be made that may be especially useful in court. In the case presented here, a plethora of skeletal features provides some insight into the unique life history of a man whose rough-and-tumble past was forever recorded in his bones. The individual's name has been changed and certain personal details of his medical history have been omitted. Steadman completed the anthropological analysis and identification, while Konigsberg has described the statistical arguments that can be used to quantify the minimum number of individuals and the probability of a correct identification in this case.

A Skull Is Found

In October 1999, a local man found a skull embedded in mud at the bottom of a creek in eastern Iowa. The location was reported to the sheriff's office and the skull was recovered by the medical examiner. Steadman was asked to examine the skull to develop a biological profile for the purposes of identification and document any evidence of perimortem trauma.

The skull was well-preserved and covered in very dark mud. It was cleaned with a toothbrush and running water and the soil was carefully removed from the cranial vault and screened for artifacts, such as insects or bullets, but none were found. Anthropological analysis of the skull indicated that the individual was a male between thirty and forty-five years of age. Discrimination between European and African American ancestry was ambiguous due to the unusual shape of the vault and face. There were several other unique features about the skull. Both nasal bones had multiple healed fractures and deformation, especially on the left side that included the maxilla (Figure 5.1). The nasal

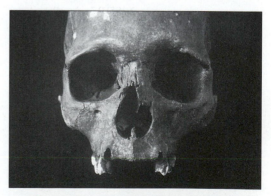

FIGURE 5.1 ANTERIOR VIEW OF SKULL
Note the healed fractures of the nasal bones with significant bony exostosis (overgrowth) on the left nasal and maxilla.

septum deviated to the left. The left orbit appeared smaller in absolute size and shape than the right, and the nasal aperture likewise appeared asymmetrical. There was a healed fracture on the right zygomatic process at its root on the temporal. Significant antemortem loss of the maxillary dentition was noted, including the left third molar, left second premolar, right first and third molars, and all of the incisors were lost. Metallic dental restorations (fillings) were present on all of the remaining teeth. There was also a healed abscess 15.8 mm above the right third molar alveolar space.

Steadman submitted a report to the sheriff's office but there were no missing persons in the tri-county area that matched this description. Investigators decided to release a portion of the report to the local newspapers with hopes that someone would come forward with information about the identity of this individual. Their efforts were immediately rewarded.

A woman saw the newspaper article about the skull and called the sheriff's office. Her recollection of the features of a close relative she hadn't seen in nearly two years closely matched the anthropological description of the skull. The individual had not been reported missing as he was known to lose contact with his family for extended periods of time but had always returned on his own accord. Her relative was a white male who was forty-four years of age at the time of his disappearance in 1997. She recounted that he had suffered several broken bones during his life and had lost his front teeth and fractured his nose multiple times from fighting. He also had an odd-shaped head, which the family attributed to the use of forceps during his birth. As the investigators began to search for dental records of the missing man, another question remained. Where was the rest of the body?

Search and Recovery

The forensic anthropologist was able to provide insight concerning the location of the postcranial remains although she was not present during the field recovery. Prior to the search, Steadman was shown photographs of the creek bed where the skull was found. The photos revealed the surrounding terrain and the proximity of specific structures to the creek, including a bridge upstream, a nearby highway, and a levee road. The photographs clearly showed that the creek was surrounded on one side by a gently sloping bank and by a steeper slope on the opposite side. Knowing the normal progression of decomposition, it seemed prudent to suggest that the officers search the steep slope first. In life, the skull only attaches to the trunk through its articulation with the atlas, or first cervical vertebra, and associated neck muscles, ligaments, and skin. Once the soft tissue decomposes, the skull easily separates from the atlas. While its own weight may cause it to roll away from the body, gravity becomes an even greater factor when the body decomposes on a slope. The skull may roll several meters away and, if it meets another transport medium, such as water or a scavenger, it may be carried a significant distance from the original deposition site. Thus, the searchers began on the steep slope and moved systematically upstream from the location at which the skull was found. A short time later, the officers discovered scattered postcranial human remains along the steep slope and creek approximately 300 feet upstream from the original recovery site of the skull.

Skeletal Inventory, Preservation, and Procedures

Inventory

A formal inventory indicated that the skeleton of what appeared to be a single individual was present and relatively complete.

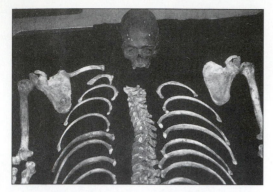

FIGURE 5.2   PARTIAL VIEW OF THE SKELETON RECOVERED FROM EASTERN IOWA

Note the color difference between the skull and postcranial bones. The skull was found in a darker soil matrix than the postcranial skeleton.

The following bones were missing: mandible, hyoid, left clavicle, two left ribs, two right ribs, left radius, left hand, first through sixth cervical vertebrae, right hand phalanges, and some foot phalanges. The skull was very dark brown while the postcranial bones were lighter brown (Figure 5.2). This indicates that the skull was in a different soil matrix for a period of time, though the length of differential exposure could not be reliably determined.

In addition to the skeletal material, soft tissue was adherent to several bones, including the pelvis, right humerus, left leg, left scapula, right ribs, thoracic vertebrae, a left rib, the right fifth metacarpal, and the right leg and foot, which were still inside a sock. Most of the soft tissue was adipocere, a soap-like substance that forms as a result of the decomposition of lipids, or fat, in warm, moist environments. Some skin was present on the right humerus, though no tattoos or other identifying marks were noted under a normal light source. Nonbiological items recovered included clothing remnants and a set of keys in the pants pocket.

The bones were well-preserved and bone damage due to recovery was minimal. There were several postmortem alterations

typical of outdoor environments. For instance, most of the postcranial bones demonstrated parallel striations consistent with rodent tooth marks (Haglund 1992).

Minimum Number of Individuals

Though there were no redundant skeletal elements (e.g., two skulls or two left femora), the context of the remains necessitated a stronger statement concerning the minimum number of individuals (MNI). This particular area of Iowa is known by police officers as a "dumping ground" for bodies. Further, homeless people camp and sometimes die in this area as well. Thus, it would be useful to calculate the probability that the skeletal elements recovered were from a single individual.

Snow and Folk (1970) have previously tackled this problem when multiple children were abducted and murdered in Oklahoma City in the 1960s (see also Snow and Luke 1984). Snow and Folk demonstrate how to calculate the probability of obtaining no duplications of individual skeletal elements *if* the collected bones actually come from two individuals. In other words, the null hypothesis is that the remains represent two individuals. If the probability is very low then we are inclined to reject the null hypothesis that two individuals are represented, and take a more parsimonious route—that the bones are from a single person.

Snow and Folk first determine how many bones are apt to survive postdepositional (taphonomic) processes and are distinguishable skeletal elements. For instance, osteologists can readily recognize a left femur or ribs 1 and 2 but cannot easily recognize side hand and foot phalanges. With these criteria in mind, the authors reduce the 200-plus bones of the adult skeleton to 98 uniquely identifiable bones. Of these, 74 bones were recovered in this case (Table 5.1). Using the calculation from Snow and Folk (1970), the probability of getting 74 bones

TABLE 5.1   LIST OF UNIQUELY IDENTIFIABLE BONES OF AN ADULT (AFTER SNOW AND FOLK 1970) AND THOSE RECOVERED FROM EASTERN IOWA

SKELETAL ELEMENT	ADULT MALE (SNOW AND FOLK 1970)	REMAINS RECOVERED FROM IOWA
Mandible	1	0
Frontal	1	1
Parietals	2	2
Occipital	1	1
Temporals	2	2
Zygomas	2	2
Maxillaries	2	2
Sternum	2	0
Vertebrae (C1, C2, C7, T1, L5, Sacrum, Cy1)	7	3
Ribs (Right 1, 2; Left 1, 2)	4	3
Scapula, Clavicles, and Long Bones of Upper Extremity	10	8
Carpals	16	8
Metacarpals	10	5
Proximal Phalanx, 1st digit—Hand	2	1
Os coxae	2	2
Long Bones of Lower Extremity	6	6
Patellae	2	2
Tarsals	14	14
Metatarsals	10	10
Proximal Phalanx, 1st digit—Foot	2	2
Totals	98	74

with no duplication of elements (assuming two individuals are represented) is about 5.6 $\times 10^{-11}$. To put it another way, the 74 uniquely identifiable bones are about 18 trillion times more likely to have been recovered if the remains belonged to one individual than if they were from two individuals.

The Problem of Bias

As a matter of protocol, many forensic anthropologists conduct an anthropological analysis "blind." That is, they do not want to know any of the investigator's theories concerning the identity of the deceased until they have completed the biological profile and perimortem trauma analysis. Forensic anthropologists are trained to avoid bias—a type of prejudice in which the observer is influenced by what they or others expect to find. Bias can creep in subconsciously, especially for cases in which certain parameters might be difficult to assess, such as age or ancestry. Many anthropologists attempt to avoid bias by shielding themselves from the facts and theories of a case until he or she forms and documents his or her own scientific opinion. In this case, the investigators recovered the missing man's dental and medical records relatively quickly, but Steadman did not accept them until after she had written a preliminary report. However, knowing when to ask specific questions can save considerable time and effort and the anthropologist must determine the appropriate moments in an investigation to gain further information.

The abbreviated anthropological report below was written prior to examining Mr. Johnson's medical and dental records. The second portion of the report compares the pathological conditions observed in the skeleton with antemortem information provided by the records. Following the protocol of pathology reports, the anthropological analysis is written in the present tense.

Anthropological Analysis of Identity

Biological Profile

The anthropological analysis of the entire skeleton indicates that the remains originated from a 35–50-year-old white male with a living stature of 68–74 inches. The determination of male sex is based primarily on the morphology of the pelvis and cranium. The size of the subpubic angle, sciatic notch, pelvic breadth, nuchal crest, supraorbital margins, glabella, mastoid process, gonial angle and chin, and the absence of a ventral arc and ischiopubic ridge are consistent with a male.

All of the epiphyses are fused, so the age range is based on the morphology of the pubic symphysis and auricular surface, and the degree of cranial suture closure. Following the descriptions of Katz and Suchey (1986), the pubic symphysis is consistent with Phase 5 for males (28–78 years). The auricular surfaces are in late stage 6 (45–50 years), according to the methods of Lovejoy et al. (1985). The cranial sutures do not offer further discriminatory power for they

give an age range of 30–45 years. Together, the age indicators suggest a range of 35–50 years.

As mentioned above, many of the morphological observations (e.g., long, narrow skull shape, slight prognathism, wide interorbital breadth, nasal guttering, rectangular orbits) indicate an individual of African American ancestry, though European ancestry cannot be ruled out. Seventeen cranial measurements are entered into a computer software program, FORDISC 2.0 (Ousley and Jantz 1996), which performs a multivariate statistical analysis to compare the measurements to those of modern individuals of known sex and ancestry. The measurements of the unknown individuals are compared to groups of white, Asian, black, and American Indian male samples from the Forensic Data Bank. Assuming that it is equally likely that the cranium came from one of these groups, the posterior probability that the cranium is from a white male is 0.85, or 85 percent. The posterior probability means the probability of obtaining the observed measurements from a white male versus getting the observed measurements from the population at large, or all of the groups considered in the analysis. However, the asymmetrical and deformed nature of the head and antemortem tooth loss most certainly affect the morphological and metric characteristics of the skull. Therefore, the individual is only tentatively assessed as a white male.

An estimate of stature from the skeleton is accomplished by applying standard sex- and population-specific regression formulae to long bone measurements. Since the estimation of ancestry is unclear, a regression analysis for both black and white males is performed, using a 90 percent prediction interval (Ousley 1995). The stature estimate for a black male is 69 ± 3 inches, while the stature for a white male is 71 ± 3 inches. Large muscle attachments on the skull and long bones indicate that the individual had a relatively robust muscle structure.

Antemortem Pathology

In addition to the pathological features of the skull, described above, there are also several well-healed antemortem fractures in the postcranial skeleton. The right tibia has two healed fractures, one in the proximal shaft and one in the distal shaft. The right tibial shaft also exhibits myostitis ossificans (ossification of the muscle) immediately superior to the proximal fracture. In addition, a previous episode of osteomyelitis (infection of the bone marrow) is indicated by the presence of three healed cloacae (channels for pus drainage) at the proximal fracture

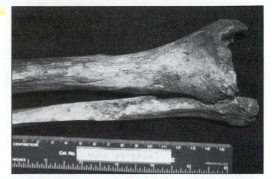

FIGURE 5.4. HEALED FRACTURES
OF THE RIGHT DISTAL TIBIA AND FIBULA

site on the posterior aspect of the proximal tibia (Figure 5.3). A healed fracture in the distal right fibula is close to the same level of the diaphysis as that of the distal tibia (Figure 5.4).

Multiple ribs have antemortem fractures in different stages of healing near the sternal ends. Healed or healing fractures are clearly indicated on the sternal ends of right ribs 5, 6, 7, 8, 9, and 10 and left ribs 6 and 11 (see Figure 5.5 on page 70). Deformation of the sternal ends of right ribs 3, 4, and 10 and left ribs 7, 8, and 9 also indicate well-healed fractures. All fractures occur on the anterior or anteriolateral aspects of the rib cage.

The right hand has two healed fractures. There is a healed fracture of the second right metacarpal head and the right fifth metacarpal exhibits a well-healed fracture of the distal shaft with subsequent bowing deformation. These types of metacarpal fractures are called "Boxer's fractures" because they are caused by an impact to the head of the metacarpal, such as when a closed fist strikes an object (Galloway 1999; Jupiter and Belsky 1992).

Several joints show signs of arthritic changes, especially those of the right shoulder, patella, and elbow. The right clavicular-acromial and clavicular-sternal joints display severe degeneration. Several ribs demonstrate moderate to severe arthritic

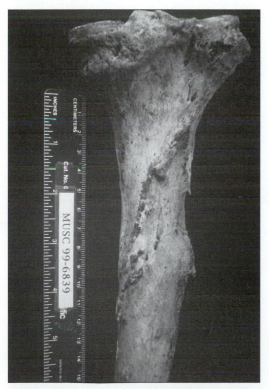

FIGURE 5.3 POSTERIOR VIEW
OF THE RIGHT PROXIMAL TIBIA

Note the healed fracture with osteomyelitis and myostitis ossificans.

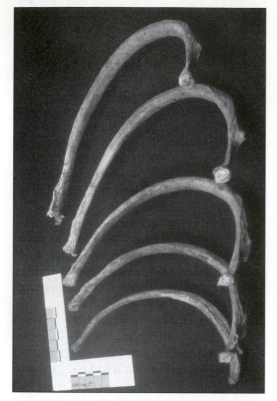

FIGURE 5.5   HEALED FRACTURES OF THE STERNAL ENDS OF SEVERAL RIGHT RIBS

lipping at the heads and at the sternal ends. Significant arthritis is also exhibited in the vertebral column and Schmorl's nodes are present in the T6–T12 and L2–L4. Schmorl's nodes are depressions in the superior and/or inferior bodies of the vertebrae and indicate disk disease and herniation (bulging of the disk).

Finally, there is a small, localized periosteal (surface) deposition of bone on the anterior right femur, approximately 21 cm proximal to the superior margin of the patellar surface (Figure 5.6). The maximum dimensions of the lesion are 15.5 x 14 mm. While the new bone is sclerotic and healing, the margins are not fully incorporated into the underlying cortical bone. The etiology of this periosteal reaction is unclear.

Perimortem and Postmortem Alterations

There are no overt signs of perimortem trauma. However, two fractures of left rib 11 and one fracture of left rib 12 may indicate perimortem damage. There is no evidence of healing and the margins and exposed trabeculae are the same color as the surrounding bone, indicating the fractures are not recent. The incomplete nature and morphology of the fractures suggests that soft tissue was still present and the bone was still "green," or fresh. Since it is unclear how rapidly the soft tissue decomposed, early postmortem damage cannot be ruled out, especially since some of the remains were likely carried by water and rodents.

Summary

The nearly complete skeletal remains recovered from a creek in eastern Iowa are those of a 35–50 year old male, probably of European ancestry, though African American ancestry cannot be ruled out. Antemortem fractures with differential healing of the nasal bones, right zygomatic arch, right tibia, right fibula, right hand, and rib cage suggest multiple past traumatic events. The individual was approximately 67 to 73 inches tall with robust musculature.

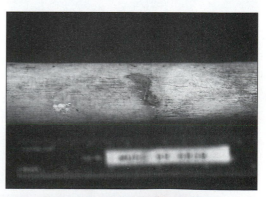

FIGURE 5.6   HEALED (SCLEROTIC) PERIOSTEAL LESION ON THE ANTERIOR SHAFT OF THE RIGHT FEMUR

Several characteristics of the face were likely distinctive in life, including a broken nose, a healed fracture of the right cheek, and loss of the upper incisors.

Identification

Comparison of the Postmortem Skeleton with Antemortem Records of W. Johnson

This case presented a rather unique problem for identification since the skull was found in a different physical context from the postcranial remains. While the statistical MNI analysis demonstrates that it is highly unlikely that the remains represent more than one individual, the first six cervical vertebrae were not recovered and the skull could not be directly rearticulated with the postcranial remains. In addition, recall that this part of the county was known as a disposal area for bodies. Thus, two separate identifications were required: one of the skull and one of the postcranial skeleton.

Identification of postcranial materials can be difficult if an individual never suffered an injury or a medical condition that required x-rays or other material documentation. Even in the absence of specific bone injuries, however, chest films are often available because physicians frequently order them to rule out certain respiratory diseases and infections. Together, the forensic radiologist and anthropologist can use antemortem chest films to compare unique bony patterns in the vertebrae, ribs, and sternum (Brogdon 1998). Fortunately, the comparison of antemortem and postmortem postcranial identification was not difficult in this case because of the wealth of medical information available from the woman's missing relative, Mr. W. Johnson (not his real name).

Mr. Johnson's medical records and radiographs were received from several hospitals and medical centers in eastern Iowa. The records span two decades, from 1977 to 1997, and document a number of traumatic events in his life. His relative also provided a significant amount of additional information. An alcohol and drug abuser since the age of fifteen, Mr. Johnson sustained a multitude of injuries from fights, falls, and vehicular accidents. After reviewing Mr. Johnson's medical records and radiographs, Steadman found multiple points of similarity and only one element of inconsistency with the cranial and postcranial skeletal remains recovered from the creek in eastern Iowa.

Dental and Cranial Comparisons

Points of similarity between the characteristics and pathological conditions of the skull and dentition and the medical history of dental and medical records attributed to W. Johnson include, but are not limited to, the following.

Dental Records

- Mr. Johnson's dental chart from early 1997 is available from a Veterans Administration (V.A.) Medical Center and shows antemortem tooth loss and restorations consistent with the maxillary dentition of the skull, including:
  - Antemortem loss of the maxillary right third and first molars, all of the incisors, left second premolar, and left third molar
  - Restorations on the occlusal and distal lingual aspect of the maxillary right second molar
- Panoramic dental radiography of Mr. Johnson dated September 1996 was compared to bite-wing views of the maxillary dentition of the skull recovered from eastern Iowa. The following points of similarity are noted:
  - Antemortem loss of the left third molar and second premolar, right first and third molars, and all incisors
  - The location and morphology of restorations, including: single metallic restorations present on the right

second molar, right first and second premolars, and left first molar; two metallic restorations visible on the left second molar and first premolar

- The boundary of the right maxillary sinus angles above the right first and second molars
- Trabecular pattern of the right first molar alveolar space

There are no inconsistencies between the dental radiographs and records belonging to W. Johnson and the dentition of the skull recovered from eastern Iowa. Further, there are several antemortem pathologies of the skull that are consistent with Mr. Johnson's medical history.

Medical Records

CRANIUM

- Medical records dated November 1978 from one V.A. Hospital include a medical history of multiple fractures of the right and left nasal bones that occurred as a result of perhaps as many as six or seven different events. Septo-rhinoplastic surgery to correct "considerable nasal deformity" had been performed in 1977. A medical history from another V.A. Hospital in 1987 indicates his nose was fractured again one month after the surgery in 1977. Septoplasty with bilateral ala cartilage implants was performed in 1987 to correct airway obstruction due to nasal trauma.
  - Though antemortem radiographs of Mr. Johnson's skull are not present for comparison, the skull recovered from eastern Iowa has multiple, well-healed fractures of the nasal bones.
- Skull trauma is reported on October of 1994. Mr. Johnson reports he struck the right side of his head on a table corner, which resulted in headaches.
  - Radiographs of the skull are not available, but this injury may correspond to the healed fracture of the right zygomatic root observed in the skull from eastern Iowa. In addition, several medical reports discuss past

cranial trauma received in motor vehicle accidents, but specific injuries are not documented.

POSTCRANIAL SKELETON   Points of similarity between the characteristics and pathological conditions of the postcranial skeletal remains and the medical history of W. Johnson include, but are not limited to, the following:

- Mr. Johnson suffered a fracture of the proximal right tibia in April 1977, when he drove his motorcycle head-on into a car. The timing of the distal tibia/fibula fracture is unclear from the medical records, but one radiological report (9-27-77) indicates they are older than the fracture of the proximal tibia. Thus, both fracture sites of the tibia (proximal and distal) apparently occurred in motorcycle accidents in 1977, but at different times.
  - The location and morphology of the fractures on the right tibia and right fibula of the skeleton is compatible with those observed on radiographs of the right lower leg of W. Johnson taken in August 1993 and April 1995 (Figures 5.7 and 5.8).
  - A radiology report in April 1992 is positive for myostitis ossificans of the right proximal leg, which is visible in radiographs taken in March and April 1994, and especially the lateral view of the right leg taken in April 1995. The location of the lesion corresponds nicely to those observed in the skeleton from eastern Iowa.
  - Mr. Johnson was treated for osteomyelitis of the right leg as noted in medical records dated October 1993. However, the exact location of the infection is not specified. The osteomyelitis visible in the posterior shaft of the proximal tibia of the skeletal remains is consistent with the physician's report that the infection may have been caused by refracturing the bone.
- Deformity of the right fifth metacarpal is noted in an August 1984 radiological

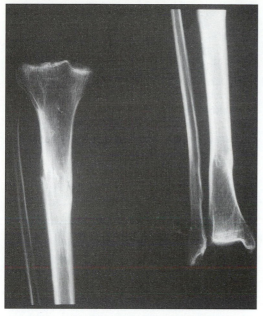

FIGURE 5.7   POSTMORTEM RADIOGRAPH
OF THE PROXIMAL (RIGHT) AND DISTAL (LEFT)
FRACTURES OF THE RIGHT TIBIA

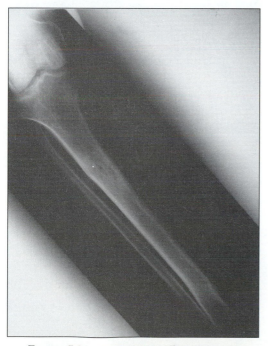

FIGURE 5.8   ANTEMORTEM RADIOGRAPH
OF MR. W. JOHNSON SHOWING PROXIMAL
AND DISTAL FRACTURES OF THE RIGHT TIBIA

report for Mr. Johnson. The deformity is visible in radiographs taken in May 1990 and March 1994 (see Figures 5.9 and 5.10 on page 74).

• The amount of healing and type and degree of deformation observed in the right fifth metacarpal of the skeleton is compatible with the radiographs and medical history.

• Fracture of the right second metacarpal head is noted in the medical records and radiographs of May 1990.

• The location, size, and morphology of the fracture are consistent with the healed fracture found in the skeleton.

• Medical records indicate that Mr. Johnson suffered a stab wound to the right upper thigh in March 1992, though an exact location of the wound is not documented.

• This injury may correspond to the periosteal reaction visible on the anterior aspect of the right femur of the skeleton.

• According to medical records, several right ribs were recently fractured in September 1992. Fresh sternal fractures of right ribs 6–9 are noted in radiographs dated 9-18-92 and healing is tracked in several radiographs through 11-25-95. These medical records indicate other rib fractures occurred in a motorcycle accident in 1977, though the report is not specific in regard to the number and location of these fractures.

• The morphology, location, and extent of healing of the right rib fractures as viewed on the antemortem radiographs are consistent with those of the skeleton. Compare Figure 5.5 (on page 70) with Figure 5.11 (on page 74). Fractures of the left ribs are also visible on the antemortem x-rays.

• Two separate radiology reports from September 1994 describe spurring of L4 and L5 with mild osteoarthritis of the lumbar spine.

• These changes are consistent with slight to moderate osteophytosis found in the thoracolumbar region of the skeleton.

- Medical records document that Mr. Johnson injured his right knee after jumping into a trash bin at work in May 1985, and subsequently underwent arthroscopy in June and again in July of 1985. Mild arthritis of the right knee joint was noted radiographically in August 1994.

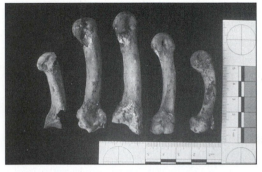

FIGURE 5.9   POSTMORTEM LATERAL VIEW
OF THE RIGHT METACARPALS

Note the curvature of the fifth metacarpal (far right).

- The arthritic changes are consistent with the moderate lipping observed on the right patella of the skeleton from eastern Iowa that is absent in the left side.
- Mr. Johnson is reported as 72 inches tall, approximately 200 pounds, with well-developed musculature.
  - This stature is within the range of variation calculated from the postcranial remains of the skeleton from eastern Iowa (71 ± 3 inches for a white male).

An Inconsistent Point?

The medical records cite only one event that could affect the skeleton but is not observed in the skeletal remains. According to an oral medical history taken at a V.A. Hospital on 5-20-94, Mr. Johnson reported a past history of a gunshot wound to the right foot. He does not provide a date for the incident. The

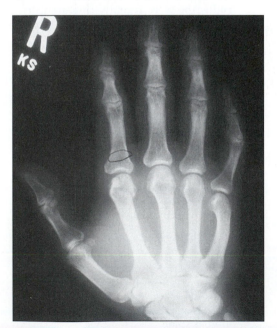

FIGURE 5.10   ANTEMORTEM RADIOGRAPH
OF MR. W. JOHNSON'S RIGHT HAND

Note the fracture of the second metacarpal and the curvature of the fifth metacarpal.

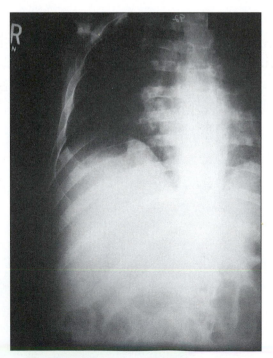

FIGURE 5.11   ANTEMORTEM CHEST FILM
OF MR. W. JOHNSON

Note the fractured right ribs.

location of the wound is not described by a physician nor is there radiographic documentation of a wound in any of the available records. One antemortem x-ray of the right foot is negative for fractures or metal. In fact, there is no skeletal evidence of a gunshot wound on either foot of the skeleton from eastern Iowa. There are two potential reasons for this discrepancy. Either the bullet did not hit bone or Mr. Johnson fabricated the story.

There are several reasons to believe the latter is correct. On 2-10-97, Mr. Johnson was hospitalized for inebriation and reported in his history that he had previously broken his neck, back, and pelvis in a motor vehicle accident. However, the physician put a question mark by this remark. This unsubstantiated claim is repeated in a medical history taken by a different physician the following month when Mr. Johnson again reported to the emergency room with a high blood alcohol level. However, there is no mention of these fractures in the medical or radiographic records. Mr. Johnson also reports inaccurate dates for surgeries and incorrectly cites previous diagnoses. Given the lack of medical substantiation of a gunshot wound to the foot, a broken pelvis, or a broken back, the oral history given by Mr. Johnson is considered suspect.

Considerations of Probability

The quantity and quality of positive similarities between the medical records of W. Johnson and the morphology of the skeletal remains suggest that the individual found in eastern Iowa is Mr. W. Johnson with a reasonable amount of scientific certainty. Quantification of scientific certainty is fraught with difficulties and requires a number of prior probabilities based on data from a population at large. To make a quantified probability statement about the uniqueness of the suite of fractures observed in Mr. Johnson and the Iowa skeleton

would require data on the number and location of fractures that occur in the population at large. Such data simply is not available. However, we can make more qualitative statements. The level of certainty in an identification case follows from our consideration of an alternative hypothesis, which in this instance is that the skeletal remains are *not* those of Mr. W. Johnson. If this alternative hypothesis is true, then we must ask how likely it is for a skeleton recovered in eastern Iowa to have the pattern of pathologies, dental restorations, and bone lengths observed in this forensic case. Subjectively, the probability of obtaining an exact match from the population at large seems vanishingly small. Consequently, it is many times more likely that we would see the observed pattern of skeletal information if the remains are those of Mr. Johnson than if the remains are not those of Mr. Johnson.

Conclusions

Mr. Johnson exemplifies the underlying principle in skeletal biology that particular events in an individual's life history are recorded in the skeleton. The location, degree of healing, and morphology of multiple rib, hand, nasal, leg, and skull fractures could easily be compared to Mr. Johnson's well-documented medical history. The medical reports from the last twenty years of Mr. Johnson's life indicate he also had a number of very serious chronic, non-skeletal conditions. At the time of his disappearance in 1997, Mr. Johnson was suffering from hepatitis C, pancreatic disease, cholelithiasis (gallstones), cirrhosis of the liver, ascites (fluid in the abdomen), and a number of other disorders related to chronic alcohol and substance abuse. Because Mr. Johnson had a "high-risk" lifestyle (drugs, fights, etc.), suffered from a variety of chronic and infectious diseases, and was often homeless, one doctor wrote in 1994 that "there is a good chance he will die on the streets." It is likely that this is what transpired three years later, in late 1997. The medical examiner ultimately classified the manner of death as "undetermined," but felt that, given the absence of perimortem trauma or other suspicious circumstances, Mr. Johnson's life of substance abuse and disease ultimately lead to his death in a field in rural Iowa.

References

Brogdon, B. Gilliam, ed. 1998. *Forensic Radiology*. Boca Raton, FL: CRC Press.

Cowger, James F. 1993. *Friction Ridge Skin: Comparison and Identification of Fingerprints*. Boca Raton, FL: CRC Press.

Galloway, Alison. 1999. *Broken Bones: Anthropological Analysis of Blunt Force Trauma*. Springfield, IL: Charles C. Thomas.

Haglund, William D. 1992. Contributions of rodents to postmortem artifacts of bone and soft tissue. *Journal of Forensic Sciences* 37: 1,459–1,465.

International Association of Identification Standards Committee. 1973. Resolution of the Standardization Committee. *Identification News*, August.

International Symposium on Fingerprint Detection and Identification. 1995. Ne'urim Israel. June 29, 1995 (see <www.latent-prints.com/Ne'urim.htm> for one editorialized summary).

Jupiter, J. B., and M. R. Belsky. 1992. Fractures and dislocations in the hand. Pp. 925–1,024 in *Skeletal Trauma Fractures, Dislocations, Ligamentous Injuries*, ed. B. D. Browner, J. B. Jupiter, A. M. Levine, and P. G. Trafton. Philadelphia: W. B. Saunders Co.

Katz, Darryl, and Judy M. Suchey. 1986. Age determination of the male *Os pubis*. *American Journal of Physical Anthropology* 69:427–435.

Lovejoy, C. Owen, Richard S. Meindl, Thomas R. Pryzbeck, and Robert P. Mensforth. 1985. Chronological metamorphosis of the auricular surface of the illium: A new method for the determination of adult skeletal age at death. *American Journal of Physical Anthropology* 68:15–28.

Ousley, Stephen. 1995. Should we estimate biological or forensic stature? *Journal of Forensic Sciences* 40(5):768–773.

Ousley, Stephen, and Richard Jantz. 1996. *FORDISC 2.0*. Department of Anthropology, University of Tennessee, Knoxville.

Shakespeare, William. 1914. *Hamlet*. In *The Oxford Shakespeare: The Complete Works of William Shakespeare*, ed. William J. Craig. London: Oxford University Press.

Snow, Clyde C., and Earl D. Folk. 1970. Statistical assessment of commingled skeletal remains. *American Journal of Physical Anthropology* 32:423–428.

Snow, Clyde C., and James L. Luke. 1984. The Oklahoma City child disappearances of 1967: Forensic anthropology in the identification of skeletal remains. Pp. 253–277 in *Human Identification: Case Studies in Forensic Anthropology*, ed. Ted A. Rathbun and Jane E. Buikstra. Springfield, IL: Charles C. Thomas.

TRIALS IN COURT

THE FORENSIC ANTHROPOLOGIST TAKES THE STAND

Kenneth A. R. Kennedy

Within recent years a number of guides have been published for the edification of forensic scientists who find themselves playing the role of expert witness in the judicial system (Brodsky 1991; Saferstein 1982). These manuals of conduct focus upon what one must do to maintain a professional decorum in what is often described as a terrifying ordeal. However, no manual of proper behavior before a judge, lawyers, and jury can surpass the reports of experienced forensic scientists who have fulfilled their civic and professional duties as expert witnesses. So while the published instructional guides may offer helpful hints, it is the well-trained forensic scientist who has taken the stand on numerous occasions that is in the best position to offer practical advice about those strategies of performance proven to be most effective under the pressures of defense and prosecution examinations.

My graduate training in biological anthropology in the early 1960s was guided by two professors at the University of California, Berkeley—Sherwood L. Washburn and Theodore D. McCown. The latter offered laboratory courses in human osteology and

maintained a forensic practice that included the identification of skeletal remains of eminent persons (Kennedy 1997, 2000; Kennedy and Brooks 1984). McCown's parallel research interest was the paleoanthropology of South Asia, and his expeditions to India influenced my decision to apply some methods of forensic anthropology to the study of ancient human populations of India, Pakistan, Sri Lanka, and their borderlands. Following an 18-month postdoctoral study in India, I was invited to join the faculty of the Department of Anthropology at Cornell University and I built a new laboratory for teaching and research in paleoanthropology and forensic anthropology. Cornell continues to be one of the training centers in the United States for these disciplines.

Not surprisingly, the development of forensic anthropology in Upstate New York over the past quarter-century has brought a considerable number of cases to my laboratory, some of which require my appearance as an expert witness in court. In these cases, I may be served a subpoena—a process involving a written order to appear in court and give testimony in person before a magistrate and other members of the court. Other cases do not require this procedure because there are no legal considerations, such as when the police bring to my laboratory a collection of nonhuman bones and teeth found by some good citizen walking along the shores of Lake Cayuga. On other occasions I have been asked by officers of the campus Safety Division to determine if a skeleton confiscated from a fraternity house after a boisterous party is human or not human, or if I can recognize it as a stolen laboratory specimen. Hoaxes to confound police have also come my way. Once the medical examiner of a neighboring county presented me with a baseball-size gummy spherical mass that he feared was a vestige of a child's brain. Upon closer gross and radiographic examination, I was able to reveal its true identity—a plastic model of a human skull available in any novelty shop, but considerably altered in shape and texture due to its long residence underground. And then there was a cobbler's metal shoe brought to me by local folks to verify their claim that it was the fossilized foot of a primitive being who had once haunted the forests of the Finger Lakes. My identification was politely rejected by the proud discoverers of the "fossil foot" who had unearthed it from behind the cabbage patch in their backyard.

Experiences of this kind are not unfamiliar to forensic anthropologists, but situations that come to court include, in my practice, those dealing with personal identification of human remains recovered under suspicious circumstances. I have been subpoenaed to give testimony about the markers of trauma on bones and teeth when the skeleton had already been identified but the nature of the assault weapon was an issue. Some of my other court cases are described below as they illustrate the diversity of challenges encountered in my practice. They relate to: (1) types of evidence that are not admitted into court because of the potentially negative effect

upon the cases tried by the attorney who has engaged my services (my client); (2) the challenge of educating both judge and jury about modern anthropology's rejection of the traditional biological race concept; and (3) a case whereby a photographic record was the critical piece of evidence for determining the identification of an alleged victim of a homicide after the body of the victim had been destroyed by legal cremation. These cases are presented as examples of how the forensic anthropologist must balance ethical issues against pressures imposed by representatives of the legal profession within our present system of justice.

Expert Testimony

That our legal system is fraught with hazards is demonstrated by the recent proliferation of published handbooks addressing a reading audience of supposedly apprehensive, guileless folks who have been ordered to serve as expert witnesses. As we read, mark, learn, and inwardly digest these testaments of acceptable court demeanor, some alarming recommendations are encountered. For example, in Dan Poynter's *Expert Witness Handbook* (1987, 99–132) the following guidelines are offered:

1. Keep your eyes open and tread carefully.
2. Do not clown around, even outside the deposition room.
3. If you become confused, ask if you may go to the bathroom.
4. Never say, "I'm doing the best I can."
5. Avoid obscenities.
6. Eat a good breakfast: It is OK not to stick to your diet on that day.
7. If you write books, stack them in a pile where the jury can see them.
8. Do not dive into the witness chair.

To these admonitions, other writers (Brodsky 1989, 113–124; Brodsky 1991, 261–264) of guides for the perplexed have added the following:

9. If you are a woman, never wear pants.
10. Do not scratch yourself.
11. Do not fall asleep while giving testimony.
12. If you are a woman, keep your knees together; if you are a man you can do whatever you like.
13. Don't mop your brow, look dejected, hang your head, or slink out of the courtroom.
14. When you truly do not know, say so.
15. Take a breath and explicitly think about questions that require thought.
16. Agree to be an expert witness only when expertise is present.

The apparent intent of some authors of these texts is that the forensic anthropologist, (probably an academic and consequently suffering from an unworldly and unstable state of mind most of the time anyway) may be encouraged to attain some level of success in the courtroom if he or she mentally recites this credo of do's and don'ts before ascending to the witness chair.

According to Richard Saferstein, former chief forensic chemist of the New Jersey State Police, the forensic scientist performs two functions: (1) the scientific activity of collecting, testing, and evaluating evidence so that an opinion may be formed about that evidence, and (2) the ability to verbally communicate that opinion and its basis to members of the court (1982, 5–13). Experts are summoned because they have the knowledge and ability to assist the jury in resolving questions outside the realm of experience of the average juror. To communicate effectively, the expert witness must translate knowledge to the court in a manner free of intellectual elitism and must direct testimony to the jury—the court's principal audience. Verbal duels with an attorney or a smart-aleck response lead to a loss of respect and support from the jury.

Among the guidelines written by forensic anthropologists for the benefit of their colleagues is T. Dale Stewart's second chapter of his text, *Essentials of Forensic Anthropology* (1979). This source is particularly helpful in preparing young forensic anthropologists for what they may expect to face in court. Stewart describes each step of the court process: advance arrangements and pretrial conference with one's client (usually an attorney), exclusion from the courtroom prior to testimony, administration of the oath, qualifying the witness, establishing the chain of possession (the documentation of every person and locality through which a specimen has passed since the time of its recovery), giving expert testimony, cross-examination, redirect examination, and dismissal of the witness. Stewart admonishes us that the forensic scientist should have no direct interest in the verdict reached by the jury. Thomas Dwight (1878), one of the pioneers of American forensic anthropology, also emphasized the avoidance of "taking sides." Over a century later Saferstein adds, "There is no reason not to tell the truth. Any deviation from this course will not only result in the expert's testimony being rendered useless, but the expert's reputation will suffer a permanent blot" (1982, 9).

A significant advance in enhancing the professional credentials of forensic anthropologists serving as expert witnesses was made in 1972 when fourteen anthropology members of the American Academy of Forensic Sciences (AAFS), founded in 1948, formed their own Section. Five years later, these forensic anthropologists established the American Board of Forensic Anthropology (ABFA), which certifies qualified persons holding an M.D. and/or a Ph.D. as Diplomates following their successful performance in rigorous written and practical examinations administered by officers and directors of the board (Kennedy 2000). As of the year 2002, there are sixty-four

Board-certified Diplomates. These persons have the advantage of presenting to the court prestigious credentials that demonstrate that their forensic anthropological peers acknowledge their expertise. However, Diplomate status is not the single qualification for serving as an expert witness, and the legality of trained biological anthropologists presenting testimony in court (some of whom may not have an affiliation with the AAFA or the ABFA) is rarely questioned.

Science and the Courts

Enlightening as published guidelines may be for the expert witness regarding proper conduct, the more overwhelming challenge for forensic anthropologists in court has to do with the transition between the rules we have mastered within our scientific and academic community to those rules established by the legal system. While forensic anthropologists and lawyers may agree that the purpose of a trial is a search for Truth, Ira Nortonson (1990, 7), editor of *Expert-at-Law Magazine* writes the following:

Let's remember what "truth" is: not in the academic setting of the classroom but in the pugilistic environment of the courtroom. There is no absolute truth. We deal with variations on the theme. It is truth born of credibility.

Courts are adversarial and, as expert witnesses, we may be provoked to conclusions we want to avoid, or at least qualify. This can happen because the public knows science by its products (medical, technological, economic) and not how science operates by the formulation of data, hypotheses, and theoretical contexts. Thus, the judge, attorneys, and jury become uncomfortable with scientific approaches involving probabilities, ranges of variation, "normal" diversity, statistical analyses, degrees of phenotypic

expression of a biological trait produced by the interaction of genetic and environmental processes, and other components of the forensic anthropologist's modus operandi. In fact, scientific data may have no role to play in a trial at all, in spite of the pro-science or anti-science attitudes of the members of the court, since judges have the authority to limit admissibility of evidence if it could cause confusion or prejudice.

The forensic anthropologist in the witness box must be familiar with these differences between the scientific and legal worlds, as has been eloquently expressed by Leslie Roberts in an article in the journal *Science* (1992, 732):

Scientists who enter the courtroom out of professional duty find their motives questioned and their integrity impugned, and they quickly find that the best scientific credentials count for little on the stand. While the scientists are there to debate the best methodologies, the proper interpretation of data, and the fine points of quality control, the lawyers are out to win—and they use any tool at their disposal. Scientists find unfavorable peer-review comments subpoenaed. Scientific mistakes and inconsistent statements from different papers are dredged up and used against them. . . . There is no room for subtlety or nuance and certainly not human error or scientific misjudgment. Instead, the normal processes of scientific debate or error and correction are used to pillory witnesses on the stand.

Peter Huber, a Fellow of the Manhattan Institute who has written a book on expert witnesses remarks that, "Good scientists hate the courtroom: the presumption is that they are lying and cheating. It is total culture shock" (1991, 12).

Two schools of thought have emerged from the U.S. legal system: (1) Trust the expert and leave decisions of validity of testimony to the jury (the *Frye* test); or (2) strictly scrutinize evidence presented to the court whereby the judge may dismiss expert witness testimony (Federal Rules of Evidence). In Scandinavian courts the judge may have expertise in particular areas of science. In the United States, the *Daubert vs. Merrell Dow Pharmaceuticals* case was the catalyst for change in establishing the standards for evidence in federal courts in the United States (Foster and Huber 1999). *The Federal Rules of Evidence* (Rule 702) aspires to higher standards of scientific knowledge by allowing judges, the legal "gate-keepers," to rule on admissibility of experts and evidence. However, the *Frye* test is still used in some states and the anthropologist should be knowledgeable about which evidentiary rules are used in their state.

Every case in which a forensic anthropologist enters the court as an expert witness challenges his or her ability to weigh scientific data and professional ethics within our country's system of justice. The following case studies in which I served as an expert witness illustrate these circumstances.

Case Histories

Case 1

In this case, forensic anthropological evidence was not admitted into court because of its potentially negative effect upon the arguments posed by the law firm that brought me into this case. My attorney client made this decision. A more detailed report of the case has been published elsewhere (Kennedy 1996). The circumstances of the trial involved the commingling of cremains of two individuals in a single mortuary container. The funeral establishment delivered this container to the family, who assumed that it contained the ashes of their daughter who had died a few hours after birth. However the father opened the receptacle to examine the cremains and decided that its contents could not have belonged to his offspring. While

some fragile bones of an infant were visible, the box also contained objects he misidentified as artificial tooth caps and inorganic debris. He then consulted a biological anthropologist at a local museum, a person unaccustomed to identifying human remains and not affiliated with the American Academy of Forensic Sciences and its Physical Anthropology Section. This anthropologist informed the distraught father that the container held the cremains of an adult. Upon being contacted by the family, the mortuary establishment admitted they made an error and delivered the wrong box and the right one was promptly sent to the family for exchange. The father refused to accept this second set of cremains, retained the first set, and began legal proceedings. He sued the funeral home for his emotional distress. Had he not opened the container, this case would not have come to court.

Shortly after these events I was contacted by the father's attorney as well as by the attorney representing the mortuary establishment. I was asked by both attorneys to identify the contents of the two containers, which were brought to me at different times within the year. I observed that the cremains in the first box (the one the father had opened) were commingled human remains. With the bones of a neonate were bones and dental fragments of a child I estimated to be around 3.5 years of age, but not an adult, as the museum anthropologist had claimed. The second container, the one that had been offered in exchange for the container first sent to the family, were those of an infant. Due to the complete cremation of the remains, it was impossible to prove that they were the remains of the family's daughter, and DNA testing was not conducted. Estimations of age from measurements of preserved long bone diaphyses and cranial fragments fell within the range of the age of the deceased infant (see Figures 6.1 and 6.2 on page 82).

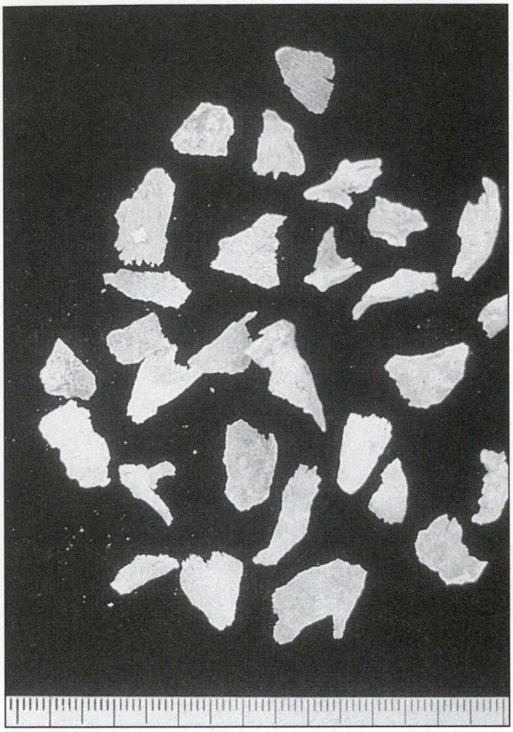

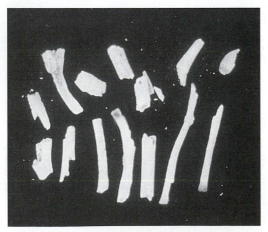

FIGURE 6.1   CRANIAL FRAGMENTS OF CREMAINS DISCUSSED IN CASE 1

The thin frontal, parietal, and occipital fragments have metrical values indicating a human neonate subject.

FIGURE 6.2   DIAPHYSEAL FRAGMENTS OF THE NEONATE DISCUSSED IN CASE 1

Measurements were qualified by shrinkage factors involved in the high temperatures of crematory furnaces (around 2,000° F).

Ultimately, the mortuary establishment's attorney subpoenaed me as an expert witness. But the damaging evidence, from my client's point of view, was the contents of the container of commingled infant and child remains. This situation would reflect negatively upon the degree of care the funeral home he was representing had taken in sorting the contents of the cremation furnaces. Here was evidence that more than one individual had been cremated at the same time, an incident that raised the question of whether this was a common practice at this establishment.

One hour before the trial began I was dismissed from the proceedings and, ironically, the forensically untrained museum anthropologist was called to testify that the first container held the remains of an adult. Here was a true case of "mistaken identity!" Ultimately, my client lost his case for the funeral home, but the father's effort to sue for a sizable sum of money was frustrated by the judge's decision to award him only payment for his court costs. Of course, things might have been worse for my attorney client had my evidence been allowed into the court record. Here is a situation in which valid scientific evidence went unheard so that the attorney could curtail further damages that might be directed against his client.

What I learned from this case was that infant cremains, and even those of neonates, may contain fragile, but preserved, skeletal structures, and radiographs reveal clear evidence of stages of bone maturation (Figure 6.3). One result of this case, and perhaps others like it, has been the recent practice of crematoria staff to pulverize all cremains prior to delivery of the powdery "ashes" to the bereaved survivors. Not only does this procedure make it nearly impossible for the forensic anthropologist to make a personal identification, but it also obscures the evidence in cases where several individuals are cremated at the same time.

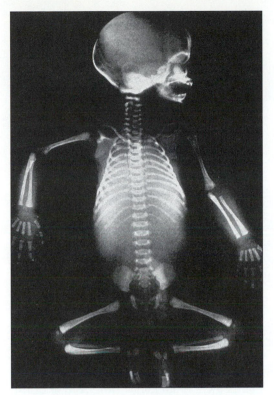

FIGURE 6.3   RADIOGRAPH OF THE COMPLETE SKELETON OF A HUMAN NEONATE
Source: Lockhart et al. (1959).

Case 2

This court episode involves the challenge of educating the judge and jury about the present-day response of biological anthropologists to the traditional race concept. In this case, a victim of a rape that occurred in the darkness of night identified the alleged perpetrator as an individual of African American ancestry. The alleged perpetrator was charged with a series of sexual assaults upon women residing in the vicinity of a university campus. During the trial, the defendant's lawyer questioned the reliability of laboratory tests that linked DNA from semen samples from the crime scene with bloodstains on a T-shirt the defendant had worn in a known previous stabbing incident. One of his alleged victims appeared in court to testify that her attacker was an African American male, but she could not verify that the defendant was that person because the incident had transpired in complete darkness.

Because of the victim's doubts on this matter, the defendant's attorney, who was my client, asked me to take the stand in order to testify to the court that the traditional race concept was defunct in systematic biology. Thus, he argued, the "race" of the accused could not be admitted as evidence. Admittedly, this was a desperate strategy on the part of the attorney to have the trial end with a hung jury. In this he was successful, although at a later court hearing the man he had defended pled guilty to these charges. In fact, he had never claimed his innocence in court. He was ultimately given a seven- to fifteen-year sentence.

This defines a situation whereby the forensic anthropologist is called into court to present a summary of a scientific concept—in this case, racial typology and its rejection by a majority of systematic biologists and anthropologists—without any direct contact or opportunity to determine the probable ancestry of the individual standing trial. This is not unethical, but it is compromised by the danger that one's legal clients may misinterpret sound scientific data. The defense attorney's efforts to demonstrate that the alleged victim could not have identified an African American assailant, either in the dead of night or at high noon, because scientists no longer adhere to a typological notion of human biological diversity, was a long shot. It could have failed had I been asked by the prosecutor to describe the protocol of ancestry estimation in forensic anthropology. This request was not made. However, neither my testimony nor the DNA tests became significant bodies of evidence once the plea agreement was achieved and the defendant confessed.

Case 3

In this case a photographic record was the only means of making a positive identification of an alleged homicide victim, "Molly," whose skeleton had been cremated prior to trial. The sequence of events was as follows, but the names have been changed.

A factory worker discovered human skeletal remains in a wooded area of upstate New York. The county medical examiner ordered that the bones be collected, then asked me to analyze them. Head hair was preserved and samples were sent to a colleague in Arizona, Walter Birkby, who is more knowledgeable than I about human hair. He reported to me that the hair was that of a person of African ancestry. My study of the skeletal remains indicated that this was an African American woman who was right-handed, had a living stature of approximately 166 to 173 cm, and exhibited skeletal markers of moderate athletic or occupational activities. An unusual feature was a gold backing of the lingual surface of the permanent right central incisor, which was a cosmetic feature rather than the consequence of remedial dental pathology (Figure 6.4). Golden incisors would have presented a striking vision to this young lady's interlocutor or embrasseur! There

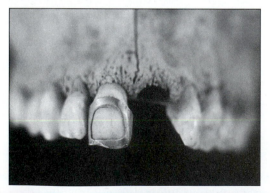

Figure 6.4   Cosmetic Gold Ornamentation of the Permanent Right Upper Central Incisor of the Individual Described in Case 3

was no evidence of trauma on any of the bones and teeth, which had been buried from two to five years, as estimated by degrees of bone diagenesis, traces of adipocere, preservation of scalp and pubic hair, and degree of clothing deterioration. Upon receiving my report, the district attorney claimed the remains were positively identified as those of Molly, who had died from undetermined causes and the medical examiner released the skeleton to her family. Cremation followed immediately at the wish of her parents.

But this is not quite the end of the story of the girl with the golden incisors. The family began to suspect that Molly had not died from unknown causes in the woods, but may have been the victim of an ex-boyfriend, "Solly." This man, once charged, found a lawyer who argued in court that Molly was not proven dead and that the medical examiner had sent the bones of some as yet unidentified person to the family. As noted above, the decomposed remains were cremated. In the course of my examination prior to the cremation event, I had taken color photographs of the skeleton and I sent these to the late Dr. William Maples of the University of Florida at Gainesville, who was also hired by the prosecutor. Maples was able to accomplish skull and portrait photo superimpositions with video comparison equipment supplied with extension tubes for adjustable levels of magnification. He found that the position and shape of facial features of my pictures of the skull and a photograph of Molly taken during life to be consistent. And there in Molly's photograph was the glistening golden incisor in the upper dental arcade clearly visible behind the parted lips of her smile. This was the young woman who met her demise at the hands of her former boyfriend, who is now serving a lengthy prison sentence following his confession.

Ethical issues may not be so obvious in this case, but the moral of the tale is that a photographic record, properly taken, may provide the key evidence in situations in which the physical evidence, including a body, has been lost. Further, as an expert witness in this trial, I needed to demonstrate to the court that the photographic superimposition and golden incisors supplemented the identifying information derived from my original examination of the bones and teeth.

Discussion

These cases are offered as examples of how forensic anthropologists must balance the ethical standards of their profession against legal practitioners who take a very different approach to scientific evidence, and the search for truth is filtered through attorneys' arguments that are tailored to protect their client. Personally, I have found the role of expert witness to be exciting and non-threatening, perhaps because of my good fortune to work with sincere, highly professional, and courteous members of the court. I have testified for both prosecution and defense in civil and criminal cases. I encounter these experiences as positive opportunities to carefully assess my own data while making a contribution to society. And while I have neither lapsed into slumber while giving testimony nor sought the refuge of a necessary room wherein to collect my thoughts, I have reflected upon those occasions when I believed that my evidence was being suppressed.

I am reminded of the final scene in that Wonderland experienced by Alice. You may recall that in the courtroom, where the participants were nothing but a pack of cards seeking to convict the knave of hearts who stole the tarts, Alice observed the following:

> One of the guinea-pigs cheered, and was immediately suppressed by the officers of the court. (As this is a rather hard word, I will just explain to you how it was done. They had a large canvas bag which (was) tied up at the mouth with strings, into which they slipped the guinea-pig head

first, and then sat upon it.) I'm glad I've seen that done, thought Alice. I've so often read in the newspapers at the end of trials, 'There was some attempt at applause, which was immediately suppressed by the officers of the court,' and I never understood what it meant until now. (Carroll 1865, 101)

Whether or not our skills as forensic anthropologists are suppressed, there is absolutely nothing like experience as an expert witness to test our integrity as scientists, sharpen our competence as teachers, and apply our expertise to society beyond the walls of the classroom and laboratory. This also provides the opportunity to work with our legal colleagues and better understand the challenges they must face in the effective practice of their profession.

References

Brodsky, Stanley L. 1989. Advocacy in the guise of scientific objectivity: An explanation of Faust and Ziskin. *Computers in Human Behavior* 5:261–264.

Brodsky, Stanley L. 1991. *Testifying in Court: Guidelines and Maxims for the Expert Witness.* Washington, D.C.: American Psychological Association.

Carroll, Lewis. [1865] 1961. *Alice's Adventures in Wonderland.* London: Folio Society.

Dwight, Thomas. 1878. *The Identification of the Human Skeleton: A Medico-Legal Study.* Boston, MA: Massachusetts Medical Society.

Foster, Kenneth R., and Peter W. Huber. 1999. *Judging Science: Scientific Knowledge and the Federal Court.* Cambridge, MA: MIT Press.

Huber, Peter W. 1991. *Galileo's Revenge: Junk Science in the Courtroom.* New York: Basic Books.

Kennedy, Kenneth A. R. 1996. The wrong urn: Commingling of cremains in mortuary practices. *Journal of Forensic Sciences* 41(4):689–692.

Kennedy, Kenneth A. R. 1997. McCown, Theodore D(oney) (1908–1969) Pp. 627–629 in *History of Physical Anthropology*, ed. F. Spencer. New York and London: Garland Publishing Inc.

Kennedy, Kenneth A. R. 2000. Forensic anthropology in the USA. Pp. 1,059–1,064 in *Encyclopedia of Forensic Sciences*. London: Academic Press.

Kennedy, Kenneth A. R., and Sheilagh T. Brooks. 1984. Theodore D. McCown: A perspective on a physical anthropologist. *Current Anthropology* 25(1):99–103.

Lockhart, R. D., G. F. Hamilton, and F. W. Fyfe. 1959. *Anatomy of the Human Body*. Philadelphia, PA: J. B. Lippincott.

Nortonson, Ira. 1990. The expert witness: Objective scientist or paid advocate? *Experts-at-Law* (March–April):6–7.

Poynter, Dan. 1987. *Expert Witness Handbook*. Santa Barbara, CA: Para Publishing.

Roberts, Leslie. 1992. Science in court: A culture clash. *Science* 257:732–735.

Saferstein, Richard. 1982. *Forensic Science Handbook*. Englewood Cliffs, NJ: Prentice Hall.

Stewart T. Dale. 1979. *Essentials of Forensic Anthropology, Especially as Developed in the United States*. Springfield, IL: Charles C. Thomas.

SEARCH AND RECOVERY

Many murderers will go to great lengths to hide their dirty deeds by disposing of their victims in a manner intended to avoid detection. Dismemberment and dispersal of body parts, burial, burning, submersion or stashing within walls, septic tanks, or under floors are just a few examples of the extremes to which perpetrators will go in order to conceal their crimes or to keep the body hidden close by to prolong their fantasies. Thus, forensic anthropologists must know how to properly detect and recover decomposed bodies or skeletal remains from a variety of contexts. The chapters in this section focus on archaeological recovery of human remains in the most common context for which forensic anthropologists are consulted—the outdoor setting. This section overview discusses some of the general principles of search and recovery, but more intensive texts and articles on the subject should also be consulted (e.g., Hunter et al. 1996; Morse et al. 1983; Skinner and Lazenby 1983; Dirkmaat and Adovasio 1997; Pickering and Bachman 1997; Killam 1990). However, no text is a substitute for formal archaeological training. Knowledge of archaeological methodology is essential to forensic anthropology casework and provides greater educational and professional breadth.

THE EPIDEMIOLOGY OF BURIALS

The Buried Body Cases Content Analyses Project (BBCCAP) provides some interesting data on the behaviors and patterns of murderers who bury their victims. The BBCCAP compiles information on recovered burial cases throughout the United States, including the length of time between deposition and recovery, relationship of the victim to the perpetrator, age and sex of victims and offenders, and burial locations (Hochrein et al. 1999). For instance, approximately half of all victim burials were placed on property owned or frequented by a perpetrator. Fewer killers identified by the study buried their victims on public lands, dumps, or on the victim's property. Fully 85 percent of victims in the database knew their killers, and 30 percent of these victims were related to the perpetrators. Sixty-nine percent of victims in the database were found within twelve months after burial. This may be related to another of the study's findings, that over half of the gravesites were found as a result of the perpetrator or an accomplice informing police of the crime.

Other burials were found because of characteristics of the grave that are most visible during the first twelve months.

It is an unfortunate fact that a burial "known" to be in a certain area may go undetected if ground cover (snow or foliage) is heavy and/or appropriate search methods are not utilized. Further, the grave becomes more difficult to find as the natural features that distinguish a grave from the surrounding soil disappear. Some of the critical elements for a successful recovery of buried human remains are, therefore, a quick response time, good intelligence information (e.g., provided by the perpetrator or witness), and proper archaeological techniques.

THE IMPORTANCE OF CONTEXT

All too often, skeletonized remains are not recognized for the important medicolegal evidence they can provide. Perhaps some feel that as the flesh decomposes the remains are somehow less human and/or have less forensic importance. Of course, neither is true. However, such misconceptions may lead law enforcement, medical examiners, coroners, and forensic pathologists to violate a number of protocols. For instance, every police investigator is trained not to disturb anything at a crime scene, *especially* the body, until the appropriate trained investigators arrive. However, it is not uncommon for forensic anthropologists to arrive at a scene and find that bones were picked up, examined, and moved. In the process, the context of the remains is compromised, which puts the anthropologist at an immediate disadvantage. Bones are also more portable than an entire body and officials have been known to disturb a scene by picking up just one bone to take to the anthropologist to identify whether it is human. If the remains are human then once again the anthropologist is working with a disturbed context. In general, forensic anthropologists would rather visit the scene than have the scene brought to them piece by piece.

In response to these and other unfortunate practices, Bass and Birkby (1978) published a paper designed to instruct law enforcement personnel about the importance of skeletal evidence, the archaeological context, and the appropriate scientific approach to buried bodies. The authors lament that, "law enforcement officers are generally unaware of how much information the careful excavation and removal of a skeleton can provide" (1978, 6). The authors also stress that, because of their broad anthropological training, many forensic anthropologists have significant archaeological experience and can work with law enforcement and crime scene technicians to preserve the context of a scene and collect evidence in a scientific manner.

All forensic search and recovery cases are multidisciplinary in nature. The scene will minimally include law enforcement personnel, crime scene technicians, and, in some cases, cadaver dogs. In addition, recovered evidence may be sent to a number of specialists for analysis, including entomologists, botanists, or agronomists. It is the responsibility of the forensic anthropologist to learn the roles of other team members in order to properly assist in the collection of all forensically important evidence.

A Brief Overview of Search and Recovery Techniques

Most search and recovery cases that require a forensic anthropologist are either surface depositions or burials in outdoor settings. A shallow grave may have characteristics of both contexts since some bones may be scattered on the surface due to erosion or disturbance, while others remain beneath the soil. No matter the context, a successful search for human remains depends on the recognition of the changes that take place between the body and the environment over time (Rodriguez and Bass 1985; Boddington et al. 1987; France et al. 1997). The environment will help determine the rate of decay while the decomposing body will likewise chemically and physically alter its immediate environment. Therefore, it is important to understand the vast number of environmental variables that affect the corpse, including ambient temperature, insect activity, soil pH, animal and human activity, clothing, and exposure (see Chapter 12).

Visual Indicators

When the body decomposes on the surface, the vegetation immediately under and around the body will die as chemicals from the body leach into the soil. This ring of dead grass and plants may be visible long after a body has been removed (Figure II.1). Wind, water, insects, scavengers, and human activity can disperse the

Figure II.1   Surface Deposition
Though scavengers have removed most of the bones, the dead grass clearly indicates that a body (in this case, a pig) had decomposed here.

remains far from their original deposition site (e.g., Haglund et al. 1989; Nawrocki et al. 1997). An appropriate search and recovery strategy must be developed based on the extent of the scatter. Searchers must remember that in the absence of sun bleaching, which turns the bones white, bones will become the color of their surrounding matrix. For instance, if the soil color is very dark, the bones will also become dark over time. Grass and certain metals, such as copper, will stain bone, providing clues about their original context if the remains had been scattered or purposefully moved.

A buried body can be detected by a different set of environmental changes. Decomposition will occur at a slower rate than surface depositions, especially if the burial is a foot or more deep (Rodriguez and Bass 1985). The act of digging a grave will change the density and color of the soil. Because the soil has been loosened and the strata (layers) mixed, it will be less compact and darker in color than the surrounding undisturbed soil. In the absence of heavy machinery, it is difficult to repack the grave fill, so a mound may form over a fresh grave. As the soil begins to settle over time, due to gravity and perhaps the action of water and surface trampling, the soil (especially fine soil) within the grave will sink below the undisturbed edges and form cracks, creating a primary depression that defines the boundaries of the pit. When the body progresses through the bloating stage, the soil will expand slightly but then sink as the abdomen collapses. Thus, a secondary depression may be visible over the torso (Morse et al. 1983; Killam 1990) (Figure II.2). Because the

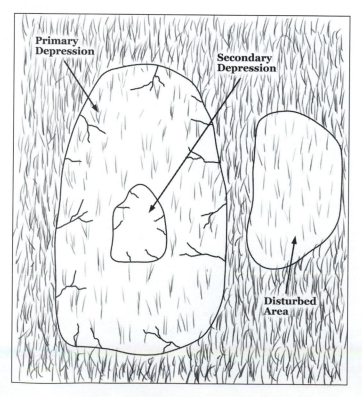

FIGURE II.2 VISUAL CHARACTERISTICS OF A GRAVE

Note the cracks along the edges of the primary and secondary depressions. The disturbed area denotes the location of the back dirt pile when the grave was being dug.

Source: Adapted from Morse et al. (1983) and Killam (1990).

consistency and density of the disturbed soil differs from that of undisturbed soil, a "soft spot" in the ground may indicate the location of a burial. Probes are often helpful in detecting these spots (Owsley 1995).

Concurrently, the decomposing body is interacting with the local flora. The plants die when a grave is first dug but the loose, well-aerated soil of the grave fill becomes extremely attractive to opportunistic plant seeds. Further, as the body decomposes, nitrogen and other chemical elements are released into the soil, which may alter the rate of plant growth, flowering, or ripening when compared to plants in the undisturbed soil surrounding the grave (France et al. 1992; Hunter et al. 1996; Killam 1990). Knowledge of the botanical species in the area is crucial, and the expertise of a local botanist may be invaluable. Finally, Morse et al. (1983) point out that vegetation under the back dirt pile adjacent to the burial pit might also be visibly damaged during the digging process, as represented in Figure II.2.

SEARCH STRATEGIES

Search and recovery strategies vary based on a number of factors, including climate, presumed mode of disposal (burial or surface), terrain (extent of ground cover and visibility), and number of available personnel. Search strategies can be divided into surface and subsurface techniques. Pedestrian searches are the most common type of surface techniques for they require little or no technology and are therefore least expensive. Techniques include zone, grid, or transect (line) search. In transect searches, for example, participating personnel form a line across an area and move forward several paces at a time using pin flags to mark the location of bones, tissue, clothing, tire marks, cultural debris, or a potential grave. The terrain dictates the spacing between the searchers and their pace. If ground cover is heavy, searchers may need to be spaced closer together and/or search on their hands and knees. While law enforcement personnel are fully capable of conducting a pedestrian search, the presence of a forensic anthropologist on the scene is still vital. The forensic anthropologist can quickly determine whether located bones are human or nonhuman, monitor how many individuals may be represented, determine which skeletal elements have been located and which are still missing, and examine any patterns to the scatter that might narrow the search area (Dirkmaat and Adovasio 1997). Specially trained dogs (cadaver dogs) can be employed during this phase of the search to help locate decomposing human remains (France et al. 1997; Killam 1990; Sorg et al. 1997).

Several subsurface imaging techniques are also useful for locating burials. Aerial searches can locate ground disturbances indicative of a burial (e.g., soil discoloration, depressions, plant changes) that may not be apparent at ground level. More technical aerial imaging devises, including thermal imaging, may also be employed (Hunter et al. 1996; France et al. 1997). Geophysical methods, including ground-penetrating radar (GPR), magnetometry, metal detectors, and other subsurface imaging devices can be incorporated if conducted by trained professionals (Killam 1990). In general, these methods detect subsoil disturbances and can therefore rule out large areas that have no subsurface changes and help pinpoint likely areas of disturbance that require further investigation.

Physical evidence should not be removed or disturbed during the search phase. Once all of the evidence and potential evidence within the search area is appropriately marked, the forensic anthropologist and/or police scene investigator should map, photograph, and, if appropriate, videotape the scene. At this point ground cover can carefully be removed and screened (sifted) through a mesh screen. If a grid has not already been established during the search stage, it must be set up prior to recovery. Within each grid, the context of every piece of evidence is documented by photography and mapping, which relates each item to a datum, a permanent point of reference. The importance of documentation cannot be overstated. Photography and detailed maps of each grid and the scene as a whole are necessary to reconstruct the context of the remains in court.

It is always appropriate to conduct a subsurface excavation, even if it appears that the individual was deposited on the ground surface. Erosion, sedimentation, wind, rain, and animal and human trampling may bury bones, buttons, rings, and bullets under the topsoil. All soil should be screened to collect evidence that may have been missed. If there is evidence of animal dispersal of the remains, the search should be extended, perhaps up to several hundred meters, and include animal burrows and hideouts (Haglund et al. 1989, Haglund 1997).

At this point it may be worth discussing the concept of evidence at an outdoor deposition scene. Unlike an indoor crime scene, in which the boundaries of the scene are well defined (e.g., a room or building), such boundaries are not immediately apparent in an outdoor recovery scene with scattered remains. Quite often investigators do not know the nature of the scene when a search begins. Did the individual die here? Was the person killed elsewhere and dumped at this location? Could this be a suicide rather than a murder? Thus, it may not be at all clear exactly what "evidence" in the area is important to the case. A cigarette butt may provide DNA evidence under good conditions, but which of the thousands of cigarette butts at a scene along a stretch of interstate highway potentially belonged to the perpetrator? Imagine how overloaded the crime labs would be if every bit of cultural debris from an outdoor scene collected was submitted for analysis! Decisions concerning the amount and type of cultural evidence to collect lie with the law enforcement investigators, though it is usually best to err on the side of collecting too much "evidence" at the outset since one can rarely return to reconstruct it later. Laboratory tests can be ordered at a later date if and when certain collected materials become pertinent.

EXCAVATION OF HUMAN REMAINS

A different methodological approach is required when a burial is located. There are also additional procedural and legal considerations. Prior to excavation, appropriate permission should be obtained, especially if the burial is located on personal property or on public property outside the jurisdiction of the investigating law enforcement unit. Such permission is typically requested before the search phase begins. In addition, when human remains have been located, the medical examiner or coroner must be contacted. It is also imperative to have all necessary equipment on hand before the recovery begins, including excavation and recording tools as well as transport and storage materials (Morse et al. 1983; Burns 1999).

It is essential to maintain the integrity of the burial so the site should be treated with the same protocols and respect as any other crime scene. Site security is required, especially if the recovery will take longer than one day. Media and the public should be kept at a respectable distance, and only authorized, *pertinent* personnel should be allowed into the burial area. A single route of access should be established to avoid trampling or disruption of dispersed evidence.

The purpose of an excavation is to understand the context of the burial, including the spatial relationship between the remains and other evidence (e.g., bullets, other individuals in the grave, clothing), the size, depth, and other characteristics of the grave, location of the grave to structures or landmarks, and to identify the tools used to dig the grave (Hochrein 2002). A proper excavation is critical, and one must have the correct tools for the job. A backhoe is not always inappropriate but certainly all use of heavy tools, including shovels, must cease when the body is reached so that the remains are not damaged. Excavation of human remains is a delicate and time-consuming process. Brushes, wood picks and other nonmetal instruments should be used to expose the remains.

An excavation should proceed by removing the soil in 10–20 cm increments. Documentation of each step of the excavation is crucial. Photographs and maps are required and videotape may be used as well. The forensic anthropologist should keep meticulous excavation notes, including a description of the stratigraphic changes at each level and an inventory of the bones and associated evidence observed. No evidence should be removed before the entire burial is exposed. The depth of the burial, the position of the body (e.g., prone or supine, extended or flexed) and the association of bones to other evidence, such as bullets, clothing, or a wallet, should be documented *in situ* by photographs and maps. Once the burial is fully exposed and documented, the bones and associated evidence may be removed and placed into labeled evidence bags. Biological materials, including bones, should be placed only in paper bags, as damp remains will mold if stored in plastic. Again, the floor of the burial should be excavated to look for additional evidence once the remains have been removed. Excellent sources that detail the painstaking process of human exhumation in a forensic context include Killam (1990), Hunter et al. (1996) and Morse et al. (1983).

Once the remains have been recovered, the anthropologist and investigators must initiate the chain of evidence—the legal documentation of who maintains custody of each piece of evidence, including human remains, from the moment of recovery until it is presented in court (Melbye and Jimenez 1997; Galloway et al. 1990). Any breach in security or break in the chain can lead to a challenge of the admissibility of that evidence. Typically the police and crime scene technicians collect physical evidence, but the body is under the jurisdiction of the coroner or medical examiner. In forensic anthropology cases, the coroner/medical examiner may give written or oral permission for the anthropologist to take custody of the remains. From that point on, the anthropologist must supply secure storage facilities and keep detailed records concerning the location of the remains and who has been granted access to them.

Professional conduct is required at all times during the search and recovery process. In addition to normal professional ethics, the scene may be under public scrutiny. An inappropriate word or action will surely be noted or recorded by the media. Typically the lead law enforcement investigator will conduct all interviews with the media because he or she coordinates the investigation and knows better than anyone what information can and cannot be released at any particular moment. As a rule, the anthropologist should not provide interviews concerning the case without specific permission from the relevant investigator.

THE CHAPTERS

In Chapter 7, David Glassman demonstrates the cooperative relationship between law enforcement and the forensic anthropologist as they search for a woman who had been missing for three years. Her killer took great pains to damage and conceal her body so that even if it were found, she would never be identified. Dr. Glassman details every aspect of the case, from the meticulous task of recovering fragmentary, burnt, and water dispersed remains from a unique (and cramped) scene, through the identification process and analysis of postmortem alterations. This case illustrates how the meticulous collection of skeletal evidence, including tiny bone fragments, can paint a concise picture of the chronology of postmortem events that was ultimately used to evaluate the suspect's version of events. Ironically, it was the suspect's own paranoia about the power of forensic science that proved his undoing.

Mann and colleagues discuss the unique circumstances that forensic anthropologists from the Central Identification Laboratory in Hawaii (CILHI) face when searching for and recovering remains of U.S. military personnel and civilians on foreign soil. The cases detail the quest for American MIAs lost in Laos during the Vietnam War. Before normal archaeological recovery techniques can be implemented, however, the CILHI teams must first conduct a search for potential crash and burial sites by interviewing local people and critically evaluating their recollections. The recovery teams face numerous obstacles, including relentless temperatures, live explosives, and the normal hostile elements of a tropical environment. Further information about the CILHI is also presented in Chapter 20.

In Chapter 9, Sauer and his colleagues present a case of a boy who was brutally murdered, mutilated, and dismembered by a person he knew and trusted. Only a full forensic anthropological and archaeological investigation could provide crucial answers to questions about the age of the burial, the spatial relationship between the grave and structures that had been on the property when the suspect lived there, and exactly how the little boy had been killed. Other forensic experts, including psychologists, used the archaeological and physical anthropological information to shed light on the behavior and motives of the perpetrator. Finally, the attorney provides the details of the prosecution's case, including a discussion of the pertinent legal precedents of the case, a synthesis of the evidence from multiple experts, and how the expert witness testimonies were structured in court to provide a coherent explanation of the chain of murderous events.

REFERENCES

Bass, William M., and Walter H. Birkby. 1978. Exhumation: The method could make the difference. *FBI Law Enforcement Bulletin* 47:6–11.

Boddington, A., A. N. Garland, and R. C. Janaway, eds. 1987. *Death, Decay and Reconstruction: Approaches to Archaeology and Forensic Science.* Manchester, UK: Manchester University Press.

Burns, Karen R. 1999. *Forensic Anthropology Training Manual.* Upper Saddle River, NJ: Prentice Hall.

Dirkmaat, Dennis, and James M. Adovasio. 1997. The role of archaeology in the recovery and interpretation of human remains from an outdoor forensic setting. Pp. 39–64 in *Forensic Taphonomy: The Postmortem Fate of Human Remains*, ed. William D. Haglund and Marcella H. Sorg. Boca Raton, FL: CRC Press.

France, Diane L., Tom J. Griffin, Jack G. Swanburg, John W. Lindemann, Vickey Trammell, Cecilia T. Travis, Boris Kondratieff, Al Nelson, Kim Castellano, and Dick Hopkins. 1992. A multidisciplinary approach to the detection of clandestine graves. *Journal of Forensic Sciences* 37:1,445–1,458.

France, Diane L., Tom J. Griffin, Jack G. Swanburg, John W. Lindemann, G. Clark Davenport, Vickey Trammell, Cecilia T. Travis, Boris Kondratieff, Al Nelson, Kim Castellano, Dick Hopkins, and Tom Adair. 1997. Necrosearch revisted: Further multidisciplinary approaches to the detection of clandestine graves. Pp. 497–509 in *Forensic Taphonomy: The Postmortem Fate of Human Remains*, ed. William D. Haglund and Marcella H. Sorg. Boca Raton, FL: CRC Press.

Galloway, Alison, Walter H. Birkby, T. Kahana, and Laura Fulginiti. 1990. Physical anthropology and the law: Legal responsibilities of forensic anthropologists. *Yearbook of Physical Anthropology* 33:39–57.

Haglund, William D. 1997. Dogs and coyotes: Postmortem involvement with human remains. Pp. 367–381 in *Forensic Taphonomy: The Postmortem Fate of Human Remains*, ed. William D. Haglund and Marcella D. Sorg. Boca Raton, FL: CRC Press.

Haglund, William D., Donald T. Reay, and Daris R. Swindler. 1989. Canid scavenging/disarticulation sequence of human remains in the Pacific Northwest. *Journal of Forensic Sciences* 34:587–606.

Hochrein, Michael J. 2002. An autopsy of the grave: Recognizing, collecting, and preserving forensic geotaphonomic evidence. Pp. 45–70 in *Advances in Forensic Taphonomy: Method, Theory, and Archaeological Perspectives*, ed. William D. Haglund and Marcella D. Sorg. Boca Raton, FL: CRC Press.

Hochrein, Michael J., Jennifer Gabra, and Stephen P. Nawrocki. 1999. The buried body cases content analysis project: Patterns in buried body investigations. Paper presented at the American Academy of Forensic Sciences, February 18, 1999, Orlando, Florida.

Hunter, John, Charlotte Roberts, and Anthony Martin. 1996. *Studies in Crime: An Introduction to Forensic Archaeology.* London: Routledge.

Killam, Edward W. 1990. *The Detection of Human Remains.* Springfield, IL: Charles C. Thomas.

Melbye, Jerry, and Susan B. Jimenez. 1997. Chain of custody from the field to the courtroom. Pp. 65–75 in *Forensic Taphonomy: The Postmortem Fate of Human Remains*, ed. William D. Haglund and Marcella H. Sorg. Boca Raton, FL: CRC Press.

Morse, Dan, Jack Duncan, and James Stoutamire, eds. 1983. *Handbook of Forensic Archaeology and Anthropology.* Tallahassee, FL: Rose Printing Co.

Nawrocki, Stephen P., John E. Pless, Dean A. Hawley, and Scott A. Wagner. 1997. Fluvial transport of human crania. Pp. 529–552 in *Forensic Taphonomy: The Postmortem Fate of Human Remains*, ed. William D. Haglund and Marcella H. Sorg. Boca Raton, FL: CRC Press.

Owsley, Douglas. 1995. Techniques for locating burials, with emphasis on the probe. *Journal of Forensic Sciences* 40:735–740.

Pickering, Robert B., and David C. Bachman. 1997. *The Use of Forensic Anthropology.* Boca Raton, FL: CRC Press.

Rodriguez, William C., and William M. Bass. 1985. Decomposition of buried bodies and methods that may aid in their location. *Journal of Forensic Sciences* 30:836–852.

Skinner, Mark, and Richard A. Lazenby. 1983. *Found! Human Remains: A Field Manual for the Recovery of the Recent Human Skeleton*. Burnaby, B.C.: Simon Frazer University, Archeology Press.

Sorg, Marcella H., Edward David, and Andrew J. Rebmann. 1997. Cadaver dogs, taphonomy, and postmortem interval in the Northeast. Pp. 120–143 in *Forensic Taphonomy: The Postmortem Fate of Human Remains*, ed. William D. Haglund and Marcella H. Sorg. Boca Raton, FL: CRC Press.

FURTHER READING

Berryman, Hugh E., William M. Bass, Steven A. Symes, and O'Brien C. Smith. 1991. Recognition of cemetery remains in the forensic setting. *Journal of Forensic Sciences* 36(1):230–237.

Brooks, Sheilagh T., and Richard H. Brooks. 1984. Problems of burial exhumation, historical and forensic aspects. Pp. 64–86 in *Human Identification: Case Studies in Forensic Anthropology*, ed. Ted A. Rathbun and Jane E. Buikstra. Springfield, IL: Charles C. Thomas.

Geberth, Vernon J. 1996. *Practical Homicide Investigation: Tactics, Procedures and Forensic Techniques*. 3rd ed. Boca Raton, FL: CRC Press.

Haglund, William D. 1998. The scene and context: Contributions of the forensic anthropologist. Pp. 41–62 in *Forensic Osteology: Advances in the Identification of Human Remains*, ed. Kathleen J. Reichs. 2nd ed. Springfield, IL: Charles C. Thomas.

Hall, David W. 1997. Forensic botany. Pp. 353–363 in *Forensic Taphonomy: The Postmortem Fate of Human Remains*, ed. William D. Haglund and Marcella H. Sorg. Boca Raton, FL: CRC Press.

Krogman, Wilton Marion, and Mehmet Yasar Iscan. (1986) *The Human Skeleton in Forensic Medicine*. 2nd ed. Springfield, IL: Charles C. Thomas.

Skinner, Mark. 1987. Planning the archaeological recovery from recent mass graves. *Forensic Science International* 34:267–287.

7

LOVE LOST AND GONE FOREVER

David M. Glassman

Students of forensic anthropology often hear their professors emphasize that each forensic case is unique, with its own set of constraints for recovery and analysis and its own history, which includes the behavior, activities, and emotions that precipitated and followed the murder. Over the past twenty-two years, I have been involved in the forensic identification of numerous homicide victims from several states in the United States and across the border into Mexico. My experience in over 250 cases yields the same conclusion: Each case *is* indeed unique. Of course, this is not true for all aspects of the case. If it were, the experience we gained from working one case would not help us increase the likelihood of successful outcomes of future skeletal recoveries and identifications. Forensic anthropologists agree that experience is an essential component in the practice of our science—so much so that prior experience is a basic requirement of board certification by the American Board of Forensic Anthropologists (ABFA).

In every state in the United States a statute can be found that addresses the legal requirements for what shall be done when human remains are found, including skeletal remains. Although the wording may differ between states, two general mandates are standard. The first states that an investigation must be made to determine the identity of the individual. The second requires an investigation to determine the manner and cause of death. Jurisdiction varies from law enforcement agencies to government agencies, medical examiners, coroners, and others as to who is directly responsible for conducting one or both of these investigations. The lead agency may call upon any forensic experts it believes may assist in the investigation of identity and cause of death. If there is any reason to suspect foul play based on the location of the body or the condition of the remains, law enforcement agencies (local, state, and/or federal) will respond immediately.

The forensic anthropologist is an expert in the interpretation of skeletal remains and may be requested to join in the investigation of the identity and/or manner and cause of death of the deceased. Knowing that the greatest chance of resolving a case is dependent upon a proper recovery procedure, forensic anthropologists often assist law enforcement officers and medical examiners at the death scene. Here, the trained and experienced forensic anthropologist will excavate buried remains, identify skeletal elements during the search phase, collect evidence useful for assessing the time since death interval, assist in the packaging of the remains in a manner most likely to limit any destruction during transport, and provide any further assistance that may potentially yield information helpful to the successful resolution of the investigation. The recognition of forensic anthropologists as experts in recovery is becoming more prevalent among federal, state, and local law enforcement agencies. Today, many agencies have developed strong ties with practicing forensic anthropologists as collaborators in cases involving human skeletal remains. This trend is certain to continue in the future.

The case presented in this chapter will describe many of the procedures and techniques used by forensic anthropologists in the recovery and interpretation phases. Like all cases, the story is unique in the behavioral and emotional circumstances that led to the murder and disappearance of the victim, the constraints associated with the recovery of the remains, and the ability to determine the identity and circumstances of death. I have chosen to change the names, dates, and geographic information of the case out of respect for the innocent relatives and friends of the victim.

Deborah's Disappearance

In 1985, a healthy sixteen-month-old female infant was found abandoned on a doorstep in Starville, Virginia. Pictures of the child were shown in the media and the viewing public was asked to help identify the child and her parents. After seeing a picture of the infant in a local newspaper, a man reported to police three days later that the baby might indeed be his. Unfortunately, the man, Bill Haley, could not say positively whether the child belonged to him or not, believing that all babies looked pretty much the same. It was not until the following day, when authorities contacted Haley's mother-in-law in West Virginia, that the identity of the baby as Bill Haley's daughter was confirmed. Haley's mother-in-law indicated to police that she could not contact her daughter, Deborah, who was the mother of the infant, and she feared something very wrong must have happened that would force her to abandon her infant on a doorstep. Instead of returning the infant to Mr. Haley, state child services placed the infant in foster care.

Police assigned to investigate the case suspected criminal activity beyond the abandonment of an infant, particularly in the disappearance of Deborah Haley. Deborah's mother told police that her daughter loved her infant dearly and would never have abandoned her under normal circumstances. When questioned about the disappearance of his wife, Bill Haley contended that he and Deborah had a very stormy marriage. He stated that it was common for the two of them to argue, after which Deborah would often leave with their daughter. He assumed that this was the current situation and that Deborah had run away and left their infant on the doorstep. Mr. Haley's mother-in-law substantiated the claim that Bill and Deborah often argued and that Deborah would leave the home. However, she further indicated that when Deborah left she would either come to her mother's house in West Virginia or call her mother by phone. Neither a visit nor a call took place the day Deborah allegedly left the house and abandoned her infant.

Once the abandoned infant was identified, the police expanded their investigation into the disappearance of Deborah Haley. Soon, Deborah's deserted car was discovered one block away from the location of the doorstep where her infant was abandoned. Deborah's purse and eyeglasses were found inside the car, adding further suspicion about her disappearance.

Detectives began to question Bill Haley about the disappearance of his wife. Searches were made at the Haley's mobile home, located in a valley near the base of Piney Mountain, and continued by car, foot, and helicopter further up the mountainside. Although detectives believed Bill Haley knew more about the disappearance of his wife than he admitted, there was no evidence to justify detaining or arresting him. After months of investigation, Deborah Haley remained missing and no new information was obtained as to her location, dead or alive. The case was becoming cold.

Sometime during the first two years that Deborah was missing, Bill Haley began a correspondence relationship with a woman in Honduras, and in late 1987 he went to Central America to be with her. Before leaving, Haley legally changed his name to Roberto Garcia. As it turned out, Bill Haley was not his original birth name either, for he had changed it once before.

Roberto Garcia remained out of the country until the following year. During this period, little progress was made in Virginia on resolving the disappearance of Deborah Haley. The Haley infant remained with a foster care family and was doing well.

After returning to Starville in 1988, Roberto Garcia rented a U-haul vehicle and attempted to rob the First National Bank. Although no money was exchanged at the bank and Garcia had apparently used an air-gun for staging the hold-up, he was charged with attempted bank robbery after being apprehended at the U-haul dealership while returning the vehicle. Mr. Garcia was subsequently transferred and processed into the Star County Jail. A routine check for prior convictions from fingerprint data led to the discovery that Roberto Garcia was, in fact, Bill Haley, father of the infant abandoned approximately three years before. Renewed interest in Deborah Haley's disappearance occurred among police investigators and the media.

While held in the county jail, Haley read an article in the National Geographic magazine that described the work of bioarchaeologists at the historic site of Jamestown. The article elaborated on the ways in which trained osteologists can determine personal information about individuals from their skeletal and dental remains. This included demographic attributes such as sex, age, and height, as well as health care information, including the prevalence of disease and prior traumatic injuries. Judging from his response, Haley must have been very impressed by the article. Haley allegedly made an interesting offer to his cellmate who was soon to be released from jail. He offered him $10,000 to locate a specific remote spot along a little-used dirt road up on Piney Mountain. He was to dig a hole and remove burned carpeting and charred skeletal remains. He further instructed his cellmate to locate and save all teeth, a request that was no doubt related to the National Geographic article, which described the importance of teeth in making identifications. Rather than accept Haley's offer and become a possible conspirator in a homicide, the cellmate told authorities all about the offer.

A few days later, I was contacted and asked to assist agents of the Virginia State Police and investigators of the Star County Police Department in locating and recovering the charred remains described by Haley.

Search and Recovery

Search Phase

At times, locating a body can be a very difficult task even when an informant provides information about where to look. I had been involved in a case in which the suspect drew a detailed map to direct us to the location of a buried child and it still took us over eight hours to find the site. Memories of where bodies have been left are often distorted due to the excitement and endorphin-rich condition of the perpetrators at the time the crime was committed. In addition, the bones of bodies that have been left to decompose on the surface of the ground are likely to be scattered for long distances by carnivorous animals and environmental processes such as rain, flooding, and high winds.

In the Haley case we knew we were dealing with buried remains. Haley's cellmate indicated that the body was located some distance up Piney Mountain. There, the charred body was supposed to have been placed near a metal drainage pipe that lay underneath the gravel road. These pipes are commonly placed at various intervals underneath gravel roads that often get heavy run-off from rains and/or melting snow. The purpose is to allow the water to drain underground without causing major damage to the road above. The locations of these drainage pipes are often included on road construction maps. The day before the search, police investigators secured a construction map that had the drainage pipes marked and began a systematic search to find the right one. They began with the most likely site, according to the vague information provided by their informant, and proceeded from that spot up and down the road to each drainage pipe. At each location, the hard ground adjacent to the road was excavated down to the level of the pipe, which in some cases extended two feet or more below the road surface. Later that day, one of the search investigators noticed a few remnants of green shag carpet poking out from the dirt. As the investigator slowed down his excavation so as not to destroy any evidence, three bone fragments appeared. I later identified the fragments as portions of a left tibia, left fibula, and right femur.

Once the probable site had been found, the investigator removed himself from the excavation unit and called in the other members of the search team. It was decided that no work would continue until the forensic anthropologist was available to examine the bones to make sure they were human and to conduct the excavation for recovery. The police acknowledged that a forensic anthropologist was best trained to provide the expertise for recovering buried skeletal remains.

When a decision is made to wait until the following day to conduct a recovery, the scene should be secured throughout the night. Securing the scene ensures that there is no destruction or disturbance of the scene or the evidence. Generally, rope or police tape is strung around the entire recovery area. This creates a visual barrier designating the death scene, and no law enforcement personnel, civilians, or members of the media should be admitted into this area unless they are specifically engaged in activities related to the recovery procedure. All other activities are to be conducted outside the perimeter. To assist in public or media control, all road entrances to the death scene may be blocked off by law enforcement agents and traffic diverted accordingly. The practice of setting up a security line is important even if it is likely that no civilians will be present or if the manpower to enforce the security is small. I have worked death scene recoveries in very remote areas and have been amazed at how fast local civilians find your location.

I arrived at the Haley recovery site early in the morning and met with the lead investigator for briefing (Figure 7.1). I was told about the carpet pieces and I examined the bone fragments. The morphology of the bones indicated they were human. Before walking into the recovery zone, a systematic recovery strategy must be developed. In this case, there was little need for a major geographical search of the surrounding

FIGURE 7.1   THE LOCATION

Here is the remote wooded location where the victim's body was buried adjacent to the dirt road. The arrow marks the excavation area.

area. Any evidence such as tire tracks or footprints that may have been associated with the perpetrator would have long since disappeared because of the annual melting of snow during the three years since Deborah's disappearance. And, as is common in cases where bodies have been buried, scattering of remains was not a factor.

Recovery Phase

Before beginning work, all of the necessary recovery equipment was assembled. The lack of appropriate equipment for securing a site, conducting the search, clearing the terrain, recovering the evidence, or transporting the remains to their transfer destination can jeopardize the investigation's objectives. If circumstances allow, it is preferable to delay a recovery for a few hours in order to retrieve the appropriate

equipment rather than to begin immediately, using only substandard tools. Notes were taken to record information about the excavation location, search and recovery strategies, and the environment and terrain. Photographs were taken of the scene to further document the site prior to any disturbance from recovery activities.

Pictures were taken continuously throughout the recovery to document all activities and evidence recovered. It is now common to document death scene recoveries using 35mm photographs, video-recordings, and digital imaging. Each format provides unique qualities, so it is suggested that they all be used together at the scene. Using acceptable practices in the recovery of homicide victims and associated evidence, and documenting these practices, have become important issues in recent high-profile cases such as the O. J. Simpson criminal trial. The activities surrounding the recovery can be as important to the legal outcome of a case as other evidence suggesting guilt or innocence of a suspect.

The actual recovery began at mid-morning. The recovery strategy called for three individuals initially to enter the recovery site. They included the anthropologist, an identification investigator, and a photographer. The vegetation was removed from around the excavation unit using garden shears, root cutters, and clippers, and sorted by hand for evidence.

The recovery excavation began by cleaning the side walls of the search phase hole with an archaeological trowel and expanding the size of the hole with small picks, shovels, and trowels. The base of the hole was leveled off to create a flat, horizontal floor. The excavation area was expanded to a 3-foot by 4-foot unit. All soil removed was collected and passed through a sifting screen constructed of 1/4-inch mesh. If it had been determined that a finer mesh screen would improve the collection of small fragments, including dental fragments, one would have been used.

Because we already knew that bone fragments had been found in the unit during the search phase, we wanted to progress slowly enough to limit any destruction of bone due to excavation artifact. If the body was found articulated, it would be left *in situ* for documenting body position, orientation, and inventory. However, if the remains were found disarticulated, fragmentary, and occurring randomly at varying depths, the site would be excavated downward in levels of ten centimeters each.

As the excavation progressed, small fragments of bone and carpet were prevalent. Some of the bone fragments were charred black, while others remained a natural color with additional brown soil-staining. Charred leaves were also noted intermixed in the soil. Bone articulation was not discernable from the fragments, although it appeared that the bones of the legs were furthest from the drainage pipe and at a higher level in the dirt matrix. This would suggest that the body was placed in, or near, the drainage pipe in a headfirst orientation.

Excavation continued down to the base of the exposed drainage pipe at a depth of approximately thirty-one inches below the surface. Additional bone and carpet fragments were located and followed a trail into the pipe. Cranial and dental fragments were noted at the pipe's entrance. This further supported the hypothesis that the body was placed headfirst into the hole. The circular pipe bore a diameter of approximately twenty-four inches, and 75 percent of its entrance was blocked by dirt and debris. The depth of the hole, combined with the heavily tree-shaded surface, resulted in darkness at the level of excavation. An electric search lantern was lowered into the excavation unit to provide light into the drainage pipe (Figure 7.2); however, the heat generated from the light was intense, and excavation progressed slowly with many needed breaks for rest. At this point, we all recognized that it was

FIGURE 7.2   THE EXCAVATION

An electric searchlight was used to assist the excavation in the metal drainage pipe.

going to be a much longer day than we had originally anticipated.

To accurately complete the recovery, the dirt that filled the entire length of pipe (approximately twenty feet) needed to be removed and sifted for evidence. This activity was complicated by the fact that the opposite end of the pipe overhung a huge drop-off in the mountain slope. Thus, there was only one way to access the pipe. The limited space for mobility forced me to enter the pipe headfirst by lying on my stomach and using my elbows to crawl along. Dirt and debris were dislodged with a trowel and dragged back along my body. Periodically, I would slide back toward the opening of the pipe, dragging the dirt with me. When outside the pipe, the dirt and debris were collected into a bucket and handed out of the excavation unit for screening.

Fortunately, the further I crawled into the drainage pipe, the less dirt and debris it contained, and by the halfway mark it covered only about 20 percent of the bottom of the pipe. Bone fragments were found throughout the length of the pipe, indicating that they had been moved by the drainage of melting snow during the past couple of seasons. The greatest concentration of bone fragments occurred near the entrance of the drainage pipe and decreased as I moved toward the pipe's exit. Virtually all of the carpet remnants were found in the excavation hole or within the drainage pipe near its entrance. When the drainage pipe was completely cleared and the dirt and debris were sifted, the excavation portion of the recovery was terminated. The open side of the pipe emptied down a vertical precipice where recovery of additional remains was not possible.

While the excavation of the pipe had been taking place, the recovered bone fragments were placed on paper and left exposed in the shade to dry. Wet or damp bones are easily prone to flaking and crumbling. Drying of damp bones will make them less likely to be damaged during packing, transport, and storage. However, attempting to dry moist bones too quickly can also result in splitting and other damage. Drying bones in direct sunlight should always be avoided. Several years ago a variety of substances were available to be painted or sprayed on bones (archaeological or forensic) to provide an impregnated coating for greater strength and protection from damage. The most common of these was polyvinyl acetate (PVA). The use of these products has diminished with the rise of DNA identification from bone samples. Chemically impregnating bones increases the risk of contaminating potential DNA samples.

An inventory of recovered evidence was tabulated, described in notes, and documented photographically prior to packaging. The fragile nature of the charred remains compounded with the roughness of the dirt road used to transport the remains made it necessary to take extra care in packaging the bones. Bones were wrapped with toilet tissue and placed together in paper bags. The bags were then placed into a cushioned cardboard box and set on the back seat of a vehicle for transport.

In all legal cases, a chain of evidence must be recorded. The chain begins in the field with the law enforcement agency in whose jurisdiction the body was found. Occasionally, it may begin with a representative of a medical examiner's office who is in attendance at the scene, or in other cases with a state or federal agency. From this point forward, all evidence must be accounted for at all times and all individuals who have been entrusted with some or all of the evidence must be documented by the chain. In the Haley case, all of the bone and dental evidence was initially transferred to the district's Office of the Chief Medical Examiner. On the following day, the skeletal remains were transferred to my custody and taken to my laboratory for anthropologic examination. The dental fragments were submitted to a forensic odontologist.

Anthropological Analysis of Fragments

Establishing Identity

When skeletal remains reach the forensic anthropologist's office they must be carefully unpacked and prepared for examination. All materials must be re-inventoried to match that which was originally recorded in the field. If the remains are complete and skeletonized, there is little, if any, preparation before the analysis begins. If they had been buried, a soft brushing may be needed to remove loose dirt and allow for examination of the bone surfaces. When remains are only partially decomposed they often must be defleshed through the process of maceration.

Skeletal preparation in single-victim cases may take a long time when the remains are highly fragmented as in the Haley case. Here, the fragments were first sorted into piles of cranial and postcranial material. The postcranial fragments were further sorted into fragment piles by skeletal element (e.g., limb bones, vertebrae, ribs, scapulae, innominates). Finally, these piles were sorted into specific bone elements and anatomical sides such as right humerus, left fibula, and thoracic vertebrae. Of course, there is always a miscellaneous pile for small fragments that cannot be identified as to specific bone or portion of the body. The size of the miscellaneous pile is directly related to the size of the fragments and the osteological expertise of the anthropologist.

The fragments of the Haley case ranged in size from crumbs to an almost complete left fibula (Figure 7.3). Approximately 20

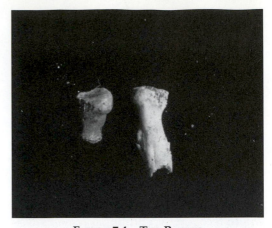

FIGURE 7.4   THE RADIUS

Proximal ends of the radius were used to establish the Minimum Number of Individuals (MNI) statistic.

FIGURE 7.3   SKELETAL FRAGMENTS

The amount of charred skeletal fragments recovered from the victim could not even fill the bottom of a 10" x 10" square box. A reconstructed knee joint is in the box in the foreground.

percent of the skeleton was recovered. Most of the fragments were less than two inches in length. After sorting, the fragments were pieced together when possible and glued, using Duco Cement. Several of the skull fragments fit together (frontal, right parietal, left parietal) and a large portion of the forehead, top, and sides of the skull were reconstructed.

The fragments were examined to determine the minimum number of individuals (MNI) statistic. The MNI is determined from the most prevalent skeletal element or area represented in the sample. In this case, the most prevalent elements were the proximal heads of radii and distal ends of tibiae. For both, two elements, one right and the other left, had been recovered (Figure 7.4). Thus, no duplication of remains occurred among the sample, resulting in an MNI statistic of one individual. A consistency of architectural size and shape of the remains further substantiated this conclusion.

The sex of the individual was determined from morphological observations of the cranium, degree of overall robustness of the bones, and size of the humeral head. The distinctive lack of brow ridges and developed forehead morphology suggested a female, as did the overall gracility of the remains in general. The right humeral head diameter measured 38 mm, also consistent with females (Dwight 1904/05; Ubelaker 1989).

Since the pubic symphyses were not available, the age of the individual was determined on the basis of epiphyseal union and suture closure. In all areas where examination of epiphyseal union was possible (distal left fibula, distal left tibia, lesser trochanter of the right femur, proximal right humerus, and distal right femur), all were fused. This suggested that the individual was of an age greater than approximately eighteen years (Ubelaker 1989). Portions of the coronal and sagittal sutures were available for examination of closure. Virtually no closure had begun on the endocranial (interior) surface, suggesting a younger adult age for the individual. However, we must be cautious when suture closure is used as an indicator of age and, in addition, anthropologists disagree on whether endocranial examination (Krogman and Iscan 1986), ectocranial examination (Meindl and Lovejoy 1985), or the combination of both (Nawrocki 1998) is the better indicator of age. The pattern of age-related endocranial morphology yielded an age range of twenty to thirty-five years.

The ancestry of the individual could not be determined because the skull was not sufficiently complete to allow metrical and morphological observations to be taken of the diagnostic areas of facial morphology indicative of ancestry.

Stature was calculated from the maximum length of the left fibula (the most complete long bone in the sample) using the Trotter and Gleser (1958) regression formula for white females. The estimate resulted in a range from 4 ft. 10 1/2 in. to 5 ft. 4 in., using a 90 percent confidence interval.

Comparison of the anthropologic results to Deborah Haley was consistent. Deborah was approximately five feet tall and twenty-three years old at the time of her disappearance. A positive identification, however, had to await the odontologic results, which came one week later and confirmed the remains as those of Deborah Haley.

Reconstruction of Postmortem Events

A very puzzling aspect of the case involved interpreting the circumstances of death and the condition of the remains. The charring of the bones clearly indicated the body had been burned at some point, but was this action involved in Deborah's death? Because burned leaves, roots, and other vegetation occurred intermixed with the burial soil and found on the ground surface, the body was most likely burned at the scene. The pattern of charring, whereby some bones were heavily charred while others were not burned at all, suggested that the fire did not encompass the whole body but was concentrated in the chest region. The fire had to be hot enough to burn through the tissue and alter the underlying bones but did not continue long enough to turn the bones to calcite (bone ash). What was curious here was the condition of the bones. The Haley bones were highly fragmentary, regardless of whether they showed charring or not. We know that bodies consumed in very hot and long-burning fires can become fragmented (Stewart 1979). However, fragmentation is much less likely to occur when either the heat or duration are reduced. In Deborah's case, the fire was not all-encompassing and did not appear to be of long duration, yet she sustained heavy fragmentation. It was therefore hypothesized that the burning of the body and fragmentation of the bones may have represented two separate actions. It was not until Bill Haley's confession that we learned exactly what had happened.

A Telling Confession

It took one week to complete the anthropologic examination and prepare the report. The evidence and report were then transferred to the district's chief medical examiner. One week later, the forensic odontologist's report was submitted. During the field recovery a small sample of dental evidence was collected. It included the natural crown from the mandibular left second molar, an artificial dental crown covered with porcelain, the roots of a mandibular molar with three metal root-canal points in place, the roots of the mandibular left first molar, and portions of ten other tooth roots. Although this sample was relatively small for identification standards, the restoration patterns and other root morphology were diagnostic and consistent with comparisons of dental records for Deborah Haley. Based on the anthropologic and odontologic reports, the chief medical examiner signed a death certificate for Deborah Haley.

Investigators and the prosecuting attorney confronted Bill Haley with the news of the discovery and identification of his wife, Deborah. After further questioning, Bill Haley confessed to murdering his wife.

At his trial, Haley offered a not-guilty plea although he intended to confess to his involvement in Deborah's death. The plea of not guilty was made to preserve his rights of appeal pending the outcome of the trial. Haley admitted that on the day of Deborah's death they had been arguing about domestic work around the house. Bill asked Deborah to make his supper but she declined and, according to Bill, told him that the only thing he was going to get was a divorce. Their argument became physical and Bill shoved Deborah to the ground and held her. During the struggle Bill indicated that he heard a snap in her neck and she died "accidentally" from the injury, presumably a broken neck.

Bill then contemplated what to do with the body so that the police would not catch him. He decided to bury his wife in the culvert adjacent to the remote dirt road on Piney Mountain where the remains were discovered. As an afterthought, once he arrived at the culvert he decided to use his tire-iron to disfigure Deborah's body, and then covered it with kindling and carpet remnants he had in the bed of his truck. Thus, it was blunt trauma to Deborah's body that was responsible for the fragmentation of bones rather than the result of fire activity. He then doused the body with gasoline, lit the fire, pushed Deborah's body toward the metal drainage pipe, and covered the hole with dirt. The burn pattern on the bones could now also be explained as the result of the gasoline accelerant not being evenly distributed on the body, and the short duration of the fire caused by the depletion of oxygen when the burial hole was filled in with dirt. Unfortunately, the remains were too incomplete to corroborate Haley's story of the strangulation and subsequent broken neck. Three days after hiding Deborah's body, Haley left his then one-year-old daughter on the doorstep of a stranger's house.

Bill Haley was convicted of first-degree murder and sentenced to sixty years in prison; however, he served only a few days after his trial. Following sentencing, Bill Haley swallowed a plastic trash-bag liner in his cell, thus committing suicide by asphyxiation.

Conclusions

This case study outlines a portion of the many roles forensic anthropologists contribute to medicolegal death investigations. The anthropologist is part of a larger team that includes medical, dental, law enforcement, and other specialists. The importance of the anthropologist's role in the present case occurred in the recovery of the remains where tiny bone and tooth fragments needed to be recognized and collected, in the piecing together of the remains to maximize the amount of information available for analysis, and the determination of age, sex, and stature of the victim. Because Bill Haley decided to confess his involvement in the death of his wife Deborah, it was not necessary for the anthropologist to testify as an expert witness. Had he not confessed, a court appearance would have been requested. Not every case assisted by a forensic anthropologist ends up with so many questions answered as were in the case of Bill Haley. But one thing is certain, every forensic anthropology case is unique and poses a new challenge!

References

Dwight, Thomas. 1904/05. The size of the articular surfaces of the long bones as characteristic of sex: An anthropological study. *American Journal of Anatomy* 4(1):19–31.

Krogman, Wilton M., and Mehmet Yasar Iscan. 1986. *The Human Skeleton in Forensic Medicine*. 2nd ed. Springfield, IL: Charles C. Thomas.

Meindl, Richard S., and C. Owen Lovejoy. 1985. Ectocranial suture closure: A revised method for the determination of skeletal age at death based on the lateral-anterior sutures. *American Journal of Physical Anthropology* 68:57–66.

Nawrocki, Stephen P. 1998. Regression formulae for estimating age at death from cranial suture closure. Pp. 276–292 in *Forensic Osteology. Advances in the Identification of Human Remains*, ed. Kathleen J. Reichs. 2nd ed. Springfield, IL: Charles C. Thomas.

Stewart, T. Dale. 1979. *Essentials of Forensic Anthropology*. Springfield, IL: Charles C. Thomas.

Trotter, Mildred, and Goldine C. Gleser. 1958. A re-evaluation of estimation of stature based on measurements of stature taken in life and of long bones after death. *American Journal of Physical Anthropology* 16(1):79–123.

Ubelaker, Douglas H. 1989. *Human Skeletal Remains. Excavation, Analysis, Interpretation*. 2nd ed. Washington, D.C.: Taraxacum.

CHAPTER

8

Unusual "Crime" Scenes

THE ROLE OF FORENSIC ANTHROPOLOGY
IN RECOVERING AND IDENTIFYING AMERICAN MIAS

Robert W. Mann, Bruce E. Anderson, Thomas D. Holland,
David R. Rankin, and Johnie E. Webb, Jr.

The U.S. government has a steadfast resolve to bring home its soldiers, airmen, sailors, and civilians listed as prisoners of war (POW) and missing in action (MIA). As most of us know, the effects of war linger long after the fighting stops. One effect of war that continues to stir strong emotions and receives considerable legal, media, political, and economic attention, even during times of peace, is the return of U.S. POWs/MIAs. Further, as many Americans feel the United States was responsible for sending its young men and women off to war, they also feel that the United States is responsible for bringing them home. Succinctly reflecting this sentiment is the MIA slogan, "You Are Not Forgotten."

The Central Identification
Laboratory, Hawaii (CILHI)

Based in part on this sentiment, the U.S. government seeks to bring home each and every one of its MIAs, regardless of where he or she might be or how long they have been missing. The organization responsible

for the recovery and return of American MIA remains is the U.S. Army Central Identification Laboratory, Hawaii (CILHI). The CILHI, located on Hickam Air Force Base and adjacent to Pearl Harbor on the island of Oahu, is the only forensic organization of its kind. State-of-the-art archaeological, anthropological, and odontological (dental) techniques are used to locate, recover, and identify as many of the remains of the nearly 90,000 U.S. service members and civilian MIAs as possible from all previous wars. To achieve this goal, the CILHI is staffed by more than 170 soldiers and civilians and deploys 12-member search and recovery (SAR) teams to such diverse places as Vietnam, Cambodia, Laos, China, Papua New Guinea, Germany, Guadalcanal, Japan, Russia, and North Korea. The teams, which include anthropologists, gather background information on each case, interview witnesses, and excavate U.S. aircraft crash sites and suspected MIA graves. Although these teams work thousands of miles from U.S. soil, they nevertheless rely on standard medicolegal (forensic) principles and techniques used in recent-death crime scenes in the United States to investigate and excavate aircraft crash sites and graves.

Whether dealing with recent homicides in New York, decade-old deaths in Louisiana, fifty-year-old military crash sites in Europe, or Vietnam-era graves in Southeast Asia, proper anthropological techniques, combined with crime scene principles and procedures, still apply. Dealing with MIA sites, what some might call "crime" scenes (Falise 1999), is similar to dealing with recent and old crime scenes in that planning, combined with the careful recovery, documentation, and handling of evidence, is still the best formula for ensuring success. The ever-increasing role of anthropology has evolved, not surprisingly, to the point where forensic anthropologists are employed by the U.S. government and are involved in every step of finding, recovering, and identifying America's MIAs.

The CILHI is the largest forensic anthropology laboratory in the world. Many of its 30 anthropologists and four odontologists (dentists) have specialized training in medical and legal matters and have worked extensively with local, state, and federal (e.g., FBI) agencies outside of the MIA arena prior to joining the CILHI. In 1992, for example, one of the authors assisted in the identification of Jeffrey Dahmer's first known victim (Owsley et al. 1993). Dahmer had picked up eighteen-year-old Steven J. Hicks and drugged and seduced him at his semirural community in Bath, Ohio. Dahmer had unsuccessfully tried to dispose of Hicks' remains by dismembering his body, smashing his bones and teeth into tiny pieces, and scattering them over his backyard. A systematic archaeological excavation of Dahmer's backyard by police, medical authorities, and anthropologists, however, led to the identification of the victim. Two other CILHI anthropologists helped identify victims of the Branch Davidian standoff in Waco, Texas (Owsley et al. 1995). Yet two other CILHI anthropologists assisted the Physicians for Human Rights organization in the excavation and analysis of 300 Moslem noncombatants recovered from three mass graves in Bosnia-Herzegovina. In August 1997, four anthropologists and one dentist from the CILHI assisted in the recovery of the victims of the Korean Airlines 801 crash on Guam. Most recently, four CILHI anthropologists assisted in the identifications of the victims of the September 11, 2001, terrorist attack on the Pentagon. The insights and experiences gained by CILHI scientists working with organizations and cases outside the MIA arena serve to enhance their expertise, increase their professional network, and render them more capable of doing their job of recovering and identifying the remains of our American MIAs.

In the Field

To highlight the unusual role of government forensic anthropologists, the authors present two examples that depict, first, how a grave believed to be associated with an escaped American prisoner of war (POW) in Laos was located and excavated, and second, how the crash site of an AC-130 airplane was excavated. Attention to detail and the implementation of standard crime scene principles and forensic anthropological methodology resulted in successful recoveries at both sites. Once the remains were taken to the laboratory, forensic anthropologists were able to rely on the evidence found *in situ* (in its proper context) to answer questions that might otherwise have gone unanswered.

The aftermath of war has, in effect, resulted in a number of large, complex crime scene–like scenarios. However, unlike most current death crime scenes, these war-related investigations involve sites that have been dramatically altered by cultural factors, mainly villagers scavenging crash sites and graves for useable items. In Southeast Asia, for example, aircraft wreckage and ordnance (explosives including bombs, grenades, and antipersonnel mines) are sold for scrap metal while human bones and teeth have been sold on the black market in the mistaken hope of monetary or other reward from the U.S. government. In addition, there are environmental variables that destroy bones and teeth, including invasion and destruction by vegetation, soil movement, pH, rockslides, wind, and flooding. These variables combine to make the already challenging task of identifying incomplete and often fragmentary human remains even more difficult. Identifications based on dental restorations, mitochondrial DNA (mtDNA), or the preponderance of the evidence from a crash or gravesite are sometimes based on only a few teeth or bone fragments.

A Grave Believed to Be Associated with an American POW

In 1963, an Air America civilian serving as a cargo "kicker" (a crewman who literally kicks supplies out the back of the airplane in flight) in a Curtiss C-46 was taken prisoner by the Pathet Lao (Communist Lao soldiers). The cargo plane, carrying rice and freshly slaughtered buffalo meat, had a crew of seven—three Americans, three Thais, and one Hong Kong Chinese (British citizen)—as it flew over the jungles of Southern Laos. With a jolt, a shell ripped through the aircraft and tore a gaping hole in the fuselage. As the airplane burned and plunged toward the ground, five of the crew strapped on parachutes and exited the aircraft. The pilot and copilot fought to stabilize the aircraft that, within seconds, crashed on flat terrain not far from the edge of a rice paddy. Rescue workers who searched the area saw no sign of life, only evidence that the airplane had crashed.

While there was little doubt that any survivors would have been taken prisoner by the Pathet Lao, all doubt vanished when, in 1964, a photo of the kicker and four other prisoners (his fellow crew members) was published and circulated by the Pathet Lao. This photograph provided proof that at least five of the seven crew members survived and were taken prisoner. Air Force helicopter crew member Duane Martin and Navy LTJG Dieter Dengler joined the five at Hoi Het prison camp in December 1965 and January 1966, respectively. They noted that the kicker and four others made a daring escape from Bun Lang Khang prison camp during the dry season in 1964 but were recaptured at a water hole shortly thereafter. In June 1966, Dengler, Martin, and the five from the C-46 escaped from Hoi Het prison. They quickly divided into three groups, according to a previously designed plan. This increased their odds of going undetected and seeking freedom. What happened next depends on to whom one speaks. What is known, however, is that Dieter Dengler is the only escapee imprisoned at Hoi Het prison to return to his family (Dengler 1979). By the time the CILHI became involved in the search for the kicker, more than twenty-five years had elapsed and, although the dense jungle in Laos had camouflaged a gravesite initially believed to be associated with the kicker, it hadn't destroyed all traces.

An initial report of the gravesite came to light during an investigation in 1992. The site was located deep in triple-canopy jungle, about forty meters from a river that winds for hundreds of kilometers through the mountainous countryside. Once at the site, the team interviewed a middle-aged Laotian man who related the following account. One day he and a few other members of the local militia heard the sound of someone chopping wood near the river. While investigating the source of the sound, they saw someone standing guard for another man (possibly both escaped POWs) chopping firewood on the other side of the river. The man reportedly fired at them and the militia returned fire, reportedly striking the man standing guard once, either in the stomach or the leg. One scenario, as reported by one of the witnesses, notes that the militia later found the wounded man sitting under a tree and, as they approached him, he placed the rifle under his chin and committed suicide to avoid recapture. Members of the militia carried the man's body along the bank of the river and buried him in soft sand near an old tree stump. When asked how deep the body was buried, the witness pointed to his waist (about one meter).

Another witness showed the team where he believed the body had been buried. Although he appeared to be mentally sharp, his memory had faded over the years and the vegetation in the area had changed dramatically. As best he could remember, the body was buried in what was then a manioc garden, about 3 or 4 meters from a tree stump located at the site. Based on this information we laid out a 4 x 4 meter area, using string and wooden stakes. We then excavated the area to a depth of two and a half meters. Unfortunately, we found nothing—no grave, no clothing, and no remains. The witness provided incorrect information about the location of the grave. We remained convinced, however, that his story was credible. After digging four trenches to the east of the 4 x 4 meter pit, we were forced to abandon the site. There was nothing to pinpoint the precise location of

the grave. The witness lost face quickly by what everyone perceived as a wild goose chase. We packed our gear and traveled to the next site. The case was returned to investigators at the Joint Task Force–Full Accounting (JTF-FA), an umbrella military organization responsible for investigating and assisting in the recovery of MIA losses in Vietnam, Laos, and Cambodia.

A New Witness Surfaces

In 1993, a CILHI team returned to the area once again. The team interviewed a new witness who said that the body had been buried slightly more to the east. Following the witness's lead, members of the team dug several long trenches in the area without finding any evidence of human remains or clothing. The witness was given four wooden stakes and asked to stake out a square where he thought the team should dig. Once the stakes were in the ground, the team probed the witness for additional information. The team anthropologist noticed that the proposed project area designated by the witness excluded a decaying bamboo fence that appeared to have been built long after the burial. The witness held firm that the grave was nowhere near the fence. Despite this assertion, the team chose to extend the excavation a few meters in all directions to include the bamboo fence. This decision was based on two factors: first, the information that the witnesses gave in 1992 and 1993 placed the grave in two different areas; and second, the bamboo fence didn't appear to be thirty years old.

The team leveled the excavation area by removing the upper meter of sand from the entire project area and sweeping it with ground penetrating radar (GPR). Ground penetrating radar is a remote sensing device that transmits radio waves into the ground and, under certain soil conditions, reveals soil layers and ground distur-bances called "anomalies." Again, there was no evidence of a grave, clothing, or re-mains. Our luck changed the following day, however, when one of the American soldiers on the team discovered an arm bone under a removed portion of the bam-boo fence. We slowed the pace of the ex-cavation and concentrated our efforts on the grave, which yielded a skeleton lying on its right side in a slightly flexed (fetal) position with arms crossed over the chest. The anthropologist identified the bone as human but was unable to determine its an-cestry. Members of the team put their shovels down and began the meticulous task of exposing the remains tooth by tooth, bone by bone, using only brushes and wooden picks so as to avoid scratch-ing the bones. Each step in the excavation was photographed. Findings were record-ed in field notes.

While less-experienced soldiers brushed away the loose sand from atop the leg re-gion of the skeleton, two forensic anthro-pologists worked on the facial region. The leg region yielded an M-1 rifle magazine with six unspent cartridges, two spent car-tridges, and several clothing buttons. The ammunition magazine and some of the buttons remained suspended in the sand, as they were located on the clothing before the cloth disintegrated. The anthropolo-gists who excavated the facial region used extreme care as they brushed away the loose sand from the facial region to deter-mine if the evidence indicated that the decedent had sustained gunshot trauma, which would be consistent with the wit-ness's story of suicide. The skull and facial bones were broken into many pieces and the teeth were in disarray. It was apparent that this pattern of trauma was consistent with a gunshot wound to the mouth or chin. The remains were carefully removed from the ground and packed in plastic bags to prevent further damage and placed in a locked, sealed container for transport to the CILHI.

Anthropological Analysis at the CILHI

At the CILHI, an anthropologist conducted an in-depth analysis of the remains and noted that the pattern of cranial fractures and disarray of the teeth found during the excavation suggested that the individual had died of a gunshot wound to the head. It was also possible, however, that the victim died of blunt force injuries to the head—the poor condition of some of the bones com-plicated our interpretation of trauma. What we could tell, however, was that the bones of the face and mandible revealed massive trauma and fractures consistent with a gun-shot wound under the chin. Lacking, how-ever, was sufficient evidence for us to determine if it was a self-inflicted injury (suicide), because a similar pattern of peri-mortem fractures could have resulted from a gunshot to other areas of the head. Re-gardless of whether it was suicide or homi-cide, the pattern of fractures supported the witness's story. We then wondered about the "cause of death" and its meaning.

The term *cause of death*, a topic in anthro-pology (forensic and otherwise) is poorly understood and often used incorrectly. *Cause of death* has different meanings for dif-ferent people and is used rather loosely by both professionals and laypersons. Unless an anthropologist is also a pathologist, he or she does not determine cause of death—a medical-legal ruling on death. Most peo-ple who talk about the cause of death refer to it as *manner* or *method* of death. These terms, *cause of death* and *manner of death* are not, however, synonymous. Cause of death deals specifically with the physiological basis of death—for example, asphyxia or exsanguination (*bleeding to death*). *Manner* of death, on the other hand, refers to whether someone died as a result of a homicide, suicide, accident, natural, or unknown. *Method* of death relates to how someone died—in other words, was he or she shot, stabbed, hanged, or the like. Armed with this information it becomes apparent that a death can be attributed to suicide (*manner*) by hanging (*method*), and the cause of death, asphyxia. Anthropologists, therefore, are often called upon to provide information on *manner* and *method* of death—such as in the case of the kicker, not the actual *cause of death.*

At the CILHI, a forensic anthropologist and forensic odontologist examined the alleged kicker's remains and determined that the dental profile did not match that of the C-46 kicker. Our thoughts then turned to the possibility that the remains could be one of the other four escaped POWs, as Dengler and Martin were accounted for. There was good information that Martin had been killed in Laos. Although we have yet to identify the remains, our investigation continues, an investigation that will eventually solve the mystery of the kicker.

An AC-130 Aircraft Crash Site in Laos

In April 1970, eleven crewmen were flying aboard an AC-130 gunship on an armed reconnaissance mission over Laos. They were escorted by two U.S. F-4 Phantoms. The AC-130 made three initial passes over the target. On the fourth pass, the pilot transmitted a message that the aircraft had been hit near its tail. No further transmission was heard. Moments later, the aircraft crashed and burned. One crewman managed to parachute from the aircraft and was rescued. The ten other crewmen were presumably killed in the crash.

A search of U.S. aircraft incident/loss reports, combined with information provided by local villagers, led JTF-FA investigators to a remote jungle area where they believed the aircraft had crashed. A preliminary survey of the area conducted by the investigation team yielded small pieces of scattered aircraft wreckage. The next step involved a joint CILHI/JTF-FA excavation team who conducted a full-scale excavation of the crash site designed to achieve the following objectives: (1) Identify the aircraft as the AC-130 gunship to the exclusion of all others; (2) recover any human remains; and (3) recover material evidence (e.g., parachute equipment, identification or dog tags, wristwatches) that could prove that the ten crewmen were actually in the airplane when it crashed. Our goal was to achieve these three objectives and resolve the case. Friends and family members of the ten MIAs could finally experience closure to a long, painful chapter in their lives.

The search and recovery team set up camp (tents) near a small Lao village and flew to and from the site daily via helicopter. The aircraft crash site was located on the side of a mountain in a remote triple-canopy jungle. Because of the low-angle impact when the AC-130 airplane crashed, no crater was visible. The aircraft, however, broke into thousands of pieces, many of which were scattered over a large area in the jungle. Since the site was so isolated and there were no villages nearby, the large, heavy Wright engines, propellers, and three 20mm guns lay where they landed. We also found the aircraft's yellow fiberglass nose cone nestled among the trees, and what was left of one of the tires. The scalloped pattern in the rubber of the tire revealed that some villagers cut away the rubber and made many "Ho Chi Minh" sandals. We photographed all items, recorded any serial numbers, and left the items in place, as they were too heavy for us to remove. Photographs, however, did provide the documentary evidence needed to identify the airplane to the exclusion of all others. As we proceeded, we photographed each significant item, noted

FIGURE 8.1   EXCAVATION SITE

Shown here is the excavation site of a large/deep (4 meters) crater caused by a cargo plane that crashed in Vietnam. Each square, marked off in white, measures 4 x 4 meters.

FIGURE 8.2   EXCAVATING A B-52 CRASH SITE IN VIETNAM

its position from a reference point (datum) on a site sketch (using distance and azimuth readings), and photographed each step in the subsequent excavation. These photos provided information that may have been overlooked while on-site and later served as the primary documentation of the team's on-site activity.

Initially, a thorough surface search and metal detector survey of a large area were made to determine the pattern, density, and dispersion of wreckage and ordnance hazard, both on the surface and below the ground. At that point, we were unsure of how large the proposed area of excavation should be. To resolve our dilemma, we used colored pin flags to mark the location of items by type (red for aircraft wreckage, yellow for life support equipment, and orange for human remains). The anthropologist then laid out the proposed excavation area (site) based on the distribution of the pin flags. We next cut and cleared the vegetation from the site and laid out a 16 x 30 meter archaeological grid system consisting of 2 x 2 meter grid squares. Each square was independently excavated. The soil was sifted through 1/4" wire mesh screens. Artifacts were separated by type, such as aircraft wreckage, remains, or personal effects. All significant material evidence was placed in separate plastic bags and marked with the date, grid square number, and site number. At the end of each day these items were inventoried, using a chain of custody form, and sealed in containers for transport to the CILHI for analysis. Insignificant aircraft wreckage and ordnance were discarded when the site was closed and no further excavation was planned.

After fifteen days of excavation we recovered a metallic cross inscribed with the words "JESUS IS LORD," assorted U.S. coins including a 1968 Kennedy half dollar, a Seiko watch housing, numerous pieces of a watchband, two survival knives, house keys, fingernail clippers, tweezers, and dog tags for seven of the ten missing crewmen. Most important, we recovered more than 1,500 human bone fragments and 5 human teeth, one with a restoration (filling). The bones and teeth had been broken in a manner consistent with a high-speed incident such as an aircraft crash. The rapid deceleration and subsequent crash of the aircraft caused extensive fragmentation of nearly all bones and some of the teeth. This extensive fracturing and commingling, or mixing, of the bones and teeth, combined with secondary explosions of ordnance and intense burning prevented scientists at the CILHI from identifying the remains of each individual. Remains that could not be identified and attributed to a specific individual were buried as group remains in a cemetery selected by family members. We also recovered parachute pieces, including 38 V-rings (3 per parachute) and 27 D-rings (2 per parachute). These items allowed us to account for fourteen of fifteen personnel parachutes carried on the airplane. After anthropological and dental analyses at the CILHI, the Armed Forces Identification Review Board (AFIRB), a panel of military officers, accepted the recommendations by the CILHI for the identifications of the ten missing crewmen. Many of the remains could not be identified as those of a particular crew member. However, those that could be identified were forwarded to the respective primary next of kin for burial.

Conclusion

As of January 2002, the CILHI has identified more than 1,000 MIA U.S. service members and civilians from previous wars. The CILHI, as part of a broader effort, has achieved the U.S. government's goal of finding, recovering, and identifying its MIAs by deploying search and recovery teams wherever necessary in the world. These teams are supervised on-site by highly experienced archaeologists and forensic anthropologists who are trained not only in anthropology, but in the handling of evidence and the conduct of investigations such as those of the kicker and members of the AC-130 aircraft. By employing state-of-the-art equipment and adhering to strict scientific and legal principles, these teams find and recover America's MIAs from some of the most hazardous and remote areas in the world. Lessons learned by the teams apply to cases in the steel and concrete jungles of the United States, and the remote jungles of Southeast Asia. In this way, methods of recovery and identification used by the CILHI echo the MIA herald, "You Are Not Forgotten."

Author's Note: The families of the MIAs and POWs discussed in this report request your assistance. If you have any questions or comments, or can provide additional information on either of these cases, please contact Robert W. Mann.

Acknowledgments

The authors thank Mr. Bill Gadoury at the CILHI and Dr. Jerry DeBruin at the University of Toledo for reading the manuscript and providing useful comments.

References

Dengler, Dieter. 1979. *Escape from Laos*. Novato, California: Presidio Press.

Falise, Thierry. 1999. Laos-MIA: The Jungle Detectives. *Nation World Times*, November 9.

Owsley Douglas W., Robert W. Mann, R. E. Chapman, E. Moore, and W. A. Cox. 1993. Positive identification in a case of intentional extreme fragmentation. *Journal of Forensic Sciences* 38(4):985–996.

Owsley, Douglas W., Douglas Ubelaker, Max Houk, Kari Sanders, William Grant, E. Craig, T. Woltanski, and N. Peerwani. 1995. The role of forensic anthropology in the recovery and analysis of the Branch Davidian Compound victims: Techniques of analysis. *Journal of Forensic Sciences* 40 (3):341–348.

Webster, Ann D. 1998. Excavation of a Vietnam-era aircraft crash site: Use of cross-cultural understanding and dual forensic recovery methods. *Journal of Forensic Sciences* 43(2):277–283.

Further Reading

DeBruin, Jerry. 1995. Personality: Gene DeBruin, POW-Laos. *Vietnam*.

Hoshower, Lisa M. 1999. Dr. William R. Maples and the role of the consultants at the U.S. Army Central Identification Laboratory, Hawaii. *Journal of Forensic Sciences* 44 (4):689–691.

Rochester, Stuart I., and Frederick Kiley. 1998. *Honor Bound*. OSD Historical Office.

Ubelaker Douglas H., Douglas W. Owsley, Max M. Houck, E. Craig, W. Grant, T. Woltanski, R. Fram, Kari Sandness, and N. Peerwani. 1995. The role of forensic anthropology in the recovery and analysis of Branch Davidian Compound victims: Recovery procedures and characteristics of the victims. *Journal of Forensic Sciences* 40(3):335–340.

CHAPTER

9

THE CONTRIBUTIONS OF ARCHAEOLOGY AND PHYSICAL ANTHROPOLOGY TO THE JOHN MCRAE CASE

Norman J. Sauer, William A. Lovis, Mark E. Blumer, and Jennifer Fillion

Forensic anthropologists normally conduct their analyses and write their reports inside the relative isolation of their labs. But how is the anthropological evidence incorporated with other lines of evidence into a compelling case that can be argued in court? Forensic anthropologists often lose sight of the fact that their contribution may be only one small part of a much larger and complex picture. Collectively, anthropologists (and probably other forensic scientists) focus on what their discipline can contribute, and artificially constrain their perspective on the larger case by not attending closing arguments or not reading final court transcripts of the cases in which they participated. To a degree this is expected. All forensic scientists balance multiple demands on their time and normally engage in more than one case at any given time. However, understanding how forensic anthropology fits into a broader criminal investigation, and consequently the development of a successful case, can be quite useful. As a learning experience, it should allow anthropologists to ask better questions of the people leading the investigation and provide insight into how they

might better interact with attorneys on both sides of the table (Sigler-Eisenberg 1985). To demonstrate the value and complexity of the multidisciplinary nature of forensic science, the case study presented here follows a forensic investigation and prosecution to completion. Because the case presented herein has been well publicized throughout the state of Michigan and the United States, via a nationally aired crime program, and because the case has been adjudicated, it is our decision to use the real names of the victim and the convicted perpetrator in this chapter.

Recovery and Identification

In August 1997, a farm worker in northern Michigan was using a backhoe to excavate a refuse pit and noticed a human skull in the back dirt. Local law enforcement agencies and the Michigan State Police (MSP) were called to the scene and conducted an excavation of the area using a Bobcat grader. They recovered approximately 70 percent of the skeleton of an adolescent.

When the anthropologists first saw the remains, they had been delivered to a local morgue and were packaged in paper grocery bags. The bones were dry, devoid of soft tissue, and soil stained. We quickly noted that all of the bones of the feet and distal epiphyses of both tibiae and fibulae were contained in a pair of socks that were found with lengths of rope knotted around the tops of the cuffs (Figure 9.1). The developmental stage of the remains indicated an age at death between thirteen and sixteen years. For example, the three primary centers of the innominates, but none of the long bone epiphyses, had fused. Because the features that are normally used to estimate sex are not completely developed until after puberty, sex estimation in adolescents is chancy. Nonetheless, the cranial and pelvic morphology suggested male. Because of the

young age of the victim, no attempt was made to estimate stature or ancestry.

Dental records and X-rays of a missing boy, Randy Laufer, had been forwarded along with the remains. The antemortem dental records were all consistent with the dentition of the skeleton and dental radiographs, taken in an orientation similar to that of the antemortem films, were identical. The identification of Randy Laufer was positive.

Eleven years earlier, Randy, a fifteen-year-old boy, was last seen when he left school to spend the weekend with a friend. The friend's father, John McRae, had once been convicted of the murder and mutilation of another young boy and was a suspect in the disappearance of two other young males. Further, McRae had owned the property where the remains were found. Given these circumstances and the fact that there was significant trauma to the skeleton, John McRae quickly became a suspect in the case.

The Skeletal Evidence for Dismemberment and Mutilation

At the time of the initial examination, it was noted that a number of the elements exhibited sharp force trauma, some of which was extensive. The left clavicle, two lumbar vertebrae, and the sacrum exhibited evidence for extensive perimortem or immediate postmortem dismemberment and mutilation. All of these bones were sent to Dr. Steven Symes at the Regional Forensic Center, Memphis, Tennessee, who is recognized as one of the nation's leading authorities on the interpretation of cut marks on bone. His conclusions were consistent with ours.

The left clavicle (Figure 9.2) displayed at least four cut marks along the superior surface of the midshaft. The deepest mark suggests a repeated rocking or sawing action. Evidence for a tension fracture on the inferior surface indicates that at least one of the cuts was delivered with sufficient force to fracture the bone.

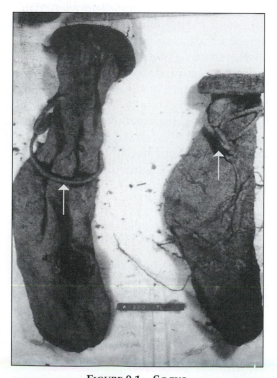

FIGURE 9.1 SOCKS

These socks contained bones of the feet and distal leg bone epiphyses. Note the knotted chords.

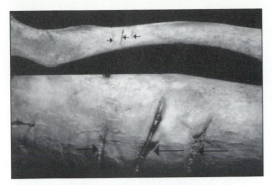

FIGURE 9.2   SUPERIOR SURFACE
OF THE LEFT CLAVICLE

The arrows indicate cut marks. The bottom of the photograph is a closer view.

A series of at least four horizontal cut marks was identified on the lateral aspect of the right inferior articular process and the spinous process of the third lumbar vertebra (L3) (Figure 9.3). Portions of both articular and spinous processes were excised and not recovered. An additional sharp instrument defect on the right side of the body was contiguous with one of the marks on the articular process and may have resulted from the same strike. Collectively, these lesions appear to represent a successful attempt to separate the right inferior articular process from the remainder of the bone.

Also apparent on L3 was a deep, vertically oriented cut that penetrated the centrum from the left side and obliquely traversed the body to the right posterior aspect. This apparently resulted from a stabbing blow with a large v-shaped knife blade.

Similar sharp force trauma was evident on the fourth lumbar vertebra (L4) (Figure 9.4), mainly on the left side. A deep cut extending along and parallel to the superior aspect of the body was contiguous with cut marks associated with the removal of the left superior articular process. These marks on the left side of L4 are associated with sharp force trauma on the left side of L3. Finally, the right superior articular process of L4 exhibited a fracture that appears to have resulted from one of the blows directed toward the right inferior process of L3 (see Figure 9.5 on page 120).

Collectively, the sharp instrument trauma identified on the lumbar vertebrae indicates that the victim's body was separated in the abdominal region, between the rib cage and the pelvis. As anyone familiar with dissection understands, separating vertebrae between their centra normally presents few

FIGURE 9.3   RIGHT SIDE
OF THIRD LUMBAR VERTEBRA

Note the excised portion of the spinous process (a); the excised inferior articular process (b); and the cut mark along the spinous process and articular process (c).

FIGURE 9.4   LEFT SIDE OF THIRD
AND FOURTH LUMBAR VERTEBRAE

On L4 note the excised superior articular process (b) and the continuous excision mark on the body (a). Note the contiguous cut marks on the left inferior articular process (c) and the spinous process (d) on L3.

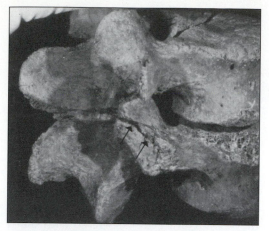

FIGURE 9.5   RIGHT SIDE OF THIRD AND FOURTH LUMBAR VERTEBRAE

Note the fracture (arrows) on the superior articular process of L4 that is contiguous with the exposed excised surface of the L3 inferior articular process.

problems. Essentially, the process involves cutting through several millimeters of fibrocartilage that lies between the two adjacent vertebral bodies. The neural arch, however, is quite a different matter. The interlocking superior and inferior processes would have to be pulled apart (a process made quite difficult by the strong diarthrodial joints and the strong, tight muscles that hold the joints together), or excised. In this case, it appears that the processes were cut. A series of blows from a sharp instrument were directed to the junction between the third and fourth lumbar vertebrae with sufficient force to excise one superior and one inferior process and a portion of the spinous process of L3. The fractured process on L4 adjacent to the transected process of L3 is further indication of the force of at least one of the blows. A small horizontal nick on the anterior surface of L4 that was made by the side rather than the tip of a sharp instrument suggests that the anterior aspect of the vertebra had been exposed at the time the defect was created.

The last series of cut marks were identified on the sacrum. A minimum of three fine,

cranial-caudally oriented cut marks were present on the anterior surface of the left ala (Figure 9.6). These marks were apparently made by a thin bladed knife, probably not the same instrument responsible for the broader lesions on the superior surface of the clavicle. In contrast to the lumbar vertebral trauma, the marks on the sacrum appear to represent mutilation rather than dismemberment. They are not associated with a joint and there is no other evidence that an attempt was made to separate the sacroiliac joint. A reasonable explanation for the position and orientation of the sacral trauma is penetration through the uro-genital area.

The Timing of the Injuries

One important consideration in the evaluation of any skeletal trauma is the timing of the injuries with respect to death. Certainly, the totality of injuries indicates that all of the events did not occur antemortem (before the death of the victim). First, there is no evidence for osteogenic reaction on any of the affected elements (Sauer 1998) and secondly, separating a body in the lumbar region is incompatible with life. A more difficult question is whether the injuries were inflicted perimortem (at or around the time of death) or postmortem (after death).

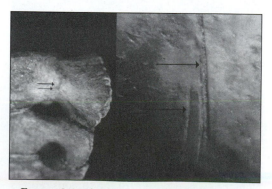

FIGURE 9.6   ANTERIOR SURFACE OF SACRUM

Arrows indicate cut marks. The right side of the photograph is a closer view.

The consistent brown stain on all of the bone surfaces indicates that they were all exposed for comparable amounts of time. If any of the bone traumas occurred during recovery by law enforcement officials or by the action of the backhoe operator who initially reported the discovery, the newly exposed surfaces would have been stained differently than the surrounding bone and easily identifiable (Ubelaker and Adams 1995, 511). There was no such evidence.

Also, the pattern of trauma to the lumbar vertebrae indicates that the bones were still tightly articulated when the apparent dismemberment took place. In addition to the placement of the marks where one would expect them to be during dissection, the position of contiguous cuts on adjacent bones only makes sense if the elements were joined. Therefore, the evidence from the skeletal material is compelling. At some point near the time of death, the remains of Randy Laufer were subjected to a series of sharp force injuries. These injuries occurred in the region of the left clavicle, between the neck and shoulder; at the level of the third and fourth lumbar vertebrae, particularly at their intersection; and on the anterior surface of the sacrum at the level of the first sacral vertebra. Evidently, the damage to the lumbar vertebrae reflects a successful attempt to separate the upper part of the body from the lower portion.

The Forensic Archaeology of the Randy Laufer Case: Establishing Context

The remains of Randy Laufer were recovered under less than ideal circumstances. The initial discovery was the result of an uncontrolled backhoe excavation, which resulted in major alteration of the original context of both the burial location and the remains prior to inspection by law enforcement personnel from the Michigan State Police. Further investigation and the subsequent recovery of additional remains by law enforcement employed heavy equipment, a Bobcat grader, as well as hand excavation, and was not performed with a view toward reconstructing the original location of the burial or its relationship to structures that existed while John McRae was still a resident on the property. As a consequence, even after the positive identification of Randy Laufer had been made it was unknown whether additional human remains might be present, whether evidence of the original burial pit was still present in the vicinity of the discovery, or what the relationship of the burial location was to structures inhabited and used by John McRae. Thus, the unusual use of archaeology *ex post facto* was focused on clarifying these several issues. Were there additional human remains present? Was there *in situ* evidence of the original burial pit? If not, then where was the most likely location from which the human remains might have derived? Could this location be associated with evidence of former structures on the property?

To achieve these ends, archaeological investigation of the McRae property proceeded with four primary field goals: first, to relocate any evidence of the original burial pit containing the human remains if traces were still present and recoverable, and if not directly recoverable then to define the larger area from which the remains most likely were recovered; second, to relocate the precise positions of former structures on the property; third to relocate the backhoe excavation that had initially uncovered the remains; and finally, to relocate the excavations that law enforcement personnel had undertaken with both heavy equipment and hand excavation. This information would then be used to make inferences about the maximum area and location from which the human remains might have derived and, if possible, to determine the most likely location within this larger area, and relative to former standing structures, that the body might have been deposited.

These goals were approached using systematic archaeological procedures, beginning with the use of available archival data. First, two series of aerial photographs, one series dating to early 1988, and the other dating to 1993/1994, were inspected. The earlier photo series showed the presence and relative position of structures on the property when McRae was in residence, and were examined to obtain information about the spatial relationships of structures at the locale, and their collective relationship to the recovery site of the burial. The second and later series was taken after the structures had been removed, and displayed the site as it was when Randy Laufer's remains were discovered and recovered. The second set of archival data consisted of insurance documents obtained from the Clare County Assessor's Office, and was contemporary with McRae's ownership of the property. These insurance records were obtained by the state and county prosecutors and revealed the number, type, and dimensions of several of the structures on the property, as well as details of their construction and value. This combination of descriptive insurance documents and aerial photographs revealed that a house trailer, a frame dwelling, and a barn with dimensions of 12' x 30' had been present in the immediate vicinity of the remains but had subsequently been demolished after McRae sold the property to his neighbor.

With this information in hand, a field investigation was initiated. A walkover inspection of the crime scene revealed that one corner of the barn foundation was still present on the site, and could be used to further guide archaeological investigation. Using the barn corner as a reference, systematic shovel skimming was employed to discover and trace soil stains reflecting areas on the interior and exterior of the 12' x 30' barn structure. These inferences were based on the presence of substantial soil color and texture differences, with loamy organic soils on the interior, and coarse inorganic sands on the exterior. Using this procedure, a second corner and parts of the south wall of the barn were revealed, allowing reconstruction of both the barn orientation and its alignment. Dimensional data recovered from these archaeological procedures closely matched those from the insurance documents. With these data it was possible to project the partial walls and relocate the alignments of missing walls and corners of the barn (Figure 9.7). This stage of field analysis revealed that the burial recovery location was either directly within the barn, or directly adjacent to it on the exterior wall.

A toothless backhoe was subsequently employed to reveal outlines of soil disturbances. This work was conducted along the southeast corner of the reconstructed barn wall in the vicinity of the initial burial recovery and police investigation. Backhoe excavations were undertaken at approximate 1-foot (30–40 cm) vertical intervals. It was possible, using this procedure, to define several of the prior excavation episodes. Specifically, the maximum extent of the initial backhoe excavations that had accidentally discovered the skeletal remains was clearly evident. In addition, areas of subsequent Michigan State Police investigation using heavy equipment and hand tools were also clearly visible as soil stains. Finally, it was possible to define both the spatial position and maximum depth of these combined excavations. Ancillary data collected during this procedure included soil color and texture changes related to a gravel driveway between the house trailer and the barn, and preparation of a compact clay pad for the house trailer. No evidence of the original burial pit was recovered. Overall, some 275 square feet of area was excavated by hand and machine during this procedure, which took a single long work day to complete. The compiled excavation

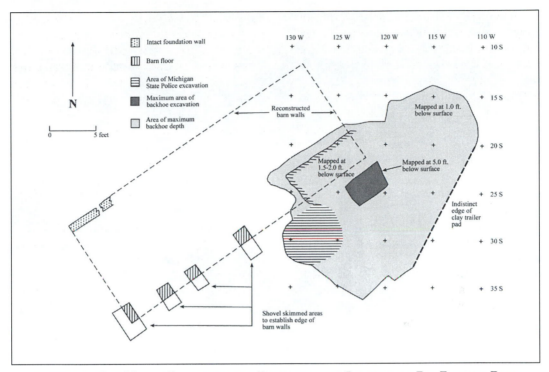

FIGURE 9.7   SITE MAP OF EXCAVATION AND RECONSTRUCTED LOCATION OF PRE-EXISTING BARN

data provided information about the maximum area from which the skeletal remains could have been derived; the location of this area relative to the barn, driveway, and trailer that existed on the property; and the area that most likely contained the human remains within this broader bounded space.

In both pretrial and trial testimony these data, in conjunction with information from a variety of other sources, were employed to demonstrate that Randy Laufer's remains derived from an area no more than 15 feet (5 m) from the front door of the defendant's trailer (see Figure 9.8 on page 124). No remnants of the original burial pit remained. However, there is a high probability that the burial was either directly within the wall of the adjacent barn or, more probably, outside the barn wall under the defendant's gravel driveway, within direct view of his front door.

The Prosecution's Case against John McRae

In 1950, at age fifteen, John McRae slashed an eight-year-old neighbor to death with a straight razor. The details of the attack clearly demonstrated a motive based upon sexual sadism. The pathologist commented on this at the autopsy, and also predicted that whoever was responsible for that attack was likely to be a repeat offender.

In 1951, McRae was caught, tried, and convicted of first-degree murder, and sentenced to life in prison without parole. However, in 1972, Michigan Governor William G. Milliken commuted his life sentence to "time served," and released him. McRae subsequently left Michigan for Florida, where he was employed as a prison guard. He eventually became the primary suspect in the disappearance of two boys. When he became the target of

FIGURE 9.8   AERIAL PHOTOGRAPH

This aerial photograph shows the pre-existing structures on the McRae property and the maximum area within which the original burial pit was contained (dashed lines).

these investigations he suddenly left Florida, eventually making his way back to central Michigan.

No one in the community of Harrison, Michigan, knew McRae's background. He became active in the community, including Boy Scouts and 4-H Clubs, and, by 1986, was fully integrated into the activities of the area. Through his son, Martin, who attended the local middle school, McRae met Randy Laufer, who eventually became a frequent guest at the McRae home.

Randy Laufer was a small, effeminate-looking child of fifteen. His classmates sometimes teased him for his short stature. Laufer was prepubescent in appearance, if not in fact. It was also reported that the boy was rebelling against a restrictive home life. On September 15, 1987, Randy Laufer was last seen leaving school at the end of the school day. For more than a year his disappearance was treated as the case of a runaway teenager. It was not until after John

McRae made a hasty middle-of-the-night departure with his family, and left his dog tied to a neighbor's tree, that the Clare County Sheriff discovered McRae's background and began to treat Randy Laufer's disappearance as a more serious event.

Failure to find the body of a victim is not, as many would believe, a fatal defect in a homicide prosecution (see *People v. Modelski*, 164 Mich App 337 [1987]). However, where circumstances do not necessarily prove death, and a reasonable alternative explanation to murder exists, a prosecution is doomed to failure. Here, there was really nothing that demonstrated death other than the suspect's history. It was still equally likely that Randy Laufer had run away from home.

In 1989 or 1990, the abandoned McRae property was purchased by a neighbor who had all the decrepit buildings torn down for safety reasons. She used the land as pasture for her horses. Apparently her horses kept tripping over some chunks of concrete from the small barn foundation, so she ordered her farmhand to dig a pit at the site and bury the debris. It was while performing this excavation operation, in August 1997, that Randy Laufer's remains were uncovered.

At first blush, this would appear to be an easy case; a convicted vicious murderer of a little boy leaves town with the body of another young boy buried on his property. The problem, in this instance, was that the case was wholly circumstantial. Under the rules of evidence, especially as interpreted by the judge in this case, it was not at all assured that the jury would hear of McRae's past during a trial. His defense was clearly to prevent his prior conviction from becoming evidence, and then to assert that the boy was buried on the property after McRae left the region.

Under *Michigan Rules of Evidence* (MRE) 404 (b), the state may not use prior misconduct to demonstrate propensity to commit crimes, and by extension, the crime in litigation. The state may use such evidence to prove certain relevant matters, such as a distinct pattern of behavior that might show the identity of the suspect, motive, etc. In a watershed case, *People v. VanderVliet*, (444 Mich 52 [1993]), the Michigan Supreme Court reinterpreted this rule to lower these barriers, which for many years had prevented prosecutors from using much of this valuable evidence. The trial judge in McRae's case, however, largely adhered to the pre-*VanderVliet* rule (based upon *People v. Golohowicz*, 413 Mich 298 [1982]) and did not allow the use of the prior case to show the identity of the murderer based upon a pattern of behavior. However, he did rule that the prior crime would be admissible to compare to the recent case in order to prove a common motive. This latitude would then support an inference of premeditation and a specific intent to kill.

The forensic evidence developed by both the forensic anthropological and archaeological investigation was important in several respects. Most important, the evidence served as foundation for the motive testimony by two behavioral experts; a specialist in forensic psychology, and another in forensic psychiatry. The behavioral testimony was the medium by which the jury was made aware of the prior crime. It came in as part of the foundation for the expert opinions of the psychologist and the psychiatrist.

Forensic anthropological observations established the identity of the victim and settled the fact that the boy met a violent death. The astonishing discoveries that the boy had been penetrated in the anal/genital region with a sharp knife, and the observation that there was preassault bondage were the stepping stones the behavioralists needed to conclude that this crime was motivated by sexual sadism. The forensic anthropologist also testified that there was peri- or immediate postmortem dismemberment of the victim. There was evidence of this type of behavior in the first McRae murder as well. The dismemberment in 1950 was incomplete, most likely because he had the wrong tool for the job.

The forensic archaeological investigation established the locus of the burial site despite severe area disturbance by the farm hand's backhoe and then by the Michigan State Police bulldozer. This evidence was also foundational to the argument that killers motivated by sexual sadism are known to collect memorabilia of their crimes to facilitate their reliving of the event. Here, because it was demonstrated that the body was buried literally one giant step from the suspect's door, the prosecution was able to argue that this was the ultimate memento of the crime. This evidence undoubtedly carried great emotional weight with the jury. The lower court judge, while ruling that there was sufficient evidence to justify a trial, commented that the relevance of all the other evidence and circumstantial conclusions would have been greatly diminished if it had not shown that the boy was twelve to fifteen feet from McRae's door.

The prosecutor structured this case to have various forensic scientists build on the testimony of earlier experts to present a comprehensive, albeit circumstantial, picture of the torture and murder of a young boy by a lifelong sexual predator. It is typical of the prosecutor's courtroom style that their arguments are spare and go directly to the point. This inevitably presents a more energetic case with a dramatic impact. The drawback to this approach is that each quantum of evidence and its staging is more critical since there is little redundancy, and each witness is scheduled with care for maximum dramatic effect. The forensic anthropological and archaeological evidence in the McRae case was of overwhelming significance to the prosecution.

Both anthropologists employed multimedia during their testimonies. This enhanced the dramatic impact of their presentations while simplifying the concepts for the lay, rural jury. It is safe to say that without the findings of these two scientists, presented as they were, the state could not have won this case. John McRae was again convicted of first-degree murder. This time he will not be released.

Conclusions

Whether as skeletal biologists or archaeologists, the role of anthropologists in forensic cases is rather routine. Forensic anthropologists typically report and testify about positive identification, including the biological profile, and, when appropriate, present evidence for the circumstances or manner of death. Archaeologists normally discuss the location and orientation of human remains and associated artifacts and details of the interment process. Both specialists may comment about time since death and deposition.

In the case presented, the forensic anthropologist described the remains, generated a biological profile, established a positive identification, and presented evidence for perimortem or immediate postmortem mutilation

of the body. The archaeologist established the location of the initial grave and its position relative to several buildings that were on the property when the remains were buried, but which had long been removed. In concert, these contributions provided a sequenced trajectory of perimortem and postmortem events related to the murder and disposition of Randy Laufer. What makes this case particularly interesting and informative is the way this information was used to develop a strong, albeit circumstantial case against a suspect.

Typically, when an expert steps down from the witness stand that is the last he or she hears of the case. This illustrates how forensic anthropology and archaeology articulate with a broader judicial framework and assists in understanding the potential impact and use of our contributions. It also underscores the importance of good communication between scientists and appropriate attorneys throughout a case.

Acknowledgments

The authors thank Steve Symes, Ph.D., for his assistance with the analysis of the cut marks and for contributing several of the photographs used in this chapter.

References

Michigan Rules of Evidence (MRE) 404 (b).
People v. Golohowicz, 413 Mich 298 (1982).
People v. Modelski, 164 Mich App 337 (1987).
People v. VanderVliet, 444 Mich 52 (1993).
Sauer, Norman J. 1998. The timing of injuries and manner of death: Distinguishing among antemortem, perimortem, and postmortem trauma. Pp. 321–332 in *Forensic Osteology: Advances in the Identification of Human Remains*, ed. Kathleen J. Reichs. Springfield, IL: Charles C. Thomas.
Sigler-Eisenberg, B. 1985. Forensic research: Expanding the concept of applied archaeology. *American Antiquity* 50:650–655.
Ubelaker, Douglas H., and Bradley J. Adams. 1995. Differentiation of perimortem and postmortem trauma using taphonomic indicators. *Journal of Forensic Sciences* 40(3):509–512.

INTERPRETATION OF TRAUMA
AND TAPHONOMY

As the 1997 fall harvest approached, a midwestern farmer walked his field to inspect the crops and made a grisly discovery. Amidst the bending corn stalks were the nearly skeletonized remains of what the farmer made out to be a man, based on the boots. Without disturbing the body, the farmer called the police who brought the remains to the medical examiner's office. The forensic pathologist laid out the remains, recognized that visual or fingerprint identification would be impossible, and asked a forensic anthropologist to conduct an analysis of identity, perimortem trauma, and time since death.

There was differential decomposition of the body. While the skull, thorax, and legs were completely skeletonized, significant soft tissue remained on the hands, though rodents had consumed the fingertips. Police officers observed that the individual was found face down with the hands tucked under the body, which considerably reduced the rate of their decomposition. The feet were still in the boots and a great amount of adipocere was present. A large number of crickets, maggots, and beetles were also found on the remains. Samples of these insects were collected and sent to an entomologist to identify the species and determine their stage of development in order to estimate the postmortem interval.

Anthropological analysis revealed the following biological profile: a white male, twenty to thirty years of age at death, height between 65 and 71 inches, with vertebral arthritis and a compression fracture of the eighth thoracic vertebra. Only one missing man fit this biological profile and his dental records matched the dental characteristics of the remains. While identification was straightforward, the next two questions were much more challenging. How long ago had he died? Are defects observed on the skeleton due to blunt or sharp trauma that occurred at the time of death or did they occur after his death as his body lay decomposing in the cornfield?

Both of these questions involve an understanding of taphonomic principles, while the latter also necessitates a strong background in bone biomechanics. Taphonomy is the study of postdepositional processes; that is, the factors that modify the body after death. Skeletal damage that occurs during and after decomposition can mimic or mask blunt and sharp trauma that transpired at the time of death. Further, bones can be completely destroyed by taphonomic processes, resulting in the loss of potential evidence. In the case described above, the skeletal wounds were inconsistent with cuts, stabs, or chopping wounds typical of sharp trauma, and there were no perimortem fractures. Based on the morphology of the wounds and the color of their margins, the wounds were attributed to postmortem damage, including plant root growth, rodent scavenging, and weathering. The issue of just how long this man had been dead was still problematic, however.

Estimation of the time since death, often called the postmortem interval (PMI), has traditionally been one of the most difficult parameters to estimate in forensic anthropology cases. Before studies began at the University of Tennessee in the early 1980s (see below), there was little information about how different environmental variables affect human decay rates. Thanks in large part to the Tennessee studies, forensic anthropologists now have a good understanding of the phases of human decomposition. Experimental studies are now conducted all around the world to examine human decay rates in various microenvironments (e.g., Lopes de Carvalho and Linhares 2001; VanLaerhoven and Anderson 1999). However, at the time the skeleton was found in the cornfield, there were no midwestern regional studies to provide guidelines as to how quickly a body might decompose on the ground surface in the late summer. Further, the anthropologist's previous experiences were from the American Southwest—a hot, arid environment quite different from the humid Midwest summers. Ultimately, investigators determined that the man had died of an intentional insulin overdose two months before his skeleton was discovered, and this was consistent with experimental anthropological studies of the postmortem interval in that region. However, this case and dozens like it each year underscore the need for local studies of human decomposition.

The chapters in this section address three principal topics—interpretation of perimortem trauma, estimation of the postmortem interval, and instances in which taphonomic processes were key to the resolution of a case. Since the chapters are quite comprehensive on their respective topics, this brief overview will consider only the basic principles of taphonomy and trauma interpretation.

PATHOLOGICAL AND ANTHROPOLOGICAL INTERPRETATION OF PERIMORTEM TRAUMA

Forensic pathologists are tasked with determining the cause, manner, and mechanism of death through an extensive external and internal analysis of perimortem trauma. According to DiMaio and DiMaio (2001) (and discussed in Chapter 8), the *cause of death* is any mechanism that leads to physiological failure to an extent that the individual dies. Therefore, a potential cause of death could be atherosclerosis, a stab wound to the chest, a gunshot wound to the head, or pneumonia. The *mechanism of death* is the actual physiological process that results in death. This process of death is initiated by the cause of death. Mechanism of death can include cardiac arrhythmia and hemorrhage. The *manner of death* is an explanation of the circumstances of death. There are five medicolegal classifications of manner of death—homicide, suicide, natural, accidental, and undetermined.

While a forensic anthropologist may make recommendations as to the cause and manner of death based on his or her interpretation of skeletal trauma, it is ultimately the medicolegal responsibility of the forensic pathologist to make the final determinations.

Forensic pathologists have developed several cause of death categories, including electrocution, asphyxia, natural diseases, blunt trauma, sharp trauma, and gunshot trauma (DiMaio and DiMaio 2001; Dix and Calaluce 1998). Since forensic anthropologists are rarely called to interpret perimortem wounds of soft tissue lacking bony involvement, they focus instead on the types of wounds that leave distinctive marks on the skeleton—sharp, blunt, and gunshot trauma.

There are dozens of different firearms and scores of projectiles available in the United States, and indeed gunshot wounds are the leading cause of violent death in this country (National Center for Injury Prevention and Control 1999). When confronted with firearms fatalities, forensic pathologists may attempt to determine the cause and manner of death by assessing the trajectory of the projectile and range of fire (DiMaio 1999). However, since the diagnostic markers of gunshot distance are on the skin and/or within the soft tissue wound track, the anthropologist typically cannot assess range of fire when soft tissue is absent. Determination of the caliber of a bullet by examining the morphology and size of the entrance wound is also unreliable (Berryman et al. 1995). However, anthropologists can make a significant contribution to a death investigation by examining fracture patterns and the beveling of entrance and exit wounds to determine the direction of fire (e.g., front to back, left to right) and the minimum number of bullets that impact a skeleton.

Blunt and sharp force trauma provide a number of challenges to a forensic team, but typically an anthropologist will examine the fracture or cut patterns to attempt to estimate the minimum number of blows or stabs, the direction of impact, and the class characteristics of the offending object. Class characteristics are those that define a particular group of objects (e.g., a long rounded item, such as a lead pipe or bat, or a sharp, pointed item such as a knife). In special cases, individual characteristics may also be elucidated from an injury pattern. Individual characteristics are those that are unique to a particular item, such as a defect in a pipe. Firearms examiners use class characteristics to determine the caliber of a bullet and individual characteristics to match a bullet recovered from a crime scene to a bullet test-fired from a suspect's weapon. While the anthropologist may be able to discern some helpful class characteristics of a blunt or sharp weapon, individualization of weapons based on the analysis of bony defects is much more rare.

Perimortem trauma must be effectively discriminated from trauma or pseudo-trauma resulting from postmortem processes, as well as antemortem pathologies that show signs of healing. It is also important to note that the absence of such markers in the skeleton does not necessarily mean that the individual did not suffer perimortem trauma. Since the ribs protect the thoracic organs, they will often show evidence of forceful trauma to the chest, yet penetrating abdominal wounds may not involve bone. Further, many skeletons are incomplete and it is always possible that the missing bones may have had evidence of perimortem trauma.

TAPHONOMY AND THE ESTIMATION OF TIME SINCE DEATH

In the broadest sense, taphonomy is the study of postmortem changes of the body. Originally developed in the field of paleontology, the study of fossils, taphonomic principles are applicable to forensic anthropology in a number of ways, including the identification of variables that affect human decomposition in different micro- and macroenvironments, the estimation of the time since death, and differentiation of postmortem changes from perimortem trauma (Bass 1984; Haglund and Sorg 1997, 2002; Mann and Owsley 1992; Micozzi 1991; Rodriguez and Bass 1983).

Forensic anthropologists have long known that particular variables such as temperature and insects affect human decay rates, yet few mechanisms were in place to systematically study them. In response to this void, Dr. William Bass initiated the Archaeological Research Facility at the University of Tennessee, Knoxville, in 1980. Researchers at this unique facility place human cadavers in various microenvironments (e.g., burial, submersion, automobile, ground surface) and then record their observations of specific variables, such as ambient temperature, insect activity, humidity, and, if the corpse is visible, the morphological changes of the body as it decays.

The earliest studies of human decomposition at the Archaeological Research Facility focused upon the impact of insect activity on decomposition (Rodriguez and Bass 1983) and the rate of decay of buried and "surface" bodies (Rodriguez and Bass 1985). Mann and colleagues (1990) summarize some of the more important decomposition variables based on collective research at the Facility (Table III.1). The authors note that, "the overwhelming majority of soft-tissue destruction is due to feeding by insect larvae" (1990, 106). They observed that a fresh body could be rendered a skeleton in only one week during hot, humid periods in eastern Tennessee. Indeed, many of the variables in Table III.1, such as temperature and clothing, are considered important because they can significantly impact insect activity.

Forensic anthropologists and entomologists have great respect for insects, not only on account of their propensity to find a deceased body in nearly any context, but because they can provide reliable information concerning the postmortem interval. The life cycle of most species is well known. For instance, flies (Diptera) are typically the first insects that are attracted to the corpse. The females lay their egg masses in natural orifices or artificial openings of the body, such as wounds (Figure III.1). The eggs hatch within one to three days, depending on the species and environmental conditions, and the larvae (maggots) immediately begin to feed on the flesh by secreting enzymes that liquefy the tissues (see Figure III.2 on page 132). Within a few days to weeks, the maggots, now fat and happy, leave the body, burrow under the ground (if in an outdoor setting) to pupate, and finally emerge as adult flies from the puparia several days later (Haskell et al. 1997). The life cycle of a fly can be used to estimate the postmortem interval if climatic data is available from a nearby meteorological station. According to Haskell et al. (1997, 431), "the approach is to identify the species collected from a corpse of unknown PMI, note the stage of development, retrospectively obtain weather records for the area in question, and calculate the amount of time that would have been required to 'drive' that insect species from the egg (or first instar larva, as appropriate) to the stage collected."

TABLE III.1   SOME VARIABLES AFFECTING THE RATE OF DECAY OF HUMAN REMAINS

VARIABLE	SCORE*	EFFECT
Temperature	5	Faster decay in high temperatures due in part to insect activity; slowed or ceased decay process in cold temperatures (below freezing)
Access by insects	5	Very rapid decay if weather conditions are warm enough for oviposition and maggot activity
Burial and depth	5	Bodies buried one foot or more will decompose much slower (months to years) than bodies laid on the surface (a few weeks to a few months)
Carnivores and rodents	4	Can consume and destroy specific tissues (e.g., face, hands) and remove smaller skeletal elements
Trauma (penetrating/crushing)	4	Increases decay rate in wound areas due to insect activity
Humidity/aridity	4	Higher humidity correlated with increased insect activity
Rainfall	3	Little or no effect on maggot activity; decreased fly activity during heavy rains
Body size and weight	3	No strong connection between body size and decay, though body composition does play a role (obese individuals lose mass quickly due to liquification of fats)
Clothing	2	Slightly increases rate of decay because it protects maggots

*Subjective criteria rating based on a five-point scale, 5 being the most influential (Mann et al. 1990).
Source: Adapted from Mann et al. (1990) and Rodriguez and Bass (1985).

FIGURE III.1   FEMALE FLIES OVIPOSIT EGG MASSES IN THE MOUTH AND NOSE OF A PIG LESS THAN FOUR HOURS AFTER DEPOSITION (AUGUST 30)

FIGURE III.2   EXTENSIVE MAGGOT ACTIVITY TWO DAYS AFTER DEPOSITION

Note the pool of liquefied decomposition products on the ground and the exposure of the mandible. The maggot mass had also moved the forelimb several inches from its original position.

The flies are not the only insects interested in feasting on the corpse. Other insect species become attracted to the remains as the maggots reduce the soft tissues of the body (Byrd and Castner 2001). Various species of beetles (Coleoptera) enter the scene to feed on the tougher connective tissues (ligaments and cartilage) and on the maggots. These may be followed by ticks, ants, and cockroaches. The corpse becomes a biota for insects, often as many as "hundreds of species and thousands of individuals" (Catts and Haskell 1990, 29). The orderly attraction of different insect species to a corpse throughout the decomposition process is called succession, and forensic anthropologists and entomologists can also use the pattern of succession to estimate the time since deposition (e.g., Goff 1993; Anderson 2001).

In addition to the postmortem interval, insects can provide clues concerning other important taphonomic factors or events. For instance, if a nonindigenous species is found on the corpse, it may indicate the corpse has been moved from a different geographic region. Since different insect species are only active during specific seasons, the presence of a certain species, or their puparia, can shed light on the season in which the body was deposited. As mentioned above, adult female flies look for body orifices in which to lay their eggs, and this is where the maggots first begin to consume the flesh. Thus, intense insect activity away from a natural orifice may suggest the presence of a perimortem wound that provided a different portal of entry into the body. Maggots will also consume whatever toxins might be present in the body, including drugs such as cocaine and heroin, which is stored in their exoskeleton. Therefore, maggots or their puparia can undergo a toxicological screening (Beyer et al. 1980; Bourel et al. 2001; Goff and Lord 1994; Introna et al. 1990). Further, Wells and colleagues (2001) and Lord et al. (1998) have successfully isolated and sequenced human mitochondrial DNA from insects that had fed upon human corpses. This has tremendous implications for forensic identifications, for insects may provide an additional source of human DNA that can be sequenced for the purposes of identification.

REGIONAL TAPHONOMY STUDIES

Forensic taphonomy is a subject ripe for research, and one of the most important areas of inquiry is the macro- and microenvironmental variables that impact human decay rates in different geographic regions. Entomological and taphonomic information from Tennessee is not readily applicable to other areas of the country. The temperate, wooded environment of eastern Tennessee is quite different from the arid Southwest, the tropics of Hawaii, or other geographic areas where there are greater climatic extremes throughout the year. Further, many of the plant, animal, and insect species observed in the Tennessee facility are region-specific. As a result, many anthropologists have initiated experimental taphonomic studies in other localities (e.g., Goff and Flynn 1991), or accumulated data from local forensic cases to provide an appropriate model for their region (e.g., Galloway et al. 1989; Manhein 1997).

If human cadavers are not available, researchers can conduct regional decomposition studies on pigs (*Sus scrofa*), which make excellent models for human decomposition. The pig integument system (skin) is much like ours, and they lack fur or thick hair. Further, the size, shape, and internal anatomy of the thorax are similar among pigs and humans. A 23–50 kg pig is typically recommended for studies that model adult human decomposition, though size does not seem to alter decompositional patterns or insect succession significantly (Hewadikaram and Goff 1991). Exciting areas of current taphonomic research using both humans and nonhuman models include technically sophisticated studies of the rate and products of soft tissue decomposition (e.g., Vass et al. 1992; Yan et al. 2001), and the effect of decomposition on nuclear and mitochondrial DNA recovery from bones (e.g., Perry et al. 1988; Rankin et al. 1996).

THE CHAPTERS

The chapters in this section represent the diversity of interpretive problems that forensic anthropologists face beyond the assessment of personal identity. In Chapter 10, Smith and colleagues provide a series of case studies that illustrate the biomechanical properties of blunt, sharp, and gunshot trauma, the most common trauma types encountered in forensic anthropological casework. While most papers and texts emphasize craniofacial trauma, the authors supply considerable documentation of postcranial trauma. The authors also illustrate the mutual benefit of collaboration between forensic pathologists and anthropologists to ensure accurate interpretation of perimortem trauma involving both soft and hard tissues.

In many cases, the identity of the deceased is known and the forensic anthropologist is asked to offer an opinion concerning the nature of perimortem trauma. A case from Hawaii, presented by Ubelaker and Smialek, is a good example of the interpretive challenges anthropologists and pathologists best face together when multiple types of perimortem injuries are evident. How many weapons were used? What was the nature of the weapon(s)? Which traumatic events occurred first? Which wounds might have proved fatal? Do the forensic results corroborate a suspect's story or implicate him or her? This chapter also illustrates the important components of a forensic case report, including the use of precise measurements and appropriate anatomical terminology to properly describe various forms of perimortem trauma.

In Chapter 12, Love and Marks provide a comprehensive overview of the most important taphonomic variables that affect human decomposition. They present a tragic case of two murdered children, found within a few meters of each other, yet in radically different stages of decomposition. What accounts for these differences? Were the children deposited at the same time or at different times? Could their deaths be linked? The authors also discuss some of the latest areas of taphonomic research, including recent anthropological interest in the earliest stages of decomposition, a topic traditionally relegated to the pathologist.

Human skulls are often found in the most bizarre places—locations that hold few or no clues about the origin or identity of the individual. Thus, anthropologists examine the characteristics of the skull itself to understand its context. In Chapter 13, Willey and Leach present an example of this relatively common yet problematic type of case. A skull found in a yard of an otherwise quiet neighborhood has distinctive biological and postmortem characteristics that the authors, based on previous experiences and research, believe are indicative of a "trophy" skull. The authors discuss the nature of trophy skulls and how they can be identified in a forensic context.

Postmortem alterations are also important in the final chapter of this section. In Chapter 14, Anderson and colleagues analyze the dismembered and incomplete remains of a man who washed up on a Hawaiian shore. Numerous cut marks are clearly visible on the femur. Utilizing a scanning electron microscope, the researchers observe that an enamel particle, perhaps a shark's tooth, is embedded in the bone. Could the shark attack be the cause of death or is this a case of postmortem scavenging? Can entomological evidence be of value when remains are exposed to both marine and terrestrial environments? The authors pursue a number of lines of inquiry to answer these and other questions, and discuss many of the taphonomic processes unique to marine postdepositional contexts.

REFERENCES

Anderson, Gail S. 2001. Insect succession on carrion and its relationship to determining time of death. Pp. 143–175 in *Forensic Entomology: The Utility of Arthropods in Legal Investigations*, ed. Jason H. Byrd and James L. Castner. Boca Raton, FL: CRC Press.

Bass, William M. 1984. Time interval since death: A difficult decision. Pp. 136–147 in *Human Identification: Case Studies in Forensic Anthropology*, ed. Ted A. Rathbun and Jane E. Buikstra. Springfield, IL: Charles C. Thomas.

Berryman, Hugh E., O. C. Smith, and Steven A. Symes. 1995. Diameter of cranial gunshot wounds as a function of bullet caliber. *Journal of Forensic Sciences* 40(5):751–754.

Beyer, J. C., W. F. Enos, and M. Stajic. 1980. Drug identification through analysis of maggots. *Journal of Forensic Sciences* 25:411–412.

Bourel, Benoit, Gilles Tournel, Valery Hedouin, M. Lee Goff, and Didier Gosset. 2001. Determination of drug levels in two species of necrophagous *coleoptera* reared on substrates containing morphine. *Journal of Forensic Sciences* 46(3):600–603.

Byrd, Jason H., and James L. Castner. 2001. Insects of forensic importance. Pp. 43–79 in *Forensic Entomology: The Utility of Arthropods in Legal Investigations*, ed. Jason H. Byrd and James L. Castner. Boca Raton, FL: CRC Press.

Catts, E. Paul, and Neal H. Haskell. 1990. *Entomology and Death: A Procedural Guide*. Clemson, SC: Joyce's Print Shop.

Center for Disease Control, National Center for Injury Prevention and Control. 10 Leading Causes of Death, United States, 1999.

DiMaio, Vincent J. M. 1999. *Gunshot Wounds: Practical Aspects of Firearms, Ballistics, and Forensic Techniques*. 2nd ed. Boca Raton, FL: CRC Press.

DiMaio, Vincent J., and Dominick DiMaio. 2001. *Forensic Pathology*. 2nd ed. Boca Raton, FL: CRC Press.

Dix, Jay, and Robert Calaluce. 1998. *Guide to Forensic Pathology*. Boca Raton, FL: CRC Press.

Galloway, Alison, Walter H. Birkby, Allen M. Jones, Thomas E. Henry, and Bruce O. Parks. 1989. Decay rates of human remains in an arid environment. *Journal of Forensic Sciences* 34(3):607–616.

Goff, M. Lee. 1993. Estimation of postmortem interval using arthropod development and successional patterns. *Forensic Science Review* 5(2):76–82.

Goff, M. Lee, and Wayne D. Lord. 1994. Entomotoxicology: A new area for forensic investigation. *American Journal of Forensic Medicine and Pathology* 15:51–57.

Goff, M. Lee, and M. M. Flynn. 1991. Determination of postmortem interval by arthropod succession: A case study from the Hawaiian Islands. *Journal of Forensic Sciences* 36:607–614.

Haglund, William D., and Marcella H. Sorg, eds. 1997. *Forensic Taphonomy: The Postmortem Fate of Human Remains*. Boca Raton, FL: CRC Press.

Haglund, William D., and Marcella H. Sorg, eds. 2002. *Advances in Forensic Taphonomy: Method, Theory, and Archaeological Perspectives*. Boca Raton, FL: CRC Press.

Haskell, Neal H., Robert D. Hall, Valerie J. Cervenka, and Michael A. Clark. 1997. On the body: Insects' life stage presence and their postmortem artifacts. Pp. 415–448 in *Forensic Taphonomy: The Postmortem Fate of Human Remains*, ed. William D. Haglund and Marcella H. Sorg. Boca Raton, FL: CRC Press.

Hewadikaram, K. A., and M. Lee Goff. 1991. Effect of carcass size on rate of decomposition and arthropod succession patterns. *American Journal of Forensic Medicine and Pathology* 12:235.

Introna, F., Jr., C. Lo Dico, Y. H. Caplan, and J. E. Smialek. 1990. Opiate analysis in cadaveric blowfly larvae as an indicator of narcotic intoxication. *Journal of Forensic Sciences* 35:118–122.

Lopes de Carvalho, L. M., and Aricio Xavier Linhares. 2001. Seasonality of insect succession and pig carcass decomposition in a natural forest area in southeastern Brazil. *Journal of Forensic Sciences* 46(3):604–608.

Lord, Wayne D., Joseph A. DiZinno, Mark R. Wilson, Bruce Budowle, David Taplin, and Terri L. Meinking. 1998. Isolation, amplification, and sequencing of human mitochondrial DNA obtained from human crab louse, *Pthirus Pubis* (L.), blood meals. *Journal of Forensic Sciences* 43(5):1097–1100.

Manhein, Mary H. 1997. Decomposition rates of deliberate burials: A case study of preservation. Pp. 469–481 in *Forensic Taphonomy: The Postmortem Fate of Human Remains*, ed. William D. Haglund and Marcella H. Sorg. Boca Raton, FL: CRC Press.

Mann, Robert W., and Douglas W. Owsley. 1992. Human osteology: Key to the sequence of events in a postmortem shooting. *Journal of Forensic Sciences* 37(5):1386–1392.

Mann, Robert W., William M. Bass, and Lee Meadows. 1990. Time since death and decomposition of the human body: Variables and observations in case and experimental field studies. *Journal of Forensic Sciences* 35:103–111.

Micozzi, Mark S. 1991. *Postmortem Changes in Human and Animal Remains*. Springfield, IL: Charles C. Thomas.

Perry, W. L., William M. Bass, W. S. Riggsby, and K. Sirotkin. 1988. The autodegradation of deoxyribonucleic acid (DNA) in human rib bone and its relationship to the time interval since death. *Journal of Forensic Sciences* 33(1):144–153.

Rankin, David R., D. S. Narveson, Walter H. Birkby, and J. Lal. 1996. Restriction fragment length polymorphism (RFLP) analysis on DNA from human compact bone. *Journal of Forensic Sciences* 41(1):40–46.

Rodriguez, William C., and William M. Bass. 1983. Insect activity and its relationship to decay rates of human cadavers in east Tennessee. *Journal of Forensic Sciences* 28:423–432.

Rodriguez, William C., and William M. Bass. 1985. Decomposition of buried bodies and methods that may aid in their location. *Journal of Forensic Sciences* 30(3):836–852.

Van Laerhoven, S., and Gail S. Anderson. 1999. Insect succession on buried carrion in two biogeoclimatic zones of British Columbia. *Journal of Forensic Sciences* 44(1):32–43.

Vass Arpad A., William M. Bass, J. D. Wolt, J. E. Foss, and J. T. Ammons. 1992. Time since death determinations of human cadavers using soil solution. *Journal of Forensic Sciences* 37(5):1236–1253.

Wells, Jeffrey D., Francesco Introna, Jr., Giancarlo Di Vella, Carlo P. Campobasso, Jack Hayes, and Felix A. H. Sperling. 2001. Human and insect mitochondrial DNA analysis from maggots. *Journal of Forensic Sciences* 46(3):685–687.

Yan, Fei, Randall McNally, Elias J. Kontanis, and Omowunmi A. Sadik. 2001. Preliminary quantitative investigation of postmortem adipocere formation. *Journal of Forensic Sciences* 46(3):609–614.

FURTHER READING

Boddington, A., A. N. Garland, and R. C. Janaway, eds. 1987. *Death, Decay and Reconstruction: Approaches to Archaeology and Forensic Science*. Manchester, UK: Manchester University Press.

Dixon, D. S. 1984. Pattern of intersecting fractures and direction of fire. *Journal of Forensic Sciences* 29(2):651–654.

Erzinclioglu, Y. Z. 1983. The application of entomology to forensic medicine. *Medicine, Science, and the Law* 23:57–63.

Galloway, Alison, ed. 1999. *Broken Bones*. Springfield, IL: Charles C. Thomas.

Gilbert, B. M., and William M. Bass. 1967. Seasonal dating of burials from the presence of fly pupae. *American Antiquity* 32:534–535.

Goff, M. Lee. 2000. *A Fly for the Prosecution*. Cambridge, MA: Harvard University Press.

Greenberg, Bernard. 1985. Forensic entomology: Case studies. *Bulletin of the Entomological Society of America* 31:25–28.

Haskell, Neal H., Wayne D. Lord, and Jason H. Byrd. 2001. Collection of entomological evidence during death investigations. Pp. 81–120 in *Forensic Entomology: The Utility of Arthropods in Legal Investigations*, ed. Jason H. Byrd and James L. Castner. Boca Raton, FL: CRC Press.

Rhine, J. Stanley, and B. K. Curran. 1990. Multiple gunshot wounds of the head: An anthropological view. *Journal of Forensic Sciences* 35(5):1236–1245.

Sauer, Norman J. 1984. Manner of death: Skeletal evidence of blunt and sharp instrument wounds. Pp. 176–184 in *Human Identification: Case Studies in Forensic Anthropology*, ed. Ted A. Rathbun and Jane E. Buikstra. Springfield, IL: Charles C. Thomas.

Schoenly, Kenneth, Karien Griest, and Stanley Rhine. 1991. An experimental field protocol for investigating the postmortem interval using multidisciplinary indicators. *Journal of Forensic Sciences* 36:1395–1413.

Smith, O'Brien C., Hugh E. Berryman, and C. H. Lahren. 1987. Cranial fracture patterns and estimate of direction from low velocity gunshot wounds. *Journal of Forensic Sciences* 32(5):1416–1421.

Smith, O'Brien C., Steven A. Symes, Hugh E. Berryman, and M. M. LeVaughn. 1991. Matching bullets to bone impact signatures. *Journal of Forensic Sciences* 36(6):1736–1739.

Ubelaker, Douglas H. 1996. The remains of Dr. Carl Austin Weiss: Anthropological analysis. *Journal of Forensic Sciences* 41(1):60–79.

CHAPTER

10

LOOK UNTIL YOU SEE

IDENTIFICATION OF TRAUMA IN SKELETAL MATERIAL

O. C. Smith, Elayne J. Pope, and Steven A. Symes

A man dies from a gunshot wound to the head. Is it suicide or homicide? A victim falls amid multiple gunshots and multiple suspects. From what direction did the bullets come? A man is beaten to death but which weapon was used? These are questions forensic pathologists and anthropologists are expected to answer, often in the complete absence of soft tissue information.

The medical examiner setting provides unlimited opportunity for the anthropologist to observe and study traumatic cases, including gunshot wounds and blunt and sharp force trauma, as well as deaths due to thermal injuries, drowning, exsanguination, asphyxia, electrocution, poisoning, drug overdose, and natural diseases. While anthropologists rarely assist in cases that do not involve skeletal tissue, they are invaluable assets to forensic pathologists when skeletal trauma is present. Anthropologists are often vital when conventional methods of identifying human remains have become obscured through decomposition, skeletonization, taphonomic changes, dismemberment, burning, or extensive trauma. Their expertise in skeletal biology becomes an important resource to

pathologists when soft tissues are absent or noncontributory (decomposed, scavenged, or mummified). Their assistance to the medical examiner and forensic pathologist addresses not only questions concerning personal identification, but also focuses on understanding skeletal trauma that may help explain events surrounding the victim's death.

During a typical year, the Regional Forensic Center in Memphis, Tennessee, averages 250 cases involving skeletal injury requiring collaborative investigation. The Medical Examiner's Office in Memphis is staffed by forensic pathologists who place a high value on forensic anthropology and recognize the important scientific contribution the discipline brings to trauma interpretation and personal identification. By including anthropologists at autopsy, they have a unique opportunity to observe and correlate the relationship between skin and soft tissue injuries with the patterns of underlying skeletal trauma.

This chapter highlights three of the most common types of trauma encountered by forensic anthropologists: ballistic, blunt, and sharp force trauma. Supporting case studies will demonstrate the material application of trauma interpretation, including the biomechanical properties of bone and expected fracture patterns associated with each trauma type.

Bone Chemistry and Biomechanics

It is fundamental to understand that the appearance, or morphology, of bony injuries reflects not only the shape, area, mass, speed, and direction of the instrument applying the external force, but also the intrinsic strength, anatomy, thickness, mineral content, and overall health of the bone. Objects capable of producing high-velocity impacts, such as gunshots, impart their energy so suddenly that bone reacts as a brittle material and shatters. Lower energy bending forces and slower impacts from blunt force trauma deliver a gradual rate of loading, causing the bone to react more as a ductile material capable of showing plastic deformation (Watkins 1999). Sharp force injuries may have a blend of characteristics involving incised bone combined with blunt force trauma. A brief overview of the biomechanical properties of bone is necessary to comprehend the unique morphology trauma produces in skeletal material.

Consider first the morphology and function of bone. Bone must support body weight and anchor muscles against their powerful contracting forces, yet be light and strong for active movement. If bone were brittle like glass, it would support weight well yet fracture the moment a muscle tried to pull that bone out of alignment with the ground. Conversely, were bones as pliable as a nylon rope our bodies would collapse from the lack of an internal framework. The heterogeneous, visco-elastic structure of bone provides adaptive responses to both extremes. Hydroxyapatite crystals and calcium salts are the stiff (viscous), unyielding, brittle component, while the collagen matrix is elastic, yielding,

and ductile. This composite structure not only demonstrates the versatility of bone as a structural material, it is also responsible for the unique morphology of fractures and defects caused by trauma.

Gunshot Trauma

During medicolegal investigations of homicides and suicides, forensic anthropologists frequently encounter gunshot wound injuries. Identification of the signature patterns of gunshot wounds is essential to determine the orientation of the victim relative to the shooter or the sequence of wounds. There are distinguishing characteristics of both entry and exit wounds in soft tissue and bone, as well as the fractures that radiate from these wounds.

Initial ballistic impact perpendicular to cranial bone produces a circular hole with a smooth, rounded border on the external table of the skull. As the bullet punches through this layer, it creates a ragged, cone-shaped *internal bevel* on the adjoining internal table of bone. This defect is typical for an entrance wound (see Figure 10.1 on page 140). A bullet with sufficient velocity will continue to travel in a straight path through the cranial vault, where it will generate a similar defect in bone when it exits. The exit will look like a reversal of the entrance since the external table of bone exhibits a ragged, cone-shaped *external bevel*. Variations in exit wound appearance can be due to decrease in velocity, projectile deformation or tumbling, and interference by entrance fractures (DiMaio 1999, Smith et al. 1993).

In addition to the primary entrance and exit wounds, ballistic trauma may create secondary fracture patterns in bone that can aid in determining the sequence of fire. Three morphologically distinct fracture types are associated with gunshot wounds: plug and spall, radiating, and heaving concentric (Smith 1996).

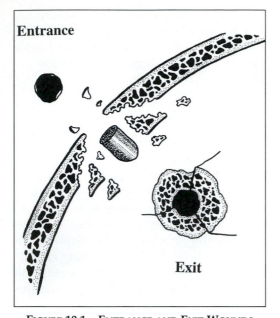

Entrance

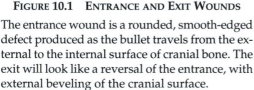

Exit

FIGURE 10.1   ENTRANCE AND EXIT WOUNDS

The entrance wound is a rounded, smooth-edged defect produced as the bullet travels from the external to the internal surface of cranial bone. The exit will look like a reversal of the entrance, with external beveling of the cranial surface.

Plug and spall fractures are the result of initial impact when the projectile punches through the external table to the internal table as it enters the bone. Minimal force may create only the plug and spall. Greater forces produce fractures that radiate from the impact site (Figure 10.2). These radiating fractures occur in response to tensile forces as pressure increases inside the skull. When radiating fractures cannot sufficiently relieve the pressure, heaving concentric fractures are produced as internal pressure sequentially levers out bones of the skull.

Interpretation of these fracture patterns will aid in understanding the sequence and direction of gunshot wounds to bone. Three basic biomechanical principles to remember include the following:

1.   Bone beveling does not lie and is the best indicator of projectile direction.

2.   Radiating fractures will continue to form and expand until pressures subside or until energy is dissipated into an existing fracture or another structure that can absorb energy, such as sutures. Thus, secondary fractures typically "T" into pre-existing fractures.

3.   Fractures that radiate from an entrance wound travel at a much faster rate than any bullet. Therefore, fractures may travel to the other side of the skull faster than the bullet can exit, which can produce an atypical fracture or exit wound morphology.

Three case studies demonstrate the biomechanical principles of typical and some atypical features of gunshot trauma in the skull and postcranial remains, as well as problems encountered during some analyses.

Case 1: Suicide or Murder?

A forty-eight-year-old male was brought to the medical examiner's office with a single gunshot wound to the head. The deceased had not been seen for five days and family members were concerned about the nature of his death since his wife had recently moved out and filed for divorce after thirteen years of marriage. Upon interviewing the wife, she did not seem surprised that her husband had been found dead and she related that he had threatened suicide on numerous occasions. He did own a gun and was in possession of it two weeks earlier when she moved out. Was this a case of suicide or murder? In this case, the pathologist was able to make this assessment by closely examining the wounds and fracture patterns created by ballistic penetration through soft tissue and bone.

The external examination of the decomposed remains did not readily reveal the direction of the bullet path since soft tissues had dried and decompositional fluids obscured the bone. In fact, the wound to the front of the head appeared to have entrance

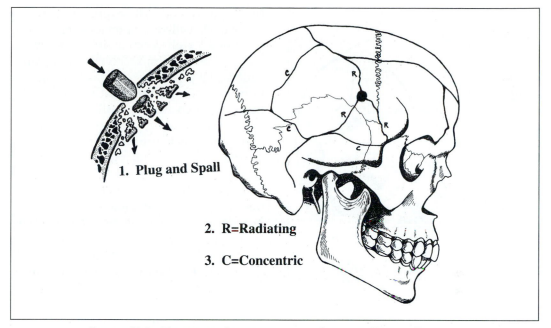

FIGURE 10.2   FRACTURES ASSOCIATED WITH GUNSHOT WOUND TRAUMA

Fractures associated with gunshot wound trauma include the plug and spall, radiating and heaving concentric fractures.

and exit beveling. Since initial examination of the tissues was confusing, an anthropologist was asked to consult.

After processing and reconstructing the cranial fragments, the anthropologist was able to determine the path of the bullet entry and exit. A smooth-edged circular hole with internal beveling, consistent with an entrance wound, was observed in the lower right portion of the occipital. A second large, externally beveled defect observed on the left portion of the frontal bone above the eye orbit was consistent with an exit wound. Based on the orientation of these features alone, the path of the bullet was determined to travel from back to front and right to left.

Closer examination of the exit site revealed the reason for confusion on initial analysis. Half of the feature is an outwardly beveled semicircle and the other half abuts a straight margin of bone. This atypical exit

formed when a radiating fracture associated with the entrance wound traveled around the skull prior to the exit of the bullet. When the bullet exited, it punched out a typical outward beveled exit, but much of the energy was immediately absorbed by the preexisting fractures from the entrance wound, thus resulting in the semicircular appearance (see Figure 10.3 on page 142).

Next, the relative position of the gun to the victim could be reconstructed. In this case, the location and appearance of the entrance wound at the back of the victim's head suggested that it was more than likely a homicide rather than a suicide due to the range and direction of fire. The shot was oriented perpendicular to the back of the victim's head. Additionally, the weapon was never recovered in the vicinity of the victim, findings unlikely in a self-inflicted injury. Based on this evidence, suicide was ruled out. Three weeks later, investigators found

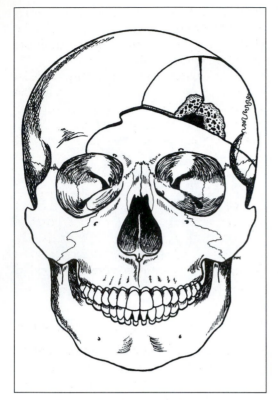

FIGURE 10.3   RADIATING FRACTURES

Radiating fractures produced by the entrance preceded the exit of the bullet. The presence of a fracture absorbed a portion of the bullet's energy, resulting in a semicircular defect as the exit.

additional evidence that implicated the victim's spouse, who ultimately confessed to firing a single shot into the back of her husband's head.

Case 2: Direction of Fire

A twenty-five-year-old man was found in his neighborhood with multiple gunshot wounds to the head. Witnesses had reported that several shots had been fired during the confrontation and multiple shooters may have been involved. During autopsy, the anthropologist recovered enough bone fragments to establish the number of bullets and direction of fire by reconstructing

the entrance and exit wounds of a single bullet track. Unlike the previous case, which exhibited a well-defined circular entrance wound, this victim received a tangential shot to the top of the head, resulting in a large and complicated exit wound of the head. In this case, the bullet entered the skull at an oblique, shallow angle rather than perpendicular to the bone. These tangential strikes are similar to a perpendicular wound at the initial impact, but as the bullet goes on edge with the bone, a fan-shaped defect is produced, commonly called a keyhole defect due to the shape of the resulting trauma (Dixon 1982; Coe 1982). The projectile not only bevels the bone inward, but also chips it to produce an outward bevel (Figure 10.4).

Features of the ballistic trauma to the skull of this victim are typical tangential gunshot wound characteristics (Figure 10.5). The entrance is a long, oval shape with a smooth, round margin soiled by bullet

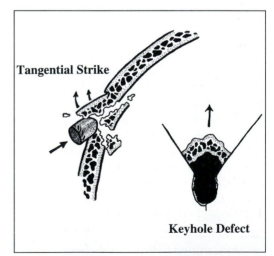

FIGURE 10.4   KEYHOLE DEFECT

A keyhole defect is the result of a tangential strike by a bullet that produces beveling of bone inward and chipping outward. The shape is created by the shallow entry of the bullet that produces an oblong opening, followed by a fan-shaped outward beveling of bone.

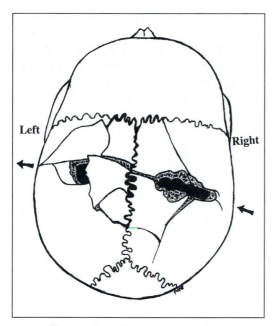

FIGURE 10.5 TANGENTIAL STRIKE

Tangential strike of the bullet on the vault produced a keyhole defect, making it possible to interpret the trajectory.

metal at one end and an externally beveled, fan-shaped edge at the other end. The smooth-edged defect is where the bullet initially punched into bone, while the opposing side of this oval defect is where the bone levered out from the shallow angle of the penetrating projectile. In addition, the bullet tunneled through and under bone, producing an irregularly shaped exit wound due to preexisting fractures from the entrance. The short distance between the entrance and exit sites, combined with the directional forces from the shallow angle of the bullet, produced a rapid outward levering of the bone. With an understanding of these biomechanics, the trajectory became clear. The bullet traveled from right to left transecting the gentle curve of the vault, just grazing the top of his head and only tunneling under the bone for inches. Of the five suspects, this implicated two who were seen standing near the right side of the victim at

the time of the shooting. It was also determined that only a single gunshot struck the victim, despite witnesses hearing multiple shots that night.

It was critical to have an anthropologist present during autopsy in this case. The shallow angle of entry and multiple exiting bullet and bone fragments at the top of the head produced complex skin wounds that were difficult to interpret. In order to assess the trajectory and direction of fire, the anthropologist had to reconstruct the cranial fragments. Recognizing characteristics of the keyhole defect in the skull made it possible to distinguish the point of entry from the exit wound. The trajectory of a bullet can also be determined from postcranial gunshot wounds, the subject of the next case.

Case 3: Postcranial Wounds—Long Bones

A defendant charged with murder testified that he and an unknown drug dealer, the victim, argued over an exchange that allegedly had just occurred in deserted woods on the edge of town. The fight escalated to the point at which the drug dealer pulled out a gun. The defendant testified that he likewise pulled a gun from his car in self-defense. Although there was no denying the presence of firearms, the defendant claimed he used his weapon purely for self-defense. When the victim cocked and raised his gun, the defendant felt threatened and fired a single shot. The defendant saw the victim fall, at which time he jumped into his car and sped off. When the shooter was picked up for questioning four months later, he stated that he had no indication of the severity of the victim's wounds, and while, yes, they were attempting to exchange illegal drugs, he did not start the conflict and was shocked to hear the drug dealer did not survive the gunshot.

Normally, soft tissue injuries possess clear indications of entrance and exit wound features. However, a delay in reporting the incident allowed the remains to decompose. Therefore, it became necessary to consult an anthropologist at autopsy to establish the direction of fire. Analysis of the ballistic injuries after processing of the remains indicated the victim had been shot in the lower right leg by a single bullet.

Features of ballistic damage to long bones are similar to those seen in the cranium, which include smooth-edged entrance defects associated with a punched out plug, as well as radiating and concentric fractures resulting from the energy of penetration. But by the time the bullet exits, the radial and concentric fractures have already reached the far side of the bone and have compromised the tubular structure. Thus, the exit wound may not be recognizable in many diaphyseal bones since fragments of bone become displaced before the bullet exits. This case was further complicated by the fact that the bone was greatly fragmented and commingled with soft tissue, which made analysis difficult. Thus, reconstruction of the fragments in order to identify the type of trauma and the direction of fire was essential (Figure 10.6).

The reconstructed tibia revealed an obvious circular entrance defect in the posterior surface of the shaft. However, a recognizable exit wound was lacking since the radial and concentric entrance-associated fractures had fragmented the exit area before the bullet impacted that surface. The direction of fire could still be determined, however. The victim was shot from the back and not from the front as the defendant maintained. Based on this evidence, it was unlikely the victim was shot in self-defense, but rather from behind. Therefore the testimony of the assailant was rejected and he was convicted of manslaughter following his confession of his intent to rob the dealer. The ensuing chase and shooting numerous times resulted in a wound to the tibia and the abdomen. No bullets were recovered so each wound was likely a through and through wound, and combined,

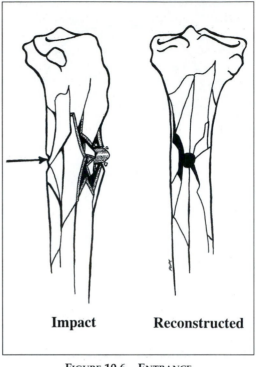

Impact   Reconstructed

FIGURE 10.6   ENTRANCE
AND EXIT IDENTIFICATION

The entrance can be identified in a tubular long bone. However, the exit may not be identifiable since the impact of the penetration causes the tubular structure to shatter before the bullet exits.

these wounds could certainly be considered fatal. This case demonstrates that biomechanical characteristics of bone fracture patterns can provide pivotal evidence and clarify certain circumstances in criminal investigations.

Blunt Trauma

Blunt force is another common type of skeletal trauma observed at the Medical Examiner's Office in Memphis. Blunt trauma typically results from motor-vehicle accidents, pedestrian accidents, falls, assaults, and workplace injuries. Investigation of these injuries is aided by interpreting fracture patterns to indicate the direction of force and the sequence of blows. Similar to ballistic trauma, blunt trauma is best understood by correlating the soft tissue injuries (e.g., contusions and lacerations) with the underlying bony defects. Forensic pathologists use sequential layers of traumatic defects, from skin to underlying soft tissue to the bone, to reconstruct the events surrounding the incident. Anthropologists, however, typically work in the absence of soft tissue, so they must be able to determine the direction and sequence of wounds using only information derived exclusively from bony injuries. Without understanding the language of fractures and biomechanical reactions of bone to blunt force injuries, accurate assessments of the traumatic events are difficult.

Skeletal responses to blunt force trauma will depend on the intrinsic properties of bone geometry, stress risers (areas resistant to stress), and bone density, which collectively determine the susceptibility to fracture (Harkness et al. 1984; Smith et al. 1987). Extrinsic factors include the shape, weight, and material of the object, the rates and duration of loading at the impact site, and relative force of the blow.

More factors go into producing a bone fracture by blunt force than with ballistic trauma, and their concepts need to be briefly presented. Much like trying to bend and break a fresh, green stick, constant external pressure to the structure of bone causes it to pass through several stages: force applied without bending or distortion (stress), resilient bending under the load (strain, elastic deformation), bending with permanent deformation (plastic deformation), and finally failure (fracture) of the structure when it separates. In other words, if a force is applied to a skeletal structure, it initially bends the bone. Due to bone's composite structure, it is able to resist low rates of compressive and tensile stresses during the initial stages of bending. During this time, bone is in the elastic

stage of deformation and can return to its natural shape when the force is removed. However, if pressure increases, the bone enters plastic deformation and can no longer regain its original shape. This transition from an elastic stage to a plastic stage occurs at its unique yield point, and maintains permanent deformation of its structure (Harkness et al. 1984). Once the extrinsic factors exceed the resisting strength of the bone, the bone will fail and a fracture will occur. Since bone is about one-third stronger in compression than in tension, failure (fracture) occurs first in tension on the weakest side, which is opposite the side of impact.

When a tubular bone receives a perpendicular impact, the first response of the bone is to bend around the insult (Currey 1984). This distortion produces compression on the concave (inside curve) of the bone and tension on the opposite, convex (outside curve) of the bone. With continued force, the bone eventually fails in compression. As bone fails in tension, and then compression, perpendicular (shearing) fractures encounter those formed by compression and are redirected longitudinally to the shaft. These mechanisms combine to create a triangular-shaped wedge of bone commonly referred to as a "butterfly fracture" (see Figure 10.7 on page 146). The tension component looks like the body of the butterfly and the angled compression fractures appear as the wings. The ability to differentiate between tension and compression makes fractures in tubular and cranial bone amenable to interpretation and allows the direction of force or impact to be established.

The skull reacts somewhat differently from long bones to blunt trauma because of its unique architecture and intrinsic properties. The skull does not fracture with the typical butterfly patterns of long bone. The cranial vault comprises two cortical bone layers separated by a spongy layer of diploe. Since bone is weaker in tension, the underlying inner table may experience the

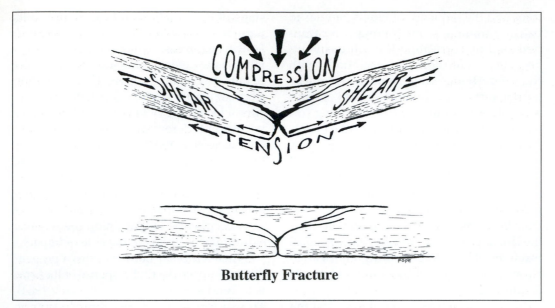

Butterfly Fracture

FIGURE 10.7 BUTTERFLY FRACTURES

Butterfly fractures in tubular long bones are produced by the tension and compression fractures. The tension fracture looks like the body and the angled compressed fractures appear as the butterfly wings.

first phase of the fracture if energy is applied through all three layers. Once initiated, the fracture will progress through the diploe and into the outer table of bone.

Fracture patterns in the skull associated with blunt trauma share some similarities to and important differences from those of gunshot wounds (Smith et al. 1987). Radiating fractures progress from the initial point of the impact and concentric fractures may also be present when sustained force drives the cranial vault (Figure 10.8). The beveling will indicate the direction of the force. In gunshots, internal forces from cavitation and expansion create an outward beveling of concentric fractures; in blunt trauma the bevel is reversed because external forces cause inward deformation and intrusion (Smith et al. 1987). Once the initial fractures are formed, subsequent blows may be recognizable through additional impact sites with fracture lines terminating into the fractures from the first blow. Therefore, a

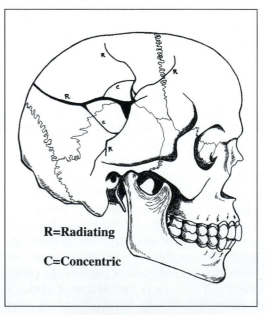

R=Radiating

C=Concentric

FIGURE 10.8 RADIATING AND CONCENTRIC FRACTURES

Shown here are radiating and concentric fractures associated with blunt force trauma.

minimum number of blows from points of impact and sequence of blows is potentially revealed when examining these patterns in bone.

The biomechanical principles influencing the characteristics of blunt force trauma of both cranial and postcranial skeletal material are illustrated in the following two case studies.

Case 4: Pedestrian Accident

A thirty-four-year-old man was struck by an oncoming van while attempting to cross the interstate after his car had stalled. Differing witness accounts made it difficult to determine if the victim was trying to leave his car (left side facing traffic) and cross to the median or suddenly attempting to return to his car after already crossing to the median (right side facing traffic). One witness saw only the victim running across to the median and could not account for why the van did not miss the pedestrian, while the van driver claimed that the victim ran across to the medium and was almost to a safe area, when he suddenly turned 180 degrees and bolted back in front of the van, leaving the vehicle operator no choice but to hit the victim. The victim sustained multiple blunt force injuries as a result of the impact. During the forensic examination at the Medical Examiner's Office, it was apparent that his right tibia and fibula had been broken, but the soft tissue injuries were difficult to interpret since the victim was struck multiple times by other vehicles once he was down. The lower leg bones were removed for anthropological analysis to determine the direction of impact.

The location of the fractures on the tibia and fibula are near the midshaft of both bones, which corresponds to the height of the van bumper. The height of leg injuries can vary due to the bumper height and to the amount of braking applied at the time of impact. If impact occurs under braking,

injuries occur lower on the leg, closer to the ankle, since the front of the car is quickly pulled downward during the sudden emergency braking (brake squat). Brake squat usually creates a very low impact on the leg, just above the ankle.

Fracture patterns present in the tibia and fibula of the vehicular accident victim exhibit the classic characteristics of tension and compression fractures. As the car bumper deformed the bones, the structure of the bone first failed in tension, opposite the point of impact (Figure 10.9). As the force was sustained, the bone continued to fail in compression on the impact side. Based on the interpretation of these injuries, it became apparent the victim had been

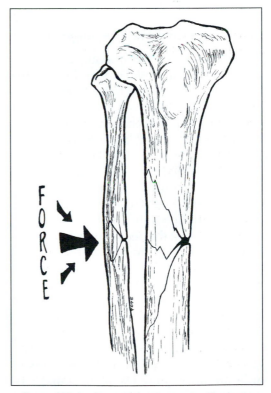

FIGURE 10.9   BUTTERFLY FRACTURE PATTERN

A butterfly fracture pattern in the right tibia and fibula of the motor vehicle accident victim shows the direction of impact after interpreting the tension and compression fractures.

struck by the offender's vehicle from the right side, indicating he did in fact, without warning, attempt to return to his car, not allowing time or distance for the oncoming traffic to react. His wallet was found lying on the passenger seat and it is assumed that the victim remembered that he had left his wallet in an unlocked car and his first reaction was to return immediately.

In this situation, cooperation between the anthropologist and the forensic pathologist established the direction of force from examining bony injuries because they understood the language of fractures. Interpreting the butterfly fracture pattern establishes the direction of the force applied to the victim's leg and the orientation of the victim to the van at the time of the incident.

Case 5: A Fall or a Jump?

Some boys were walking along an old train bed just outside of the city and found the body of a man who had fallen from an overhanging bridge that was about forty feet above the ground. Although death was due to multiple injuries, it became important to determine what portion of his body struck first. According to acquaintances and relatives, he ran with a rough crowd who were notorious for instigating local bar fights and other disturbances. In addition, investigators learned that the deceased had made offhand threats to kill himself in order to get back at his ex-wife. Although his actual intent will never be known, it was important to establish the approximate posture and orientation of his body at impact.

At autopsy most of his extremities exhibited multiple fractures. The anthropologist studied the nature of the fractures in order to identify the mechanism that produced them. Axial loading is when the forces of impact are directed through the long axis of the bone. This type of loading is most commonly seen in the leg bones following vertical falls if someone lands on

their feet. Axial loading is also seen in motor vehicle accidents, in which the horizontal femur of the driver or passenger is forced into the dashboard during impact. However, if the individual lands at an oblique angle or falls flat against the ground, the stresses are perpendicular to the long bone, producing the compression and tension fractures discussed above.

In this case, the anthropologist was given the task of recovering the bone and performing a fracture analysis. The fracture patterns of the left knee provided the most useful information concerning the nature of the fall. The distal portion of the femur and proximal portion of the tibia had impacted each other, creating significant damage. The femur demonstrated a typical "teacup" fracture produced by axial forces in the center of the knee that drove the two condyles apart, splitting them up the middle (Figure 10.10). The proximal tibia exhibited a similar axial loading injury because the tibial plateau had been vertically sheared from the joint. Axial compression of a bone may result in either an oblique fracture, between 30–45 degrees, or a longitudinal fracture along the axis of the bone. The latter was found in the tibial plateau fracture. The teacup fracture is also the result of axial forces. Based on these observations, the anthropologist concluded that the victim landed on his feet. Although it does not rule out the possibility of being maliciously thrown off a bridge, it does support the theory that he may have made the conscious decision to jump.

Sharp Force Trauma

Sharp force injury is the third major type of trauma commonly encountered in medical examiner's offices. It is important to understand from the outset that sharp force trauma (SFT) is a blunt force blow delivered by a sharp object. Like ballistic and blunt force injuries, the wound must be considered as a whole. The path of the

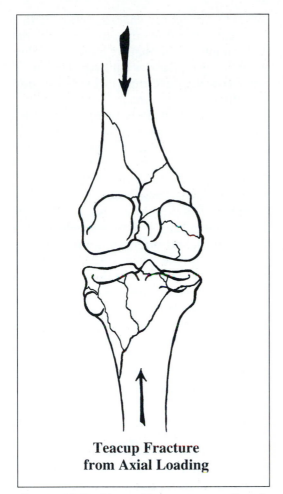

**Teacup Fracture
from Axial Loading**

FIGURE 10.10   TEACUP FRACTURE FROM CASE 5

anatomical region (head, chest, neck, abdomen, or extremities) each sharp force injury may produce extensive damage to soft tissue while failing to contact bone. When anthropologists are asked to examine skeletal material devoid of soft tissue to evaluate sharp force injuries, valuable information from the skin, soft tissues, and organs is absent. In some cases, the smallest nick on the inner surface of a rib may reflect the only bony evidence of a knife penetrating the chest cavity. Additionally, it is important to understand that the blunt fracture of a rib may reflect the force used to stab a person, without actually incising the bone. With so many potential variables involved in sharp trauma it becomes important for the anthropologist to recognize and understand the mechanisms behind sharp force injuries.

Skin, soft tissue, organs, cartilage, and bone are materials with different properties, each capable of capturing different characteristics of sharp instruments. Skin is highly elastic, flexible under tension, and receives varying support from underlying bone. These properties must be considered when making estimates of knife orientation, type of edge (sharp, dull, straight, or serrated), not to mention the size and shape of the blade. Soft internal tissues (arterial walls, pleura, or pericardium) are also somewhat elastic, while organs, such as the liver, may retain the shape of the knife tip or even record tooth striations. Cartilage possesses both malleable and compact properties that have the ability to retain characteristics of tool marks (Symes et al. 1999). Examination of cartilage is especially important since knife attacks often involve the anterior neck and chest. Finally, it is the uniform and compact nature of bone combined with its ease of preservation that gives it the potential to be some of the more accurate and durable evidence reflecting both class and individual characteristics of the weapon.

wound should be correlated through all penetrated layers, from clothing to bone. Further, sharp force wounds in soft tissue and bone each have diagnostic value. Soft tissue injuries can provide accurate information about the depth and angle of penetration by a sharp object, while sharp trauma in bone has a tendency to present greater interpretive challenges.

Medical examiners and forensic pathologists focus on documenting the number, location, pattern, direction, and depth of wounds at autopsy. Depending upon the

Before learning what sharp force injuries look like in bone, it is important to understand the responsible actions and mechanisms that may create wounds in soft tissue. There are six separate types of wounds produced in knife attacks (Department of the Army 1992). The *slash* is an incised wound longer than it is deep. The *stab* is deeper than it is wide. Chopping action with the edge of the blade produces the *hack*. The *flick* is a minor injury produced by point contact with the tip of the knife to skin. Drawing the tip of the knife across skin produces the *drag*. Finally, the *butt* is a strike with the knife handle. Of these, the stab, hack, and slash are likely to produce sharp trauma in bone. Additionally, with substantial application of force, the stab, hack, and butt are likely to have a component of blunt force.

As implied above, edged weapons may produce sharp force injuries, blunt fractures, or a mixture of both. The cutting edge produces smooth, roughened, or irregular margins, depending on knife design and the type of motion. Sharp blades and a slicing motion produce the smoothest margins. These wounds become progressively roughened with knife dullness and forceful wedging that occurs in hacking wounds. Blunt fractures may be adjacent to SFT, especially when there is increased force to the blow, impacts with the knife guard, or when these are combined with thick, heavy blades. The rules of blunt force injury apply and the fractures follow the same tension and compression mechanics.

Tool marks in defects are usefully divided into two categories of features. The first of these are class characteristics reflecting the manufacturer's general design of the knife, such as single-edged, double-edged, length, width, thickness, serrated, straight, spine features, and hilt shape. These features may also vary along the length of the blade, such that the angle and depth of penetration may influence the wound morphology. Besides class characteristics,

individual or "type" characteristics are the other category of features that are specific and unique only to that weapon. Examples would be irregularities left from the manufacturer's edge grinding or blade use defects after manufacture.

Experience will show that it is easier to look at a knife and predict the wound it may produce than it is to do the reverse. Unfortunately, it is usually the latter task that burdens the forensic scientist. Application of intuition beyond observation can be the downfall of an examiner. It is only through an understanding of tissues involved, the SFT location and orientation in the body, and recognition of accurate size and shape characteristics that allows the examiner to narrow the field of suspect weapons.

The construction, water content, and Lines of Langer, or the grain of the skin, influences soft tissue injuries. These lines of tension affect the physical appearance of incised skin wounds. Costal cartilage, with its high water content, is slightly brittle, and may fracture instead of incise when impacted by a dull blade, making a distinction between blunt and sharp force trauma almost impossible. The composition of some bone, particularly ribs, possesses a significant grain in its structure, similar to wood. This means that bone has a tendency to split preferentially along the grain when penetrated. Orientation of the blade relative to the grain of the bone may alter the dimension of the defect. A knife penetrating with its spine and cutting edge parallel to the grain will cause splitting along the grain (Figure 10.11). This may create a wound longer than the blade width. While this longitudinal splitting of the grain may influence accuracy in predicting blade width, wound thickness does correlate well with knife spine thickness at the level of penetration since the flat of the spine is oriented across the grain and crushes the bone instead of splitting it. Splitting is minimized when the knife is oriented across the grain

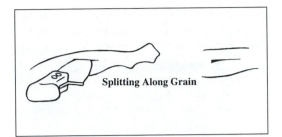

FIGURE 10.11   BONE PENETRATION
PARALLEL TO THE GRAIN

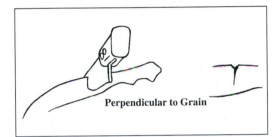

FIGURE 10.12   BONE PENETRATION
PERPENDICULAR TO THE GRAIN

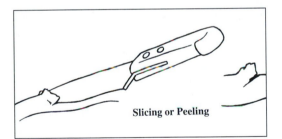

FIGURE 10.13   ANGLED PENETRATION OF BONE

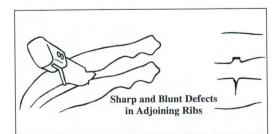

FIGURE 10.14   INTERCOSTAL PENETRATION
PRODUCING WOUNDS IN ADJOINING RIBS

of long bones or in stab wounds to cranial bone, making thickness and sometimes width measurements accurate (Figure 10.12). Orientation may be further refined as penetration by the knife displaces fragments of bone in the direction of the force or from angled slicing and peeling of the bone surface (Figure 10.13).

Questions concerning minimum number of stab wounds must be approached with caution and can be estimated from the skeleton once it is rearticulated and examined under magnification. Maximum numbers of stab wounds cannot be determined solely from skeletal remains. Blades cutting two ribs at an angle could cut both ribs in one blow, but not simultaneously, and may not accurately reflect blade width. Additionally, two defects can be created when the sharp edge creates a characteristic cut, while the spine of the blade creates blunt crushing or shaving of the adjoining rib (Symes et al. 2002) (Figure 10.14). Also keep in mind that it is not unusual for an examiner to go back to a specimen(s) and find more incised wounds than were recorded in an initial report. Rule of thumb: Incised wounds to bone are difficult to see and therefore easy to miss.

Obviously, a conservative approach is key to SFT analyses. Blade measurements are substantiated when there are numerous confirming examples, and all measurements and descriptions of wounds in bone must be couched by the third dimension, depth. Depth must be considered to substantiate width and length measurements. And, as with all trauma analysis, knowledge of the insulted tissues is essential before assessments truly become accurate.

Case 6: Multiple Stab Wounds

This victim arrived at the city morgue with numerous stab wounds. Her husband, who was known to have a violent temper, was still at large but a broken knife blade was

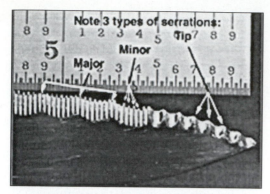

FIGURE 10.15   BROKEN KNIFE BLADE
FOUND NEAR THE CRIME SCENE

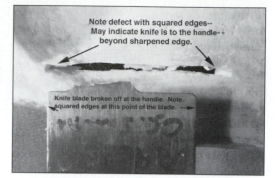

FIGURE 10.16   COMPARISON
OF CHARACTERISTICS OF BONE WOUND WITH
A BROKEN KNIFE FOUND NEAR THE SCENE

recovered near the scene (Figure 10.15). The anthropologist (SAS) was called to the autopsy since a wound penetrated the posterior right shoulder blade (scapula) with continuation to posterior ribs 2 and 3. There were also stab wounds to the face and abdomen. While many of the wounds exhibited different SFT characteristics, the skin, organs, and each bone contributed to the narrowing of the field of suspect weapons.

The scapula wound was interesting in that the puncture into the thin fan of bone was rectangular in shape, with no beveled edges as would be expected for a knife stab wound. Cuts to ribs 2 and 3 obviously represent the borders of the knife stab wound after it went though the scapula. Although confusing, the scapula accurately mimics the blade dimensions when you consider what part of the blade it represents. A knife is defined as a blade that has an edge bevel, or a sharpened edge. This sharpened edge extends for most of the blade, but may discontinue before the knife guard or the beginning of the handle. Commonly, the knife blade has not been sharpened at the handle and is therefore rectangular in shape. The rectangular blade impression in bone most likely represents the knife blade dimensions beyond the sharpened edge (Figure 10.16).

The defect in rib 3 has a shaved (polished) appearance (Figure 10.17a) while rib 2 had an incised wound appearance (Figure 10.17b). Even though the rib defects are associated with the same stab wound, differences between these wounds

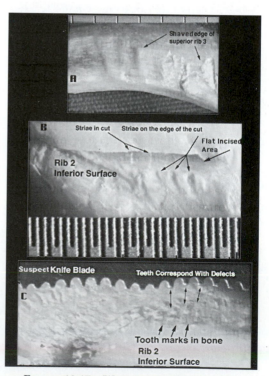

FIGURE 10.17   WOUND CHARACTERISTICS

suggest that the blade used has differing designs on each edge and the blade cuts differently on one edge than on the other. While the scapula did not demonstrate a single or double-edged blade, characteristics on the lower rib suggest a weapon with a nonsharpened edge (knife spine), and the upper rib reveals a beveled (sharpened) edge. These bones indicate a single-edged knife with width and thickness dimensions consistent with the blade recovered.

Microscopic examination of the bottom of right rib 2 also revealed striations and gouges. When examined, they appear patterned and regular. This strongly suggests a manufactured tooth pattern on the suspect weapon used in this stabbing. Figure 10.17c illustrates the consistent match between the suspect knife teeth and scratches in the bone.

Not to be outdone by characteristics revealed only in bone, the medical examiner in this case (OCS) also found dimensions in the incised skin wounds consistent with the suspected blade, as well as revealing characteristics in the sectioned liver of the victim. This tissue revealed a picture-perfect image of the in and out stab wound with depth measurements and also revealed patterned striations created by more coarse teeth manufactured in the tip of the weapon (Figure 10.18).

In this case, different bones and tissues from a single victim were used to collectively describe a weapon. These tissues indicated a long, single-edged knife with at least two types of manufactured serrations. While this does not describe any particular individual weapon, these characteristics narrowed the range of class characteristics, which matched that of the recovered broken blade. This blade, in turn, was eventually matched to a handle that retained the husband's fingerprints and blood.

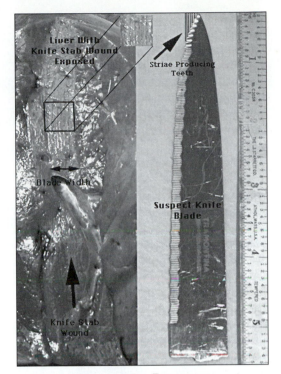

FIGURE 10.18   PATTERNED
CHARACTERISTICS OF THE WEAPON

Conclusions

Anthropologists trained in the language of fractures contribute much to the interpretation of skeletal trauma and have a direct bearing on the outcome of criminal investigations. The anthropologist must comprehend the biomechanical properties of bone and be able to interpret the bony responses in order to recreate traumatic events. In many cases, the anthropologist can contribute accurate descriptions of the circumstances surrounding the injury based on observations of injury pattern. Therefore, the ability to distinguish fractures associated with high velocity ballistic trauma from fractures created by lesser energy from blunt force trauma is crucial for narrowing not only the type of trauma, but, in some cases, the suspect weapon. The same rules apply when examining sharp force injuries, for each defect in bone and surrounding tissues contains signature information about the traumatic event. It is the responsibility of the anthropologist to recognize and appreciate the significance of each feature in bone in order to produce credible and testable information for a medicolegal case.

Acknowledgments

For their support and comments, the authors are indebted to: Cindy Gardner, M.D., Teresa Campbell, M.D., and the entire supportive staff at the Regional Forensic Center, Memphis TN; Richard Jantz, Ph.D., Linda Parsons Marion, M.A., and Brian Pope, Knoxville, TN; and Jerome C. Rose, Ph.D., Katherine Murray, M.A., Peter Ungar, Ph.D., and Mary Jo Schneider Ph.D., University of Arkansas, Fayetteville, AR.

References

Coe, J. 1982. External beveling of entrance wounds by handguns. *American Journal of Forensic Medicine and Pathology* 3(3) September.

Currey, J. D. 1984. *The Mechanical Adaptations of Bones*. Princeton NJ: Princeton University Press.

Department of the Army. 1992. "Combatives" Field Manual #FM21-150.

DiMaio, Vincent. 1999. *Gunshot Wounds: Practical Aspects of Firearms, Ballistics, and Forensic Techniques*. 2nd ed. Boca Raton, FL: CRC Press.

Dixon, D. 1982. Keyhole lesions in gunshot wounds of the skull and direction of fire. *Journal of Forensic Sciences* 27(3):555–566.

Harkness, James, William Ramsey, and B. Ahmadi. 1984. Principles of fractures and dislocations. Chapter 1 in *Fractures in Adults*, ed., C. Rockwood and David Green. Vol. 1. Philadelphia, PA: Lippincot Company.

Smith, O. C. 1996. Ballistic bone trauma. In *Bones: Bullets, Burns, Bludgeons, Blunders and Why*, ed. Steven A. Symes. Proceedings of the Bone Trauma Workshop: American Academy of Forensic Science, Feb. 19–24, Nashville, TN.

Smith, O. C., Hugh Berryman, Steven A. Symes, Jerry Francisco, and Violet Hnilica. 1993. Atypical gunshot exit defects to the cranial vault. *Journal of Forensic Sciences* 38(2):339–343.

Smith, O. C., Hugh Berryman, and Craig Lahren. 1987. Cranial fracture patterns and estimate of direction from low velocity gunshot wounds. *Journal of Forensic Sciences* 32(5):1416–1421.

Symes, Steven A., O. C., Smith, C. D. Gardner, J. T. Francisco, and G. A. Horton. 1999. Anthropological and pathological analyses of sharp trauma in autopsy. *Proceedings of the American Academy of Forensic Sciences* 5:177–178.

Symes, Steven A., John A. Williams, Elizabeth A. Murray, J. Michael Hoffman, Thomas D. Holland, Julie Saul, Frank Saul, and Elayne J. Pope. 2002. Taphonomical context of sharp trauma in suspected cases of human mutilation and dismemberment. Pp. 403–434 in *Advances in Forensic Taphonomy: Method, Theory, and Archaeological Perspectives*, ed. William D. Haglund and Marcella H. Sorg. New York: CRC Press.

Watkins, J. 1999. Mechanical characteristics of musculoskeletal components. Pp. 285–293 in *Structure and Function of the Musculoskeletal System*. Glasgow, Scotland: Human Kinetics.

THE INTERFACE OF FORENSIC ANTHROPOLOGY AND FORENSIC PATHOLOGY IN TRAUMA INTERPRETATION

Douglas H. Ubelaker and John E. Smialek

With the growth of forensic anthropology as a subdiscipline of both physical anthropology and forensic science, physical anthropologists increasingly become involved in the analysis of human remains recovered in a medicolegal context. Usually, the material for this analysis consists of skeletal remains, although at times other materials can be analyzed as well. In the examination of human skeletal remains, anthropologists not only seek information about age at death, sex, ancestry, and living stature, which can facilitate identification, but also offer opinions on skeletal evidence for antemortem trauma and disease, postmortem change, and foul play, including perimortem trauma interpretation. The goal of this work is to assist in the identification of the decedents and to help determine what happened to them.

Because of their experience with both archeological and forensic samples, physical anthropologists can be especially useful in trauma interpretation. In evaluating this type of evidence, investigators must distinguish the important perimortem evidence from normal anatomical variants, pathological conditions, antemortem trauma, and taphonomically produced alterations.

Although forensic anthropologists provide significant input into the investigation of death, it is important to remember that their results are used in conjunction with those of other forensic specialists and investigators. Responsibility for the overall interpretation of the medicolegal aspects of a case usually rests with the forensic pathologist or another medically trained specialist in such a role. Whereas the forensic anthropologists, with their knowledge of skeletal anatomy and taphonomic processes, may find and interpret the evidence for foul play in a case, the forensic pathologist will use that and other information to determine cause and manner of death. The anthropologist and pathologist, either directly or indirectly, work as a team to document and interpret relevant forensic evidence.

An example from Hawaii represents a case in point of how this dynamic interface between forensic anthropology and forensic pathology works and how it can lead to final interpretations that would not likely be attained independently by either discipline. In our opinion, it offers an example of the value of interdisciplinary research and collaboration.

Discovery and Anthropological Analysis

In March of 1992, incomplete human remains were found on the ground surface near an apparent animal trail on an undeveloped lot in Kona, Hawaii. Positive identification of the adult male decedent was established relatively quickly through comparison with dental records. The remains were then sent to the central FBI Laboratory in Washington, D.C., for additional analysis and trauma interpretation. Following normal protocol, the remains were processed through the Hair and Fiber Unit (now referred to as Trace Evidence) of the FBI and subsequently delivered to the first author at the Smithsonian Institution for anthropological analysis.

Inventory revealed that the remains consisted of one human cranium, mandible, and the first three cervical vertebrae. Twelve teeth were present, in addition to artificial restorative crowns and related evidence of dentistry. Four of the natural teeth displayed fractured surfaces, but it was not clear if the fractures were sustained perimortem or postmortem.

The cranium displayed a rugged face with well-healed trauma (as evidenced by fractures) in the nasal area, left frontal (Figure 11.1) and right maxilla. Some green algae-like stain was present on the occipital and the left side of the cranial vault. Some desiccated soft tissue was present, although the remains were not odiferous.

Observations of postmortem changes included evidence of animal scavenging. Crushing, compression-type localized fractures, consistent with animal chewing, were detected on the posterior aspects of both mandibular condyles (Figure 11.2) and on areas of the first and third cervical vertebrae.

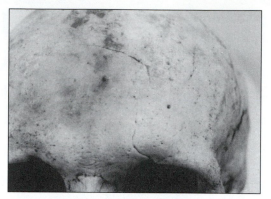

FIGURE 11.1   WELL-REMODELED ANTEMORTEM TRAUMA IN THE LEFT FRONTAL BONE ABOVE THE ORBIT

FIGURE 11.2   EVIDENCE OF PROBABLE ANIMAL CHEWING ON THE CONDYLE OF MANDIBLE

Perimortem Trauma

Evidence for perimortem trauma was found on the cranium and the third cervical vertebra. A fracture was detected extending through the right temporal, right parietal, and right sphenoid with the area of the superior anterior squamosal temporal broken and missing (Figure 11.3). A small fracture was also noted extending in an anterior-inferior direction on the outer surface of the right malar bone from the midpoint of the suture between the malar and temporal bones on the zygomatic

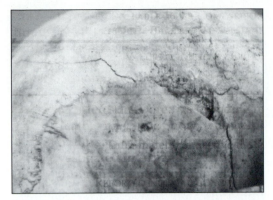

FIGURE 11.3   PERIMORTEM CRANIAL FRACTURES
ON THE RIGHT TEMPORAL AND PARIETAL

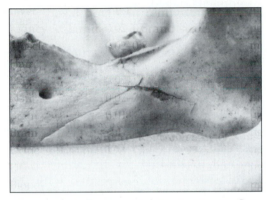

FIGURE 11.4   PERIMORTEM FRACTURE AND CUT
MARK ON THE LEFT SIDE OF THE MANDIBLE

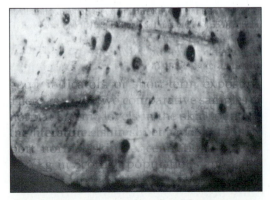

FIGURE 11.5   PERIMORTEM CUT MARKS ON THE
CENTRUM OF THE THIRD CERVICAL VERTEBRA

arch. The morphology of these fractures suggested they resulted from perimortem blunt-force trauma to the right side of the cranial vault.

A fracture was also noted located on the left horizontal ramus of the mandible (Figure 11.4) in the area of the premolars and molars, mostly confined to the buccal (outside) surface. It extended from the area immediately lingual to the missing left first molar across the alveolus to a point on the buccal surface 14.5 mm below the first molar and then inferior and anterior to a point on the inferior border just below the mental foramen. The fracture then extended posteriorly along the inferior border to a point directly below the third molar area.

In addition, a deep (estimated 2 mm) cut extended across the fracture on the mandible described immediately above (Figure 11.4). The cut was oriented horizontally in the area of the first molar just below the point where the fracture bent anteriorly and inferiorly. The cut measured 21.6 mm in length with only about 5.5 mm of the cut located anterior to the fracture.

Three additional areas of cuts (sharp-force trauma) were detected on the ventral surface of the centrum of the third cervical vertebra (Figure 11.5). These cuts were also oriented horizontally. One area of injury measured 7.7 mm in length and was located 5 mm below the superior margin of the centrum. Microscopic examination of this area revealed evidence of two cuts, one slightly deeper but contiguous with the other (see Figure 11.6 on page 158). Another single cut measured 5.1 mm in length and was located 5 mm superior to the inferior margin of the centrum. This cut was located 6 mm right of the midline.

An additional cut was located on the inferior anterior margin of the centrum in the

FIGURE 11.6   MICROSCOPIC VIEW
OF CUTS ON VERTEBRAL CENTRUM

midline. This cut measured 5.6 mm in length. In contrast to the other cuts on the vertebra, this one was oriented anterior-posterior. Morphology of this alteration suggests that the instrument producing it penetrated between the third and fourth cervical vertebrae from the right side, striking the anterior aspect of the inferior surface of the centrum of the third cervical vertebra. This incision penetrated the edge of the bone 5.6 mm, partially separating a thin sliver of bone that was still connected to the centrum on the left side. The sliver of bone measured 2.3 mm in width.

The previous discussion reveals that anthropological analysis of the recovered remains exhibited evidence of ante-mortem trauma (fractures to frontal, maxilla, and nasal area), postmortem trauma (animal chew marks), and perimortem trauma (the fractures and incisions described above). Collectively, the perimortem alterations suggested blunt-force trauma to the right side of the head, deep, sharp-force trauma with an associated fracture on the left side of the mandible, and multiple, fine, sharp-force trauma on the third cervical vertebra.

Forensic Pathology Analysis

After initial anthropological examination, the remains were submitted to the second author for a forensic pathological examination. The forensic pathologist noted the alterations described above and agreed with the anthropological interpretation. He also felt that the similarity and parallel relationship of the vertebral cuts suggested that the victim was immobile when they were inflicted. Their anatomic location indicated that considerable force would have been involved to cut through the trachea, esophagus, and musculature of the neck before the vertebral column could be damaged.

Following standard practice in forensic pathology, the second author sectioned the superior portion of the calvarium to study the contents and inner morphology of the cranial vault. This procedure revealed a circumscribed mass of dark, red-brown desiccated material adherent to the right temporal bone, directly beneath the fracture. The pathologist interpreted this finding as representing the remnants of an epidural hematoma associated with the cranial fracture that apparently involved a torn, right middle meningeal artery. In the pathologist's opinion, this represented a perimortem injury and constituted the cause of death. The pathologist subsequently classified this death as a homicide.

The pathologist believed that the pattern of the cuts on the vertebra indicated a thin, sharp-bladed instrument had been employed. He also thought that the assault involved a blow to the left side of the jaw and another to the right side of the head. In his opinion, death would not have been immediate. Rather, several hours would have been necessary for bleeding to enlarge an epidural hematoma to a size that would cause death due to increased intracranial pressure. During the interval, the victim would likely have remained unconscious, but breathing. He felt that the cuts on the vertebrae were consistent with postmortem injuries inflicted during decapitation.

Statements made by a suspect suggested that he had used a machete-type blade to strike the victim in self-defense. This event occurred in February of 1991, approximately one month before the remains were discovered. Analysis of the perimortem alterations by the forensic anthropologist and forensic pathologist provided important, relevant information that allowed a jury to fairly evaluate all of the evidence. Both of the authors offered court testimony regarding their interpretations in the subsequent trial. The jury found the defendant guilty of manslaughter based on "reckless conduct."

Summary

This case provides an example of how the expertise and experience of an anthropologist and pathologist complement and support each other. Working together, the two specialists can achieve interpretations, conclusions, and specific details that they would be less likely to reach independently. Anthropologists bring to the cases unique experience in skeletal anatomy and familiarity with the diverse factors that can affect skeletal indicators. Pathologists offer unique experience with soft tissue wound interpretation, pathology, and a cause of death analysis. Constructive integration of observations and results of investigation in these two subdisciplines leads to strengthened overall interpretation.

12

TAPHONOMY AND TIME

ESTIMATING THE POSTMORTEM INTERVAL

Jennifer C. Love and Murray K. Marks

Estimating time since death is a difficult component of the death scene investigation. Decay rates are influenced by numerous factors, including temperature, insect and carnivore activity, and perimortem trauma. Each of these variables must be considered when estimating a postmortem interval. Both forensic pathologists and forensic anthropologists are called upon to estimate the time between death and discovery. In order to accurately evaluate a decomposing body they turn to the research of various disciplines, including entomology and biochemistry.

As a clinical science guided by autopsy dissection, forensic pathology is a specialized branch of medicine that primarily deals with the postmortem evaluation of the mechanical cause of violent death in the recently deceased (for reviews see Knight 1996: Spitz 1993; DiMiao and DiMiao 1989). The focus is upon the remarkable soft tissue trauma and anomalies of the victim. In addition to the interpretation of cause and manner of death, the pathologist is called upon to estimate postmortem chronology. Traditionally, this has been subjectively assessed by means of algor, livor, and rigor mortis changes in the recently deceased.

As a natural science, physical anthropology has long nurtured an interest in death and disease processes through paleopathology and, more recently, forensic anthropology. By assessing disease patterns in the odontoskeletal tissues of the population (an epidemiological perspective), paleopathologists evaluate frequencies of infection, trauma, neoplasms, etc., as a consequence of culture change, warfare, or biological evolution/adaptation in prehistoric and historic groups (see Aufderheide and Rodriguez-Martin 1998; Larsen 1998; Ortner and Putschar 1981; Steinbock 1976).

During the last quarter-century, skeletal biology has become increasingly applied to medicolegal casework. This new direction raises novel questions and research foci that have ultimately led to the development of forensic anthropology as a legitimate subdiscipline of physical anthropology (Thompson 1982). Because of its historical roots, forensic anthropology is able to provide a comprehensive understanding of the growth, development, and trauma of the odontoskeleton to the forensic pathologist (Galloway 1999; Haglund and Sorg 1997; Reichs 1998). The forensic anthropological autopsy is a flexible protocol dictated by the nature of the scene, wounds to the victim, and time since death. Regardless of the scene or medical examiner facility, the anthropologist is an invited consultant by the pathologist or law enforcement agent.

As more and more forensic anthropologists collaborate with and/or become employees within the medical examiner system, our knowledge must be well-grounded in the entire process of decomposition and not just the latter stages of skeletonization that has characterized traditional forensic anthropology. An accurate estimation of how long a victim has been dead prior to discovery is often as important as the identity of the individual. The success or failure of many investigations hinges directly upon an accurate assessment of the postmortem interval. Thus, one goal of the anthropologist is to comprehensively evaluate death as a complex series of cascading events that systematically reduce a fresh corpse to a skeleton and beyond (e.g., Gill-King 1997; Haglund and Sorg 1997).

Both forensic pathology and forensic anthropology have independently evolved research agendas to better understand the postmortem process (see Knight 1996; Reichs 1998). As the postmortem interval increases and soft tissue decomposes, cases become more "anthropological," with the attention of the investigator shifting from soft tissue pathological evidence to hard tissue anthropological evidence. This is not to imply that pathologists are not interested in hard tissue biology and trauma, albeit clinical (e.g., Dorfman and Czerniak 1998; McCarthy and Frassica 1998; Wold et al. 1990), and that anthropologists are not interested in soft tissue trauma (e.g., Galloway 1999).

The following case studies exemplify the role of the forensic pathologist and anthropologist in estimating the postmortem interval and the research and methodologies they use.

Recovery of Human Remains

In late October 1998, detectives from a central Tennessee sheriff's department requested anthropological recovery and examination of a decomposing body discovered by turkey hunters in a rural, wooded section of the county. Arriving at the scene, the anthropologist was guided to the remains, which were almost completely concealed under a brush pile in some dense undergrowth. This deposition site was adjacent to a dry feeder stream of a large nearby creek. The individual was lying face down and in an advanced stage of decomposition. The remains were partially skeletonized, and several elements were scattered (see Figure 12.1 on page 162). The remaining soft tissue was mummified. A preliminary (at the scene) examination of the scattered elements indicated carnivore disturbance. The skull was discovered near the original location of body deposition. Several silver amalgam restorative therapies were present on the maxillary molars. Dental records and radiographs of a thirteen-year-old adolescent male and a fourteen-year-old adolescent female missing for exactly six weeks to the day were summoned for odontoskeletal comparison.

Surprisingly, within minutes of initiating the anthropological survey of the surrounding woods for missing bones and clothing of the victim, another body was discovered approximately 290 meters to the southeast within the same drainage ravine (see Figure 12.2 on page 162). The nude body was in a much earlier stage of decomposition than the first person, as evidenced by moderate to advanced bloating,

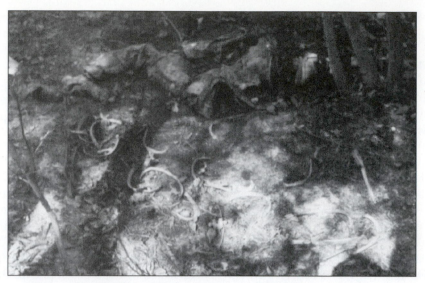

FIGURE 12.1   VICTIM 1: ADVANCED DECOMPOSITION WITH SUBSEQUENT SKELETAL SCATTER

FIGURE 12.2   VICTIM 2: EARLY DECOMPOSITION REVEALING BLOATING, MARBLING, AND SKIN SLIPPAGE

epidermal sloughing of all surfaces, extensive vascular marbling of the abdomen and limbs, and darkened discoloration and drying of the head. There was remarkable odor and fly activity with some egg masses. First instar maggot activity was noted in the ears, hairline of the scalp, and along the ground-body interface. An *instar* refers to an arthropod or insect whose development is between successive molts (shedding of the skin) (see Haskell et al. 1997; Byrd and Castner 2001). Second and third instar maggot activity was especially remarkable throughout the anterior neck region with skeletonization of the laryngeal structures and near skeletonization of the entire cervical spine. Second and third instar maggots were also very active within a darkened perineum (genital region).

While the first victim represents the traditional outdoor anthropological recovery case with skeletonization and disarticulation, the second victim is a case for a forensic pathologist, whose findings may be achieved through routine autopsy methods. The initial division of labor of the two crime scenes fell along traditional lines. Working with the skeletonized victim, the anthropologist conducted an intense ground search for scattered remains, clothing, and the primary site of decomposition. The primary site of decomposition was marked by dark greasy soil and often dead or yellowing vegetation caused by the highly acidic decomposition fluids. A soil sample was taken from the decay site and a control soil sample was taken from nearby, but outside, the decay site. Law enforcement then combed the scene with metal detectors.

Having completed the skeletal and evidence recovery, the anthropologist returned with the materials to the laboratory to begin the analysis. The condition of the skeleton was first documented and photographed. The skeleton was then processed to remove the remaining soft tissue to assess trauma, age, and sex. Finally, a forensic odontologist was summoned to compare the dental records to the dentition.

The forensic pathologist processed the second crime scene. Along with a medical investigator and blood spatter expert, they searched the area for evidence of perimortem events, photographed the scene and the body *in situ*, and then sent the body to the county morgue for a routine autopsy. The condition of the body, although decomposing, was fresh enough for an external and internal examination. A reliable rule of thumb for the anthropologist to follow when the medical examiner, medical investigator, or coroner is not at the scene is to direct the body to those experts when the soft tissue integrity of the thoraco-abdominal boundaries have not been perforated. Law enforcement scene personnel do not always recognize when remains are at the pathological or anthropological phase of decomposition. Regardless, it is their duty to alert the county medical examiner/coroner that remains have been discovered and that the anthropologist will process the scene. During the external examination of the second victim the pathologist documented the external signs of trauma and decomposition and collected several maggot samples from the various populations found on the body. During the internal examination she retained all bone that was impacted by trauma and removed the dental arches for identification.

The basic pathological and anthropological autopsies were completed when the pathologist declared cause and manner of death in both cases. Both deaths were ruled homicide (manner) due to the sharp force trauma to the anterior neck. However, only the second victim could be diagnosed with a cause of death (exsanguination) given the discovery of discernable deep wounds to the musculature and deep vessels of the left lateral neck. Working together and pulling from various areas of research and methodologies, the scientists began to establish the postmortem interval.

Progression of Decomposition

At death, vertebrate organisms systematically begin the decay process by passing through a physiochemical and gross continuum of tissue breakdown from fresh to skeletal and beyond. Though systematic, the transition through several well-documented stages (created for scientific convenience) is unique to each case, guided by an interrelat 1 combination of body composition, caus   nd manner of death, depositional contexι, and environmental conditions that, in concert, may serve to temporarily arrest, retard, or accelerate this process.

At a basic level, the physical reduction of remains is the result of two processes—internal decomposition and external decomposition. Insects aside, decay can be considered as a highly competitive external environmental contest between moisture and aridity that progressively reduces remains by decomposition or desiccation, respectively (Aufderheide 1981; Nielsen et al. 1994). Meanwhile, internal reduction is caused by cell death and exponential proliferation of colonic microbial activity (bacteria normally inside the intestines) (Coe 1993; Gill-King 1997; Clark et al. 1997).

Autolysis

The earliest biochemical process of decomposition is autolysis. This is the irreversible cascading event of cell death that destroys cellular integrity and the cell-to-cell junctions that progressively result in widespread tissue necrosis (death). The byproducts of autolysis subsequently fuel putrefaction, the consumption of the body tissues through the progressive proliferation of endogenous bacteria. Given appropriate time and environmental conditions, these two internal processes are sufficient, even in the absence of insects and carnivores, to reduce a body to a skeleton.

An understanding of decomposition is born from a fundamental knowledge of the normal biochemical function of the living cell. Adenosine triphosphate (ATP) provides the energy for most of the biochemical and physiological processes of the cell. In aerobic organisms, ATP is produced by respiration, which fuels the oxygen-dependent extraction of energy from food (Berne and Levy 1993). In the anaerobic environment produced at death, an organism produces ATP through fermentation, converting pyruvate to lactate, thereby reducing the intracellular pH. The anaerobic pathway of ATP production is inefficient and the net gain is insufficient to maintain cellular physiology (Gill-King 1997; Tobin and Morrel 1997).

At death, circulatory stasis and the consequent loss of aerobic ATP synthesis insults cellular integrity leading to microscopic (cellular) and eventual macroscopic (tissue) morphologic changes. First, via a concentration gradient, the membrane begins to deteriorate and the cell swells. This allows extracellular matrix to leak into the cell. Next, the cellular organelles that house the hydrolytic enzymes that monitor intracellular digestion deteriorate, and the liberated enzymes leak into the cytoplasm. Activated by the lowered pH of the cytoplasm, the enzymes begin to consume the cell (Junqueira et al. 1995). During this stage, decomposition becomes observable at the gross level as tissues become more pale in color. Also, breakdown of the cellular junction occurring between the layers of epidermis and dermis may result in skin slippage of the epidermis (Figure 12.3). This process was evident on the second body found in the Tennessee case.

FIGURE 12.3   SKIN SLIPPAGE (GLOVING)

As the junction between the epidermis and dermis deteriorates, the epidermis sheds from the body.

In addition to skin slippage and generalized tissue necrosis, circulatory stasis and autolysis trigger several gross morphologic changes traditionally targeted by the pathologist during external examination: algor mortis (cooling of the body to ambient temperature), livor mortis (blood pooling), and rigor mortis (muscle stiffening). During life, normal metabolic pathways maintain the body at a core temperature around 98.6°F. When these pathways diminish, the body begins gradually, then more rapidly, to cool to ambient levels. Loss of body heat is typically measured through the "deep core" rectal temperature using a standard thermometer. Historically, a questionable rule of thumb used by some pathologists is a body temperature loss of 1.5°F per hour (Henssge et al. 1995). Unfortunately, however, bodies do not cool at consistent rates. Initially, the core temperature drops slowly, creating an early temperature plateau. With time, the rate increases. Recent research aims at developing mathematical models to predict the cooling curve with the goal of extrapolating the time since death from rectal and ambient temperatures (Henssge et al. 1995). However, algor mortis as a time since death indicator remains complicated by variable rates of temperature loss in different individuals perishing under a wide variety of contexts.

Livor mortis, or hypostasis, is discoloration of the body due to circulatory stasis. Blood pools in the capillaries where the body is experiencing gravitational pull, e.g., the feet of a hanging victim. Initially, livor is unfixed, meaning pressure will force the collected blood out of the capillaries, allowing the tissue to blanch. With time, the capillary blood coagulates and the surrounding fat cells solidify, thereby inhibiting the tissue to blanch under pressure (Figure 12.4). Lividity can be observed between one and two hours postmortem and can become fixed between eight and twelve hours postmortem (Coe 1993; DiMiao and DiMiao 1989; Clark et al. 1997). Once lividity becomes fixed it can no longer be used as a specific indicator of the postmortem interval. Research on

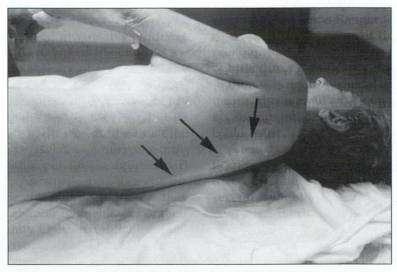

FIGURE 12.4   FIXED LIVOR MORTIS

The arrows demonstrate areas of blanching that remain white despite the release of pressure.

quantifying livor mortis as a time since death indicator has concentrated on measuring blood pooling rates via light absorbing properties of blood. As a time since death indicator, livor mortis is limited by the short length of applicability until fixation and complicated by dark(er) pigmented skin where observation is more difficult.

Rigor mortis, the most commonly utilized time since death indicator in forensic pathology, is the stiffening of muscles from the biochemical binding together of muscle fibers. During the decay process muscles do not contract, as commonly seen in movies when cadavers sit up, but simply lock in place. With time, the fibers break away from their anchoring site at the end of the cell, gradually causing rigor mortis to dissipate. Like algor, the rate and extent of rigor is dependent on many environmental factors, including the level of the perimortem physical activity and postmortem environmental conditions. A rough timeline for rigor mortis is initial development at one to two hours after death, complete stiffness at twelve hours postmortem, and waning over the resulting twelve-hour (or longer) period (DiMiao and DiMiao 1989; Spitz 1993; Knight 1996; Clark et al. 1997). Researchers have tried to "fine-tune" this generalization by measuring force of muscle contraction initiated by electric current but have found high occurrence of intra- and inter-muscle group variation (Madea and Henssge 1988; Madea et al. 1995).

Putrefaction

Putrefaction is the degenerative biochemical pathway of organism destruction from internal bacteria. The release of nutrients from autolyzed cells coupled with the decreased intercellular pH from loss of the buffer system creates a rich environment for endogenous bacterial proliferation. The largest bacterial population during life and the early postmortem period lies in the cecum, located in the lower right quadrant of the abdominal cavity. Because of the large size of the cecum and its proximity to the skin surface of the abdominal wall, putrefaction is often first recognized in this area (Knight 1996; Spitz 1993). A by-product of this exponential bacterial proliferation is the production of a large quantity of hydrogen sulfide gas that easily diffuses through the soft tissue. The gas reacts with the iron of hemoglobin in the blood to form the black precipitate, ferrous sulfide. The precipitate causes observable discoloration of the dermis over the cecum. Discoloration progresses through the remaining regions of the abdominal wall from the same precipitate formation as well as through the release of pigments from the breakdown of biliary (gallbladder) structures. Hydrolytic enzymes released from pancreatic cells attack biliary structures releasing various colored pigments into the circulatory system and wall of the abdomen. With time, the color of the entire body will progressively advance from normal to green to purple, and through various shades of brown (Gill-King 1997; Knight 1996) (Figure 12.5).

Endogenous bacteria are not confined to the large intestine, but spread to the lungs and, to a much lesser degree, throughout the entire body. Since bacteria colonize fluids with ease, their growth and hydrogen sulfide gas-producing capabilities (forming ferrous sulfide) invade the circulatory system initially and systematically blacken the blood vessels. This event, termed intravascular hemolysis or "marbling," is easily seen in the superficial vessels on the body surface (Figure 12.6) and was obvious in the second victim.

While some gases produced in the intestines diffuse through the lining of the organs and the abdominal wall proper, other gases remain trapped within the abdomen and other tissues. The collection of the gas causes the abdomen and other regions to bloat and increase several times in size (see Figures 12.7 and 12.8 on page 168). In males,

FIGURE 12.5   LATE DISCOLORATION

The body becomes reddish-brown due to endogenous bacterial proliferation and exposure of the dermis from epidermal slippage.

FIGURE 12.6   MARBLING

The by-product of bacterial proliferation produces ferrous sulfide, a black precipitant, in the vascular system.

abdominal gas buildup often pushes into the scrotum, causing it to balloon. With time, the abdominal gases cause tissues to rupture or subside naturally, leaking from the body orifices and reducing it to the perimortem size and smaller (Galloway 1997). The second victim found at the crime scene was bloating.

Estimating the Postmortem Interval (PMI)

Gross Examination

Having reviewed the basic mechanics of decay and the gross changes resulting from the process, the second victim was clearly in a relatively early stage of decomposition.

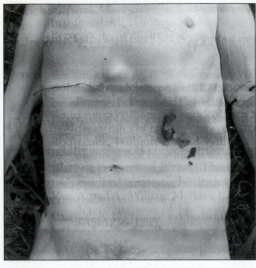

FIGURE 12.7   BLOATING   FIGURE 12.8   BLOATING

The gas by-products of bacterial growth throughout the body cause an increase in size. Here, the same individual was photographed at two and six days postmortem. Notice the xiphoid process, ribs, clavicle and anterior iliac crest in the left image that become obliterated in the right image.

The core body temperature was equivalent to the ambient temperature. Rigor was completely absent from the body and livor was fixed. As previously mentioned, the body was bloated, marbled, discolored, and the skin was slipping. In sum, the observable gross changes were the result of putrefaction as opposed to autolysis.

There is an inverse relationship between the interval between death and discovery and the accuracy in estimating that interval. While the initial internal changes resulting from autolysis are rapid and fairly consistent, the rules governing putrefaction are much less chronologically fixed. During the early stage of decomposition while the body cools, livor mortis is unfixed, and rigor mortis is waxing and waning, the estimation of the postmortem interval can be accurate to within a few hours. In addition to the previously mentioned techniques, many sophisticated methods have been developed to monitor the biochemical progression of early decay (Henssge et al. 1995; Kaatsch et al. 1994; Lange et al. 1993; Madea and Henssge 1988).

In order to understand the highly variable rate of putrefactive decay for standard utilization, researchers (Reed 1958; Rodriguez and Bass 1983; Galloway et al. 1989; Rhine and Dawson 1997; Galloway 1997; Clark et al. 1997, among others) have broken the progression of decay into stages following the soft and osseous tissue destruction characteristic of their geographic/climatic region. Although each researcher has developed his or her own stages and sequence of the advancement of decay, they can be melded into the following scheme: fresh, discoloration, bloating, skeletonization, and skeletal decomposition (Table 12.1) (Marks et al. 2000).

Based on the literature, the pathologist and anthropologist described the second, more fresh body as in the bloating stage of decomposition. The first victim discovered was nearly completely skeletonized and several of the disarticulated elements were scattered. However, a small amount of mummified tissue was present. Because some soft tissue adhered to the skeleton, the anthropologist

TABLE 12.1 STAGES OF DECAY AND ASSOCIATED GROSS MORPHOLOGIC CHANGES

STAGE OF DECOMPOSITION	EXTERNAL SIGNS
Fresh	Algor mortis
	Livor mortis
	Rigor mortis
Discoloration	Initial skin slippage
	Abdominal discoloration
	Progressive discoloration of thorax and neck
	Marbling
Bloating	Abdominal distention
	Bloating progresses throughout the body
	Initial skeletalization of face
Skeletonization	Bloating completely subsided
	Soft tissue continues to deteriorate
Skeletal Decomposition	All soft tissue consumed
	Skeleton completely disarticulated
	Cortex of bone begins to crack and age

placed this victim in the skeletonization stage. Once the bodies were defined in terms of stage of decomposition, the scientists turned back to the literature in an attempt to correlate the stages to time since death.

Researchers have sought to extrapolate the postmortem interval from the decompositional stage through two sometimes correlated avenues of study: (1) data compiled from cross-sectional accounts of medical examiner records and (2) longitudinal studies with data recording the progression of decay from fresh to skeletonized. Galloway et al.'s work (1989; Galloway 1997) is an excellent example of the cross-sectional approach. They correlated date of discovery, date last seen, and stage of decomposition for 468 medical examiner cases from Arizona and plotted the stage of decomposition against the postmortem interval illustrating the variability of the decay rate of a corpse in an arid environment. Rhine and Dawson (1997) developed a similarly ingenious plot illustrating the variability in decay rates from fifty medical examiner cases in New Mexico.

Equipped with a unique open-air research laboratory designed exclusively for longitudinally studying decomposition in East Tennessee, Bass and coworkers at the University of Tennessee have analyzed hundreds of bodies progressing through all stages of decomposition, and documented the postmortem interval at each stage (see Bass 1997; Rodriquez and Bass 1983; Mann et al. 1990) (see Figures 12.9–12.14 on page 170). Although the results of these studies are generally invaluable to the development of an understanding of the time since death phenomena in forensic anthropology, they lack the focus of correlating time since death to temperature and humidity. This perspective has become central in current research (Barshick et al. 2000; Marks et al. 2000).

The speed at which a body passes from fresh to skeletal is dependent on bacterial activity/growth, which, in turn, is more temperature- than time-dependent. Colonic bacteria are most active between the temperatures of 60 and 95°F (Micozzi 1997). Bacterial activity remarkably decreases at

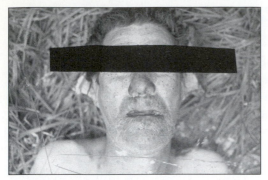

FIGURE 12.9   TWO DAYS POSTMORTEM

The fresh face with egg masses (white) in the nostrils, adjacent to right of nose and on neck.

FIGURE 12.12   TEN DAYS POSTMORTEM

Note the increased maggot size and activity and the discoloration and blackening (drying) of the skin during late bloating.

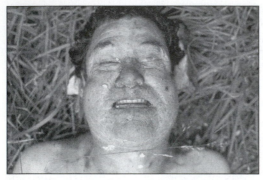

FIGURE 12.10   FOUR DAYS POSTMORTEM

Note the enlarged cheeks due to maggot activity and early bloating.

FIGURE 12.13   THIRTEEN DAYS POSTMORTEM

The maggots continue to reduce the soft tissues of the face.

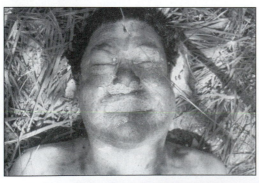

FIGURE 12.11   SIX DAYS POSTMORTEM

Note the active maggot mass in the lower face during advanced bloating.

FIGURE 12.14   SEVENTEEN DAYS POSTMORTEM

Note decreased maggot activity and beginning of skeletonization.

temperatures below 55°F and above 100°F. During the later stages of decay, insects play a large role in the rate of decomposition while bacteria plays a diminishing role. Insect activity is also influenced by temperature (Haskell et al. 1997). An alternate method to measure the rate of decomposition that incorporates the effects of temperature is accumulated daily degrees (ADD). ADD is the sum of consecutive average daily temperatures. In 1992, Vass and colleagues were the first to correlate ADD with advancing decay. Recent research on rates of decomposition have turned the focus from correlating stages of decomposition with time to correlating stages of decomposition against accumulated daily degrees. Marks and colleagues (2000) recently digitally recorded progression of decomposition while measuring temperature and humidity. Following Galloway (1997; Galloway et al. 1989) and Rhine and Dawson (1997), Marks et al. plotted each stage of decomposition against ADD. This pilot study currently involves data from five bodies with the goal of correlating the rate of decomposition to temperature and humidity, while illustrating variability of decay rates.

In practice, the association of the stage of decay to the postmortem interval is a relatively new method of time since death estimation. The scientists in the Tennessee cases reviewed both Galloway et al.'s (1989, Galloway 1997) and Marks et al.'s (2000) work but did not feel confident in either method to estimate time since death of the two victims. They ruled out Galloway's data because of the vast climatological discrepancies between Tennessee and Arizona. Furthermore, Marks et al.'s (2000) pilot study did not yet have sufficient data to obtain a reliable time since death estimation. Fortunately, the pathologist collected a representative sample of maggots from the various populations

found on the second victim and the anthropologist collected a soil sample of the primary decay site. The samples were sent to a forensic entomologist and biochemist, respectively, for analysis.

Entomology and Soil Analysis

Forensic entomology is a crucial component in the evaluation of the postmortem interval by providing a chronological "gold standard" for other perspectives, such as anthropology and criminalistics (Byrd and Castner 2001; Catts and Haskell 1990; Haskell et al. 1997). To date, the succession, activity, and longevity/maturity of a variety of arthropods reflect the stage of decay to a more accurate degree than assessment of gross morphological change of the decedent. Larval maturity, for example, although temperature influenced, is an excellent measuring tool of time since death. For example, in many settings, the *Calliphoridae* (blow fly) is the first carrion insect interested in a corpse. This insect is present on a corpse within the first hour of deposition and oviposition (egg laying) has been observed immediately (Rodriguez and Bass 1983). If death occurred near the time of deposition, the maturity level of the *Calliphoridae* larvae is the most sensitive indicator of time since death (Catts and Haskell 1990).

Three larval samples were taken from the hairline, cervical region, and perineum of the second victim and sent to a forensic entomologist along with climatological data of the crime scene for a postmortem estimation. The larvae were identified as blow flies. The samples taken from the neck and abdominal region were estimated to be three to four weeks old. The larvae sampled from the hairline were estimated to be one to two weeks old.

Vass et al. (1992) developed a method to correlate the concentration of volatile fatty acids (VFA) and pH found in the soil under a decomposing body to the accumulated degree days. Volatile fatty acids are the by-product of putrefactive breakdown of fat and muscle. The method is complicated by the fact that the concentration of VFA is proportional to the mass of the individual. In this case the first victim was unidentified at the time the soil analysis was done so exact weight was unknown, but the skeletal profile indicated the victim was a mature female. Vass reported three postmortem estimations based on three weight categories, 100–150 lbs., 150–200 lbs., 200–250 lbs. Choosing the lighter weight categories, the results indicated a postmortem estimation of eight months to one year.

Case Study Resolution

Soft and hard tissue analysis showed both victims died from sharp trauma to the neck. The first victim had several cutmarks that horizontally incised the body and left greater wing of the hyoid bone and the transverse processes of several cervical vertebrae located inferior and lateral to the hyoid. It was actually the differential decomposition of the head, neck, and post-crania of the second (fresh) victim that provided perimortem trauma clues to look for on the first victim, though this is not to say that the cutmark wounds would not have been discerned during anthropological analysis of the first victim had there not been a second body. It was just coincidence that both suffered sharp-force trauma.

Recall that a thirteen-year-old male and a fourteen-year-old female had been reported missing for exactly six weeks prior to the recovery of the bodies. The anthropologist determined that the long bones of the first victim revealed no evidence of epiphyseal activity (e.g., were completely fused) and the roots of the molar teeth were completely developed. Finally, decomposition status was far too advanced for a period of only

six weeks for the missing teenagers. However, always keep in mind that a "missing" date does not imply a date of death. Our assessment of time since death for the first victim was between eight months and one year. That estimation considers many variables from the state of decomposition, desiccation, cortical bone quality, arthropod and climatological evidence, carnivore activity, and soil analysis. The missing teenagers could be excluded because the skeleton was that of an adult. Ultimately, the first victim was identified as a twenty-nine-year-old white female who had been reported missing from a halfway house in Louisville, Kentucky, two years prior. Positive identification was achieved through frontal sinus patterning from an A-P (anterior-posterior) radiograph of the head taken six years before her disappearance.

The second victim was positively identified through dental records as the thirteen-year-old male who had been reported missing. However, the degree of decomposition was not consistent with the six-week period of time, given the warm late summer and early fall. Using the oldest insect population found on the victim, the time since death estimation was between three to four weeks.

A suspect in the death of the adult female was in another state and could not have been implicated in the second killing. That suspect received a life sentence. To date, no one has been arrested (or questioned) in the death of the young male.

Conclusion

The focus of forensic pathology has traditionally been and will continue to remain on the interpretation of perimortem events and their biological consequences in recently deceased victims. There has been a burgeoning practical need and resultant research focus into time since death questions by those investigators dealing with decomposing remains. Research in this field is essentially in its infancy even though as many prolonged postmortem environmental situations as imaginable have been explored to some degree by anthropologists. From a research perspective in pinpointing postmortem chronology, forensic pathology is primarily concerned with the process of autolysis while forensic anthropology is concerned with the putrefactive and later stages of decomposition.

After slight to significant natural processes reduce soft tissues through decomposition, the pathologist relies on the anthropologist to not only supply the more traditional odontoskeletal–demographic evaluations, but also trauma and time since death assessments. There is no reason to think that, as long as research and case-based experiences are shared between pathologists and anthropologists, this mutual alliance will not continue to flourish. In fact, the forensic researchers at the University of Tennessee who observe human decomposition, and our colleagues utilizing nonhuman models, have moved forensic anthropology toward center-stage in many areas of experimental taphonomic research. Since the majority of those forensic anthropologists studying these phenomena do not have access to an outdoor research facility to longitudinally quantify human decomposition processes, they must compile and quantify cross-sectional data from medical examiner sources to define the regional seasonal and climatic variation in specific geographic regions. We owe much of our present baseline knowledge about decomposition to the case-by-case database. Those real life (or death) forensic scenarios with known chronological parameters provide the litmus test for what we discover experimentally.

Given that pigs are the most appropriate nonhuman models, well demonstrated by entomological research (Byrd and Castner

2001; Haskell et al. 1997), longitudinal decomposition experimentation employing pig models are needed to provide quantification of regional/geographic variation. While the general gross trends in decomposition are recognized in a broad sense, the biochemical pathways producing those macroscopic results are poorly understood. Future research into these processes, macroscopic or microscopic, must concentrate upon the biochemistry of fresh and decomposing tissues, soils, odors, and continued appreciation and testing for differing depositional contexts against the two most important variables, temperature and humidity.

References

Aufderheide, Arthur C. 1981. Soft tissue paleopathology: An emerging subspecialty. *Human Pathology* 12:865–867.

Aufderheide, Arthur C., and Conrado Rodriguez-Martin. 1998. *The Cambridge Encyclopedia of Human Paleopathology*. Cambridge: Cambridge University Press.

Barshick, Stacy-Ann, Arpad A. Vass, Gary Sega, John Caton, Jennifer C. Love, and Murray K. Marks. 2000. Measurement technologies for determining time since death. *Proceedings of the American Academy of Forensic Science*, 187.

Bass, William M. 1997. Outdoor decomposition rates in Tennessee. Pp. 181–186 in *Forensic Taphonomy: The Postmortem Fate of Human Remains*, ed. William D. Haglund and Marcella H. Sorg. Boca Raton, FL: CRC Press.

Berne, Robert M., and Matthew N. Levy. 1993. *Physiology*. 3rd ed. St. Louis, MO: Mosby Year Book.

Byrd, Jason H., and James L. Castner. 2001. *Forensic Entomology: The Utility of Arthropods in Legal Investigations*. Boca Raton, FL: CRC Press.

Catts, Paul W., and Neal D. Haskell. 1990. *Entomology and Death: A Procedural Guide*. Clemson, SC: Joyce's Print Shop.

Clark, Michael A., Michael B. Worrell, and John E. Pless. 1997. Postmortem changes in soft tissues. Pp. 151–164 in *Forensic Taphonomy: The Postmortem Fate of Human Remains*, ed. William D. Haglund and Marcella H. Sorg. Boca Raton, FL: CRC Press.

Coe, John I. 1993. Postmortem chemistry update: Emphasis on forensic applications. *American*

Journal of Forensic Medicine and Pathology 14(2):92–94.

DiMiao, Dominick J., and Vincent J. M. DiMiao. 1989. *Forensic Pathology*. New York: Elsevier.

Dix, Jay, and Michael Graham. 2000. *Time of Death, Decomposition, and Identification: An Atlas*. Boca Raton, FL: CRC Press.

Dorfman, Howard D., and Bogdan Czerniak. 1998. *Bone Tumors*. St. Louis, MO: Mosby.

Galloway, Alison, ed. 1999. *Broken Bones—Anthropological Analysis of Blunt Force Trauma*. Springfield, IL: Charles C. Thomas.

Galloway, Alison. 1997. The process of decomposition: A model from the Arizona-Sonoran Desert. Pp. 139–149 in *Forensic Taphonomy: The Postmortem Fate of Human Remains*, ed. William D. Haglund and Marcella H. Sorg. Boca Raton, FL: CRC Press.

Galloway, Alison, Walter H. Birkby, Allen M. Jones, Thomas E. Henry, and Bruce O. Parks. 1989. Decay rates of human remains in an arid environment. *Journal of Forensic Science* 34(3):607–616.

Gill-King, H. 1997. Chemical and ultrastructural aspects of decomposition. Pp. 93–108 in *Forensic Taphonomy: The Postmortem Fate of Human Remains*, ed. William D. Haglund and Marcella H. Sorg. Boca Raton, FL: CRC Press.

Haglund, William D., and Marcella H. Sorg. 1997. *The Postmortem Fate of Human Remains*. Boca Raton, FL: CRC Press.

Haskell, Neal H., Robert D. Hall, Valerie J. Cervenka, and Michael A. Clark. 1997. On the body: Insects' life stage presence, their postmortem artifacts. Pp. 353–363 in *Forensic Taphonomy: The Postmortem Fate of Human Remains*, ed. William D. Haglund and Marcella H. Sorg. Boca Raton, FL: CRC Press.

Henssge, Claus, Bernard Knight, Thomas Krompecher, B. Madea, and Len Nokes. 1995. *The Estimation of the Time Since Death in the Early Postmortem Period*. Boston, MA: Arnold.

Junqueira, Luiz C., Jose Carneiro, and Robert O. Kelley. 1995. *Basic Histology*. Norwalk, CT: Appleton and Lange.

Kaatsch, H. J., E. Schmidtke, and W. Nietsch. 1994. Photometric measurement of pressure-induced blanching of livor mortis as an aid to estimating time of death. Application of a new system for quantifying pressure-induced blanching in lividity. *International Journal of Legal Pathology* 106(4):209–214.

Knight, Bernard. 1996. *Forensic Pathology*. 2nd ed. London: Arnold.

Larsen, Clark S. 1998. *Bioarchaeology—Interpreting Behavior from the Human Skeleton*. Cambridge: Cambridge University Press.

Madea, B., and Claus Henssge. 1988. Determination of the time since death II. Electrical excitability of skeletal muscles. Current state and recent development. *Acta Medical Legal Society* 38(1):91–108.

Madea, B., Thomas Krompecher, and Bernard Knight. 1995. Muscle and tissue changes after death. Pp. 138–171 in *The Estimation of the Time Since Death in the Early Postmortem Period*, ed. Claus Henssge, Bernard Knight, Thomas Krompecher, B. Madea, Len Nokes. Boston, MA: Arnold.

Mann, Robert W., William M. Bass, and Lee Meadows. 1990. Time since death and decomposition of the human body: Variables and observations in case and experimental field studies. *Journal of Forensic Sciences* 35(1):103–111.

Marks, Murray K., Jennifer C. Love, and Sandra K. Elkins. 2000. Time since death: A practical guide to physical postmortem events. *Proceedings of the American Academy of Forensic Sciences*, 181–182.

McCarthy, Edward F., and Frank J. Frassica. 1998. *Pathology of Bone and Joint Disorders with Clinical and Radiographic Correlation*. Philadelphia: W. B. Saunders.

Micozzi, Marc S. 1997. Frozen environments and soft tissue preservation. Pp. 171–180 in *Forensic Taphonomy: The Postmortem Fate of Human Remains*, ed. William D. Haglund and Marcella H. Sorg. Boca Raton, FL: CRC Press.

Nielsen, Henrik, Jan Engberg, and Ingolf Thuesen. 1994. DNA from arctic human burials. Chapter 8 in *Ancient DNA*, ed. B. Hermann and S. Hummel. New York: Springer-Verlag.

Ortner, Donald J., and Walter G. J. Putschar. 1981. *Identification of Pathological Conditions in Human Skeletal Remains*. Vol. 28. Washington, D.C.: Smithsonian Contributions to Anthropology.

Reed, H. B. 1958. A study of dog carcass communities in Tennessee with special references to the insects. *American Midland Naturalist* 34(3):213–245.

Reichs, Kathleen J. 1998. *Forensic Osteology: Advances in the Identification of Human Remains*. 2nd ed. Springfield, IL: Charles C. Thomas.

Rhine, Stan, and J. E. Dawson. 1997. Estimation of time since death in the Southwestern United States. Pp. 145-159 in *Forensic Osteology: Advances in the Identification of Human Remains*, ed. Kathleen J. Riechs. 2nd ed. Springfield, IL: Charles C. Thomas.

Rodriguez, William C., and William M. Bass. 1983. Insect activity and its relationship to decay rates of human cadavers in East Tennessee. *Journal of Forensic Science* 28(2): 423–432.

Spitz, Werner U. 1993. *Medicolegal Investigation of Death—Guidelines for the Application of Pathology to Crime Investigation*. 3rd ed. Springfield, IL: Charles C. Thomas.

Steinbock, R. Ted. 1976. *Paleopathological Diagnosis and Interpretation: Bone Diseases in Ancient Human Populations*. Springfield, IL: Charles C. Thomas.

Thompson, David D. 1982. Forensic anthropology. Pp. 357–370 in *History of American Physical Anthropology*, ed. F. Spencer. New York: Academic Press.

Tobin, Allan J., and Richard E. Morrel. 1997. *Asking about Cells*. Fort Worth, TX: Saunders College Publishing.

Vass, Arpad A. et al. 1992. Time since death determinations of human cadavers using soil solution. *Journal of Forensic Sciences* 37(5): 1236–1253.

Wold, Lester E. 1990. *Atlas of Orthopaedic Pathology*. Philadelphia: W. B. Saunders.

THE SKULL ON THE LAWN

TROPHIES, TAPHONOMY, AND FORENSIC ANTHROPOLOGY

P. Willey and Paulette Leach

On October 1, 1992—less than a month before Halloween—officials were called to a home in Happy Valley, Shasta County, Northern California. That day some of the residents were unhappy. After picking up her grandchildren from school, a woman returned home and let the children play outside. Soon the children entered the house and told her that they had seen a skull in the front yard. Imaginary friends are one thing, perhaps, but bones are a different, very real matter. More than happy to prove their point, the children brought a skull and mandible into the house. The grandmother immediately notified the authorities.

When Shasta County detectives arrived, the grandmother assured the officers that she knew of no missing persons in the area and that there were "no problems with the neighbors." The grandmother further told investigators that she thought that perhaps the bones had been carried onto the lawn by one of the dogs that freely roamed the neighborhood. The officers assured her that the investigation would continue and took the bones into custody.

Skeletal remains of an unknown individual found under suspicious circumstances—these are the types of cases in which forensic anthropologists are consulted. The only thing this early Halloween case lacked was a dark and stormy night combined with a ghoul or two. Over the years, the Chico State Human Identification Laboratory has developed a good working relationship with the Shasta County Sheriff-Coroner's Office and the bones were transferred to us, eighty-five miles away.

When the bones arrived at Chico State, they were "clean," dry, and required no preparation by our laboratory before analysis began. One of us (PW) had seen similar skulls before, so hypotheses and alternate hypotheses were being generated even before the chain of custody tags were signed. The hypothesis that seemed most likely was that the remains were that of a trophy skull. Trophy remains are those that are originally acquired under suspect circumstances and kept as a memento of the event. Many assessments would have to be made to confirm such a conclusion, however, and that evidence was gathered in the usual systematic way.

Snow (1982) has suggested a useful checklist and sequence of assessments to conduct a formal analysis. The first critical step is to determine whether or not the remains are human. If not, then the remains are no longer of forensic interest, although there are exceptions, such as illegal trafficking of animal parts, poaching, or other criminal activities involving animals (Owsley et al. 1992). If they are human, the next step is to determine if the remains are from a single individual or the commingled remains of several people. The third assessment is the time interval between death and discovery. Fourth, the deceased's biological parameters are determined. These parameters are the traditional osteological assessments—age at death, sex, ancestry, stature, and diseases or injuries. Finally, evidence of disease and trauma is considered to individualize the subject and to suggest a possible cause and manner of death.

To Snow's list, we always add another assessment—taphonomy. Taphonomy consists of the events and processes that modify remains following a person's death. These observations may be extremely important in assessing the manner of death and the importance of the remains in a court of law. Taphonomic determinations may be helpful in establishing the postmortem interval, the sequence of perimortem trauma, and the intent to destroy, modify, or conceal the remains. The taphonomic processes indicated by the remains from Happy Valley proved critical in resolving this case.

Analysis

Species and Number of Individuals

The human-nonhuman assessment is a humdrum but always essential beginning. A large proportion of remains submitted for analysis are not human. In a summary of 1,845 cases reported by members of the American Board of Forensic Anthropology in their 1995 annual updates, 4.7 percent of the cases were not human (Reichs 1998, 27). As Reichs notes, however, that figure is probably much lower than the actual number because many members fail to include nonhuman remains in their records or their annual updates. Here at Chico State during the past ten years, approximately one-fourth of the cases have been either nonhuman remains (19.1 percent) or cases that include both human and nonhuman elements (6.3 percent). None of those nonhuman specimens were of any further relevance to a court of law.

When the remains are identified as human, the next step requires determining what skeletal elements are present and how many individuals are represented. In other words, we note what human parts escaped the ravages of taphonomy, what has been preserved and recovered, and what is present for analysis.

In the Happy Valley case, the remains present were clearly a human mandible and skull of a single individual. No nonhuman elements were recovered. The skull was incomplete, however, missing the left zygomatic bone and zygomatic process of the left temporal, and portions of the right zygomatic arch, left maxilla, and alveolar process (see Figure 13.1 on page 178). All of the teeth whose alveolar portions were preserved had been lost following death. It is not too unusual to encounter fragmented and missing elements. The causes of these losses and breaks proved critical in resolving the skull's origin and helped to assess our hypothesis of the case's origin.

Interval since Death

The time period between death and recovery is almost always a difficult assessment. The presence of decomposition odor, adhering soft tissue, oozing grease, and insect remains may aid the estimation. But none

178

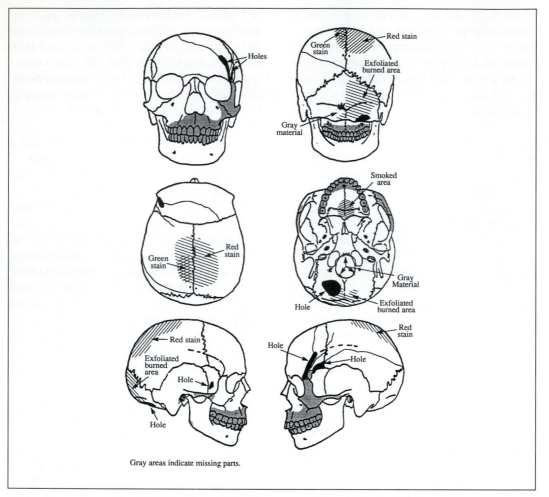

Gray areas indicate missing parts.

FIGURE 13.1   SCHEMATIC DIAGRAM OF HAPPY VALLEY SKULL

of these diagnostic characteristics were present in this case, so the interval since death was inexact. Based on the taphonomic changes and lack of soft tissue, we estimated that death had occurred years, perhaps decades, before the remains were recovered. This, too, contributed to the evaluation of our working hypothesis.

Age at Death

One of the vital biological parameters forensic anthropologists address is age. One source of confusion in this area is the fact that people don't always feel or act their age. Sometimes they feel they are physically ready or able to engage in activities that are incompatible with their chronological age. They are too young to cross the street, too young to drink alcohol legally, too young to retire, or too old to do the things that they once did more ably—or at least wish they had been able to do. Age at death is a snapshot of the last stage of maturation a person has achieved before the time of his or her departure.

This "snapshot" has two aspects. One aspect is chronological age—how much time has occurred between the time of birth and death, measured in some chronometric interval, such as months or years. It is chronological age that is calculated from our driver's license or birth certificate. The other aspect of age is biological. Biological age is related to how fast or slowly we grow, develop, and, once achieving maturation, how rapidly or slowly we deteriorate. Biological age is influenced by our environment, genetics, and lifestyle. Forensic anthropologists estimate chronological age based on the biological age of the remains.

Age at death is estimated using a variety of skeletal changes. The most accurate indicators of adult age are histological (including the percentage of circumferential lamellar bone, osteons, and osteon fragments) and postcranial macroscopic ones (such as pubic symphysis and rib sternal end morphologies). But in this case, none of those more accurate approaches could be applied, because the only remains present were a skull and mandible. When the skull is all that is available for age estimation, suture closure is used out of necessity. Employing Todd and Lyon's (1925) method for endocranial suture closure, the age of the skull was estimated to be younger than 36 years and possibly younger than 27 years.

Meindl and Lovejoy's (1985) vault observations gave a minimum age of 19 years, while their lateral-anterior observations placed the skull between 21 and 42 years. The application of these techniques and other age estimation techniques to the present case is summarized in Table 13.1.

The basilar suture of the Happy Valley skull, one of the more reliable age-indicating sutures (McKern and Stewart 1957), showed complete union, suggesting an age of at least fourteen years, while the other ectocranial sutures were completely open, suggesting an adolescent or youthful adult. The sutures of the maxilla were inspected. All of the preserved sutures were open, although the incisive suture, which may have been the most useful age indicator in this case, was lost from postmortem damage. Based on contemporary cadaver and forensic collections (Mann et al. 1991), such palatal suture closure is typical of someone younger than middle age, probably younger than thirty years.

Dental development provided a useful technique for age estimation. The sockets for the third molars were porotic and indicated that the tooth apices were incompletely developed, the roots perhaps 75 percent or more complete (Moorrees et al.

TABLE 13.1   AGE AT DEATH ESTIMATION TECHNIQUES, THEIR EXPRESSION IN THE HAPPY VALLEY REMAINS AND THE AGE ESTIMATIONS

OBSERVATION	EXPRESSION	AGE AT DEATH	REFERENCE
Endocranial suture closure	All open	≤ 36 years	Todd and Lyon 1925
Ectocranial vault suture closure	All open	≤ 19 years	Meindl and Lovejoy 1985
Ectocranial anterior-lateral suture closure	All open	21–42 years	Meindl and Lovejoy 1985
Basilar suture closure	Closed	≥ 15 years	McKern and Stewart 1957
Palatal suture closure	All present open	25–30 years	Mann et al. 1991
Root development of third molar	Root ca. ¾ complete	≤ 30 years	Moorrees et al. 1963

1963). This development suggested an age of late adolescence or early adulthood.

When all of the age indications were evaluated together, we had an individual who died in late adolescence or early adulthood. In terms of years, an age interval of 15 to 35 years seemed most likely, although a broader age interval could not be excluded. This age was consistent with our hypothesis that the skull was a trophy.

Sex

Sex is another important biological parameter. By accurately assessing sex, the analyst can exclude half of the population from further consideration. Parenthetically, we do try to determine *sex*, usually not gender. Sex is the biological characteristic that divides the species in two. Social roles and behavior determine gender. Because we usually assess the biological aspects, we determine sex, not gender.

A final qualification is needed. Sexual dimorphism (the morphological differences in overall size and shape between the sexes) differs from one population to the next. Some populations display great sexual dimorphism, making sex assessment fairly easy and accurate to estimate. But even in the most dimorphic populations, there is considerable overlap between the sexes. Further, some populations are more gracile, others more robust. We believed this specimen was from a more gracile population, a group with little dimorphism, making sex assessment more difficult and less accurate than in a more dimorphic population.

Table 13.2 summarizes the osteological observations used to determine the sex of the Happy Valley remains. Unfortunately, those characteristics suggesting the skull was of one sex were balanced by an equal number of characteristics suggesting it was the other sex. The morphological observations were supplemented by metric analysis to estimate sex.

Employing the sex discriminant function in *FORDISC 2.0* (Ousley and Jantz 1996) for twenty-four measurements, the Happy Valley skull was classified as female (Table 13.3) with a posterior probability of 0.756, and a typicality of 0.000. The posterior probability

TABLE 13.2   SELECTED SEX CHARACTERISTICS
AND THEIR APPLICATION TO THE HAPPY VALLEY SKULL AND MANDIBLE

CHARACTERISTIC	OCCURRENCE IN HAPPY VALLEY REMAINS		SEX INDICATED			COMMENTS
	PRESENT	ABSENT	FEMALE	MALE	UNKNOWN	
Round orbital margin	X			X		
Supraorbital development	X			X		Slight
Nasion indentation	X			X		Slight
Large mastoid process	X			X		
Robust nuchal area		X	X			
Sloping forehead		X	X			
Acute gonial angle		X	X			
Square chin		X			X	Round, not pointed
Overall large size		X	X			Medium-sized

Source: After Bass 1987.

TABLE 13.3   FORDISC 2.0 RESULTS FOR THE HAPPY VALLEY SKULL AND OTHERS
(OTHER THAN THE HAPPY VALLEY SKULL, FORDISC 2.0 IS APPLIED
TO MEASUREMENTS PREVIOUSLY PRESENTED IN THE ORIGINAL PUBLICATIONS)

	SEX (POSTERIOR PROBABILITY/ TYPICALITY)	MOST LIKELY ANCESTRY (POSTERIOR PROBABILITY/ TYPICALITY)	SECOND-MOST LIKELY ANCESTRY (POSTERIOR PROBABILITY/TYPICALITY)
Happy Valley (Shasta Co. 92-766)	Female (0.756/0.000)	American Indian female (0.489/0.261)	Vietnamese male (0.354/0.231)
Japanese soldier (Bass 1983)	Female (0.975/0.740)	Japanese female (0.466/0.890)	White female (0.246/0.745)
Japanese pilot (Bass 1983)	Male (0.906/0.318)	White male (0.452/0.254)	Black male (0.213/0.158)
Vietnamese (1987.3107.02) (Sledzik & Ousley 1991)	Female (0.925/0.013)	Japanese female (0.616/0.566)	Chinese male (0.100/0.287)
Vietnamese (1987.3107.03) (Sledzik & Ousley 1991)	Male (0.863/0.000)	Vietnamese male (0.928/0.000)	Japanese male (0.044/0.000)
Vietnamese (1987.3107.05) (Sledzik & Ousley 1991)	Female (0.710/0.089)	Black female* (0.284/0.159)	Japanese female* (0.284/0.159)
Vietnamese (1987.3107.08) (Sledzik & Ousley 1991)	Male (0.735/0.281)	Japanese male (0.418/0.406)	Chinese male (0.148/0.265)
Vietnamese (1987.3107.09) (Sledzik & Ousley 1991)	Female (0.622/0.533)	Japanese female (0.281/0.785)	Black female (0.257/0.764)
Vietnamese (1987.3107.23) (Sledzik & Ousley 1991)	Male (0.896/0.033)	Chinese male (0.396/0.580)	Vietnamese male (0.275/0.517)
Vietnamese (Taylor et al. 1984)	Male (0.771/0.931)	Japanese male (0.314/0.980)	Hispanic male (0.213/0.954)

* Each identification is equally likely.

indicated that, assuming the skull is from one of the base samples, there is a 75.6 percent chance that it was from the group identified by the discriminant function—in this case, female. The typicality of zero, however, meant that the skull is atypical of the individuals in the reference sample. The *FORDISC* sex discriminant function was established on black and white reference samples (Jantz 1999), groups with considerable sexual dimorphism and of relatively larger size than most Asian populations. The lack of typicality of the Happy Valley skull indicated it is unlike either of those reference samples. As a consequence, this application of *FORDISC* may have been inappropriate for the case at hand and the resulting sex assessment unreliable.

Although the overall size of the skull was medium and it displayed some gracile characteristics, the rounded orbital margins, supraorbital ridge, nasal indentation and mastoid processes appeared masculine. If the skull represented an individual from a gracile and sexually nondimorphic population, these features would be the better indicator of sex than the results of the multivariate discriminant function, which was based on more dimorphic populations. The skull was finally determined to be male and this assessment was consistent with the trophy skull hypothesis.

Ancestry

Race is a dirty word. A person's race, ancestry, or heritage may have few biological indicators or definitive morphological characteristics, even with soft tissue present. Still, there may be modal, normative morphological expressions of ancestry, whereby certain anatomical characteristics are present in many individuals of a group from a certain geographic area.

Using standard morphological characteristics (Rhine 1990), the Happy Valley skull seemed to be of Asian descent. This conclusion was supported by the presence of wormian bones, rectangular eye orbits, projecting zygomatics, curved zygomatico-maxillary sutures, a parabolic dental arcade, and a vertical chin. Other characteristics of the skull were consistent with this assessment. Table 13.4 provides a summary of the features used to determine ancestry. Note that Rhine's ancestry terms (American Caucasoid, Southwestern Mongoloid, and

American Black) have been employed in abbreviated form in Table 13.4.

A metrical assessment was also used. The most reliable discriminant functions for determining ancestry employ cranial measurements, which are then entered into the same *FORDISC 2.0* program that was used to estimate sex. Fourteen cranial measurements of the Happy Valley skull were taken and inserted into the *FORDISC* functions, which then placed the individual into statistical space and classified it into one of the reference groups. The reference groups included black, Japanese, Native American, and white females and males, and Hispanic, Chinese, and Vietnamese males.

The Happy Valley specimen was identified as a Native American female (posterior probability 0.489, typicality 0.261), a Vietnamese male (posterior probability 0.354, typicality 0.231) being the second-most-likely identity, and other groups being less likely (see Table 13.3 on page 181). Both of these assessments indicated a general Asian ancestry, Vietnamese being the more gracile and less sexually dimorphic of the two populations. It is noteworthy that only some of the better discriminating facial measurements were possible on the Happy Valley cranium.

TABLE 13.4   SELECTED ANCESTRAL CHARACTERISTICS
AND THEIR EXPRESSION ON THE HAPPY VALLEY SKULL

Characteristic	Expression	American Caucasoid	Southwestern Mongoloid	American Black
Wormian bones	Present		X	
Rectangular orbits	Present		X	
Indentation at nasion	Present—slight	X		
Shape of nasals	Quonset			X
Zygomatic bones	Projecting		X	
Zygomaxillary suture shape	Curved		X	
Dental arcade shape	Parabolic		X	
Oval window visible	One visible, other not	X	X	X

Source: After Rhine 1990.

A final ancestry assessment included both the results of the morphological characteristics and the discriminant function. These combined results were most consistent with a male of Asian ancestry, possibly Vietnamese. This conclusion, too, supported our trophy skull hypothesis.

Stature

The forensic anthropologist typically uses long bone limb lengths in appropriate regression formulae by sex and race to estimate stature (e.g., Trotter and Glesser 1958). Height is generally not estimated from cranial and mandibular remains alone, so no attempt to establish stature was made in this case.

Antemortem and Perimortem Pathology

Sticks and stones may break your bones, and skeletal manifestations result from them. Disease and trauma that occur both long before death and around the time of death often manifest themselves in the skeletal system. In the Happy Valley specimen, there were notable perimortem defects superior and lateral to the left orbit (Figures 13.1 and 13.2). The larger defect (55 mm x 6.5 mm) was linear, extending from the left orbit superiorly and posteriorly across the vault and forehead. The smaller defect (21 mm x 8.5 mm) was also linear, extending posteriorly from the margin of the larger fracture. Both defects had fractures radiating from their posterior edges and the defects' edges were stained, indicating a considerable time interval since the breaks occurred. The nature of the defects and the associated fractures were consistent with a blow or multiple blows to the cranial vault.

In addition to the fractures extending posteriorly from the two major defects, there was a linear fracture that was probably associated with these blows that coursed

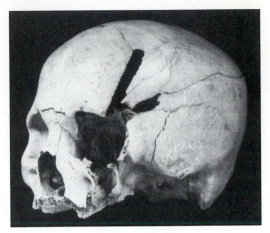

FIGURE 13.2 BONE DAMAGE TO LEFT FACIAL AND FRONTAL AREA OF HAPPY VALLEY SKULL

transversely from the left orbit across the glabellar region to the right orbit. It did not continue through the right zygofrontal process or the pterygoid plates.

Finally, there was a perimortem defect in the greater wing of the right sphenoid. This defect was smaller (9 mm x 6 mm) than either of the previous two. There were no fractures radiating from this defect.

If these blows occurred while the person was alive, then they could have been associated with the cause of death. Much caution is warranted in making such determinations, however. Stewart (1979, 76) stated that cause of death—the initiation of the cessation of the physiological processes necessary to sustain life—is rarely, if ever, possible to determine from skeletal remains. Even if physiological processes could be inferred from the bone, forensic anthropologists rarely have the specialized training required to identify and interpret those processes. Cause of death is the purview of the pathologist or physician, a determination codified in most jurisdictions by the coroner or medical examiner. While pointing out trauma, suggesting possible causes for it, and assessing whether it occurred ante-, peri-, or postmortem may be appropriate, a forensic anthropologist does not determine cause of death from the skeleton. Such a determination is a "rookie" error of the worst kind, one not made in the Happy Valley case.

Along with injuries, the remains were also examined for indications of antemortem disease. Medical records or family recollections of an individual's health may be useful in including or excluding a possible identification. Unfortunately, there were no major anomalies or indications of antemortem disease on the Happy Valley specimens.

Taphonomic Processes

Taphonomic events were the key to resolving this case. Postmortem alterations included staining, heat, drilling, recent breaks, and polishing—all characteristics shared by trophy skulls.

A red stain, perhaps left by contact with paint or rust, was present on the posterior portion of the vault (see Figure 13.1 on page 178). Within the boundaries of the red stain, there was also a blue-green discoloration that may indicate previous contact with copper or brass. A gray substance—perhaps clay, putty, or caulk—was present on the occipital and scattered elsewhere on the skull.

Evidence of contact with heat was also present (Figures 13.1 and 13.3). Depending on the intensity and duration of the heat, a variety of manifestations may occur (Buikstra and Swegle 1989). The lightest degree of heating is "smoking," when gray or black soot settles on the bone. The Happy Valley skull's palate and an area on the occipital (Figure 13.3) displayed such smoking. Exfoliation, the peeling away and loss of a bone surface, from charring is indicative of more intense heat. Adjacent to the smoked area, a portion of the Happy Valley occipital was exfoliated. This region bordered a hole that was perhaps caused or modified by the heat. Finally, the greatest degree of

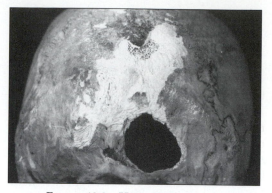

FIGURE 13.3   HOLE, EXFOLIATION, AND BURNING ON OCCIPITAL OF HAPPY VALLEY SKULL

burning is calcination—the loss of organic materials from heat. This degree of heating results in a white or light gray color, and brittle, china-like bone. No calcination was noted on the remains.

Drilled holes were present on both of the mandibular condyles (Figure 13.4) and on the skull immediately anterior to both of the mastoids. The internal diameters of the holes were between 2.0 and 2.8 mm, with most being approximately 2.4 mm. The locations and sizes of the holes suggested that they were most likely made in order to attach the mandible to the skull with a thin

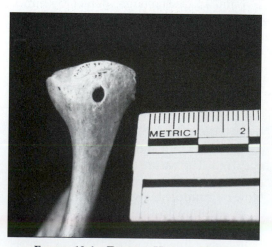

FIGURE 13.4   DRILLED HOLE IN HAPPY VALLEY RIGHT MANDIBULAR CONDYLE

wire or perhaps a thread. Such attachments are usually done for displaying skulls with articulated mandibles. This modification is commonly seen in biological supply skeletons used for instructional purposes and in trophy skulls.

The recent postmortem breaks were noted earlier, but bear comment here in the context of taphonomy. Breaks occurred in the anterior maxillary alveolus. These breaks were typical of careless handling or perhaps chewing by dogs or other canids, although no definite gnaw-marks were present. The rest of the breaks (zygomatic bone and processes) were typical of rough, careless handling that poorly "curated" trophies experience.

Burnishing or polishing was also present. Much of the external vault had developed a patina from being burnished. Generally such burnishing occurs incidentally with much touching and handling. It is commonly found on specimens used in osteology and forensic anthropology laboratories. In instructional laboratories, just before important quizzes, students handle the study specimens as often and repetitiously as rosary beads, praying for a passing grade. A material result of such handling of "curated" specimens is a burnish or polish, and similar burnishing occurred on the Happy Valley remains.

Comparisons

As mentioned earlier, there was a familiarity to the remains and much of this familiarity was related to the taphonomic processes the remains exhibited. The Happy Valley remains were similar to skulls we had analyzed before, as well as seen in published descriptions of similar specimens identified as trophy skulls. Therefore, early in our analysis we hypothesized that the Happy Valley bones were trophies.

Most reminiscent of the Happy Valley case were two Japanese soldiers' skulls,

which were accessioned in the 1970s and curated in the Bass Osteological Collection at the University of Tennessee. Like the Happy Valley specimen, those remains bore paint and were missing bony projections. Bass (1983) published an article describing the skulls, in which he warned forensic anthropologists that additional trophy skulls might be arriving in their laboratories. He noted that a generation was passing and that such materials were being discarded or redistributed to others. As Bass predicted, such trophies were found elsewhere, and descriptions of several other trophy skulls have been published. Taylor et al. (1984) responded the year following Bass's publication with a description of a Vietnamese female that was recovered during the search of a suspect's New York home. Sledzik and Ousley (1991) followed with descriptions of six Vietnamese skulls confiscated as U.S. military personnel attempted to bring them into the country. Gill-King (1992) has reported on another Japanese trophy skull, although published details concerning that specimen are limited.

Table 13.5 (on page 186) shows how the postmortem treatment of the Happy Valley remains compares to these trophy cases. The elements present (skull and/or mandible), the age at death (usually older adolescent or younger adult), the ancestry (Asian, possibly Vietnamese) and the sex (male) were mostly similar. Nearly all—if not all—displayed burnishing from frequent handling. In addition, they suffered presumably accidental "curatorial" breaks of some fragile bones. There was postmortem loss of teeth, indicated by the sharp alveolar margins surrounding the tooth sockets. In most ways, these characteristics compared favorably with the anatomical supply specimens employed in osteology classes. In addition, the trophy skulls displayed other features not usually found on study specimens. They typically had paint or pigment spatter on them from careless application of pigments

TABLE 13.5   CHARACTERISTICS OF WAR-RELATED TROPHY SKULLS

	HAPPY VALLEY (PRESENT CASE)	WWII JAPANESE (BASS 1983)	VIETNAMESE (TAYLOR ET AL. 1984)	VIETNAMESE (SLEDZIK & OUSLEY 1991)
Number of individuals	One	Two	One	Six
Elements	Skull & mandible	Cranial vaults	Skull	Skulls
Age	Young adult	"Military age"	Young adult	Adolescents & young adults
Sex	Male	Males	Female [?]	Mostly males
Perimortem damage	Present in vault	Possible in face	Gunshot wound	Present in some specimens
Postmortem damage	Present	Present	Present	Present
Burning	Present	Absent from bones	Present	Present in some specimens
Pigments or graffiti	Present	Present	Not reported	Present on most specimens
Burnishing, patina	Present	Not reported	Not reported	Present
Teeth	All absent postmortem	Faces absent	All absent postmortem	Nearly all lost postmortem
Soft tissue	Absent	Absent	Absent	Absent

near the trophies or purposeful painting directly on them. Some had smoked or burned surfaces, or wax, suggesting modifications from Halloweens past. The key to understanding and interpreting all of these specimens was their "curated" appearance.

FORDISC 2.0 is applied here to the comparative specimens to assess sex and ancestry (see Table 13.3 on page 181), employing the previously published measurements. The results of FORDISC were generally what are expected given the FORDISC results for the Happy Valley remains. Sex is identified as male in approximately half of the cases. It is noteworthy that the Vietnamese "female" described by Taylor et al. (1984) is identified as a male using FORDISC 2.0; the possibility of sex misidentification by the original analysts must be considered a possibility. FORDISC's ancestry identification of the other trophy skulls is as eclectic as its

identification of the Happy Valley remains (Table 13.3). Most of the other trophy skulls are identified as being Asian or of Asian ancestry as the original analysts concluded. However, the FORDISC results contradict some of the original assessments, identifying a few of the trophies as being black, white, or Asian groups other than their presumed identity.

The Rest of the Story

When the mother of the Happy Valley children was later questioned concerning the remains, she suggested an explanation that was consistent with these osteological observations. She said that when her husband returned from a tour of duty in Vietnam, he brought mementos home with him. Among his souvenirs were a human skull and jaw. He kept the skull in their garage, displaying it at Halloween and other such times. She demanded that he rid their home of the bones. When he failed to do that—and presumably for other transgressions and incompatibilities as well—she divorced him. As a part of their separation, he moved to Southern California. Although he vacated the house, some legacies remained—among them the bones, which are now curated by the Chico State Human Identification Laboratory.

There are still a number of poorly answered or unanswered questions concerning this case.

- How did the skull get from the garage to the yard? It is likely that the children found the bones in the garage, moved them to the lawn, and then denied their involvement.

- Were the bones from a Vietnamese individual who died a natural death or was this a war-related casualty? The defects suggest a homicide, but lacking soft-tissue evidence, it is also possible that the defects happened after the person's death.

- What instruments and actions caused the perimortem damage to the vault? They appeared to have been made by an elongated instrument and may have been associated with the cause of death, but these inferences were neither confirmed nor denied by the informants.

- How were the bones defleshed? The burning on the occipital suggests that heat may have been employed in the process, but the heating may have occurred long after the flesh was removed.

- How were the bones smuggled into the United States? Presumably the children's father sneaked them into the country but that supposition was neither confirmed nor denied.

All cases leave questions, even the relatively simple, resolved cases. Rarely do we know for sure that the events reconstructed from the bones, the version accepted by the court, or even the story told in a confession are what actually happened. It is these uncertainties that keep the field interesting, challenging, and rewarding.

Acknowledgments

Ray Bailey of the Shasta County Medical Examiner's Office provided information concerning the remains and their context, and authorized their donation to Chico State. An earlier version of this manuscript was presented as a paper titled "Vietnamese Trophy Skull from Northern California" to the Physical Anthropology Section, American Academy of Forensic Sciences Annual Meeting, February 1994, San Antonio, Texas. Since then, Paul Sledzik provided bibliographic resources, Richard L. Jantz gave insights into the application of the *FORDISC 2.0* program and discriminant functions in general, and Judy Stolen drew the schematic illustrations of the skull and mandible (Figure 13.1 on page 178).

References

Bass, William M. 1983. The occurrence of Japanese trophy skulls in the United States. *Journal of Forensic Sciences* 28(3):800–803.

Bass, William M. 1987. *Human Osteology: A Laboratory and Field Manual*. Columbia, MO: Missouri Archaeological Society.

Brooks, Sheilagh T. 1955. Skeletal age at death: The reliability of cranial and pubic age indicators. *American Journal of Physical Anthropology* 13:567–597.

Buikstra, Jane E., and Mark Swegle. 1989. Bone modifications due to burning: Experimental evidence. Pp. 247–258 in *Bone Modification*, ed. R. Bonnichsen and Marcella H. Sorg. Orono, ME: Center for the Study of the First Americans.

Gill-King, H. 1992. A Japanese "trophy skull" from the Battle of Saipan. Program and abstracts of the American Academy of Forensic Sciences annual meeting, February 1992, New Orleans. Colorado Springs, CO: American Academy of Forensic Sciences. Page 162.

Jantz, Richard L. 1999. Personal communication. Electronic message addressed to the first author, dated December 11, 1999.

Mann, Robert W., Richard L. Jantz, William M. Bass, and P. S. Willey. 1991. Maxillary suture obliteration: A visual method for estimating skeletal age. *Journal of Forensic Sciences* 36(3):781–791.

McKern, Thomas W., and T. Dale Stewart. 1957. *Skeletal Age Changes in Young American Males. Analyzed from the Standpoint of Age Identification*. Natick, MA: Environmental Protection Research Division, Quartermaster Research and Development Center, U.S. Army. Technical Report EP-45.

Meindl, Richard S., and C. Owen Lovejoy. 1985. Ectocranial suture closure: A revised method for the determination of skeletal age at death based on the lateral-anterior sutures. *American Journal of Physical Anthropology* 68:57–66.

Moorrees, C. F. A., E. A. Fanning, and Edward E. Hunt, Jr. 1963. Age variation of formation stages for ten permanent teeth. *Journal of Dental Research* 42:1490–1502.

Ousley, Stephen D., and Richard L. Jantz. 1996. *FORDISC 2.0*: Personal computer forensic discriminant functions. Knoxville, TN: The University of Tennessee.

Owsley, Douglas W., E. D. Roberts, and E. M. Manning. 1992. Field recovery and analysis of horse skeletal remains. *Journal of Forensic Sciences* 37(1):163–175.

Reichs, Kathleen J. 1998. Forensic anthropology: A decade of progress. Pp. 13–38 in *Forensic Osteology: Advances in the Identification of Human Remains*, ed. Kathleen J. Reichs. 2nd ed. Springfield, IL: Charles C. Thomas.

Rhine, Stanley. 1990. Non-metric skull racing. Vol. 4, pp. 9–20 in *Skeletal Attribution of Race*, ed. George W. Gill and Stanley Rhine. Albuquerque, NM: Maxwell Museum of Anthropology; Anthropology Papers.

Sledzik, Paul S., and Stephen Ousley. 1991. Analysis of six Vietnamese trophy skulls. *Journal of Forensic Sciences* 36(2):520–530.

Snow, Clyde C. 1982. Forensic anthropology. *Annual Review of Anthropology* 11:97–131.

Stewart, T. Dale. 1979. *Essentials of Forensic Anthropology*. Springfield, IL: Charles C. Thomas.

Taylor, J. V., L. Roth, and A. D. Goldman. 1984. Metropolitan Forensic Anthropology Team (MFAT) case studies in identification: 2. Identification of a Vietnamese trophy skull. *Journal of Forensic Sciences* 29(4):1253–1259.

Todd, T. Wingate, and D. W. Lyon, Jr. 1925. Cranial suture closure: Its progress and age relationship. Part II. Ectocranial closure in adult males of white stock. *American Journal of Physical Anthropology* 8:23–45.

Trotter, Mildred, and Goldine C. Gleser. 1958. A re-evaluation of stature based on measurements taken during life and of long bones after death. *American Journal of Physical Anthropology* 16:79–123.

A DEATH IN PARADISE

HUMAN REMAINS SCAVENGED BY A SHARK

Bruce E. Anderson, Anthony Manoukian,
Thomas D. Holland, and William E. Grant

On a sunny January day in 1994, a tranquil, white sand beach along the Hamakua coast on the island of Hawai'i revealed something out of the ordinary. Police dogs had sniffed out the partial and decomposing remains of an individual—possibly one of two missing persons that local authorities were attempting to locate in this tropical paradise. That these remains were human was evident to the police officers, but determining the identity of this person and the circumstances surrounding his or her death would become the responsibility of several forensic scientists and fall under the auspices of the forensic pathologist for the island.

Multidisciplinary Teamwork

Forensic Pathology

The role of the forensic pathologist in this case was first to recognize its multi-disciplinary challenges. Secondly, the forensic pathologist would be required to certify the identity of the remains, as well as certifying the cause and manner of death. Upon initial examination, the forensic pathologist constructed a crude postmortem interval (PMI) of between one and eight weeks, which would bracket the dates of disappearance of both missing local residents. This PMI takes into account that the postmortem environment could have been aquatic and/or subterranean, in addition to the beach's sandy, warm, and sunny surface. Dr. M. Lee Goff, the renowned forensic entomologist at the University of Hawai'i, would eventually calculate a more precise PMI.

During autopsy, the forensic pathologist was able to observe that these remains, consisting of the lower back, pelvis, and thighs of a single person, had multiple deep, serrated, linear grooves on both femora. Deeply embedded within one of these grooves was a minuscule, gray-white enameled particle. At this point, the possibility that this enameled particle was a fragment of a tooth was strongly considered, and a shark was deemed the most likely contributor. Personal identification of these remains would prove to be more problematic, as

189

they were nearly skeletonized and did not include the cranium, mandible, or teeth.

Forensic Anthropology

The pathologist recognized that the remains warranted further attention by a forensic anthropologist. Therefore, after the forensic pathologist completed the postmortem examination of these remains at Kona Hospital, an anthropological examination was conducted at the U.S. Army's Central Identification Laboratory, Hawai'i (CILHI). Located on Hickam Air Force Base and near the mouth of Pearl Harbor, the CILHI has made an unparalleled contribution to the personal identification of military personnel killed in past wars. However, most individuals are unaware of the CILHI's contribution to local law enforcement in the resolution of some of their more difficult cases.

The forensic anthropologists at the CILHI who examined these remains—none of whom had any previous experience with shark-altered human remains—were immediately impressed with the size and scope of these "bite marks." While many forensic anthropologists, and human osteologists in general, are quite familiar with the gnaw marks of rodents, canids, and even bears, witnessing the possible effects of shark bites upon human remains was a new variation upon this taphonomic theme. The forensic anthropologists agreed with the forensic pathologist's assessment that a portion of a tooth that caused these deep grooves might still be present in the right femur. No additional tooth fragments were noted, and prior to any additional analyses it was decided to macerate these remains to remove the remaining soft tissue. Two vertebral elements—the first and second lumbar vertebrae—were removed prior to maceration and returned to the forensic pathologist because an extraction

of DNA was to be attempted on these skeletal elements and their adherent soft tissues. One of the factors that can greatly reduce the successful extraction of usable DNA from biological tissues is significant exposure to heat, and because our maceration technique included heating water to near-boiling temperatures, we removed the two vertebrae.

After the skeletal remains were freed of adherent soft tissue, the following elements were further examined: the left twelfth rib, the twelfth thoracic vertebra, the third, fourth, and fifth lumbar vertebrae, the sacrum, fused coccygeal vertebrae, both os coxae, the complete left femur, and the proximal right femur (Figure 14.1). Anthropological analyses revealed that these remains represented a human male, likely of white or Asian ancestry, who was probably nineteen or twenty years of age and stood between sixty-five and seventy inches in height. The determination of sex was based upon the morphology of the pelvis, which lacked any female characteristics and was clearly male. The determination of ancestry, here admittedly imprecise, was based upon the intermediate degree of anterior femoral bow, which was inconsistent with most individuals of African American ancestry (Gilbert 1976). The presence of incompletely fused epiphyses on the rib head, iliac crests, and several vertebral transverse processes made the determination of age quite straightforward, with a young adult being indicated by these near-mature growth areas. The stature determination was based upon the morphological length of the left femur (Sjovold 1990).

While none of the more common unique identifying features (e.g., surgical hardware or healed fractures) were noted during the postmortem examination, an anatomic aberration was present. The left

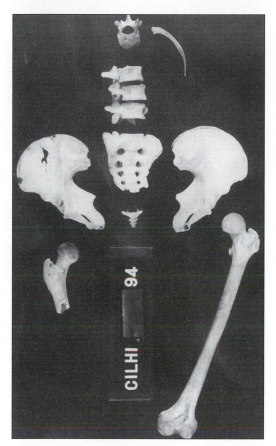

FIGURE 14.1   LAYOUT OF SKELETAL ELEMENTS
IN STANDARD ANATOMICAL POSITION

transverse process of the fourth lumbar vertebra was markedly underdeveloped in comparison to the contralateral process and to the transverse processes of the adjacent vertebrae. This skeletal anomaly could speak loudly as to identity if described or depicted in medical records for either of the two missing persons. Unfortunately, no antemortem records, radiological or written, were known to exist for either person. Alas, as is well known to medicolegal investigators, unless antemortem records are made available for comparison, all the anatomical peculiarities in the world become mute. Simply put,

such comparisons—be they radiological, molecular, or anthroposcopic—require both postmortem *and* antemortem records.

Forensic Entomology and PMI

Included in the residue of the maceration process performed by the forensic anthropologists were several insect pupal casings. These casings were submitted to Dr. Lee Goff, professor of entomology at the University of Hawai'i and resident expert on determining the PMI from insect infestation of human remains. The field of forensic entomology is a steadily growing endeavor in which its practitioners can not only identify the specific insect that infested the remains, but also provide an estimate of the time that any particular insect colonized the remains. In addition, forensic entomology has further aided medicolegal investigations by detecting illicit drugs (e.g., cocaine) and human DNA in the tissues of insects that have fed upon decomposing human remains.

In our case, Dr. Goff was only asked to estimate a PMI. He determined that these pupal casings could be identified as *Chrysomya megacephala*, a species of fly that is frequently associated with decomposing remains in the Hawai'ian Islands. It would normally take this insect nearly five days to attain this developmental stage. However, Dr. Goff had learned from experience that exposure to salt water usually serves to delay colonization by an additional day—possibly because this particular species of fly finds salt unappetizing. Thus, Dr. Goff determined that a minimum of six days would be required for the flies to have matured to the larval stage present prior to the discovery of the remains by the police dogs. Therefore, at least six days had elapsed from the time the remains became accessible to the flies and the time of discovery.

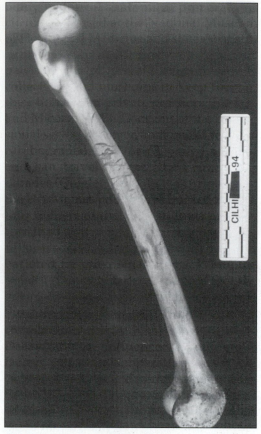

FIGURE 14.2   LATERAL VIEW OF THE LEFT FEMUR

This minimal time period was consistent with the forensic pathologist's estimate of between one and eight weeks for a PMI, as the remains would be inaccessible to flies if underwater or buried by beach sand. If the recovered remains were from an individual who had drowned offshore, they would have subsequently been washed onto shore where flies would have had access to the decomposing flesh.

Analysis of Taphonomic Processes

While the forensic entomologist was studying the insect larvae, the forensic anthropologists focused their attention on the fractured skeletal remains and serrated linear grooves of both femora (Figures 14.2 and 14.3). No other traumata were observed. The right femoral portion (Figure 14.4), containing the embedded gray-white enameled particle, was fractured distal to the lesser trochanter. The morphology of this fracture strongly suggested that the distal portion of the femur had been fractured, or literally snapped off from the proximal portion. In addition,

FIGURE 14.3   CLOSE-UP OF DIAPHYSIS OF LEFT FEMUR (NOTE BITE MARKS)

deep, serrated, linear grooves were observed just proximal to this fracture, and within one of these grooves was the suspected tooth portion (Figure 14.5). It was reasoned that a shark could have "clamped on" to the right thigh at this location and during the fracturing of the femur, deposited a portion of tooth. Because the forensic anthropologists lacked experience in the analysis of shark bites, it was decided to elicit the aid of those with the appropriate expertise.

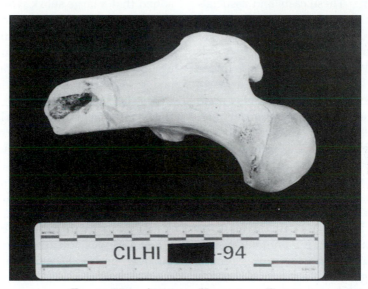

FIGURE 14.4   ANTERIOR VIEW OF THE RIGHT FEMUR (PROXIMAL PORTION ONLY)

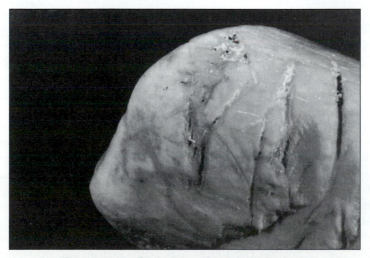

FIGURE 14.5   CLOSE-UP OF POSTERIOR SURFACE OF RIGHT FEMUR (NOTE TOOTH FRAGMENT)

Cut Mark Analysis

Plaster and dental stone casts of the cut marks on the left and right femora were made by the U.S. Army Dental Unit at Tripler Medical Center (on the island of O'ahu and near the CILHI) and submitted to shark experts. These casts and associated photographs were initially shown to Steve Kaiser, Curator of Fishes at Sea Life Park, a local marine biology enterprise. It was his opinion that the serrated, linear grooves were indeed produced by a shark, with the possibility of that shark being none other than a Great White (*Carcharodon carcahrias*). This assessment was partly based upon the morphology of the grooves, which seemed to correspond to the morphology of the serrated teeth of a Great White shark, and partly on the fact that the human remains had been recovered from the north shore of the island of Hawai'i. Hawai'i, or the Big Island as it is more commonly called, is a known haunt for migrating Great Whites during December, which was the presumed time of disappearance for this unidentified individual. These sharks do not usually swim to the inner islands during their migration, thus making Great White sightings from O'ahu a relatively rare occurrence. Incidentally, we learned that because tourism is such an integral part of the local Hawai'ian economy, a confirmed sighting—or a tooth fragment in a human femur, for that matter—of a Great White shark off the otherwise inviting beaches of O'ahu could have devastating economic repercussions. On the other hand, Tiger sharks (*Galeocerdo cuvier*) are known to inhabit Hawai'ian reefs and usually peacefully co-exist with humans utilizing the coastal waters. We left Sea Life Park with a greater appreciation for shark diversity and a sense that the Hawai'i Visitors Bureau would prefer that the fish that deposited the tooth fragment in the femur be a Tiger shark rather than a Great White.

A set of casts and photographs had also been mailed to Dr. George Burgess, director of the International Shark Attack File, at the University of Florida. It was the opinion of Dr. Burgess that a Tiger shark, on the order of eight feet in length, produced the deep, linear grooves in the femora. He reasoned that a large shark would very likely have done more extensive damage to the skeletal elements. Thus, the most likely candidate to have done this amount of damage observed in the femora was a Tiger shark. Dr. Burgess also cautioned that because sharks are scavengers, the most likely scenario in which a shark and human come into contact is one of scavenging, and not an attack on a living person. In the case of these human remains, neither the forensic pathologist nor the forensic anthropologists were able to state definitively whether this unidentified person was attacked by a shark, or met his demise by a different mode and was subsequently fed upon by the neighborhood scavengers.

Analysis of the Embedded Particle

Our next avenue of inquiry was to try to determine if the gray-white enameled particle embedded in the right femur was indeed a tooth fragment. To address this question, the femoral portion was submitted to Dr. Don Magee, at the University of Hawai'i, for analyses by a scanning electron microscope (SEM). To avoid the possibility of destroying the suspected tooth, it was left in place within its femoral matrix. After the necessary treatment of the femoral specimen, a photomicrograph was produced of the femur and suspected tooth fragment (Figure 14.6). Several sites upon the suspected tooth were then sampled for compositional analysis. Elevated amounts of both calcium and phosphorous were revealed and this was deemed by shark expert Dr. Burgess to be consistent with the

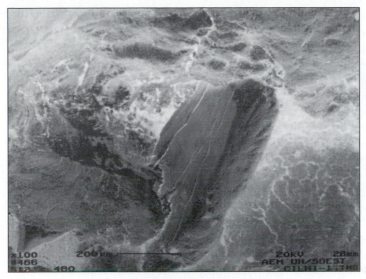

**FIGURE 14.6   SCANNING ELECTRON MICROGRAPH
OF EMBEDDED TOOTH FRAGMENT**

teeth of cartilaginous fishes. Thus, SEM analyses seemed to confirm what the forensic pathologist had proposed from the beginning—that the gray-white enameled particle embedded within a deep groove in the right femur was very likely a portion of shark tooth.

Is an Identification Possible?

Since the bite marks present on the femora were rather conclusively attributed to feeding by a shark—or sharks—we next turned our attention to the identification of the remains and an explanation of the circumstances of the death and postmortem scavenging of this individual. By comparing the results of our biological profile to that of missing persons from this area, it was the opinion of the forensic pathologist that these remains were most probably those of DM, a twenty-year-old white male who was last seen surfing in rough water off the coast of Waipio Valley, along the north shore of the Big Island. While the cause and manner of death remain undetermined, a scenario based upon the preponderance of evidence was proposed.

DM was the last of several surfers to remain in the threatening waters off Waipio that winter day. The human remains discovered on the beach some twenty-six days later were determined to be consistent with the PMI, as well as DM's age, ancestry, and stature. Deep, serrated, linear grooves seen on several of the skeletal elements and the presence of a tooth fragment embedded in the right femur were consistent with postmortem shark (species undetermined) predation. Thus, the cause and manner of death, as determined by the pathologist, are *most likely* to have been drowning and accident, respectively. The results of this medicolegal investigation were presented to DM's mother who accepted the remains for burial. Included with these remains was the tooth fragment, still embedded in DM's right femur.

Conclusions

A positive identification of DM was not possible due to the lack of any dental remains, or antemortem radiographs of the lower back, pelvis, or thighs. Extraction of DNA from the submitted lumbar vertebrae proved unsuccessful. In cases such as this, sometimes the circumstances surrounding the disappearance of an individual are utilized in effecting identification. Through the combined efforts of those with expertise in forensic pathology, forensic anthropology, forensic entomology, shark anatomy and behavior, dental casting, scanning electron microscopy, and those police officers with their trained dogs, a case of a missing person was resolved. Given that the biological profile generated by the forensic anthropologists was in close agreement with the missing surfer, the forensic pathologist rendered a circumstantial identification. Once again, the multidisciplinary nature of the forensic sciences was utilized to effectively resolve a medicolegal case.

As an aside, this investigation indirectly led to the recovery and identification of the second of the two missing men from the area. A local suspect stepped forward and led police detectives in Kona's Criminal Investigation Section to a sandy grave where the remains of the other victim were recovered. He had been shot twice in the torso. This grave was located approximately fifty yards from where the remains of DM were recovered.

References

Gilbert, Miles. 1976. Anterior femoral curvature: Its probable basis and utility as a criterion of racial assessment. *American Journal of Physical Anthropology* 45:601–604.

Sjovold, Torstein. 1990. Stature estimation from long bones. *Human Evolution* 5(5):431–447.

Further Reading

Catts, E. Paul, and Neal H. Haskell. 1990. *Entomology and Death: A Procedural Guide*. Clemson, SC: Joyce's Print Shop.

Goff, M. Lee. 2000. *A Fly for the Prosecution: How Insect Evidence Helps Solve Crimes*. Cambridge, MA: Harvard University Press.

Haglund, William D., and Marcella H. Sorg. 1997. *Forensic Taphonomy: The Postmortem Fate of Human Remains*. Boca Raton, FL: CRC Press.

Iscan, Mehmet Yasar, and Barbara Q. McCabe. 1995. Analysis of human remains recovered from a shark. *Forensic Science International* 72:15–23.

Rathbun, Ted A., and Babette C. Rathbun. 1984. Human remains recovered from a shark's stomach in South Carolina. *Journal of Forensic Sciences* 29:269–276.

ANALYTICAL TECHNIQUES
IN FORENSIC ANTHROPOLOGY

The chapters in this section demonstrate some of the analytical techniques that extend beyond the normal gross analysis of skeletal materials. The techniques incorporated in these case studies are quite diverse—genetic analysis, computer facial superimposition, histomorphology, tool mark analysis, mass spectrometry, and scanning electron microscopy—and exhibit the increasing breadth of anthropological research and work in the forensic sciences. The purpose of this brief overview is to provide a theoretical basis for two of the more complex and anthropologically relevant methods emphasized in the following chapters, mitochondrial DNA analysis and histomorphology.

FORENSIC DNA

DNA AND MTDNA

Genetic analyses have many forensic applications, such as the comparison of biological evidence from a crime scene (blood stains, sperm, hair) to a purported offender or victim, the determination of parentage, or to link serial crimes. Since forensic anthropologists may work with forensic DNA analysts to help determine the identity of unknown human remains, they should be very familiar with the applications, statistics, and limitations of DNA evidence.

Our genetic code is carried in our cells as two forms of DNA. Within the cell nucleus we find chromosomal or nuclear DNA, and inside the mitochondria, or powerhouses of the cell, is mitochondrial DNA (mtDNA). Humans share over 99 percent of their genetic material, but forensic molecular biologists and molecular anthropologists are interested in the small percentage of the DNA code that differentiates one person from another. To that end, forensic scientists focus on polymorphisms—sites in nuclear or mitochondrial DNA that vary among individuals.

There are several important differences between nuclear DNA and mtDNA (see Table IV.1 on page 198). Nuclear DNA is organized into forty-six chromosomes, half of which are inherited from an individual's biological mother and the other half from the biological father. MtDNA, on the other hand, is inherited only from the mother. Due to differences in the mode of inheritance, selection of a comparative or

TABLE IV.1   COMPARISON OF NUCLEAR AND MITOCHONDRIAL DNA

CHARACTERISTIC	NUCLEAR DNA	MTDNA
Size	~3 billion base pairs	~16,569 base pairs
Structure	Linear chromosomes (23 pairs)	Closed circular molecules
Number per cell	2 complements of chromosomes per cell	Hundreds to thousands
Inheritance	Biparental	Maternal only
Unique	Yes	No
Preferred Samples	Semen, blood, saliva	Bone, teeth, hair

"reference" sample may differ in forensic cases depending upon whether nuclear or mitochondrial DNA is tested. If a missing individual's own DNA is not available (e.g., preserved blood, hair, or pathological samples), any biological relative can be compared in a nuclear DNA analysis to give the statistical likelihood that two individuals are related, but typically two or more relatives are required. Although mtDNA is not a unique identifier because maternally related individuals will share the same sequence, the amount of human mtDNA variation is enormous. Therefore, in most cases, about 98–99 percent of individuals can be excluded as contributors of questioned samples, leaving a high statistical probability that an unknown genetic sample comes from the matched individual. Since mtDNA is often recoverable from bones and teeth, the typical materials with which forensic anthropologists work, mtDNA analysis has been a welcome addition to the investigation of human skeletal remains.

ANALYSIS OF DNA

Forensic scientists use a variety of techniques to analyze DNA and mtDNA. The most recent technique, the polymerase chain reaction, or PCR, is frequently used in forensic contexts because it is fast and provides a greater quantity of DNA with which to work. PCR makes thousands of copies of a small section of DNA, which enables accurate analysis of small or degraded portions of DNA. There are several analytical systems using PCR-amplified DNA in forensic applications, the most common of which is short tandem repeats (STRs). In this system, short repeats, which are 2–6 base pairs long, are amplified from several different loci, or regions of nuclear DNA. STR testing has allowed analysis of smaller fragments of nuclear DNA, which provides a benefit for minimal and degraded samples. MtDNA analysis is also based in PCR, but this step is followed by sequencing, or determination of the actual DNA sequence (order of the chemical bases) that comprises an individual sample.

The polymorphic STR loci provide powerful results. For instance, the FBI currently uses 13 STRs to test human identity. "The average random match probability for unrelated individuals for the 13 STR loci is less than one in a trillion, even in populations with reduced genetic variability" (Budowle et al. 2000, 2). This statistical power will become even greater as forensic and population geneticists gather more STR data from populations around the world (e.g., Huang et al. 2000; Pagano et al. 2001).

The development of local, state, and national forensic nuclear DNA databases has greatly increased the value and utility of genetic evidence in criminal cases. In 1994, the FBI instituted the Combined DNA Index System (CODIS), which consists of two indices. The Convicted Offender index (based on 13 STR loci) includes nuclear DNA profiles of felons convicted of violent crimes. The second CODIS index is the Forensic Case index, which contains nuclear DNA collected from crime scenes. Qualified laboratories across the nation can access CODIS to compare DNA samples from trace evidence left at crime scenes to check for matches. Some states have recently proposed or passed legislation to expand the number of offenses incorporated into their databases. For instance, in 1999, the governor of New York increased the range of felony crimes that can be admitted into the state DNA identification index, a jump from 8 percent to 65 percent of all violent felonies. As a result, the number of DNA samples collected annually will increase from 3,000 to approximately 30,000 (*New York Times*, 1999).

Nuclear DNA and mtDNA analysts must measure the similarity between the evidence sample and the reference sample. As Inman and Rudin (1997) state, there are three possible conclusions—exclusion (the evidence and reference samples did not originate from the same source), inclusion (they could have originated from the same source), and inconclusive. The principle goal of genetic analysis is exclusionary, as inclusion alone does not determine identity. Inclusion only means that the individual could not be ruled out as a DNA match. For nuclear DNA, the analyst must next accurately depict the likelihood that a particular genetic profile is specific to a single individual. The methods of determining the significance of the DNA results are too complex to present here, but one method is to compare the results to appropriate population databases. For instance, several laboratories, including the FBI and Armed Forces DNA Identification Laboratory, contribute data to a mtDNA population database. This database provides population genetic data that are used to estimate the relative population frequency of the submitted mtDNA profile. Ubelaker and colleagues (Chapter 3) and Melton (Chapter 15) discuss some of the statistical parameters used to interpret genetic data.

FORENSIC ANTHROPOLOGY AND DNA ANALYSIS

People often ask if forensic anthropology is still relevant in this modern age of DNA. Why do we need skeletal analyses, which can be ambiguous, if we can conclusively identify someone from their DNA? Isn't DNA 100 percent accurate? Shouldn't a forensic anthropologist be consulted only if DNA fails?

Most forensic anthropologists will argue that, for a number of reasons, the relevancy of forensic anthropology has not been compromised with the widespread forensic application of DNA technology. First, DNA may not always be preserved, especially after cremation and other taphonomic processes. Second, DNA cannot speak to perimortem trauma or postmortem alterations that can prove critical in forensic cases. Further, nuclear and mitochondrial DNA can build a genetic profile but it cannot construct a biological profile. Although sex can be determined from nuclear DNA and ancestry may be statistically inferred, other important aspects of the biological profile, such as stature, antemortem pathologies, and age, cannot be gleaned from genetic data. The biological profile is used to reduce the quantity of potential matches so that a reasonable number of comparative genetic samples can be obtained. Further, the difference between the biological and genetic profile is particularly significant when comparative DNA data are lacking. The purpose of a genetic analysis is to compare DNA of an unknown individual to DNA from a blood relative or good source of the missing individual's DNA, such as hair, tissue samples, or preserved blood. Thus, in order for DNA analyses to be useful, investigators must have some idea of the identity of the individual so appropriate comparative samples (e.g., siblings, parents, children) can be obtained and tested. Currently there are no national missing person DNA databases, though the FBI is beginning to develop such a databank for mtDNA as of this writing.

Other problems may limit the utility of DNA analysis in unidentified person cases. Given the sheer number of offender and case profiles that must be entered into CODIS, state and local DNA laboratories are severely backlogged. According to a government source (U.S. Department of Energy 1999), crime labs across the nation are collectively facing a backlog of approximately 600,000 samples. In addition, DNA labs must adhere to strict and demanding standards for every sample tested since genetic evidence must comply with the rules of evidentiary admissibility. Thus, DNA testing may take weeks or even months, especially if the number of comparative samples has not been narrowed significantly. While the backlog does not detract from the importance or utility of DNA evidence in any way, it does illustrate the necessity for forensic anthropologists, odontologists, and radiologists to work together to make presumptive identifications that may then be efficiently tested using DNA technology.

CASE STUDY—THE IDENTIFICATION OF JESSE JAMES

An example of the value of forensic anthropological and genetic collaboration is illustrated by the identification of outlaw Jesse James (Finnegan and Kysar 1998; Stone et al. 2001). There are a number of tall tales concerning whether James was assassinated in 1882 or lived to a ripe old age under a pseudonym. Many people have claimed to be direct descendants of Jesse James, or even James himself. Originally buried near his family farm in St. Joseph, Missouri, the remains were exhumed and reburied in 1902 in a marked grave next to his wife in Kearney, Missouri. An unsystematic excavation of that grave in 1978 resulted in the removal of some bones, but the rest of the skeleton remained buried (Finnegan 1984). To resolve the historical debate concerning James' whereabouts and true descendants, the grave in Mount Olivet Cemetery in Kearney was exhumed in 1995 to determine the identity of the occupant.

Following a three-day exhumation, a forensic anthropologist analyzed the skeletal materials, while bone and tooth samples were sent to the Pennsylvania State

University for mtDNA analysis. The skeletal analysis determined that the individual in the grave was a white male who stood between 67–71 inches tall and was between 34 and 41 years old at the time of death. Reliable historical information about Jesse James indicates that he was white, 68–70 inches tall and died at the age of 34 years. In addition, the forensic anthropologists found a single gunshot wound in the back of the skull, thus corroborating the story that James was assassinated. The time since death was estimated to be less than 150 years (Finnegan and Kysar 1998).

James had a sister, Susan, who would share a copy of his mtDNA. Susan had two living descendants whose relationships to her are not in dispute, a great-grandson and a great-great-grandson, who volunteered their mtDNA as comparative samples. MtDNA was isolated from the tooth samples and the sequence was compared to that of the living maternal relatives of Jesse James (Stone et al. 2001).

As expected, the mtDNA profiles of the two descendants were identical to each other since they both inherited their mtDNA through a common maternal lineage. Further, the mtDNA from the cemetery remains was identical to that of the living relatives. Stone and colleagues (2001) compared the mtDNA to the FBI's forensic mtDNA database and determined that the sequence had never been observed before in 2,426 individuals from different ethnic groups of North America. The anthropological team concluded that the remains were therefore likely to be Jesse James or a close maternal relative, though the latter was deemed unlikely given the strength of the other biological and historical evidence that places Jesse James in that grave.

ANALYSIS OF BONE MICROSTRUCTURE

The gross or "macro" structure of bone was discussed in Chapter 1, which emphasized the relationship between form and function. However, forensic anthropologists do not devote their attention only to the gross (macro) aspect of the human skeleton. The microscopic study of human bone, histomorphology, provides a whole new world of information and source of variation that is useful for identification and, in some cases, holds clues concerning the circumstances of an individual's death.

Bone microstructure reflects its biological function related to maintaining both biomechanical competence and mineral homeostasis. Bone is a physiologically active tissue and an engineering marvel. Bone grows, modifies its shape to meet biomechanical demands, and renews itself. These complex functions are met through the spatially and temporally coordinated activities of the two basic bone cells, osteoblasts and osteoclasts. Osteoblasts are cells that form bone, while osteoclasts resorb bone and are considered the garbage disposals of the skeletal system. Osteoblasts and osteoclasts continually work together to remodel bone to maximize the biomechanical efficiency of an entire bone or a particular area of a bone. Osteocytes are mature osteoblasts and function to regulate physiological activity and maintain the structural integrity of bone. Osteocytes reside in lentil-shaped cavities, called lacunae, and communicate with each other and surrounding bone by way of cytoplasmic extensions that travel through small canaliculi, branching channels in bone.

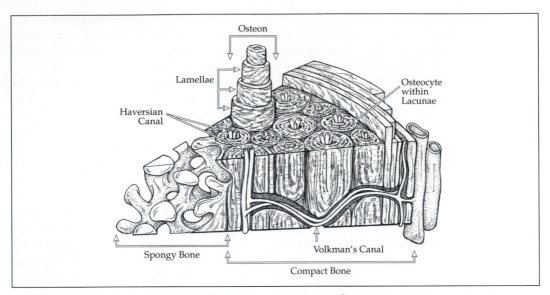

FIGURE IV.1   STRUCTURE OF AN OSTEON

The basic structural unit of compact bone is called an osteon. Osteons are arranged in columns that run parallel to the long axis of the bone. At the center of each osteon is a Haversian (or central) canal. This canal contains an artery, vein, and nerve that deliver the nutrients bone requires. The Haversian canal is surrounded by rings of lamellar, or mature bone (Figure IV.1). The size, number, and degree of remodeling of osteons are useful for aging adult bones, an area of study called histomorphometry (e.g., Kerley 1965; Kerley and Ubelaker 1978; Robling and Stout 2000). Further, human osteons are readily differentiated from those of many nonhuman mammals (Jowsey 1968; Owsley et al. 1985).

THE CHAPTERS

Sometimes mysteries take generations to resolve. Questions may remain unanswered until novel technological advances provide an opportunity to re-examine evidence. The case of Anna Anderson, presented by Terry Melton, was one of the most enduring and contested mysteries of the twentieth century. Anna Anderson went to her grave in 1984 still professing to be Anastasia, the daughter of Czar Nicholas of Russia, purportedly assassinated with the rest of her family in 1918. Melton shows how mitochondrial DNA, skeletal evidence, and historical research merged to offer the final word on Anna Anderson's true identity.

As Willey and Leach demonstrated in Chapter 13, a number of questions arise when human skulls lack contextual information. In Chapter 16, Steadman shows that many questions remain even when the skull has a face. Investigators were baffled when an unidentified but well-preserved mummified head appeared in a Des

Moines pawnshop. The anthropologist was tasked with determining if this case was a matter of immediate forensic significance, archaeological importance, or historic interest. Steadman conducted tool mark experiments and chemical analyses to determine the medicolegal context of the head.

In Chapter 17, Gill-King discusses the evolving technique of computer superimposition in a heart-wrenching case from Texas. While he deftly demonstrates the comparative points useful for identification, the impact of the story lies in the ethical dilemma presented by the "incidental" information the anthropologist can garner from skeletal remains. Sometimes the bones tell secrets that are not meant to be shared. Gill-King takes a poignant look at biological paternity and ethical issues concerning if, when, and how potentially harmful incidental information should be released to family members.

Finally, Stout demonstrates the use of histomorphology to identify a homicide victim. In this case, the killer believed that he had sufficiently disposed of a body and cleaned the crime scene, yet tiny fragments of bone and blood were found when the scene was discovered two years later. While most of the bones were too small to glean much information from the gross structure, Stout discovered that these tiny fragments of bone still held a considerable number of clues in their microstructure. The skeletal and genetic evidence led to the identification of the victim, an understanding of the circumstances of her death, and, ultimately, the perpetrator's own demise.

REFERENCES

Budowle, Bruce, Ranajit Chakraborty, George Carmody, and Keith L. Monson. 2000. Source attribution of a forensic DNA profile. *Forensic Science Communications* 2(3) (www.fbi.hq/lab/fsc/backissu/july2000/sources.htm).

Finnegan, Michael. 1984. Forensic analysis of osseous material excavated at the James site, Clay County, Missouri. Pp. 380–391 in *Human Identification: Case Studies in Forensic Anthropology*, ed. Ted A. Rathbun and Jane E. Buikstra. Springfield, IL: Charles C. Thomas.

Finnegan, Michael, and Daniel A. Kysar. 1998. The third exhumation of Jesse Woodson James: Implications for the analysis of historic figures. Pp. 533–555 in *Forensic Osteology: Advances in the Identification of Human Remains*, ed. Kathleen Reichs. Springfield, IL: Charles C. Thomas.

Huang, Dai Xin, Lin Zhang, and Mei Yun Wu. 2000. Allele frequency distributions for three STR loci in the Han and Thai populations. *Journal of Forensic Sciences* 45(6):1352.

Inman, Keith, and Norah Rudin. 1997. *An Introduction to Forensic DNA Analysis*. Boca Raton, FL: CRC Press.

Jowsey, J. 1968. Age and species differences in bone. *Cornell Vet* 56 (Suppl):74–94.

Kerley, Ellis R. 1965. The microscopic determination of age in human bone. *American Journal of Physical Anthropology* 23:149–164.

Kerley, Ellis R., and Douglas H. Ubelaker. 1978. Revisions in the microscopic method of estimating age at death on human cortical bone. *American Journal of Physical Anthropology* 49:545–546.

New York Times. 1999. Governor signs bill expanding DNA database. October 19.

Owsley, Douglas W., Ann Marie Mires, and M. S. Keith. 1985. Case involving differentiation of deer and human bone fragments. *Journal of Forensic Sciences* 30(20):572–578.

Pagano, Sinthia, J. Carlos Alvarez, Carmen Entrala, Jose A. Lorente, Miguel Lorente, Bruce Budowle, and Enrique Villanueva. 2001. Uruguayan population data for eight STR loci (Using the PowerPlex 1.2 Kit). *Journal of Forensic Sciences* 46(1):178.

Robling, Alexander G., and Sam D. Stout. 2000. Histomorphometry of human cortical bone: Applications to age estimation. Pp. 187–213 in *Biological Anthropology of the Human Skeleton*, ed. M. Anne Katzengerg and Shelley R. Saunders. New York: Wiley-Liss.

Stone, Anne C., James E. Starrs, and Mark Stoneking. 2001. Mitochondrial DNA analysis of the presumptive remains of Jesse James. *Journal of Forensic Sciences* 46(1):173–176.

U.S. Department of Energy. 1999. Human Genome Project (http://www.ornl.gov/hgmis/elsi/forensics.html).

FURTHER READING

Burr, D. B., C. B. Ruff, and D. D. Thompson. 1990. Patterns of skeletal histologic change through time: Comparison of an archaic Native American population with modern populations. *Anat Rec* 226:307–313.

Butler, John M. 2001. *Forensic DNA Typing: Biology and Technology Behind STR Markers*. San Diego, CA: Academic Press.

Dudar, J. C., S. Pfeiffer, and Shelley R. Saunders. 1993. Evaluation of morphological and histological adult skeletal age-at-death estimation techniques using ribs. *Journal of Forensic Sciences* 38:677–685.

Federal Judicial Center, National Institute of Justice. 2001. Reference Manual on Scientific Evidence (http://air.fjc.gov/public/pdf.nsf.lookup/sciman00.pdf/$file/sciman00.pdf).

Frank, W. E., and B. E. Llewellyn. 1999. A time course study on STR profiles derived from human bone, muscle, and bone marrow. *Journal of Forensic Sciences* 44(4):778–782.

Holland, M. M., D. L. Fisher, L. G. Mitchell, W. C. Rodriquez, J. J. Canik, C. R. Merril, and V. W. Weedn. 1993. Mitochondrial DNA sequence analysis of human skeletal remains: Identification of remains from the Vietnam War. *Journal of Forensic Sciences* 38:542–553.

Isenberg, Alice R., and Jodi M. Moore. 1999. Mitochondrial DNA analysis at the FBI laboratory. *Forensic Science Communications* 1(2) (www.fbi.hq/lab/fsc/backissu/july1999/dna-text.htm).

Perry, W. L., William M. Bass, W. S. Riggsby, and K. Sirotkin. 1988. The autodegradation of deoxyribonucleic acid (DNA) in human rib bone and its relationship to the time interval since death. *Journal of Forensic Sciences* 33(1):144–153.

Rankin, David R., S. D. Narveson, Walter H. Birkby, and J. Lal. 1996. Restriction fragment length polymorphism (RFLP) analysis on DNA from human compact bone. *Journal of Forensic Sciences* 41(1):40–46.

Rudin, Norah, and Keith Inman. 1997. *An Introduction to Forensic DNA Analysis*. 2nd ed. Boca Raton, FL: CRC Press.

Stout, Sam D. 1986. The use of bone histomorphometry in skeletal identification: The case of Francisco Pizarro. *Journal of Forensic Sciences* 31:296–300.

Stout, Sam D., and R. R. Paine. 1992. Brief communication: Histological age estimation using rib and clavicle. *American Journal of Physical Anthropology* 87:111–115.

Ubelaker, Douglas H. 1986. Estimation of age at death from histology of human bone. Pp. 240–247 in *Dating and Age Determination of Biological Materials*, ed. M. R. Zimmerman and J. L. Angel. London: Crook Helm.

MITOCHONDRIAL DNA

SOLVING THE MYSTERY OF ANNA ANDERSON

Terry Melton

With the availability of forensic DNA typing, all kinds of biological materials that previously held secrets of human identity are now being examined for clues to both genealogical links and historical mysteries. Nowhere has this been truer than for the application of mitochondrial DNA (mtDNA) testing to old skeletal remains. From the ancient Neanderthal humerus studied by Krings et al. (1997), to the Iceman (Handt et al. 1994), the Romanovs (Gill et al. 1994), and the American outlaw Jesse James (Stoneking and Stone 1996), mtDNA analysis of bones and teeth have revealed more fascinating answers to interesting historical and anthropological questions than ever believed possible. While skeletal materials have given up their secrets a number of times in the last few years, rarely have other aged biological materials been used for similar forensic investigations. In 1994, the Penn State Anthropological Genetics Laboratory performed a mitochondrial DNA analysis on six hairs to help solve a seven-decade-old mystery of whether a woman named Anna Anderson was the missing Grand Duchess Anastasia, daughter of the last Czar and Czarina of Russia (Gill et al. 1995).

Case History

In 1917, the Russian royal family, including the Czar, Czarina, their four daughters, son, and a small retinue of servants, were sent into exile near Ekaterinburg, Russia, after the Bolsheviks took control of the government. On July 16, 1918, all were taken into the basement room of a house and shot on the orders of Vladimir Lenin. Accounts given by those involved said that the bodies of the two youngest children were later burned, while the remains of the others were thrown down a mine shaft and perhaps later retrieved for burial (Maples and Browning 1994). Those who were involved in the assassination never disclosed the location of the bodies.

The preface to the story of Anna Anderson's unmasking began in 1994 with the publication of an article in *Nature Genetics* about the identification of the skeletal remains of the Romanov family that were found in a shallow grave in Ekaterinburg in

1991 (Gill et al. 1994). This fascinating account of the recovery and DNA testing of nine skeletons comprising the royal family and their servants laid the groundwork necessary to determine the true identity of the woman who, for over seventy years, claimed to have survived the Romanovs' assassination. Although all of the skeletons were ultimately identified through anthropological and genetic testing, the bodies of two of the children were not recovered. Alexei, the young son, was definitely absent; which one of the four daughters was missing was less certain.

When the mitochondrial DNA sequence of Prince Philip, Duke of Edinburgh, was published in Gill's article, all the information necessary to exclude Anna Anderson as claimant to the Romanov name was in the public domain. Philip is a second cousin of Anastasia, maternally related through his great-grandmother and her grandmother, Princess Alice, the second daughter of Queen Victoria.

Anderson appeared in Berlin in 1920 after World War I, where she was hospitalized after she attempted suicide by drowning. Although she claimed to have amnesia, those caring for her noted a resemblance to Anastasia, the youngest daughter of the Czar and Czarina. Rumors about the possible survival of at least one of the Romanov children had been rife in Europe since the Romanovs disappeared in 1918, and many were convinced that this young woman was, indeed, Anastasia. Although she never spoke Russian, the hospitalized woman who later called herself Anna Anderson was "recognized" by some visitors familiar with the royal family. What ensued were nearly eight decades of contesting her identity, marked by very public warring of factions loyal to or opposed to her, and a series of court trials, books, and movies documenting her struggle for recognition. During this time, forensic science played a big role in trying to uncover her true identity. Among

other tests, there were attempts to correlate her scars with those from a possible assassination scenario, photographic facial comparisons using points of the ear, handwriting analyses, and, of course, endless questioning about her memories of life as a Grand Duchess (Kurth 1985).

Toward the end of her life, Anderson married an American, Jack Manahan, a retired history professor from the University of Virginia. She never received any official recognition of her claim of identity, and lived out her life in relative obscurity in Charlottesville, Virginia, although she had a number of loyal supporters until her death in 1984. One supporter was Marina Schweitzer, the granddaughter of Dr. Eugene Botkin, the royal family's private physician who was assassinated with the family, and whose body was also identified from the Ekaterinburg grave. Schweitzer and her husband, who lived in Great Falls, Virginia, were lifelong believers that Anderson was Anastasia, and began a quest to prove her claims posthumously. During 1994 this quest became more heated as factions opposed to knowing a final answer as well as those who wanted closure for this story became aware that mitochondrial DNA could provide conclusive proof that Anderson was not the Grand Duchess.

mtDNA Analysis

Basis of mtDNA Analysis

Mitochondrial DNA, an ~16,569 base-pair circular molecule found in all cells of the human body, provides a valuable locus for forensic DNA typing in certain circumstances. The large number of sequence variants in two hypervariable portions of the noncoding control region may allow discrimination among individuals and/or biological samples (Figure 15.1). The likelihood of recovering mtDNA in small or degraded biological samples is greater

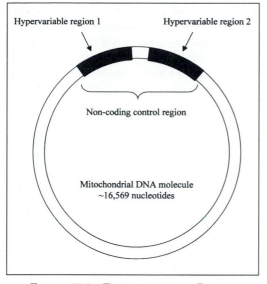

FIGURE 15.1   DIAGRAM OF THE CLOSED CIRCULAR MITOCHONDRIAL DNA MOLECULE

This diagram shows the location of the hypervariable regions typically sequenced in a forensic analysis. Each region is approximately 350 base pairs in length.

An mtDNA analysis begins when total genomic DNA is extracted from biological material, such as a tooth, blood sample, or hair. The polymerase chain reaction (PCR) is then used to amplify, or create many copies of, the two hypervariable portions of the noncoding region of the mtDNA molecule, using flanking primers. Primers are small bits of DNA that identify and hybridize to or adhere to the ends of the region one wishes to PCR amplify, thereby targeting a region for amplification and subsequent analysis. When adequate amounts of PCR product are amplified to provide all the necessary information about the two hypervariable regions, sequencing reactions are performed. These chemical reactions use each PCR product as a template to create new complementary strands of DNA in which some of the nucleotide bases that make up the DNA sequence are labeled with dye or radioactive materials. These strands are separated according to size by an automated sequencing machine that uses a laser to "read" the sequence, or order, of the nucleotide bases. An alternative acceptable method is to use a manual sequencing electrophoresis rig, which results in the production of an autoradiogram, or x-ray film (see Figure 15.2 on page 208). In either case, the end result is a DNA sequence of around 780 bases which may be used to compare samples, and hence individuals.

Mitochondrial DNA analysis is more rigorous and time-consuming than nuclear DNA typing because of the often difficult nature of samples, such as small hair fragments or old skeletal material that contain minimal DNA, rather than blood or semen. In addition, redundancy is built into the analysis for duplicate confirmations of the DNA substitutions that characterize each sequence; whereas the final result may contain around 780 bases, each of these bases may be sequenced up to four times. Because sample contamination with either human DNA or PCR product is an ever-present concern in an mtDNA lab, care is taken to eliminate

than for nuclear DNA because mtDNA molecules are present in hundreds to thousands of copies per cell compared to the nuclear complement of two copies per cell. Therefore, muscle, bone, hair, skin, blood, and other body fluids, even if degraded by environmental insult or time, may provide enough material for typing mtDNA. In addition, mtDNA is inherited from the mother only, so that in situations in which mtDNA of a missing individual is not available for a direct comparison with a biological sample, any maternal relative may provide a reference sample. Barring an unlikely mutational event that changes the sequence between generations, the DNA sequences from both individuals will match. Conversely, mutations that have occurred over thousands of years and generations provide the sequence differences that allow discrimination among individuals.

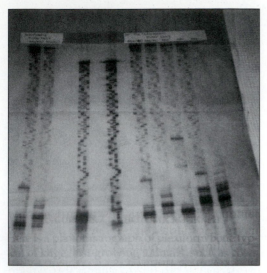

FIGURE 15.2 AUDIORADIOGRAPH OF DNA
PROFILES FROM THE ANNA ANDERSON CASE

the introduction of exogenous DNA during both the extraction and amplification steps, via methods such as the use of pre-packaged sterile equipment and reagents, aerosol-resistant barrier pipette tips, gloves, masks, and lab coats. Pre- and post-amplification areas in the lab are separated using dedicated reagents for each, equipment is irradiated with ultraviolet light, and tubes and reagent stocks are autoclaved. In forensic casework, questioned samples are always processed before known samples or they are processed in different laboratory rooms. All individuals working in an mtDNA lab have their own sequence types on file for identification of potential contaminants; a cough or sneeze over questioned samples or a single flake of skin could result in contamination with exogenous DNA.

The Pursuit of Samples: Anna Anderson's mtDNA

In the Anna Anderson case, the maternal reference sequence for the Tsarina's lineage was already published, so the mitochondrial DNA typing of a sample from Anderson was the only portion of the analysis that needed

to be done. However, it was determined that Anderson was cremated after her death, and the only available known tissue was a small portion of bowel embedded in a formalin-fixed paraffin block collected in 1978 from Anderson during a hospital biopsy for an illness. A battle quickly erupted over who had legal rights to this tissue. The Schweitzers sued the hospital in 1994 to have the tissue released as quickly as possible, while the hospital maintained that no living next-of-kin survived to give permission for the testing, since Jack Manahan had died in 1990. The Russian Nobility Association opposed any testing, since they had always disputed Anderson's claim to the title of Grand Duchess. While this legal tussling occurred in the summer of 1994, another sample appeared unbeknownst to the parties involved.

During the latter stage of Anderson's life, it was known that Manahan saved her hairs to give to admirers from around the world. After his death, a number of books from his estate were sold to a used bookstore in Chapel Hill, North Carolina. An amateur historian named Susan Burkhart, who had had a lifelong interest in the Romanovs, discovered an envelope labeled "Anna's hairs" in one of these books. Ironically, Burckhart's husband was a molecular biologist, and he instructed her not to touch the hair in the envelope, as it might become valuable genetic evidence in proving the identity of Anderson. Burckhart contacted Sid Mandelbaum, an advocate for DNA testing in New York. In turn, Mandelbaum contacted Dr. Mark Stoneking at Penn State University, who had pioneered the use of mitochondrial DNA in forensic testing (Stoneking et al. 1991). An arrangement for mtDNA testing at Penn State was made during the summer of 1994.

Analysis of the Evidence

On receiving six hairs in our lab in Penn State's Anthropology Department on September 9, 1994, Stoneking passed them on to me, his graduate student at the time, for analysis. Up to this point, we primarily had experience with the robust, freshly plucked anagen hairs (roots present) used for human population studies on groups such as African pygmies. As a relatively noninvasive sampling method, this way of collecting biological material was nearly ideal for the physical anthropologist in the field. If anything, the hairs presented to us in the Anderson case were classic telogen hairs, rootless or with just the suggestion of a root bulb present. They were also fine and hypopigmented like those that might be collected from an elderly person with white hair. Hairs such as these were not ideal candidates for mtDNA testing, since it is known that telogen hairs may contain as few as 100 copies of mtDNA. Since chain of custody was tenuous at best, we were faced with analyzing difficult samples that could or could not actually be from Anderson, although circumstantial evidence favored the possibility that the hairs were hers.

In our lab, each hair was analyzed individually. A high salt DNA extraction method that had been developed for hair roots was used to purify genomic DNA away from the cellular debris. In this method, the entire hair is incubated in dithiothreitol and proteinase K that break disulfide bonds and then digest cellular protein around both the nuclear and mitochondrial DNA. In hair shafts it is presumed that some mtDNA survives the death and compacting of cells during hair growth, and that in a fresh hair hundreds to thousands of copies may be available as targets for analysis, whereas nuclear DNA is minimal and even degraded. For this reason most hairs available from forensic cases were, until the availability of mtDNA typing, virtually useless for nuclear DNA typing unless they had a visible robust root.

Once extraction of DNA from each hair was complete, we targeted the first hypervariable region for PCR amplification. After creating a PCR template in one fragment encompassing nucleotides 15997–16400, we sequenced both strands using two primers, L15996 and H16401. This region had been reported in the 1994 Gill paper on the Romanov remains analysis, and therefore we intended to make comparisons between the sequences of the hairs and that of Prince Philip, Anastasia's maternal relative. The analysis took three weeks, and while the second and third hairs gave complete sequence for all of hypervariable region 1, hairs 4, 5, and 6 gave only partial sequence for this area. Hair 1 was found to contain insufficient DNA for an analysis. The complete sequence observed for hairs 2 and 3 and the portions obtainable for 4, 5, and 6, were in agreement. However, the sequence we observed did not match that of the maternal lineage expected from Anastasia. There were six sequence differences in the 404 bases obtained overall from the six hairs (see Table 15.1 on page 210). Clearly, if these were hairs from Anna Anderson, she could not have been the Grand Duchess Anastasia.

The End of the Debate?

The results from this test were released three days before Dr. Peter Gill, from the U.K.'s Forensic Science Service, held a press conference to reveal the results of his own testing of the intestinal tissue, which had finally been released for mtDNA analysis. When Gill was notified that our test results had resulted in an exclusion, his reaction was to share his results with us. His tests of the tissue had given the same sequence as our tests of the hair, with an exact match at all common positions. Gill had gone further to make an mtDNA comparison with a Polish family that had stepped forward in the 1920s to claim, and then later deny, that Anderson was their missing sister. Indeed, this comparison was fruitful: Anderson's sequence matched exactly that of the Schanzkowska family from Poland. It is

TABLE 15.1 NUCLEOTIDE SUBSTITUTIONS IN THE FIRST HYPERVARIABLE REGION
OF mtDNA IN THE ANNA ANDERSON IDENTIFICATION CASE

		POSITION WITHIN THE FIRST HYPERVARIABLE REGION					
ORIGIN OF SAMPLE	*DNA SOURCE*	*16111*	*16126*	*16266*	*16294*	*16304*	*16357*
Prince Philip (great nephew of Czarina)	Blood	T	T	C	C	T	C
Anna Anderson	Intestinal tissue	C	C	T	T	C	T
Anna Anderson	Hair	C	C	T	T	C	T
Carl Maucher (great-nephew of Schanzkowska)	Blood	C	C	T	T	C	T

now believed that Anderson was Franzisca Schanzkowska, a Polish munitions factory worker who disappeared in Berlin around the time of Anderson's appearance in 1920. Based on the relative rarity of the mtDNA type that was found and the replication of our results by another laboratory, we could not exclude the possibility that the hairs we had typed were indeed those of Anderson, née Schanzkowska. An additional later test on the intestinal tissue by the Armed Forces DNA Identification Laboratory in Rockville, Maryland re-confirmed the Anderson mtDNA sequence.

While the forensic tests done in this case were rigorous, and later published in a refereed scientific journal (Gill et al. 1994), supporters of Anderson as Anastasia, or the "Anastasians," even today cannot be convinced that Anderson, with her mystique and regal bearing, could have been a Polish factory worker. In spite of three laboratories conducting independent tests on two different kinds of biological material, Anastasians have spoken of conspiracies to explain the results. However, in the eyes of science, these results have allowed a conclusion to be written to one of the most fascinating historical mysteries of human identity of this century.

References

Gill, Peter, P. L. Ivanov, Colin Kimpton, R. Piercy, N. Benson, Gillian Tully, Ian Evett, Erika Hagelberg, and Kevin Sullivan. 1994. Identification of the remains of the Romanov family by DNA analysis. *Nature Genetics* 6:130–135.

Gill, Peter, Colin Kimpton, R. Aliston-Greiner, Kevin Sullivan, Mark Stoneking, Terry Melton, J. Nott, Suzanne Barritt, Rhonda Roby, Mitchell Holland, and Victor Weedn. 1995. Establishing the identity of Anna Anderson Manahan. *Nature Genetics* 9:9–10.

Handt, Oliva, Martin Richards, M. Trommsdorff, C. Kilger, J. Simanainen, O. Georgiev, K. Bauer, Anne Stone, Robert Hedges, W. Schaffner, G. Utermann, Bryan Sykes, and Svante Pääbo. 1994. Molecular genetic analyses of the Tyrolean ice man. *Science* 264:1775–1778.

Krings, Matthias, Anne Stone, R. W. Schmitz, H. Krainitski, Mark Stoneking, and Svante Pääbo. (1997) Neanderthal DNA sequences and the origin of modern humans. *Cell* 90:19–30.

Kurth, Peter. 1985. *Anastasia: The Riddle of Anna Anderson*. Vol. 1. New York: Little, Brown, and Company.

Maples, William R., and Michael Browning. 1994. *Dead Men Do Tell Tales: The Strange and Fascinating Cases of a Forensic Anthropologist.* New York: Doubleday.

Stoneking, Mark, D. Hedgecock, Russell G. Higuchi, Linda Vigilant, and Henry A. Erlich. 1991. Population variation of human mtDNA control region sequences detected by enzymatic amplification and sequence specific oligonucleotide probes. *American Journal of Human Genetics* 48:370–382.

Stoneking, Mark, and Anne C. Stone. 1996. Mitochondrial DNA analysis of the exhumed remains from Mount Olivet Cemetery. Abstract, Proceedings of the American Academy of Forensic Sciences annual meeting, Nashville, Tennessee, February 1996.

Further Reading

Budowle, Bruce, D. E. Adams, Catherine T. Comey, and C. R. Merrill. 1990. Mitochondrial DNA: A possible genetic material suitable for forensic analysis. Pp. 76–97 in *Advances in Forensic Sciences*, ed. H. C. Lee and R. E. Gaensslen. Chicago, IL: Year Book Medical Publishers.

Ivanov, P. L., M. J. Wadhams, Rhenda K. Roby, Mitchell M. Holland, Victor W. Weedn, and Thomas J. Parsons. 1996. Mitochondrial DNA sequence heteroplasmy in the Grand Duke of Russia Georgij Romanov establishes the authenticity of the remains of Tsar Nicholas II. *Nature Genetics* 12:417–420.

Klier, J., and J. Mingay. 1997. *The Quest for Anastasia: Solving the Mystery of the Lost Romanovs.* New York: Carol Publishing Group.

Massie, Robert K. 1976. *Nicholas and Alexandra.* New York: Dell Publishing Company.

Massie, Robert K. 1995. *The Romanovs: The Final Chapter.* New York: Random House.

Pääbo, Svante, J. A. Gifford, and Alan C. Wilson. 1988. Mitochondrial DNA sequences from a 7000-year-old brain. *Nucleic Acids Research* 16:9775–9778.

Sullivan, Kevin M., R. Hopgood, and Peter Gill. 1992. Identification of human remains by amplification and automated sequencing of mitochondrial DNA. *International Journal of Legal Medicine* 105:83–86.

Wilson, Mark R., Mark Stoneking, Mitchell M. Holland, Joseph A. DiZinno, and Bruce Budowle. 1993. Guidelines for the use of mitochondrial DNA sequencing in forensic science. *Crime Laboratory Digest* 20:68–77.

Wilson, Mark R., Joseph A. DiZinno, Deborah Polanskey, J. Replogle, and Bruce Budowle. 1995. Validation of mitochondrial DNA sequencing for forensic case work analysis. *International Journal of Legal Medicine* 108:68–74.

Wilson, Mark R., Deborah Polanskey, John Butler, Joseph A. DiZinno, J. Replogle, and Bruce Budowle. 1995. Extraction, PCR amplification, and sequencing of mitochondrial DNA from human hair shafts. *Biotechniques* 14:662–669.

CHAPTER

16

THE PAWN SHOP MUMMIFIED HEAD

DISCRIMINATING AMONG FORENSIC, HISTORIC, AND ANCIENT CONTEXTS

Dawnie Wolfe Steadman

A forensic anthropologist is often called upon to identify partial, fragmentary, burnt, and skeletal remains from some rather unusual locations. However, forensic anthropologists also receive human remains with no known temporal or spatial context. Since legal issues differ depending on the time period in which an individual lived and died, the anthropologist must quickly determine whether the case is of medicolegal, historical, or archaeological importance. Though some protocols may differ across the United States, cases less than a century old are typically regarded as forensic, and remains between 100 and 500 years old are considered historic. Prehistoric remains antedate the arrival of Europeans in North America (~AD 1500). Both prehistoric and historic American Indian remains are handled under the guidelines of Public Law 101-601 (1990), commonly known as the Native American Graves Protection and Repatriation Act (NAGPRA). Additionally, each state has its own regulations and codes designed to protect human remains. Thus, anthropologists must be fully aware of the legalities

in the state(s) in which they provide forensic services.

When a forensic anthropologist receives remains of uncertain temporal context, reliance on past experiences and creative scientific approaches are required to determine the antiquity of the remains and assess the medicolegal significance of the case. The methods will vary depending on the skeletal elements present, the nature of the remains, and the state of preservation. In the case presented here, tool mark and chemical analyses were conducted to determine the origin and antiquity of mummified human remains that lacked any contextual information.

Case History

On May 21, 1998, the Des Moines Police Department confiscated a mummified human head from a local pawnshop. The owner of the establishment reported that he purchased the head for $100 and displayed it in his store to entertain customers. The exhibit became an instant attraction due to the excellent soft tissue preservation, including

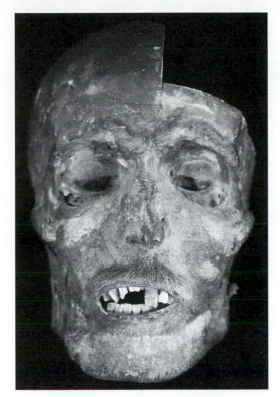

FIGURE 16.1 MUMMIFIED HUMAN HEAD, FRONTAL VIEW

the individual, the police allowed local television news stations and newspapers to broadcast photographs of the head. There was an immediate public response. While some older Iowans professed to have seen the head in traveling carnival shows or museums around the turn of the twentieth century, others claimed to have used it in satanic cult rituals and demanded its immediate return. As none of these leads seemed promising, the county medical examiner obtained custody of the remains and sent them to the author for analysis. Iowa has a statute (Iowa Code section 331.802) requiring a county medical examiner to investigate any death "which affects the public interest," including any death in which the decedent's identity is unknown. Thus, at the medical examiner's request, the anthropological goals were to place the head in its rightful temporal and legal context, determine if foul play was involved, and, if possible, establish personal identity.

Establishing a Biological Profile

The case consists of a relatively complete head and articulated mandible of an adult human. Soft tissue preservation of the face is remarkable (see Figure 16.2 on page 214). The skin is dark brown, hard but not brittle, and the exposed masseter (jaw closing) muscles are relatively pliable. The desiccated eyes lie deep in the sockets and the eyelids, eyelashes, and muscles around the eyes are well-preserved. The cartilage and skin of the nose are present, though the distal end of the nose is pinched, polished, and deviated to the left due to postmortem handling. A full, trimmed mustache extends to the level of the mouth crease bilaterally and is light brown in color with darker roots. Short whiskers are relatively dense on the chin and scattered on the cheeks. There is no postmortem tooth loss, though the anterior teeth are broken from previous rough

eyelashes, skin, and a full mustache, which gives the face a quite startling appearance (Figure 16.1). The owner placed the head atop a mounted human skeleton with an "Otis Elevator" hat, worn by elevator stewards early in the twentieth century, atop the head. The remains subsequently received the nickname of "Otis" in the tremendous media attention the case garnered. Unamused, the police were concerned with the legal status of the remains. Perhaps the individual had been murdered or looted from a historic or prehistoric cemetery. While police investigators could determine that several people had obtained possession of the remains, the trail died with the last known owner in 1970. With hopes of receiving some leads as to the identity and history of

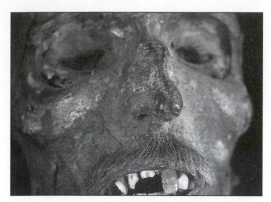

**FIGURE 16.2   PRESERVATION
OF MUMMIFIED FACE**

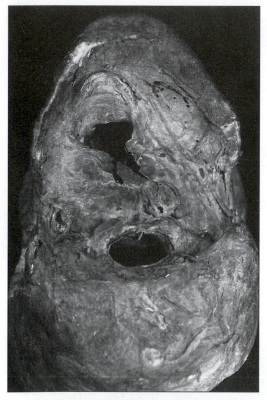

FIGURE 16.3   BASE OF SKULL

death. The masseter muscles, tongue, and superior pharyngeal muscles are well-preserved and the hyoid is embedded in the inferior surface of the tongue (Figure 16.3). The nuchal, sternocleidomastoid, and right temporalis muscles are cut closely at their attachments on the skull.

The scalp and hair have been removed and the external and internal vaults are medium to dark brown in color. The left side of the vault has been sectioned and the brain is absent, though the dura mater (outermost covering of the brain) remains *in situ* (Figure 16.4). Foreign objects within the braincase include a piece of Styrofoam under the right falx cerebri as well as dust and remnants of packing materials, including an undated newspaper scrap. Evidence of soil or other indications of burial is lacking. There is no evidence of paint, wax, graffiti, or burning typical of trophy skull treatment (Bass 1983; Sledzik and Ousley 1991; see also Willey and Leach Chapter 13). Postmortem excavation of the right mastoid region is obvious (Figure 16.5). Other postmortem modifications are described below.

handling. The left and right maxillary second molars and the left mandibular second premolar and first molar were lost before

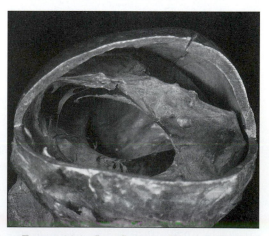

FIGURE 16.4   LEFT LATERAL VIEW OF HEAD
Note the preservation of intact dura mater.

FIGURE 16.5   POSTMORTEM ALTERATION
OF RIGHT MASTOID REGION

Biological Profile

The preservation of facial hair, including a full mustache, indicates the individual is male. All of the skeletal indicators are consistent with this rather obvious assessment of sex. The nuchal crests are quite robust and the left mastoid process is broad and long. The supraorbital ridge is very heavy and the supraorbital margins are thick. Cranial sutures are the only morphological indicator of age available. All of the external and internal cranial vault sutures are obliterated. Following Meindl and Lovejoy (1985), the individual was likely older than forty years of age at death.

Both morphological observations and cranial measurements are used to estimate ancestry. The soft tissue morphology is indicative of European ancestry. The nose is long, straight, and narrow, the eyes lack epicanthic folds common in those of Asian ancestry, and, though the skin is now dark, it was likely much lighter in life. In addition, the face is narrow and long and lacks prognathism. Additional features of the skull are suggestive of European ancestry, including oval orbital shape, retreating zygomatics, and a prominent chin (Rhine

1990). A discriminate function analysis based on cranial measurements is produced using *FORDISC 2.0* (Ousley and Jantz 1996). The results indicate that when all male groups in the database are compared (white, black, Hispanic, American Indian, Vietnamese, Chinese, and Japanese), those of Asian and African ancestry can quickly be eliminated given their low posterior probabilities. Of the Hispanic and white males in the database, the cranial measurements were most closely associated with those of the white male group (posterior probability of .967). Thus, an estimate of European ancestry is consistent with the cranial and soft tissue morphology.

No skeletal, soft tissue, or dental pathologies, including caries or enamel hypoplasias, are observed upon gross or radiographic examination. In addition, artificial restorations or other dental modifications are absent. There is no evidence of perimortem trauma. Cut marks on the base on the occipital condyles or elsewhere on the cranial base indicative of forceful decapitation are lacking (Reichs 1998).

While the ancestry results effectively eliminate concern that the head was looted from an ancient American Indian cemetery or collected as an Asian trophy skull, the analysis provides little information concerning the temporal, and therefore legal, context of the individual. Thus, attention shifted to the type, mode, and skill of the postmortem alterations of the head with the purpose of determining the antiquity of the individual and the context (e.g., clandestine or medical) of the alterations.

Postmortem Alterations

Postmortem alterations to the head include scalp removal, hemisection of the cranial vault, extraction of the brain, excavation of the right mastoid region, bilateral subcutaneous punctures around the chin, and probable intentional preservation of soft tissues. The cut marks on the skull lack color changes, which indicate that the procedures are not recent. Contrary to a typical modern autopsy protocol in which a single circular- or wedge-shaped section of the top of the skull is removed, only the left half of the skull vault was sectioned in this case (see Figure 16.3 on page 214). A sagittal cut begins 3.0 cm above Glabella (the most anteriorly projecting point at the midline of the frontal) and ends 2.5 cm above Opisthocranion (the most posterior point of the skull that is not on the external occipital protuberance; Bass 1995). This section consistently runs 1.5 cm to the left of the sagittal suture, thereby leaving the superior attachment of the dura mater intact along the sagittal sulcus. The cut is extremely "clean" and precise. The starting kerf on the frontal is 6.2 mm deep while the occipital kerf is only 3.1 mm. A kerf is a well-defined cut in the bone. The second cut is an even, radial section around the inferior aspect of the left frontal and parietal and intersects the sagittal cut on the superior occipital squama, leaving only a slight residual kerf on the occipital (1.3 mm deep) and none on the frontal. Striations within the cross-section of the sagittal cut are oriented parallel to the anterior and posterior kerfs near these endpoints, though they change direction near the apex of the vault. This may reflect repositioning of the head or new angle of approach of the saw as the section proceeded posteriorly.

A different tool was used to remove the entire right mastoid region, affecting a 3.36 x 2.68 cm area immediately posterior to the external auditory meatus (outer entrance to the ear canal). Excavation extends approximately 2.13 cm into the skull from the external surface. Though deep, the excavation did not reach the inner ear region, and the internal auditory meatus and vestibular apparatus were not compromised. The tool left semilunar notches on the outer rim with parallel, horizontal grooves lying within each notch. Smaller, secondary flakes were removed with most of the external primary cuts.

Experimental Models: Establishing Context

Toolmark Analysis

To determine the context of the alterations, and, perhaps, the antiquity of the preparation as well, a tool mark analysis was conducted to identify the classes of instruments used. If the tools are typical of household or other nonmedical contexts it becomes more pertinent to consider murder, mutilation, or clandestine experimentation. Nonmedical or nonfunerary personnel could use crude or common household tools to dissect, dismember, or disfigure an individual who was murdered or stolen from a grave. However, if only specialized medical tools were used, such sordid situations are less likely (though not inconceivable). Further, by determining the patent date of the tools, it is possible to estimate the earliest date in which the alterations could have occurred.

Controlled experiments were conducted on human cranial bones from a modern reference collection to determine the class characteristics and, if possible, the type of tools utilized to section the skull and dissect the mastoid area. Class characteristics are those that can be associated with a particular group of tools. These characteristics can be used to exclude particular instruments from consideration, but they cannot identify an individual tool (Saferstein 2001). In the case of saw marks, however, class characteristics may provide information concerning the power source (hand or mechanical), blade and tooth size and set, and the shape of the saw that produced the cut mark (Symes et al. 1998; Reichs 1998).

Steven Symes (1992; Symes et al. 1998) has conducted numerous tool mark experiments and recommends using kerf morphology for a comparative analysis of saw marks. As the floor and sides of the kerfs in the vault could not be visualized *in situ*, negative impressions of each kerf were produced using vinyl polysiloxane dental casting materials (Reichs 1998). The morphology of the kerfs was compared to those made on dry human crania by two electrically powered saws (one band saw and one electric autopsy saw), four handsaws (two meat, one pruning, one hacksaw), and two hand-powered bone saws from an autopsy room (Figure 16.6). The marks on the right mastoid region were compared to those produced on dry human vaults and mastoid processes by medium and small bone ronguers, needle-nosed pliers, and utility pliers, as well as reference skeletal materials that display rodent gnaw marks.

Since fresh human bone would be the preferred experimental material, the cut marks produced experimentally in dry bone were compared to those made in fresh animal bone and reference cut marks in fresh human material. The morphological characteristics were clearly identifiable and similar across species as well as in

fresh and dry bone samples. It was therefore assumed that the particular tools used in this experiment produced cut marks in dry bone comparable to that in fresh bone. Since cut marks on the vault suggest the scalp was removed prior to sectioning, experimental bone samples free of soft tissue were used.

Elemental Analysis

Elemental analysis was conducted to determine if the soft tissue was embalmed and what types of chemicals were used. If chemical elements found in embalming fluids are detected in greater than expected concentrations for normal body tissues, it may be assumed that they were introduced after death. Further, many embalming chemicals have known usage dates in the United States and, if present, can be used to estimate the antiquity of the preparation.

Small samples (< 0.05 g) of dura mater, masseter muscle, and superficial skin of the left cheek were removed by scraping and cutting with sterile glass. The samples were submitted to Dr. Sam Houk of the Department of Chemistry, Iowa State University, for elemental analysis by inductively coupled plasma mass spectrometry (ICP-MS). The methods and procedures of ICP-MS are fully described in Houk (1994). This analytical procedure is ideal for a case such as this since only a very small sample of each tissue type is required, multiple chemical elements can be analyzed simultaneously, and the specific concentrations of every element can be quantified.

Results

Toolmark Analysis

FIGURE 16.6   EXPERIMENTAL SAWS
From left: hacksaw, meat saw, modern bone saw, backed bone saw.

Experimental kerfs produced by six different saws were compared with those of the sagittal section on the skull. Marks created experimentally by the band saw, hacksaw, and pruning saw, all commonly found in the public sector, are inconsistent with the saw marks observed on the specimen. For instance, the band saw, which is a continuous action saw, produces polish but no stroke striae or directional changes (Symes 1992). The striations from the band saw are vertically oriented and much more fine and regular than that on the specimen (Figures 16.7 and 16.8.)

In contrast, the electric autopsy and hand-powered bone saws created kerf patterns most similar to those of the unknown skull (Figure 16.9). The marks left by each saw appear quite similar in cross-section, and differentiation between the two classes is difficult. According to Symes (1992), these saw types have alternating tooth sets with chiseling teeth and are both classified as Kerf Class B. The directional changes in the striations and lack of bending striations are more consistent with the hand-powered bone saw (Symes 1992; Reichs 1998). Since both saws are more commonly found in medical rather than nonmedical contexts, the context of the preparation was becoming less mysterious.

FIGURE 16.8   NEGATIVE IMPRESSION OF A KERF FROM THE FORENSIC SKULL
Note the horizontal, widely-spaced striations.

FIGURE 16.9   NEGATIVE IMPRESSION OF EXPERIMENTALLY IMPLEMENTED BACKED BONE SAW

FIGURE 16.7   NEGATIVE IMPRESSION OF AN EXPERIMENTALLY IMPLEMENTED BAND SAW KERF
Note the very fine striations.

The morphology of the marks on the right mastoid region is inconsistent with rodent gnaw marks because the outer notches are much wider and longer than would be expected for rodent incisors and canines (Haglund 1997). In addition, gnaw marks lack horizontal striations within the notches. Comparative tool mark analysis indicates that a bone ronguer is more consistent with the marks on the mastoid than utility pliers. Bone ronguers, or bone forceps, create secondary bone chips with each primary cut and leave horizontal groves within each cut. The result of each primary cut is a crescent-shaped notch that extracts only a few millimeters of bone at a time. Surgeons utilize bone ronguers to remove thin pieces of bone, while medical schools may use them to demonstrate the mastoid air sinuses and/or achieve the middle and inner ear organs from the outside rather than perforating the petrous from within the cranial cavity (Wadsworth 1916). Such a procedure in the temporal area could be performed to examine pathological conditions—such as otitis media, meningitis, or mastoiditis—and/or to demonstrate the route of small nerves and vessels. The purpose of the deep excavation in the mastoid region in this case is unclear, however. There is no evidence of either chronic or acute infection or other overt cause for an invasive examination. It is possible that the head was used to demonstrate the mastoid air sinuses and then the recesses of the inner ear but the procedure was abandoned well before even the middle ear cavity was achieved.

The location, morphology, and purpose of the postmortem alterations described above are consistent with a medical preparation. The classes of tools used, the clean cuts, lack of false starts, and careful preservation of the dura mater suggest a trained professional prepared the head. Characteristics of traumatic alterations, such as throat slashing, forceful decapitation, or other craniofacial or mandibular trauma is absent.

While amateur preparation, ancient grave robbing, and modern backyard mutilation may be presumptively ruled out, the antiquity of the head has yet to be determined since the tools cannot be tightly dated. Bone ronguers and bone saws are commonly found in medical and funerary kits that antedate the Civil War. Backed bone saws are also known from historical collections of surgical sets from the Revolutionary War in the United States and the Renaissance in Europe (Bennion 1979; Davis 1981). All of the tools are also still used today in medical and mortuary schools. Therefore, analysis of the chemicals used to preserve the soft tissue holds the most promise to accurately date the preparation of the head.

Elemental Analysis

Table 16.1 (on page 220) presents the concentrations of twenty-six of the elements present in each tissue type sampled in the forensic case. Of particular importance is the concentration of mercury (Hg), arsenic (As), and zinc (Zn), which are found in embalming fluids before the turn of the century. Mendelsohn (1940) describes a typical solution of embalming fluid in 1903 prior to legislative mandates prohibiting the inclusion of arsenic, mercury, and other toxic elements and compounds (see Table 16.2 on page 220). These chemical combinations were used to significantly retard bacterial growth that leads to decay (Berryman et al. 1991). Both arsenic and mercuric chloride also had the effect of rapidly and completely desiccating fresh tissue. Mercuric chloride was also used in topical solutions and local tissue injections to bleach postmortem skin discolorations resulting from congestion. High concentrations of sulfur, bromine, and aluminum in the tissues of the head are indicative of different salts used as drying agents, anticoagulants, surfactants, and humectants during the embalming procedure (Mayer 1996; Mendelsohn 1940).

TABLE 16.1   CONCENTRATIONS OF
ELEMENTS DETECTED BY ICP-MS ANALYSIS
OF THE SKIN, MASSETER MUSCLE,
AND DURA MATER OF THE HEAD

ELEMENT	MUSCLE (PPM)	DURA MATER (PPM)	SKIN (PPM)
Na	508.500	700.600	649.000
Mg	189.200	133.200	470.200
Al	**2.890**	**17.000**	**62.200**
Si	3.100	4.180	24.400
P	39.000	65.100	47.900
S	**16287.800**	**20219.000**	**32364.000**
K	544.400	971.700	1480.300
Ca	633.600	2762.500	48823.500
Sc	0.371	0.414	2.190
Ti	2.954	5.770	36.600
Mn	4.940	20.400	38.300
Fe	307.600	456.300	1791.200
Ni	1.090	7.590	8.450
Cu	0.000	16.120	20.400
Zn	**129.800**	**111.400**	**1332.800**
As	**0.137**	**0.450**	**1.020**
Br	**31.300**	**30.500**	**18.200**
Rb	1.480	1.820	3.160
Ag	0.364	2.520	5.280
Cd	0.597	3.870	3.550
Sn	1.080	3.140	5.710
I	0.450	1.670	1.640
Ba	5.600	18.900	4.140
Ce	21.000	0.960	77.800
Hg	**8.510***	**45.100***	**11.500***
Pb	5387.000	50.300	101.100

Note: Elements found in embalming fluids are in bold type.
*Hg was measured by standard addition method (see Houk 1994).

measurement (ppm, mg/L and µg/g) are reported in the tables as they are given in the literature but the values have been converted such that they all are equivalent and directly comparable. Each element occurs in at least one tissue type in much higher concentrations than expected for normal humans. Table 16.3 shows that the concentration of mercury in the masseter muscle is over twelve times that reported in the literature for normal muscle. More dramatically, the concentration of mercury in the dura mater is over three times greater than the highest level reported in any normal tissue. The extremely high concentration in the dura mater may indicate more than one exposure to embalming fluids—once while the brain was present and again after the brain was removed—as the dura was purposefully treated for long-term preservation. The distribution of highly concentrated mercury is inconsistent with poisoning or dietary intake.

The concentration of arsenic is also greater than expected in the tissue samples (see Table 16.4 on page 222). While trace amounts of arsenic are essential to growth in vertebrates (e.g., 0.04–1.4 mg/day), doses above 70 mg are considered lethal (Bowen 1979; Subramanian 1988). In life, arsenic concentrates in the skin, hair, and nails due to its affinity for keratin, so these tissues are

TABLE 16.2   TYPICAL EMBALMING
FLUID COMPONENTS IN 1903

COMPOUND	AMOUNT
Carbolic acid	48.0 g
Arsenious acid	2.0 g
Mercuric chloride	2.5 g
Alcohol	8.0 g
Glycerin	20.0 g
Water	120.0 g

Source: Mendelsohn (1940), 33.

Following a review of the literature, the sampled and normal biological levels of mercury, arsenic, and zinc can readily be compared. For example, Tables 16.3 and 16.4 compare the concentrations of mercury and arsenic, respectively. The units of

TABLE 16.3 COMPARISON OF MERCURY CONCENTRATION IN THE SAMPLED TISSUES AND IN NORMAL BIOLOGICAL TISSUES

VALUES OF MERCURY OBTAINED FROM THE MUMMIFIED HEAD

SAMPLE SOURCE	CONCENTRATION OF Hg
Skin	11.50 ppm
Muscle	8.51 ppm
Dura mater (connective tissue)	45.10 ppm

REPORTED NORMAL CONCENTRATIONS OF MERCURY IN THE HUMAN BODY

SAMPLE	CONCENTRATION*	UNITS**	RANGE	LITERATURE SOURCE[†]
Bone	0.45	mg/kg		1
Liver	< 0.1	µg/g		2
Kidney	0.02–0.8	µg/g		3
Muscle	0.02–0.7	mg/kg		1
Hair	1.2–7.6	mg/kg		1
Hair	0.001	mg/g		3
Nail	0.07–7	mg/kg		1
Brain	0.01	µg/g	0.01–1 µg/g	3
Brain	< 1	µg/g		2
Urine	1	µg/L	1–5 µg/L	3
Urine	< 5	µg/L		2
Blood	0.0012	µg/L	20–100 µg/L w/exposure	3
Blood	0.0083	µg/g	0.001–0.013 µg/g	4
Plasma	0.0065	mg/L		1

*All concentrations increase in samples with amalgam fillings, high fish diet, and/or occupational exposure.
**All units are equivalent and directly comparable.
[†]1, Bowen (1979, 104); 2, Boiteau & Pineau (1988, 554); 3, Schutz et al. (1994, 406–408); 4, Hamilton (1979, 172).

good indicators of short-term exposure. There are only two comparative samples of normal arsenic levels in the skin found in the literature. Ishinishi et al. (1986, 56) report normal skin concentrations of 0.09 mg/kg in Scottish populations and 0.064 mg/kg in Japanese samples. The level of arsenic detected in the skin sample of the head is eleven times higher than expected from the published samples. The levels of arsenic in the masseter muscle appear to be slightly greater than expected in normal muscle tissue, though the normal values reported by Subramanian (1988) are consistently higher than those given by other researchers. Therefore, based on the available sources, it appears that arsenic is present in greater than expected levels for normal tissue and was most likely applied to the tissues after death.

TABLE 16.4   Comparison of the Concentrations of Arsenic from the Sampled Tissues and Normal Biological Levels

VALUES OF ARSENIC OBTAINED FROM THE MUMMIFIED HEAD

Sample Source	Concentration of As
Skin	1.020 ppm
Muscle	0.137 ppm
Dura mater (connective tissue)	0.450 ppm

REPORTED NORMAL CONCENTRATIONS OF ARSENIC IN THE HUMAN BODY

Sample	Concentration	Units*	Range	Literature Source[†]
Bone	0.08–1.6	mg/kg		1
Skin	0.09	mg/kg	0.009–0.590	2
Hair	0.06–3.17	mg/kg		1
Hair	< 1	μg/g		3
Nails	0.2–3	mg/kg		1
Nails	0.3	mg/kg		2
Muscle	0.009–0.65	mg/kg		1
Muscle	0.063	mg/kg	0.012–0.431	2
Liver	0.023–1.6	mg/kg		1
Kidney	0.007–1.5	mg/kg		1
Brain	0.012	mg/kg	0.001–0.036	2
Lung	< 0.1	μg/g		3
Whole Blood	0.0017–0.09	mg/l		1
Whole Blood	< 0.0005–0.004	μg/g		3
Urine	2–20	μg/l		3

*All units are equivalent and directly comparable.
[†]1, Bowen (1979, 103–105); 2, Ishinishi et al. (1986, 56); 3, Stoeppler & Vahter (1994).

Although zinc is an important and necessary element in all mammalian biological systems, it was present in greater than normal quantities in the forensic samples, which strongly suggests that the zinc is from a nondietary source. According to Mendelsohn (1940), zinc was used in embalming fluids for arterial injection and/or in solutions for hypocutaneous injection to bleach tissue both before and after the disuse of mercuric chloride. Zinc chloride and zinc sulphate were used to dry, harden, and bleach local tissues. Perfusion with zinc compounds appears to be the most plausible explanation for the extremely high concentrations of zinc in the soft tissues of the specimen and may explain the bilateral puncture marks observed on the chin.

Discussion

Embalming became well established in the United States during the Civil War. President Lincoln proclaimed that the bodies of deceased soldiers should be preserved so that they could be transported to their hometowns for burial. As a result, physicians began embalming dead soldiers in the field. Though the chemical components and concentrations varied by individual fluid preparation, the use of arsenic, zinc, mercury, and aluminum compounds were common in nineteenth century embalming fluids (Strub and Frederick 1989). The first commercial embalming fluids introduced into the United States were arsenic and mercuric solutions in the 1880s. Chemical embalming began in Iowa by 1879. To protect embalmers from toxic exposure, arsenic and mercury were prohibited from use in commercial embalming fluids, beginning in Michigan in 1901 and spreading to New York by 1906, Iowa in 1910, and the rest of the United States between 1915 and 1920. However, various medical schools, funeral homes, and hospitals continued to mix their own chemicals, a procedure that remained unregulated until 1920 (Konefes and McGee 1996; Mayer 1996). Therefore, it is likely that the preservative fluid was applied to the head after 1860 and before 1920, or between 1879 and 1910 if the head was prepared in Iowa. Formaldehyde and formalin were not in general use until the twentieth century after the toxic elements were banned (Sledzik and Micozzi 1997).

Radiocarbon dating is the preferred method to estimate the age of ancient biological materials. Studies by Taylor et al. (1989) indicate that radiocarbon dates can discriminate between pre- and post-1950 skeletal remains (see also Ubelaker 2001). Further, accelerated mass spectrometry (AMS) method uses only a small amount of bone (30 grams or less) and is highly accurate for materials older than 300 years. However, the author consulted with multiple laboratory directors who felt that because the sample is likely quite recent, radiocarbon dating techniques ultimately would not help refine the time range inferred from the

chemical analysis so it was not attempted in this case.

While other sources for arsenic and mercury in the forensic head could stem from environmental contamination either before or after death, contamination seems unlikely in this case. The specific suite of chemicals found and their high tissue concentrations are more consistent with embalming than poisoning or postmortem environmental contamination. Further, contamination from arsenious soils, an ever-increasing problem in nineteenth century cemeteries, is unlikely since there is no evidence that the head had ever been buried.

The embalming process in this case probably included both arterial infusion and localized hypocutaneous perfusion. Two small punctures on the chin are consistent with postmortem injections of embalming fluid to perfuse local tissues (Mayer 1996). The lack of funeral preparation devices indicates the head was probably not prepared for funerary viewing. There are no clamps, wires, or sutures to close the jaw and lips. Similarly, there is no evidence that eye caps were used in the orbits. Finally, the lack of artificial sutures around the cranial section indicates that no attempt was made to restore the cranium.

Given the chemical evidence and postmortem dissection techniques and tools, it is most likely that this head was prepared for anatomical teaching purposes prior to 1920. Both funeral and medical schools in the nineteenth century legally utilized and embalmed human cadavers for teaching purposes (Quigley 1998; Sledzik and Micozzi 1997). The preparation was also similar to those of known anatomical preparations curated at the National Museum of Health and Medicine in Washington, D.C. (Sledzik and Micozzi 1997). Unfortunately, a more exact date or location of the preparation cannot be determined from the evidence at hand. It is also unclear as to how the head entered the public sector. Paul Sledzik has analyzed many historical anatomical preparations currently housed at the National Museum of Health and Medicine and states that students and even physicians will donate prepared skulls to private or professional collections and museums or keep them at their homes and private practices (Sledzik and Micozzi 1997). Once out of the professional sector, however, anatomical remains can be traded, sold, or presented as gifts, and can travel around the country for decades (Quigley 1998). In the current case, the Des Moines police have tracked the last four owners of the head in Iowa and determined that it had been purchased for $100, traded for a pinball machine, and bartered for other small items. While the police investigation demonstrated that the head has been in the private sector for three decades, the chemical analysis indicates that the antiquity of the individual is much greater.

Not surprisingly, the personal identity of the mummified head has not been established. The only lead thus far stems from a Des Moines resident who sent investigators a postcard bearing a photograph of "Sylvester," a mummified cadaver displayed in Ye Olde Curiosity Shop in Seattle, Washington (Figure 16.10). Sylvester died in the desert near Yuma, Arizona, after suffering a gunshot wound to the abdomen in or before 1895. Quigley (1998, 92) details Sylvester's fascinating postmortem tour of the United States. However, Sylvester mummified naturally in the arid desert environment and was not embalmed. Further, his head was not autopsied and the current owners report that Sylvester does indeed still possess his own head, thus closing that lead. It is unlikely that personal identity will be determined since the chemical and mechanical treatment of the head strongly suggests that the individual could have died a century or more ago.

**FIGURE 16.10 "SYLVESTER,"
A NATURALLY MUMMIFIED BODY**

Note that the head has not been autopsied. (*Photo courtesy of Ye Olde Curiosity Shoppe.*)

Conclusions

The case presented is a well-preserved mummified head of a middle to older aged, adult white male that lacks evidence of premortem pathology or perimortem trauma. The head was autopsied and embalmed with arsenic and mercury, toxic elements that were prohibited from use in embalming fluids in the United States by 1920. The embalming chemicals and demonstrative form of autopsy strongly suggest that the individual was not a victim of a recent murder. The head was probably professionally prepared before 1920, perhaps in a medical school, mortuary school, or museum.

The anthropologist can often make recommendations to the medical examiner concerning disposition and treatment of unclaimed human skeletal remains. In this case, the remains do not have any medicolegal significance and the state of Iowa does not explicitly prohibit ownership of non-forensic human remains. However, the author recommended that the head not be returned to the public sector for purposes of exploitation, curiosity, or profit. While the identity of the head will most likely never be determined, the display of any human material in a disrespectful or exploitative manner is beyond common decency and does not serve either the medical community or the public. Though unclaimed remains are often buried in pauper's cemeteries, I recommended that the head be retained in a professional teaching or medical facility such that the remains continue to serve the community as a source of education, not spectacle. The Polk County medical examiner granted the request and "Otis" is once again utilized for anatomical teaching purposes, this time in an osteology laboratory.

Acknowledgments

I am indebted to Dr. Steven Symes of the Regional Forensic Center in Memphis, Tennessee, for his assistance in analyzing the saw marks and providing comparative samples. Mr. Paul Sledzik provided valuable comparative information of medical specimens from the National Museum of Health and Medicine. Dr. Sam Houk and Mr. Zhiyang Du, Department of Chemistry, Iowa State University conducted the ICP-MS analysis. Special thanks also go to Dr. James M. Edmonson, Curator of the Dittrick Museum of Medical History, Dr. Francis Garrity, Polk County Medical Examiner, Dr. Ronald Myers and Dr. Elizabeth Riedesel of the Iowa State University School of Veterinary Medicine, Mr. Jim Fullerton of Fullerton Funeral Associates, and Dr. John Frasco, DDS. Andy James and James Ofrancia from Ye Olde Curiosity Shoppe in Seattle kindly granted permission to use the photograph of Sylvester. This paper was originally presented at the American Academy of Forensic Sciences in 1999.

References

Bass, William M. 1983. The occurrence of Japanese trophy skulls in the United States. *Journal of Forensic Sciences* 28(3):800–803.

Bass, William M. 1995. *Human Osteology: A Laboratory and Field Manual.* 4th ed. Columbia, MO: Missouri Archaeological Society.

Bennion, Elisabeth. 1979. *Antique Medical Instruments.* Berkley, CA: University of California Press.

Berryman, Hugh E., William M. Bass, Steven A. Symes, and O. C. Smith. 1991. Recognition of cemetery remains in the forensic setting. *Journal of Forensic Sciences* 36:230–237.

Boiteau, Henri L., and Alain Pineau. 1988. Mercury. Pp. 553–560 in *Quantitative Trace Analysis of Biological Materials,* ed. H. A. McKenzie and L. E. Smythe. Amsterdam: Elsevier.

Bowen, Humphrey J. M. 1979. *Environmental Chemistry of the Elements.* London: Academic Press.

Davis, Audrey B. 1981. *Medicine and Its Technology: An Introduction to the History of Medical Instrumentation.* Westport, CT: Greenwood Press.

Haglund, William D. 1997. Rodents and human remains. Pp. 405–414 in *Forensic Taphonomy: The Postmortem Fate of Human Remains,* ed. William D. Haglund and Marcella H. Sorg. New York: CRC Press.

Hamilton, E. I. 1979. *The Chemical Elements and Man: Measurements, Perspectives and Applications.* Springfield, IL: Charles C. Thomas.

Houk, R. S. 1994. Elemental and isotopic analysis by inductively coupled plasma mass spectrometry. *Accounts of Chemical Research, American Chemical Society* 27(11):333–339.

Ishinishi, Noburu, Kenzaburo Tsuchiya, Marie Vahter, and Bruce A. Fowler. 1986. Arsenic. Pp. 43–83 in *Handbook of the Toxicology of Metals,* ed. Lars Friberg, Gunnar F. Nordberg, and Velimir B. Vouk. Vol. 2. Amsterdam: Elsevier.

Konefes, John L., and Michael K. McGee. 1996. Old cemeteries, arsenic, and health safety. *Cultural Resource Management* 19(10):15–18.

Mayer, Robert G. 1996. *Embalming: History, Theory and Practice.* 2nd ed. Stamford, CT: Appleton and Lange.

Meindl, Richard. S., and C. Owen Lovejoy. 1985. Ectocranial suture closure: A revised method for the determination of skeletal age at death based on the lateral-anterior sutures. *American Journal of Physical Anthropology* 68:47–56.

Mendelsohn, Simon. 1940. *Embalming Fluids.* New York: Chemical Publishing.

Ousley, Stephen, and Richard L. Jantz. 1996. *FORDISC 2.0.* Department of Anthropology, University of Tennessee, Knoxville.

Quigley, Christine. 1998. *Modern Mummies.* Jefferson, NC: McFarland and Company.

Reichs, Kathleen J. 1998. Postmortem dismemberment: Recovery, analysis and interpretation. Pp. 353–388 in *Forensic Osteology: Advances in the Identification of Human Remains,* ed. Kathleen J. Reichs. 2nd ed. Springfield, IL: Charles C. Thomas.

Rhine, Stanley. 1990. Non-metric skull racing. Pp. 9–20 in *Skeletal Attribution of Race,* ed. George W. Gill and Stanley Rhine. Anthropological Papers No. 4. Albuquerque: Maxwell Museum of Anthropology.

Saferstein, Richard. 2001. *Criminalistics: An Introduction to Forensic Science.* 7th ed. Upper Saddle River, NJ: Prentice Hall.

Schutz, Andrejs, Gunnar Skarping, and Staffan Skerving. 1994. Mercury. Pp. 403–467 in *Trace Element Analysis in Biological Specimens,* ed. R. F. M. Herber and Markus Stoeppler. Amsterdam: Elsevier.

Sledzik, Paul S., and Stephen Ousley. 1991. Analysis of six Vietnamese trophy skulls. *Journal of Forensic Sciences* 36:520–530.

Sledzik, Paul S., and Marc S. Micozzi. 1997. Autopsied, embalmed, and preserved human remains: Distinguishing features in forensic and historic contexts. Pp. 483–496 in *Forensic Taphonomy: The Postmortem Fate of Human Remains,* ed. William D. Haglund and Marcella H. Sorg. New York: CRC Press.

Stoeppler, Markus, and Marie Vahter. 1994. Arsenic. Pp. 291–320 in *Trace Element Analysis in Biological Specimens,* ed. R. F. M. Herber and Markus Stoeppler. Amsterdam: Elsevier.

Strub, Charles G., and L. G. Frederick. 1989. *The Principles and Practice of Embalming.* 5th ed. Dallas, TX: Professional Training Schools, Inc. and Robertine Frederick.

Subramanian, Kunnath. 1988. Arsenic. Pp. 573–580 in *Quantitative Trace Analysis of Biological Materials,* ed. Hugh A. McKenzie and Lloyd E. Smythe. Amsterdam: Elsevier.

Symes, Steven A. 1992. *Morphology of Saw Marks in Human Bone: Identification of Class Characteristics.* Ph.D. Dissertation, Department of Anthropology, University of Tennessee.

Symes, Steven A., Hugh E. Berryman, and O. C. Smith. 1998. Saw marks in bone: Introduction and examination of residual kerf contour. Pp. 389–409 in *Forensic Osteology: Advances in the Identification of Human Remains,* ed. Kathleen J. Reichs. 2nd ed. Springfield, IL: Charles C. Thomas.

Taylor, R. E., Judy M. Suchey, L. A. Payen, and P. J. Slota. 1989. The use of radiocarbon (^{14}C) to identify human skeletal remains of forensic science interest. *Journal of Forensic Sciences* 34:1196–1205.

Ubelaker, Douglas H. 2001. Artificial radiocarbon as an indicator of recent origin of organic remains in forensic cases. *Journal of Forensic Sciences* 46(6):1285–1287.

Wadsworth, William S. 1916. *Post-mortem Examinations.* Philadelphia, PA: W. B. Saunders.

AN INCIDENTAL FINDING

H. Gill-King

A Routine Analysis

The face in the monitor belonged to a smiling child—twelve-year-old Rosemarie Lynn Gilley (not her real name). As the face slowly faded, freckles and strawberry blond hair disappeared, revealing the outlines of a skull known in our lab by its case number, ME 94-107 (see Figure 17.1). Two inverted digital triangles persisted as the face vanished, leaving the geometric figures over bleached bone. Examination of the lateral angles also confirmed an acceptable frontal overlay. A lateral view of the child's face had been enhanced from a Polaroid snapped at a backyard twelfth birthday party a week prior to her disappearance.

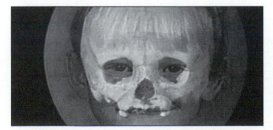

FIGURE 17.1   UNIDENTIFIED SKULL

The frontal view had been taken as a class picture earlier that year, though well within the six-month limit required by our lab protocol for skull-to-photo superimposition in child cases. The lateral overlay was equally effective. The soft tragus of the ear lay atop the auditory meatus (the bony entrance to the middle ear) as a benchmark while the contours of the brow, nasal bridge, and maxilla followed the outlines of the skull like an artist's tracing (George 1987).

Of greater importance than the congruence between skull and soft tissue features in the frontal and lateral views were the dental details. The broad smile revealed six maxillary teeth, numbers 6 through 11. Along the incisal (occlusal) edges of numbers 8 and 9 were several mammilons—small blunt serrations which, though not uncommon, vary from one individual to the next when they are present. Video close-ups of the teeth in the skull and photo revealed that these anatomical details, along with the embrasures (outlines of the front teeth), were congruent as well. Tooth number 10, the left lateral maxillary incisor, was equally informative. It was rotated almost 90° laterally and clearly seen in both the skull and photo, as they superimposed perfectly.

In a variation of the video superimposition technique performed in this case, two triangles were digitized upon the skull after sizing (Figure 17.2). These triangles were defined by base angles at the frontomaxillary sutures and vertices at the nasal spine and the central diastema, respectively. A second set of triangles was digitized in the form of faint lines on the facial photograph. These were defined by base angles at the ectocanthia (outer corners of the eyes) and vertices at the bulb of the nose and the diastema, or gap between the teeth, which showed in the smiling mouth. Application software was used with a digital mixer to "fade" one image over the other to determine whether the

two sets of digital triangles would be congruent. The same approach was used with the lateral view of the skull and the lateral photo, using different soft and hard tissue markers, including the features of the ear (e.g., Caldwell 1981) (Figure 17.3).

Timing is important when photographs of children are used for superimposition techniques. Most laboratories performing this and similar techniques accept photos taken no more than six months prior to the disappearance of a child because of the rapid velocity of growth in facial features (Burke and Hughes-Lawson 1989).

The quantity and condition of the scavenged bones suggested a postmortem interval of at least several years. The skeletal and dental remains, together with associated clothing remnants, had been sufficient to indicate a female child of approximately twelve years of age. The video superimposition had narrowed the search, and the dental comparison had produced a conclusion: ME 94-107 and Rosemarie Lynn Gilley were one and the same person beyond reasonable doubt.

Two mechanical defects (unspecified tool marks) were easily distinguishable from the characteristic scissoid (scissor-like) markings of carrion birds as well as the typical gnawing of canids and rodents. These defects could be seen near the midpoint of the arcs of two scavenged left true ribs—the first, a punctation made by a single-edged blade; the second, a slice across the upper rib margin made as the blade passed into, or out of, the body. Two more punctations were to be found on the laminae of two adjacent thoracic vertebrae. Other perimortem injuries might have been present on other skeletal elements that were not recovered or obscured by scavenging. The injuries would eventually be described as the "result of a sharp object forcibly applied"—language designed

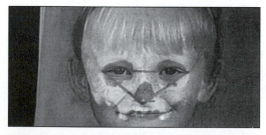

FIGURE 17.2   SUPERIMPOSITION OF PHOTOGRAPH AND SKULL, WITH TRIANGLE

FIGURE 17.3   SUPERIMPOSITION OF PHOTOGRAPH AND SKULL, WITHOUT TRIANGLE

to describe in the most encompassing and defensible terms possible the means and circumstances that ended a young life.

Justice Served

The search for Rosemarie had begun almost immediately following her disappearance in 1986 when a nervous clerk had recorded the license number of an unfamiliar vehicle outside his convenience store at about the same time Rosemarie had appeared for her customary purchases—a bag of Jolly Ranchers and a *TV Guide* for her mother. Noticing her abandoned bicycle a short time later, he retrieved the suspicious plate number and called the authorities. A few weeks after Rosemarie's apparent abduction, her small coin purse had been found in the rear floor of the suspect's car. During extensive questioning, the suspect admitted to "stealing the purse from the bicycle basket," but steadfastly denied having seen Rosemarie. No more than a cursory search of the suspect's vehicle was conducted, perhaps out of investigative inexperience, perhaps on the assumption that the intervening weeks would have erased any usable evidence which might have linked the child to the vehicle. In the absence of remains or any other direct evidence of harm, the investigation of the suspect was reluctantly dropped with no charges filed. Four years later the local sheriff was notified that the suspect had perished in a fiery crash involving no other persons in another part of the state. As word spread, most assumed that justice had been done as they closed a sad chapter in the history of their little community. Only an unfillable emptiness and gnawing imaginings of the last dreadful hours and minutes of a daughter's life remained.

A Child Comes Home

The remains had arrived at the lab by referral from the medical examiner in January of 1994, following their discovery by surveyors laying out cross-country power lines. Upon preliminary inspection of the remains and examination of antemortem photographs, some concerns had arisen: The photographs of the suspected match revealed a blue-eyed, fair-skinned, freckled, blond-to-light-red-haired subject. By contrast, the four maxillary incisors of ME 94-107 were markedly shoveled, a trait originally associated with northeast Asian populations and their descendants and, as often noted, in the highly admixed immigrant Mestizo population of the Southwestern United States (Hinkes 1990). The intact hard palate revealed a dorsally bulging posterior transverse suture. Finally, some experience with "known" Mexican crania—a happenstance of practicing in border country—had resulted in the occasional observation of multiple symmetric ossicles in the lambdoid suture, in this case three on each side. These initial observations had been sufficiently surprising to prompt an informal inquiry of the Texas Ranger following the case about the ancestry of the girl in the photographs. Although ancestry would be of little direct significance once an identification was made by dental or other direct means, this was an amalgam of traits that no serious student of human variation could resist.

A few days after the analysis and identification had been complete, I was informed that a briefing would be arranged for the several law enforcement officers who had been most directly involved in the case from the beginning. A media conference was scheduled two days hence in the victim's community, and this was to be the final update for law enforcement before meeting the press. The group, which consisted of the local sheriff, the Ranger, and an FBI agent, would fly in early by charter for a quick turnaround to West Texas.

Two days later, I entered the small cluttered conference room adjoining our lab, where the little group and their pilot were already seated around the long table piled with journals, papers, and boxes of slides. A demonstration skeleton wearing a deerstalker and perpetually chewing a pencil hung like a sentry in the corner, warily eyeing a Beauchenne ("exploded") skull on a shelf against the opposite wall. Skipping formalities in the interest of time, I killed the lights and proceeded through the analysis, illustrating conclusions with 35 mm slides projected on the wall at the end of the table. The small group sat quietly as I reviewed the findings: biological profile, postmortem interval, and lastly, the injuries. The only other illumination in the room was the red light on the coffee maker and the dim glow of the sheriff's filterless Camel. On these occasions I often wonder about the thoughts of those around me. How many of these men were fathers? How many had a daughter? Had any lost a child? In almost all child homicide cases there is a point, usually early in the investigation, often in the field at the scene, when one by one each adult male offers a vivid account of what should befall the assailant. These narratives usually take the form of a description of what one might do if left alone in a room with the suspect. In the telling, these short dramas would seem clichéd, but they are real expressions of something fundamental, something universal. And now, with the likely murderer dead and the fact of the child's death long accepted, their thoughts might be more mundane—"I don't like small planes." "Will there be time to get the dog to the vet after the media thing?" "Two more years to retirement and I'll never have to run for office again."...

Turning on the lights and offering hours-old coffee, I began loading the cassette of the superimposition. Perhaps because of time constraints, or because I had worked many times with these men, I omitted the usual warning concerning the undesirability of showing such a tape to the parents or loved ones of a victim. The psychological rationale is not unlike that of emergency room staff or mortuary professionals who discourage the viewing of a badly mangled, burned, or decomposed body of a loved one. Such images are stamped indelibly upon the memory and are not easily painted over. Such trauma is worsened by the duress of observing a loved one go from live to dead to live again as a face, captured in happier times, melts into a universal symbol of death in real time. The tape ended as I reviewed the signature dental details.

Blinking as the fluorescents came on, Threadgill, the FBI agent, spoke first. "So how sure are we on the ID?" Stifling a side discourse into the statistical theory of positive identification, I replied, "Beyond reasonable doubt," . . . then added, "In fact, this will be an excellent teaching case when everything is settled. Anything else? Everyone OK with the injury pattern?" I asked, looking at each person in the room.

The man I had taken to be the pilot spoke up softly, "Thank you for all you've done . . . I think Rosie's mother and I can do a little better now." Suddenly, time slowed and my own words went through me—"In fact, this will be an excellent teaching case" . . . "Everyone OK with the injury pattern?" What nightmarish images had I imposed on the little girl's father with the video and my remarks? Words and pictures *never* meant for a parent's fragile sensibilities. Images of other times and places; other conference rooms and lecture halls where strangers would sit, mulling the small details of their own lives, some sipping coffee, others listening attentively, others seizing upon the cool dark to nap, as a child from another place and time smiled-faded-died on the monitor.

I shook the rough hand and now examined the man carefully for the first time. Still numb from what had happened, I was beyond placing blame. His skin was permanently red and creased with the look of those whose lives are passed in hot arid places. What had once been blond hair was now mostly grey and closely cropped, and he had sad, reddened eyes that had sought hope but never found it. He had arisen early that day, shaved clean, and, perhaps moved by the purpose of his forthcoming journey and by what he was to hear, had dressed in a manner that he likely reserved for special occasions. He would hear the words, he would finally know, that his only child, taken from him in that special time of life when all daughters are "daddy's girl," would not return.

Only rarely does the awful task of reporting the news of death to a loved one befall the forensic anthropologist, and virtually never under such circumstances. In private moments, when we would undo the harm we have caused others, the events of that morning always return. When I muse over photographs of my own daughters, I am in that moment again.

The Incidental Finding

As the somber little group walked away down the hall, the father now flanked by Tom and the sheriff, Ned, the Texas Ranger, motioned me back into the conference room. "I checked out the situation with the grandparents," he said. "Dad's people are from Michigan, been there forever—Couldn't get much from the mother's side, but she was runnin' with the Bandidos when she met the girl's dad." He continued, "You know, the girl was born right at seven months after they were married." The shoveled incisors and symmetric wormians flicked across my mind as he continued his account. The Bandidos, as they were known in the seventies and eighties, were an ethnic motorcycle gang. The members were Mexican nationals, braceros, some illegal immigrants who had disappeared into North American infraculture, or individuals of recent Mexican descent. The child's mother, born in Wisconsin to a farming family of German extraction, had fallen in with the gang as a "concubina" after passing through a series of foster homes in the late sixties. She abandoned the gang under uncertain circumstances, and soon thereafter married Rosemarie's father, an oilfield worker. The couple had settled in the small West Texas town where Rosemarie's father secured work as a tractor mechanic. The early arrival of the fully developed baby girl apparently passed without comment. It is unclear whether the mother had shared her favors with gang members and her future husband concurrently for a time or, whether the "father," ignorant of the details of gestation, had accepted the child as his own without question. Perhaps he simply chose to move ahead. In any case, the source of the child's dental and cranial traits now seemed clear.

During the twelve years following her birth, Rosemarie and her father had been a constant pair, a fixture at school events, Campfire Girls' outings, and the undisputed champions of the three-legged race at the county livestock fair. He had arranged a ride on the town's only fire truck for Rosie and her cohorts on the day of her twelfth, and final, birthday party.

At the time of the analysis, standard DNA comparisons between the remains and the suspected parents would likely have proved futile, given the condition of the remains, and were rendered unnecessary by the dental comparison. PCR-driven mitochondral technology, now often preferred in bone cases, was then in its nascency. In any event, had it been available, it would not have informed the issue of paternity.

A Time to Speak and a Time to Refrain

Forensic anthropologists and others who examine human remains sometimes encounter what have come to be known as "incidental findings"—unusual anatomical variations, old traumatic or medical artifacts, or other desiderata that come to light in the course of a thorough examination, but that add no pertinent information to the investigative questions at hand. Perhaps it is an old bullet, now overgrown with bone, imbedded in the thigh of a World War I veteran who died of exposure after straying from a care facility. On one occasion when bulldozers unearthed a nun buried beyond remembrance on the campus of a Catholic girls' school, all took pause at the presence of the standard triad of parity indicators on the woman's pelvic bones. There was relief all around when discreet inquiries revealed that women often entered this particular order after rearing families and surviving spouses. A twenty-four-year old female homicide victim, identified dentally, bore scars of pregnancy although her parents and spouse insisted that she had never been pregnant. A sister revealed that her older sibling had given birth during a "runaway" interval spanning her fifteenth and sixteenth years. Tattoos which speak of old loves, past adventures, or ports of call. . . . The list goes on; some findings point the way to an identification or an understanding of the circumstances of death while most are no more than footnotes to a life concluded. Others, as in this instance, if revealed, may reach backward from death to stir painful emotions among the living.

"Above All, Do No Harm"

Much of the work in our morgues and laboratories is, in the final analysis, performed on behalf of the living; or, put another way, in the interest of "justice," "equity," or some such abstraction perceived to benefit the ongoing human condition. In the case described, it would appear that issues of justice have been foreclosed by chance. There remained no issues of jurisprudence, no need for a legal remedy. One must ask whether an incidental finding, in this case of likely mistaken paternity, should be reported. Indeed, issues of long-mistaken parentage may become a legal commonplace in the era of molecular analysis together with all that they may bring—questions ranging from matters of estate to the inheritance of medical disorders, or possibly even motivation for crimes. Postmortem revelations may leave living parties to deal with the emotional aftermath of such findings. In this instance, or wherever paternity may be the incidental issue, love and nurture of long standing may collide with hard genetic evidence. In such hypothetical instances, the living parties may reach some resolution; perhaps years of nurture and presumed relatedness and all that goes with them will prevail. But what purpose is served when affected parties cannot speak? When the love felt by a child toward a parent, presumed or real, cannot be voiced? Where, in this instance, would the needs of the living be served by revealing the incidental finding of questioned paternity? The reader is challenged to think of other incidental findings that might by their revelation produce devastating grief or concern unnecessarily.

Some will find fault with the general question, citing the need to scrupulously report all observations, while others will reject the issue as too abstract or irrelevant.

In any event, it is almost a certainty that anthropologists and others who deal with reasonably large case loads will, from time to time, encounter such incidental findings. We maintain that in the absence of clear legal or ethical guidelines, the preferred course of action is that which "does no harm." When the appropriate standards of forensic investigation have been applied, when the queries put to the forensic investigator have been answered, personal notations made, photographs and other evidence stored, it is time to think of the needs of the living.

Issued circa 410 BC, the words of Hippocrates, contained within the now famous oath named for him, ". . . above all, do no harm," seem timely. In the final analysis, in the nexus where science and conscience meet, these words provide a valuable and worthy guide.

References

Burke, P. A., and C. Hughes-Lawson. 1989. Developmental changes in the facial soft tissue. *American Journal of Physical Anthropology* 79(3):281–288.

Caldwell, Peggy C. 1981. The relationship of the details of the human face to the skull and its application in forensic anthropology. MA Thesis, University of Arizona.

George, R. M. 1987. The lateral craniographic method of facial reconstruction. *Journal of Forensic Sciences* 32(5):1305–1330.

Hinkes, Madeleine J. 1990. Shovel-shaped incisors in human identification. Pp. 21–26 in *Skeletal Attribution of Race in Forensic Anthropology*, ed. George W. Gill and Stanley Rhine. Anthropological Paper No. 4. Albuquerque, NM: Maxwell Museum of Anthropology.

18

SMALL BONES OF CONTENTION

Sam D. Stout

In the spring of 1988 I received a call from local law enforcement investigators asking me to examine human remains recovered from a crime scene. This was not an unusual request; as director of the Department of Anthropology's Human Skeletal Identification Laboratory at the University of Missouri, I routinely undertook skeletal analyses for law enforcement agencies. But this case would turn out to be one of the most unusual and challenging of my career. In this case, testimony by a team of experts, including a forensic anthropologist, pathologist, serologist, and an electron microscopist, along with careful collection of evidence by law enforcement and crime scene investigators, led to a murder conviction without a victim's body. Convictions without a body, eyewitness, or confession are rare. The prosecution had to convince a jury that a death occurred and that the defendant was responsible, even though a body was never recovered.

A Mysterious Disappearance

In June of 1986, two days after she was last seen leaving work in her 1985 red Ford Escort,

a woman was reported missing by her mother. Because there was a record of domestic problems, the husband was considered to be a suspect in her disappearance. Both local and national searches, however, failed to locate either the woman or her car, and the woman's disappearance remained a mystery for the next two years.

A major break in the case occurred in March of 1988 when the missing woman's car was discovered at a storage facility approximately thirty miles from where she was last seen. When rental payments for the facility became delinquent, an attendant entered the locked storage unit where he discovered a red 1988 Ford Escort. Because of the condition of the car, with its front windshield cracked, its driver's window missing, and a large quantity of glass and other debris inside, suspicion was aroused and law enforcement officials were contacted. The serial number and license number of the car revealed that it belonged to the missing woman and her husband. Further, records showed that the husband rented the space on the same day his wife was last seen.

FIGURE 18.1 THE FORD ESCORT
Here is the missing woman's red 1988 Ford Escort, recovered from a storage facility.

A search warrant was obtained and investigators examined and photographed the car (Figure 18.1). In addition to the missing driver's window and damage to the windshield, debris that appeared to be body tissue was observed on the dash, headliner, and front floorboard. The fragments of broken glass were inside the car but not on the garage floor, indicating that the damage probably did not occur while the car was in storage. Several shotgun pellets, possible bone fragments, and dried blood were also recovered from inside the vehicle. Deodorizers were found on the dashboard and on the rear ledge of the car and there were wipe patterns on the windows, indicating that there had been an attempt to clean the car. In an interview with investigators, an employee of the rental facility recalled that the person who stored the car was sweating profusely, felt ill, and asked to use the bathroom. Ultimately, more than eighty pieces of evidence were recovered from the automobile.

A search of the husband's house yielded additional evidence, including a 12-gauge shotgun that Alcohol, Tobacco and Firearms (ATF) records indicated was purchased by him the day his wife disappeared. In addition, there were two partially filled boxes of

12-gauge ammunition, two sets of keys to the red Ford Escort, a key to the padlock at the storage unit, cancelled checks to the storage facility, and his wife's diamond ring in a folded stapled envelope in an office desk.

After all of the evidence was collected, specific items were sent to a forensic anthropologist, a pathologist, and a serologist for further analysis. This chapter will focus on the forensic anthropologist's contribution to the successful prosecution of this case.

When officers delivering the evidence arrived at the Skeletal Identification Laboratory, I expected to be presented with a box or some similar container holding an assortment of bones and asked to determine whether they were human. In such a case, I was prepared to undertake a routine forensic osteological analysis. But the detectives carried no such containers. Instead, one of them reached into his coat pocket and removed several small matchboxes. These tiny containers held debris recovered from the missing woman's car. Along with small chards of glass and several shotgun pellets, the contents of the matchboxes consisted of thirty-one small fragments of what appeared to be bone (see Figure 18.2 on page 236).

Anthropological Analysis

Are the Fragments Really Bones?

The largest of the fragments measured approximately 27 mm^3 and the total weight of all of the fragments was only 700 mg. Given their small size, the first question to be addressed was whether they were indeed bone. To answer this question, two of the fragments were examined microscopically. If they were bone, the fragments should show the characteristic microstructure (histomorphology) of bone tissue.

In order to examine their microstructure, the fragments that had been selected for histological analysis were first embedded

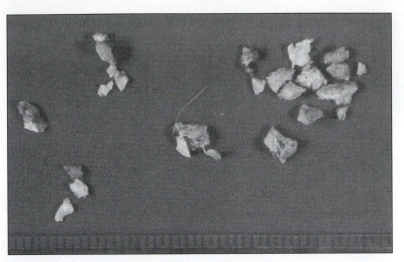

FIGURE 18.2   BONE FRAGMENTS

Shown here are suspected fragments of bone recovered from the missing woman's car.

in blocks of plastic resin. Embedding serves to keep bone samples intact during the sectioning and grinding processes that are used in the preparation of thin-sections of mineralized bone for microscopic analysis. Several 1–2 mm-thick wafers were removed from each of the embedded suspected bone fragments using a special petrographic thin-sectioning saw fitted with a diamond-coated blade (Figure 18.3). Using fine grit silicon carbide sandpaper, the wafers were then ground to a final thickness of 80–100 micromillimeters (μm) (one micromillimeter is 1/1000 of a millimeter) and mounted on microscopic slides.

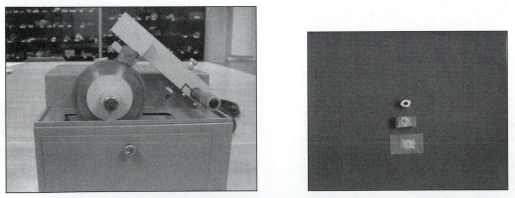

FIGURE 18.3   MICROSCOPIC ANALYSIS

Petrographic saw used to cut sections from bone samples (left), and examples of unembedded, embedded, and a sectioned wafer of bone positioned on a sheet of silicon carbide sandpaper used to further grind the sample to its final thickness for microscopic analysis.

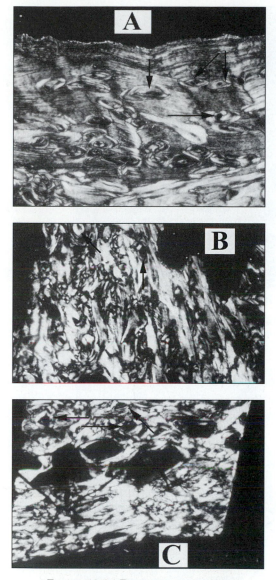

FIGURE 18.4   PHOTOMICROGRAPHS

(A) A photomicrograph of a thin section from one of the suspected bone fragments recovered from inside the missing woman's car. Note the lamellar pattern, presence of birefringence, and osteons indicative of bone (polarized light, x 2.5 magnification). The arrows denote osteons. (B) A photomicrograph of a thin section taken from the temporal bone of a human skull. (C) A photomicrograph of a thin section taken from the orbit region of a human skull.

When the thin-sections from the fragments recovered from the crime scene were examined under the microscope, a definite lamellar pattern typical of adult bone was observed (Figure 18.4). In addition, when the thin-sections were viewed under polarized light, birefringence was observed. In bone, birefringence is a pattern of adjacent light and dark lamellae. This characteristic is caused by the interaction of the polarized light with the alternating pattern of the collagen fibers that form the organic matrix of bone.

In addition to the distinctive birefringence of bone, histomorphological structures known as secondary osteons or Haversian systems (Figure 18.4, left, and Figure 18.5, page 238) were observed. Throughout life, bone is continually removed by specialized cells called osteoclasts, and then replaced by cells known as osteoblasts. This metabolic process is called bone remodeling. In the cortical bone of humans and most other large vertebrates, secondary osteons are the by-product of bone remodeling. Not all of the bone removed during remodeling is replaced, resulting in a net loss of bone. This loss accounts for the age-associated bone loss seen in humans. In some individuals, especially females after menopause, the loss is great enough to weaken the bones so much that nontraumatic fractures (e.g., fractures resulting from normal physical activity) can occur. This condition is called osteoporosis.

Figure 18.6 (on page 238) illustrates how the process of bone remodeling relates to histomorphological features of cortical bone. During the early phase of remodeling, osteoclasts resorb a discrete volume of bone that produces a distinct feature called a resorptive bay, or cutting cone. After a short reversal phase that leaves behind a distinct feature called a reversal line, the bone-resorbing osteoclasts are replaced by bone-forming osteoblasts. The osteoblasts

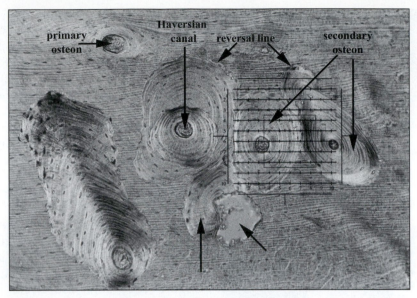

FIGURE 18.5   PHOTOMICROGRAPH

Here is a photomicrograph illustrating the typical histomorphology of a human long bone. The grid of an eyepiece reticule is superimposed on the image.

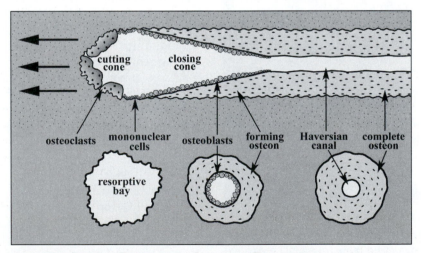

FIGURE 18.6   SCHEMATIC DIAGRAM

Here is a schematic diagram of the remodeling process in cortical bone as viewed in both longitudinal and transverse planes of view.

refill the existing resorptive bay with bone, with the exception of a Haversian canal containing two capillaries. Soon after death, cellular activity ceases and osteoclasts and osteoblasts disintegrate, but the histological features (osteons) resulting from the bone remodeling process persist. This life-long creation of osteons is the basis for histological methods used to estimate age at death for skeletal remains (Kerley and Ubelaker 1978; Stout and Paine 1992). Because of the small size and inexact anatomical location of the bone fragments from the crime scene, a histological-based estimation of age at death was not possible. For a review of histological methods to estimate age at death, see Stout (1998) and Robling and Stout (2000). Since it has been demonstrated that the microstructure is often preserved in archaeological and paleontological bone, histomorphological analysis can also be applied to relatively ancient skeletal remains (Abbott et al. 1996; Stout and Simmons 1979; Stout and Lueck 1995; Martin et al. 1981; Grupe and Garland 1993; Goldman et al. 1996; Pfeiffer and Zehr 1996; Ramsay 1997; Streeter et al. 2000).

Histomorphological analysis provided conclusive evidence that the fragments recovered from the crime scene were indeed bone. These findings were also independently confirmed by subsequent x-ray microanalysis of one of the fragments.

But Are They Human?

The next question to be addressed was whether these bone fragments were of human origin. The presence of secondary osteons eliminates from consideration some species, such as birds and very small mammals (e.g., rats), because their bone microstructure does not exhibit secondary osteons. In those species that typically exhibit secondary osteons, the average size of these structures increases in proportion to body size for animals smaller than humans (Jowsey 1968). The cross-sectional areas (the area of bone contained within a secondary osteon, including its central Haversian canal) of several clearly identifiable osteons in the bone samples in question were measured using a simple "point count" method (Parfitt 1983). To do this, an eyepiece reticule, which is a grid of known dimensions, is inserted within one of the eyepieces of the microscope. This grid appears superimposed on the surface of a bone as it is observed under the microscope (Figure 18.5). The cross-sectional area of a secondary osteon is determined by counting the number of grid points (hits) that fall within its delimiting boundary. This boundary is demarcated by the presence of a reversal line, a feature that distinguishes secondary osteons from similar histomorphological structures, such as primary osteons and vascular canals. The number of hits that fall within the reversal line of a secondary osteon is divided by the total number of possible hits for the grid, and the quotient is multiplied by the known area of the grid to determine the actual area of the osteon. To illustrate, consider the osteon that falls completely within the grid in Figure 18.5. Fifty-five of the 100 hits of the grid fall within its delimiting reversal line. If we assume that the area of the grid when viewed at this magnification is 0.069 mm^2, the cross-sectional area of this osteon is $55/100 \times 0.069$ mm$^2 = 0.038$ mm^2. Sixteen observable secondary osteons in the fragments from the crime scene were measured and yielded a mean osteonal cross-sectional area of 0.049 ± 0.010 mm^2. This size is larger than would be expected in animals smaller than a human. For example, it is greater than two standard deviations above the average cross-sectional area of secondary osteons of dogs (0.019 ± 0.01 mm^2) reported in the literature (Jowsey 1968). Statistically, this means that with repeated random samplings of dogs, an average cross-sectional area of secondary osteons this large or larger would be expected to occur in only about 2 out of 100 samplings. The mean osteonal cross-sectional area measured for the fragments falls within the extreme ranges for humans (0.045 ± 0.007 mm^2 and 0.033 ± 0.007 mm^2) reported for the decades of life between the ages of 5 and 65 years (Pirok et al. 1966). The cortical thickness of the bone fragments and the lack of evidence

FIGURE 18.7   PHOTOMICROGRAPH

Here is a photomicrograph of plexiform bone typical of large, fast-growing animals, such as cows and pigs. (*Image provided by Matt Vennemeyer.*)

of plexiform bone (Figure 18.7) also eliminate large, fast-growing animals, such as cow and pig, from consideration.

From What Part of the Human Skeleton Did the Fragments Come?

Small core samples were removed from various bones of a known human skeleton. Histological sections were prepared as described above, and their histomorphology was compared to that of the samples in question.

Long bones typically exhibit relatively round osteons when viewed in a cross-section taken in the transverse plane. This is because osteon formation tends to parallel the direction of the major biomechanical forces, such as compression and tension, that are exerted on the bone. The weight-bearing role of long bones subjects them to biomechanical forces that are roughly longitudinal in orientation. In flat bones, such as those of the skull vault, however, the biomechanical forces are not predominately longitudinal, and result in relatively eccentric shapes to the osteons. By comparing the

histomorphology of the crime scene fragments (Figure 18.4a) to known samples from the human orbit (Figure 18.4b), temporal (Figure 18.4c), and a human long bone (Figure 18.5), it was determined that the bone fragments were not from a long bone. More specifically, the shape and orientation of the osteons of the bone fragments from the crime scene were consistent with non–weight-bearing flat bones of the human skeleton, and most likely originated from the skull.

The gross morphology of two additional fragments was also suggestive of bone from the skull. One resembled a bone from the orbit, such as the lacrimal. Another exhibited a foramen, a possible suture line, and a surface curvature that would only be observed in bones of the skull (Figure 18.8). None of the fragments exhibited gross or microscopic features that were inconsistent with the skull.

Additional evidence relating to the identity of the victim and manner of death was provided by the microscopic analysis of the bone fragments. Several faint brown lines were observed during the histological examination of the bone sections. When the sections were examined using fluorescent-light microscopy, the lines emitted a bright yellow florescence (Figure 18.9). Such lines occur in the bones of individuals who have consumed compounds called fluorochromes, which include the common antibiotics called tetracyclines. Tetracyclines become incorporated in sites of active bone formation and remain there as long as the bone mineral is intact, even after death. When viewed under ultraviolet light, areas of bone that have incorporated the drug autofluoresce (glow). These properties of tetracyclines allow biomedical researchers to use them to determine dynamic rates of bone formation by sequential administration of a fluorochrome drug (*in vivo* labeling). For example, tetracycline is administered for two

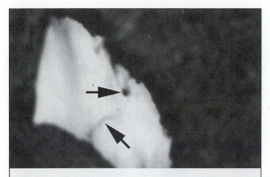

[A]

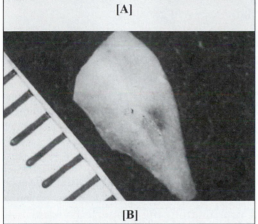

[B]

FIGURE 18.8   BONE FRAGMENTS

Shown here are two of the bone fragments recovered from the missing woman's car for which there are morphological features characteristic of bones of the human skull. Fragment A exhibits a foramen and suture line, and fragment B resembles a lacrimal bone from the orbit region.

periods of time (labeling periods), which are separated by five-day intervals during which no drug is administered. A bone biopsy is then taken, usually a small core from the hip (iliac crest), and the distance between the sequential fluorescing labels is measured using a fluorescent light–microscope. The distance between the labels indicates the amount of bone formed during the time interval between the labeling periods. Some researchers report finding fluorochrome labels in the bones of ancient Nubians living

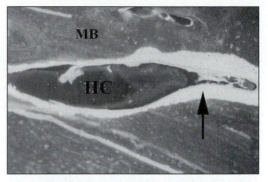

FIGURE 18.9   PHOTOMICROGRAPH

Here is a photomicrograph of a thin section from a bone fragment from the missing woman's car exhibiting a tetracycline label (arrow). MB and HC indicate mineralized bone and a Haversian canal, respectively (x 10 magnification, fluorescent light).

some 1,500 years ago. In these people, the labeling of their bone occurred as a consequence of consuming tetracycline-like compounds present in their beer as a result of its contamination with the common mold-like bacteria, streptomycetes, during the brewing process (Bassett et al. 1980).

Not only did the presence of the labels in the bone fragments from the crime scene indicate that the individual had taken tetracycline, but it was determined that the antibiotic had been administered relatively close to the time of death. This was deduced because all of the labels were observed to be on bone surfaces, such as Haversian canals, rather than being completely surrounded by bone. Since the time period required for an osteon to be completed (referred to as Sigma) is approximately three months, the fluorochrome was probably administered within three months prior to death. The missing woman's medical records corroborated these deductions, revealing that she had been prescribed tetracycline within three months of her disappearance.

Scanning Electron Microscopic Analysis and Manner of Death

Several of the bone fragments exhibited dark areas on their surfaces that appeared to be lead stains (Figure 18.10). In order to determine whether these areas were composed of lead, two of the fragments exhibiting the dark areas, along with a shotgun pellet and a piece of glass recovered from the car, were submitted for further analysis. A scanning electron microscope (SEM) equipped with an energy-dispersive X-ray spectrometer (EDS) was used to determine the chemical composition of these samples and the dark stains. In agreement with the histological analysis, the fragments exhibited a typical calcium and phosphorous signature of bone. When the areas of dark staining were isolated and analyzed, they were found to contain a significant amount of lead and a small amount of antimony (~99 percent lead and 1 percent antimony). The shotgun pellet produced similar results. Antimony is a principal component of gunshot residue produced by the ammunition's primer. It is usually found on objects at close proximity to a discharged firearm, such as the hands of the shooter and the wound of a victim. Neither lead nor antimony was detected on the sample of glass, or areas on the bone fragments that did not exhibit dark staining.

Serology: The Blood Evidence

The most convincing evidence as to the identity of the individual who died in the car was provided by DNA analysis of the blood evidence recovered from the vehicle. Samples of the dried blood from the car were submitted for DNA analysis. It was established that the dried blood samples contained sufficient amounts of genetic material for DNA fingerprinting. The fact that no known sample of the deceased's blood was available for comparison with the blood evidence posed an apparent

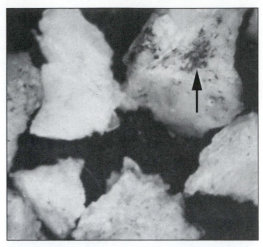

FIGURE 18.10   LEAD STAIN

Here is a lead stain (arrow) on the surface of one of the bone fragments recovered from the missing woman's car.

dilemma. One possible solution was paternity testing. The DNA of the blood evidence could be compared to that of her parents. Unfortunately the suspected victim was adopted and the identity of her biological parents was unknown. Collecting blood from the defendant and the deceased's two children for comparison with the unknown blood samples from the crime scene solved this problem. When the DNA characteristics of the father, the defendant, were eliminated from the genetic profile of the children, the remaining DNA was contributed by the mother. It was determined that the chances that the blood from the car came from anyone other than the children's mother were 1 in 22 billion (Dix et al. 1991).

Conclusions

It was concluded from the results of the histomorphological and scanning electron microscopic (SEM and EDS) analyses that the fragments recovered from the missing woman's car were from the skull of a person who had taken a tetracycline-like antibiotic within approximately three months of death. In addition, these bone fragments had been impacted with lead similar to that from shotgun pellets also recovered from the car.

The Trial and Expert Testimony

The successful prosecution of this case depended upon proving, beyond a reasonable doubt, that a fatal injury occurred in the car and that the defendant's wife was the person who died. But proving the *corpus delicti* in a murder case without the *corpus* is a challenge. A jury might accept the circumstantial proof, but juries sometimes interpret the burden of proof to mean proof beyond any doubt whatsoever.

In this case, proof was based upon the expert testimony involving forensic anthropology, forensic pathology, and DNA fingerprinting. First, the serologist testified that human blood was found in the car. The forensic anthropologist next testified that the thirty-one fragments found in the car were human bone that most likely were from a skull, and had been impacted by lead pellets. Given the amount of blood in the car, coupled with the presence of human skull fragments and shotgun pellets in the car, along with his own observations, the medical examiner was able to testify that a fatal injury had occurred in that automobile. In this case, a homicide could not have been proven without the combined testimony of all of the expert witnesses. The defendant was found guilty of the murder of his wife and sentenced to death by means of lethal injection. He was executed in the spring of 1999.

Acknowledgments

This chapter was adapted, with permission, from the *Journal of Forensic Sciences* 36, no. 3, copyright American Society for the Testing and Materials, 100 Barr Drive, West Conshohocken, PA 19428 (Dix et al. 1991; and Stout et al. 1991). L. M. Ross Jr., senior electron microscope specialist of the Department of Geological Sciences at the University of Missouri, Columbia, MO, performed the SEM analysis. Cellmark Diagnostics performed the DNA analysis.

References

Abbott, Stephen, Erik Trinkaus, and David B. Burr. 1996. Dynamic bone remodeling in later Pleistocene fossil hominids. *American Journal of Physical Anthropology* 99:585–601.

Bassett, Everett, Margaret Keith, George J. Armelagos, Debra Martin, and Antonio Villanueva. 1980. Tetracycline- labeled human bone from Prehistoric Sudanese Nubia A.D. 350. *Science* 209:1532–1534.

Dix, Jay D., Sam D. Stout, and Joe Mosley. 1991. Bones, blood, pellets, glass, and no body. *Journal of Forensic Sciences* 36(3):949–952.

Ducy, Patricia, Thursten Schinke, and Gerard Karsenty. 2000. The osteoblast: A sophisticated fibroblast under central surveillance. *Science* 289:1501–1504.

Goldman, Havica M., Timothy G. Bromage, and Chris B. Stringer. 1996. A histological analysis of a mid-shaft femoral section of an archaic *Homo sapiens* from Broken Hill (abstract). *American Journal of Physical Anthropology Suppl.* 22:114.

Grupe, Gisela, and A. Neil Garland, eds. 1993. *Histology of Ancient Human Bone.* New York: Springer-Verlag.

Jowsey, Jenifer. 1968. Age and species differences in bones. *Cornell Veterinarian* 58:74–94.

Kerley, Ellis R., and Douglas H. Ubelaker. 1978. Revisions in the microscopic method of estimating age at death in human cortical bone. *American Journal of Physical Anthropology* 49:545–546.

Martin, Debra L., George J. Armelagos, James H. Mielke, and Richard S. Miendl. 1981. Bone loss and dietary stress in an adult population from Sudanese Nubia. *Bull. et Mem. de la Soc. d'Anthrop. de Paris* 13:307–319.

Parfitt, A. Michael. 1983. Stereologic basis of bone histomorphometry: Theory of quantitative microscopy and reconstruction of the third dimension. In *Bone Histomorphometry: Techniques and Interpretations*, ed. R. R. Recker. Boca Raton, FL: CRC Press.

Pfeiffer, Susan, and Marie K. Zehr. 1996. A morphological and histological study of the human humerus from Border Cave. *Journal of Human Evolution* 31:49–59.

Pirok, D. J., J. R. Ramser, Hideaki Takahashi, Antonio R. Villanueva, and Harold M. Frost. 1966. Normal histological parameters in human mineralized bone sections. *Henry Ford Hospital Medical Bulletin* 14:195–217.

Ramsay, Heather L. 1997. Bone histology in the Le Moustier Neandertal. M.A. Thesis, Wake Forest University.

Robling, Alex R., and Sam D. Stout. 2000. Methods of determining age at death using bone microstructure. In *Biological Anthropology of the Human Skeleton*, ed. M. Anne Katzenberg and Shelley R. Saunders. New York: Wiley-Liss.

Stout, Sam D. 1998. The application of histological techniques for age at death determination. In *Forensic Osteology: Advances in the Identification of Human Remains*, ed. Kathleen J. Reichs. Springfield, IL: Charles C. Thomas.

Stout, Sam D., and Rhonda Lueck. 1995. Bone remodeling rates and maturation in three archaeological skeletal populations. *American Journal of Physical Anthropology* 98:161–171.

Stout, Sam D., and Robert R. Paine. 1992. Histological age estimation using rib and clavicle. *American Journal of Physical Anthropology* 87:111–115.

Stout, Sam D., and Lou M. Ross. 1991. Bone fragments a body can make. *Journal of Forensic Sciences* 36(3):953–957.

Stout, Sam D., and David J. Simmons. 1979. The use of histology in ancient bone research. *Yearbook of Physical Anthropology* 22:228–249.

Streeter, Margaret, Sam D. Stout, and Erik Trinkaus. 2000. Histological stress indicators in Late Pleistocene hominid diaphyseal bone (abstract). *American Journal of Physical Anthropology Suppl.* 30:295.

Teitelbaum, Steven L. 2000. Bone resorption by osteoclasts. *Science* 289:1504–1514.

SECTION V

APPLICATIONS OF FORENSIC ANTHROPOLOGY

QUEEN ELIZABETH: Ay me, I see the downfall of our house!
The tiger now hath seized the gentle hind;
Insulting tyranny begins to jet
Upon the innocent and aweless throne:
Welcome, destruction, death, and massacre!
I see, as in a map, the end of all.

—King Richard III, Act II, scene IV

Forensic anthropologists have always provided their professional services to local authorities within the United States. Over the past two decades, however, forensic anthropologists have expanded their scope beyond the local landscape and traditional laboratory roles. The chapters in this final section highlight three principal directions in which forensic anthropological applications have expanded—mass fatality incidents, search and recovery of U.S. war dead, and human rights investigations.

Mass Fatality Incidents

Earthquakes, floods, airline crashes, tornados, bombings, and hurricanes are all disasters in which people are often injured or killed. We watched our televisions in horror as burned and bleeding victims were carried from the Murrah Federal Building in Oklahoma City and the images of the World Trade Center attacks are indelibly etched in our collective consciousness. The toll in human lives can seem too much to bear yet forensic anthropologists and other specialists quickly respond to these disasters to assist in the identification of the victims. From a medicolegal perspective, however, each disaster varies in magnitude depending on the number of fatalities and the amount and type of local resources available to respond to the disaster. For instance, an earthquake in southern California can cause extensive devastation and loss of life while an earthquake of similar magnitude in southern Alaska may not incur the same degree of death and destruction because the area is not as densely populated. Similarly, the fatal crash of a two-passenger airplane into a field will not require the same response from the medicolegal community as if a fully loaded 747 airplane crashes into the same field. Thus, a *mass disaster* is a relative term and hinges upon the capabilities of the local community to administer to the injured and dead.

The U.S. government has recognized that the scale of any particular mass fatality incident may vary and, in 1992, created the Disaster Mortuary Operational Response Teams, or DMORT. There are currently ten regional teams designed to assist local jurisdictions in responding to an MFI (Figure V.1). Each team is composed of anthropologists, pathologists, radiologists, odontologists, dental assistants, mortuary officers, coroners, medical examiners, fingerprint experts, x-ray technicians, law enforcement personnel, medical record and database experts, and an administrative support staff. Since all mass fatality responses are multidisciplinary in nature, these responders work together to recover, identify, and facilitate the ultimate disposition of the victims' remains. This is extremely difficult work, full of mental and physical stresses, and each team incorporates mental health personnel to assist its members during and after deployment.

Forensic anthropologists had responded to mass fatality incidents as part of multidisciplinary teams for many years prior to the development of DMORT (Stewart 1970). The 1979 crash of American Airlines Flight 191 in Chicago provides an example. This DC-10, carrying 271 passengers and crew, departed from Chicago O'Hare airport around 3 P.M. on May 25, destined for Los Angeles. The plane lost a left engine as it took off. The aircraft winged over and ultimately turned upside down and skidded into some buildings near the airport. All aboard were fatally wounded and two people on the ground were killed (NTSB Report NSTB-AAR-79-17). Though

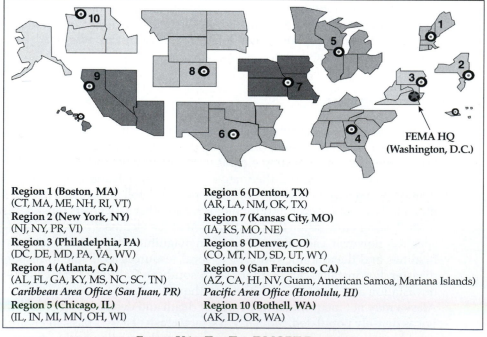

Region 1 (Boston, MA)
(CT, MA, ME, NH, RI, VT)

Region 2 (New York, NY)
(NJ, NY, PR, VI)

Region 3 (Philadelphia, PA)
(DC, DE, MD, PA, VA, WV)

Region 4 (Atlanta, GA)
(AL, FL, GA, KY, MS, NC, SC, TN)
Caribbean Area Office (San Juan, PR)

Region 5 (Chicago, IL)
(IL, IN, MI, MN, OH, WI)

Region 6 (Denton, TX)
(AR, LA, NM, OK, TX)

Region 7 (Kansas City, MO)
(IA, KS, MO, NE)

Region 8 (Denver, CO)
(CO, MT, ND, SD, UT, WY)

Region 9 (San Francisco, CA)
(AZ, CA, HI, NV, Guam, American Samoa, Mariana Islands)
Pacific Area Office (Honolulu, HI)

Region 10 (Bothell, WA)
(AK, ID, OR, WA)

FIGURE V.1   THE TEN DMORT REGIONS

the Cook County Medical Examiner's Office in Chicago was well-suited to handle the daily volume of local cases, this mass fatality incident clearly required the assistance of the forensic community at large. A temporary morgue was established in an airport hangar and an early form of an incident command system was established to coordinate efforts between the morgue, the recovery site, and other points of operation. The multidisciplinary identification teams worked for six weeks and ultimately identified all but thirty victims. The lessons and systems learned during this and other high fatality incidents (especially the crash of United Flight 232 in Sioux City a decade later) contributed to the formal structure of DMORT.

In 1996, the Aviation Disaster Family Assistance Act was signed into law. This law was created to help provide consistency in the treatment of families who lose a loved one in a major aircraft accident. The law tasks the National Transportation Safety Board with the responsibility of coordinating victim identification processes. In response to this assignment, the NTSB may rely on the DMORT teams and their standardized processes and procedures to address these needs (Sledzik 1996).

CILHI

The Central Identification Laboratory, Hawaii (CILHI), is a unique team of over 170 military and civilian personnel who work to recover and identify the remains of soldiers and civilians who died on foreign soils during past conflicts. CILHI teams have been deployed to nations throughout the Middle East, Europe, Southeast Asia, South America, and the Pacific. In addition to their quest to identify those missing and killed in action, CILHI teams have also been deployed to assist in the recovery and identification of mass fatality incidents, including the 1983 bombing of a Marine Corps barracks in Lebanon and the September 11, 2001, disaster sites. The lab's recent identification of the occupant of the Tomb of the Unknown Soldier from Vietnam underscores the importance of the work of this unique organization. Table V.1 provides a list of unannounced identifications by conflict era and year. This information is current as of April 2002.

TABLE V.1 IDENTIFICATIONS ESTABLISHED BY THE **CILHI**, 1998–2002, AS OF APRIL **2002**

YEAR OF IDENTIFICATION	VIETNAM	COLD WAR*	KOREAN WAR	WWII	TOTAL
1998	27	11	0	30	68
1999	41	0	2	24	67
2000	63	2	5	39	109
2001	52	0	6	36	94
2002	4	0	2	5	11
Totals	187	13	15	134	349

*Defined as the period between 1945 and the end of the "Iron Curtain" in 1991.

Source: www.cilhi.mil.army

The CILHI has utilized the skills of forensic anthropologists since it was established in 1947 to assist in the identification of war dead from WWII. The first anthropologist to serve at the CILHI was Charles E. Snow from the University of Kentucky. In 1948, Snow was succeeded by Mildred Trotter, whose efforts to conduct research on the remains of the war dead lead to her seminal work on skeletal stature estimation (Trotter and Gleser 1952). The Korean War escalated the workload of the CILHI and another identification laboratory was established in Japan. Significant research on the war dead was conducted at the identification laboratories in both Hawaii and Japan, leading to, among other advances, a refinement of the earlier stature estimates (Trotter and Gleser 1958; Trotter 1970) and the development of a new skeletal aging technique (McKern and Stewart 1957). An identification laboratory was also established in Saigon during the Vietnam War. Given the scope of research books, papers, and symposia organized by forensic anthropologists at the CILHI and other identification laboratories, T. Dale Stewart, a pioneer of forensic anthropology, largely attributes the modern development of the discipline to the study of American war dead (Stewart 1979).

As of early 2002, the CILHI employs thirty anthropologists and, in collaboration with molecular geneticists of the Armed Forces DNA Identification Laboratory (AFDIL), identifies MIAs even when only very small bone fragments are present. The CILHI requests that mtDNA samples be provided from all maternal relatives of those missing and killed in action (MIAs and KIAs) during past wars and conflicts. A presumptive identification undergoes a rigorous review process. If the identification stands, the results are presented to the family, who can choose to accept or reject the findings and/or can have an independent expert review the results. If the family accepts the findings, the remains are given a military escort to a burial location of the family's choice. If rejected, the file is sent to the Armed Forces Identification Review Board (AFIRB), which then determines if CILHI must provide further evidence or if the identification is indeed final. While this process may take a number of years following the recovery of the remains, the ultimate disposition of the remains to the correct family is of the utmost importance.

HUMAN RIGHTS INVESTIGATIONS

> Bosnian Muslims will disappear off the face of the earth.
>
> —Radovan Karadzic, ex-president of Bosnia, Parliamentary speech, 10/14/91

Since WWII, the world has witnessed approximately 250 armed conflicts and wars resulting in 170 million war-related casualties (Bassiouni 1999). In the year 2000 alone there were at least 20 recognized wars (Stover and Ryan 2001). The nature of all of the recent wars is brutal, but in very different ways. The Argentine military *Junta* conducted secretive "disappearances" of purported subversives in Argentina, while military leaders in the former Yugoslavia put forth a very public and unambiguous call for genocide. While less technologically advanced, the machete warfare of Rwanda exacted a human toll that was even more devastating than that of the ethnic cleansing in the Balkans (Ball 1999). Guatemala, El Salvador, and other Central and South American countries also continue their struggle to secure sociopolitical stability while seeking justice for the thousands of victims of massacres and disappearances (e.g., Danner 1993; *La Foundación de Antropología Forense de Guatemala* 2000). From a global perspective we are faced with two overriding questions—what happened to the victims and how can those who commit human rights atrocities be brought to justice?

In 1993 the United Nations International Criminal Tribunals for the former Yugoslavia (ICTY) was instituted to prosecute all military personnel and civilians accused of committing "crimes against humanity" and other war crimes in the Balkans. Only a year later, a second UN Criminal Tribunal was formed in response to the atrocities in Rwanda (ICTR). As in any trial, the Tribunal prosecutors must present evidence in court that satisfies the legal requirements of proof of a defendant's guilt. Forensic scientists, including anthropologists, have assisted in this endeavor to gather evidence through scientific death investigations. The exhumation of mass graves and/or recovery of unburied bodies typically has three main goals— to provide an objective and scientific reconstruction of events independent of political rhetoric or the "official story," collect evidence that can be used in court, and identify the dead. The relative emphasis of these goals varies from mission to mission. For instance, some missions may be *evidentiary* in nature, whereby the collection of basic demographic information and physical evidence from a scene, such as a mass grave, is of prime importance. Other cases have no legal implications in national or international courts but identification of the dead is the central issue. These may be referred to as *humanitarian* missions.

Human rights investigations are inherently multidisciplinary, and most teams include the services of anthropologists, archaeologists, radiologists, odontologists, and ballistics experts. Attorneys, physicians, statisticians, and other professionals have also contributed to these investigations (Burns 1998). Over 100 physical anthropologists and archaeologists from more than twenty countries have participated in human rights investigations in the 1990s (Steadman and Haglund 2001). Their primary roles are fairly traditional—exhumation of graves, identification of the dead, and assessment of perimortem trauma—but new roles and responsibilities are developing. Increasingly, anthropologists are the leaders of these multidisciplinary teams and are responsible for the logistics and assessments of each mission. In addition, anthropologists help educate and train local forensic scientists in the field and the lab such that the investigations can continue after the international teams depart. Burns (1998) provides a good overview of the nature and procedures of human rights missions as well as the principal roles of the anthropologist (see also Ferllini 1999).

Forensic anthropological involvement in human rights investigations did not begin in Europe or Africa in the 1990s, but rather in Argentina in 1984. Between 1976 and 1983, thousands of people were illegally seized, tortured, and murdered by the military *Junta* who wielded power over the Argentine people. While the government's "official story" was that the military was only combating leftist guerrilla groups, in reality no one was safe. Power among the combatants was certainly one-sided, and this "Dirty War" was waged in secret detention centers. In 1976, the governor of Buenos Aires Province made the *Junta*'s agenda frighteningly clear. "First we kill all the subversives; then we will kill their collaborators; then . . . their sympathizers; then . . . those who remain indifferent; and finally we will kill the timid" (General Iberico Saint Jean 1976).

The methods of repression were especially brutal. Detainees were mercilessly tortured in a number of barbaric ways, including the application of electric prods to the eyes, teeth, and genitals, hanging, rape, constant beatings, and near drowning (called the *submarino*). The military was also extremely proficient in the tactics of psychological abuse, such as forcing a parent to witness the torture of their child, or vice versa. A detainee might be forced to watch the execution of a spouse or child and then told that the death was the prisoner's own responsibility because he or she would not give the soldiers the information they wanted (CONADEP 1986).

Hundreds, then thousands of sons, husbands, and daughters went missing. Mothers of the missing began to meet at the Casa Rosada, the official presidential building in downtown Buenos Aires, to demand the return of their loved ones. They were told that their missing had simply disappeared and that the military had no responsibility in such matters. Unsatisfied, the mothers began to march in angry protest at the front door of one of the most repressive regimes of the twentieth century (Figure V.2). The international community began to listen to the collective cry of the Madres de la Plaza de Mayo (Mothers of the Plaza de Mayo, named after the square facing the Casa Rosada where they march). Unfortunately, the fate of the disappeared would not be investigated until after democracy returned to Argentina in 1983.

FIGURE V.2   PLAZA DE MAYO, 1991

Mothers of the Disappeared marching on the Plaza de Mayo in 1991. The Casa Rosada (Presidential House) is in the background. (*Photo by D. Steadman*)

During their regime, the *Junta* had to address a thorny issue—what should be done with the tortured and bullet-ridden bodies of those who were illegally detained and executed? While some were returned to families with improbable explanations for their death (suicide or a gun battle with police), most bodies were "disappeared." As corroborated by a navy pilot, some victims were drugged, put into a military aircraft, and thrown into shark-infested ocean waters (Verbitsky 1996). Others were tossed into the rivers or burned, but many were buried. The military thought burial was a particularly safe and effective mode of disposal, for who could tell anything from a bunch of bones?

When Raul Alfonsín was democratically elected to the presidency in 1983, he quickly formed the National Commission on Disappeared People (CONADEP) to investigate the fate of the *desaparecidos* ("disappeared"). In early 1984, acting on an appeal from the Grandmothers of the Plaza de Mayo and others, CONADEP formally requested the assistance of forensic scientists from the American Association for the Advancement of Science (AAAS) to identify the remains of the thousands of *desaparecidos*. Clyde Snow, a forensic anthropologist already famous around the world for his work in aviation disasters as well as historical and criminal cases, issued a challenge to his colleagues at the AAAS meeting in 1984:

> Of all the forms of murder, none is more monstrous than that committed by a state against its own citizens. And of all murder victims, those of the state are the most helpless and vulnerable since the very entity to which they have entrusted their lives and safety becomes their killer. . . . Maybe it's time for the forensic scientists of the world to heed the old call of our favorite fictional prototype: "Quick, Watson, the game's afoot!"—and go after the biggest game of all.

With these words, Clyde Snow began the first forensic anthropological investigation of human rights atrocities and ultimately changed the landscape of how human rights investigations are conducted and the directions in which forensic anthropology would move by the end of the twentieth century.

Sponsored by the AAAS, Dr. Snow led a multidisciplinary team of forensic experts to Argentina in June of 1984. They visited morgues and conducted legal exhumations of the dead. As most of the remains were skeletonized, or nearly so, the expertise of the forensic anthropologist was particularly crucial. During this mission, the delegation trained a group of anthropology and medical students in the methods of exhumation and skeletal identification. Soon this group of extraordinary young people became the Argentine Forensic Anthropology Team (Joyce and Stover 1991).

In 1985, Dr. Snow returned to Argentina to testify in War Crimes Trials, which ultimately led to the conviction of past presidents and other military personnel for war crimes atrocities during the Dirty War. After the trials, the Argentine Forensic Team continued to exhume graves, perform identifications, and document perimortem trauma despite the overt threats by the still-powerful military that was wary of the evidence the Team was collecting. Soon, however, the Team's work began to attract the attention of people across Central and South America, Africa, the Middle East, and Europe, whose recent histories were also marred by human rights abuses. The Team began to work with local forensic and nonforensic scientists in these countries, training them as Dr. Snow and his team had taught them. Ultimately, the Argentine Team became a model for the development of local teams in Guatemala and Chile.

By the late 1980s, a number of forensic anthropology and multidisciplinary human rights teams were working around the globe. The AAAS continues to sponsor forensic science investigations, as does Physicians for Human Rights (PHR), a nongovernment organization based in Boston. In addition to the United Nations, other international human rights organizations have begun to incorporate forensic science, including anthropology, into their missions. Dr. Snow also continues to work as a consultant in human rights investigations. It is unlikely that Snow, the other participants of the AAAS delegation, or the members of the Argentine Forensic Team could have predicted in 1984 the impact that forensic anthropological contributions would have on international human rights investigations in less than twenty years. Collectively, the scientific exhumation and identification of human remains around the world have empowered local populations, given human rights groups and prosecutors better legal leverage in prosecuting the accused, and provided thousands of families the answers they need and the peace they desire when their loved ones are identified and properly buried. Given the state of affairs in many areas of the world, it is likely that the application of forensic anthropology to human rights investigations will become even more important in the future.

THE CHAPTERS

Two chapters in this section provide a good perspective of the range of mass fatality incidents to which forensic anthropologists are deployed. In Chapter 19, Sledzik and Willcox describe the very first DMORT deployment in Hardin, Missouri, where the floods of 1993 disinterred caskets from a local cemetery. At first glance this seems an unlikely role for DMORT personnel since the "victims" were dead prior to the incident. However, it is not the nature of the disaster but the number of dead that initiates a mass fatality response. The authors illustrate the anguish felt by the close-knit Hardin residents as hundreds of their family members' caskets were unearthed and floated away. Sledzik and Willcox discuss how DMORT personnel worked with the community to recover, identify, and ultimately rebury the remains. The authors also provide a list of DMORT deployments subsequent to Hardin.

In Chapter 20, Frank Saul and Julie Mather Saul describe several mass fatality incidents in which they have participated, including airline crashes, a train crash, and an explosion. The authors give a sense of the chaos that pervades the early moments of a mass disaster, yet the disaster responders are charged with the task of calmly and scientifically identifying each victim and returning the remains to the families. This chapter also discusses the inner workings of DMORT's mobile morgue, or Disaster Portable Morgue Unit (DPMU), and the family assistance center.

Bunch and Shine provide a unique perspective of the efforts of the CILHI. Colleen Shine is the daughter of an Air Force Captain who was classified as Missing in Action in 1972. In a touching account, the authors examine the archaeological and physical anthropological methods utilized to recover and identify Shine's remains, but also include the thoughts and reactions of the Shine family. This personal perspective reminds us that it is more difficult to have a loved one who is missing than one who is deceased.

The constant battle between hope and despair described by Bunch and Shine is shared by thousands of people around the world whose lives have been shattered by wars, unlawful disappearances, and ethnic cleansing. In the final chapter, Mercedes Doretti, a founding member of the Argentine Forensic Anthropology Team, and Clyde Snow, who helped move forensic anthropology into the venue of human rights inquiries, examine three cases that the Argentine Team has investigated in Argentina, El Salvador, and Ethiopia. While each case is tragic, they differ in a number of important points, including what antemortem information is available, how it is collected, and the sociopolitical complications that must be managed. In addition, the authors stress that the role of forensic anthropology in human rights investigations cannot be limited to exhumations and skeletal analyses but requires extensive historical research and family interviews that continue for years after the field and lab work are complete. In all, these chapters serve as a poignant reminder that forensic anthropologists may work with human calamity on a grand scale.

REFERENCES

Ball, Howard. 1999. *Prosecuting War Crimes and Genocide: The Twentieth-Century Experience*. Lawrence, KS: University of Kansas.

Bassiouni, M. Cherif. 1999. *Crimes against Humanity in International Criminal Law*. 2nd ed. Dordrecht, Netherlands: Kluwer Law International.

Burns, Karen R. 1998. Forensic anthropology and human rights issues. Pp. 63–85 in *Forensic Osteology: Advances in the Identification of Human Remains*, ed. K. J. Reichs. 2nd ed. Springfield, IL: Charles C. Thomas.

CONADEP, The National Commission on Disappeared People. 1986. *Nunca Mas*. London: Faber and Faber.

Danner, Mark. 1993. *The Massacre at El Mozote*. New York: Vintage Books.

Ferllini, Roxana. 1999. The role of forensic anthropology in human rights investigations. Pp. 287–302 in *Forensic Osteological Analysis: A Book of Case Studies*, ed. Scott I. Fairgrieve. Springfield, IL: Charles C. Thomas.

Joyce, Christopher, and Eric Stover. 1991. *Witnesses from the Grave: The Stories Bones Tell*. Boston, MA: Little, Brown and Co.

La Foundación de Antropología Forense de Guatemala. 2000. *Informe de las Investigaciones Antropólogico Forenses e Históricas*. Report of investigations, 1997–1998. Guatemala City: *Editorial Serviprensa*.

McKern, Thomas, and T. Dale Stewart. 1957. *Skeletal Age Changes in Young American Males*. Technical Report EP-45, Natick, MA: U.S. Army Quartermaster Research and Development Center, Environmental Protection Research Division.

National Transportation Safety Board. Aircraft Accident Report—American Airlines, Inc. DC-10-10, N1100AA, Chicago-O'Hare International Airport Chicago, Illinois, May 25, 1979. Rpt. no. NSTB-AAR-79-17.

Shakespeare, William, with Tom Baldwin, ed. 2001. *King Richard III*. Cambridge, UK: Cambridge University Press.

Sledzik, Paul S. 1996. Federal resources in mass disaster response. *Cultural Resources Management* 19(10):19–20.

Snow, Clyde C. 1984. Forensic anthropology in the documentation of human rights abuses. Paper presented at the Annual Meeting of the American Association for the Advancement of Science, New York, May 27, 1984.

Steadman, Dawnie W., and William D. Haglund. 2001. The scope of anthropological contributions to human rights investigations. *Proceedings of the American Academy of Forensic Sciences*, Seattle, Washington, February 22, 2001. 7:237–38.

Stewart, T. Dale, ed. 1970. *Personal Identification in Mass Disasters*. Washington, D.C.: Smithsonian Institution Press.

Stewart, T. Dale. 1979. *Essentials of Forensic Anthropology*. Springfield, IL: Charles C. Thomas.

Stover, Eric, and Molly Ryan. 2001. Breaking bread with the dead. *Historical Archaeology* 35(1):7–25.

Trotter, Mildred. 1970. Estimation of stature from intact long bones. Pp. 71–83 in *Personal Identification in Mass Disasters*, ed. T. Dale Stewart. Washington, D.C.: Smithsonian Institution Press.

Trotter, Mildred, and Goldine C. Gleser. 1952. Estimation of stature of American Whites and Negroes. *American Journal of Physical Anthropology* 10:463–514.

Trotter, Mildred, and Goldine C. Gleser. 1958. A re-evaluation of estimation of stature based on measurements of stature taken during life and of long bones after death. *American Journal of Physical Anthropology* 16:79–123.

Verbitsky, Horacio. 1996. *The Flight: Confessions of an Argentine Dirty Warrior*. New York: New Press.

FURTHER READING

Danner, Mark. 1993. The truth of El Mozote. *The New Yorker*. December 6, 1993, 50–133.

Didion, Joan. 1983. *Salvador*. New York: Vintage Books.

Goldstone, Richard J. 2000. *For Humanity: Reflections of a War Crimes Investigator*. New Haven, CT: Yale University Press.

Haglund, William D., Melissa Connor, and Douglas D. Scott. 2001. The archaeology of contemporary mass graves. *Historical Archaeology* 35(1):57–69. (Note that this volume of *Historical Archaeology* is dedicated to Archaeologists as Forensic Investigators.)

Owsley, D., D. Ubelaker, M. Houk, K. Sanders, W. Grant, E. Craig, T. Woltanski, and N. Peerwani. 1995. The role of forensic anthropology in the recovery and analysis of the Branch Davidian Compound victims: Techniques of analysis. *Journal of Forensic Sciences* 40(3):341–348.

Owsley, Douglas. 1993. Identification of the fragmentary, burned remains of two U.S. journalists seven years after their disappearance in Guatemala. *Journal of Forensic Sciences* 38:1372–1382.

Prunier, G. 1995. *The Rwanda Crisis: History of a Genocide*. Kampala, Uganda: Fountain Publishers, Ltd.

Scott, Douglas D. 2001. Firearms identification in support of identifying a mass execution of El Mozote, El Salvador. *Historical Archaeology* 35(1):79–86.

Skinner, Mark. 1987. Planning the archaeological recovery from recent mass graves. *Forensic Science International* 34:267–287.

Snow, Clyde, and Maria J. Bihurriet. 1992. An epidemiology of homicide: Ningun Nombre burials in the Province of Buenos Aires from 1970 to 1984. Pp. 328–363 in *Human Rights and Statistics: Getting the Record Straight*, ed. Thomas B. Jabine and Richard P. Claude. Philadelphia, PA: University of Pennsylvania Press.

Snow, Clyde C., Eric Stover, and Kari Hannibal. 1989. Scientists as detectives: Investigating human rights. *Technology Review* 92(2):42–49.

Stover, Eric. 1995. In the shadow of Nuremberg: Pursuing war criminals in the Former Yugoslavia and Rwanda. *Medicine and Global Survival* 2:140–147.

Stover, Eric, and Gilles Peress. 1998. *The Graves: Srebrenica and Vukovar*. Zurich: Scalo.

Stratton, Sabine U., and Owen B. Beattie. 1999. Mass disasters: Comments and discussion regarding the Hinton train collision of 1986. Pp. 267–286 in *Forensic Osteological Analysis: A Book of Case Studies*, ed. Scott I. Fairgrieve. Springfield, IL: Charles C. Thomas.

Tedeschi, L. 1984. Human rights and the forensic scientist. *The American Journal of Forensic Medicine and Pathology* 5:295–296.

Wright, Jaime. 1998. *Torture in Brazil: A Shocking Report on the Pervasive Use of Torture by Brazilian Military Governments, 1965–1979*. (translation of *Brasil: Nunca Mas* by the Archdiocese of Sao Paulo, 1985). Austin, TX: University of Texas Press.

WEBSITES OF HUMAN RIGHTS, DMORT, AND CILHI ORGANIZATIONS

AFIP (Armed Forces Institute of Pathology)
www.afip.org

CILHI (Central Identification Laboratory, Hawaii)
www.cilhi.army.mil

DMORT (Disaster Mortuary Operational Response Team)
www.dmort.org

EAAF (Argentine Forensic Anthropology Team)
www.eaaf.org.ar

FAFG (Guatemalan Forensic Anthropology Team)
garnet.acns.fsu.edu/~sss4407/EAFG.htm

NDMS (National Disaster Medical System)
www.ndms.dhhs.org

PHR (Physicians for Human Rights)
www.phrusa.org

United Nations, Human Rights
www.un.org/rights

19

CORPI AQUATICUS

THE HARDIN CEMETERY FLOOD OF 1993

Paul S. Sledzik and Allison Webb Willcox

But let judgment run down as waters,
and righteousness as a mighty stream

       —Amos 5:24 King James Version

In 1993, the waters of the Mississippi River flooded a large enough area of the Midwestern United States to make it a sixth Great Lake. This flood exacted a heavy toll on lives, property, and entire towns. But the floodwaters that rolled their way into Hardin, Missouri, brought about a new kind of devastation. The torrent nearly obliterated the town cemetery. Of 1,756 graves, 769 were washed away. These graves dated from the nineteenth century to just a few weeks before the disaster. As authorities recognized the immense task of recovering and identifying the bodies washed out by the flood, forensic anthropologists were called to aid in the effort. As a result, the Hardin cemetery flood was a watershed moment for forensic anthropology in disaster response.

Forensic anthropologists are trained to identify the dead, whether from aircraft accidents, mass graves, or a single skeleton, and often work with human remains that are less than perfect—decomposed, fragmented,

mutilated, or burned. As a general rule, the less complete the remains, the more time-consuming and difficult the identification becomes. The forces acting upon the human body in mass disasters can result in a wide variety of preservational states. However, no matter the nature of the remains, identifying the unknown dead is a deeply held value of our culture and an important tenet of our legal system. Further, there is a palpable urgency to identify and return the dead as quickly and efficiently as possible so that families may grieve.

Disasters create many needs: Medical assistance, infrastructure, communications, and transportation are just a few. Locating, recovering, and identifying the dead, and taking care of the next of kin, require skills that typically are not available in the local jurisdiction. Most fire, rescue, and police agencies work with the living, while the medicolegal agencies deal with individual deaths. When the number of dead exceeds the capacity of local agencies to manage them, the term *mass fatality incident* (MFI) is used. MFIs present an entirely new set of problems to the disaster responder, who is trained to help the living, but who is usually unsure what to do when faced with large numbers of dead. Responders to mass fatality incidents must have a different mindset, in addition to calling on a unique set of resources and personnel. MFIs draw on forensic scientists and federal and state medicolegal investigators, professionals who are rarely involved in issues of disaster medical care, food, housing, and infrastructure. Although it may sound like a simple word change, when a search and rescue operation turns to a search and recovery operation, the mind-set of the responder also changes.

Forensic Anthropology in Mass Disasters

Traditionally, forensic anthropologists have focused on one case at a time—an unidentified individual skeleton. The anthropologist analyzes the skeleton's biological attributes and unique features, and the resulting biological profile is compared to missing persons' reports, with the ultimate goal of making an identification. In a disaster setting, however, the forensic anthropologist may manage hundreds of cases simultaneously, work that is complicated by disaster-specific factors, such as burning, commingling, fragmentation, and decomposition. The anthropologist is also often asked to assist in search and recovery, processing of records, and other critical activities.

Forensic Anthropological Skills for the Mass Fatality Incident

At the Scene

- Set up grid system for search and recovery of remains.
- Locate, recognize, and recover human remains, especially burned and fragmented remains.
- Document location of remains within grid units.
- Devise search criteria based on size and scope of disaster.

In the Morgue

- Assist in "triage" of remains.
- Describe incomplete/fragmentary remains and condition of remains.
- Conduct analysis to determine sex, age, ancestry, stature, and distinguishing characteristics.
- Separate commingled remains.
- Obtain radiographs for age estimation and unique skeletal features.
- Reassociate body parts based on biological profile and descriptions of missing parts.
- Determine minimum number of individuals based on remains recovered.
- Assist in organizing identification exclusion/inclusion matrix.
- Compare antemortem and postmortem data (e.g., radiographs, skeletal information).
- Assist in age determination of complete remains/bodies.
- Analyze trauma patterns/evidence and incident-related injuries.

In addition, the attention of the media, politicians and, most important, the next of kin, is focused on the identification process. As part of a team of forensic responders, anthropologists must coordinate their work with a variety of other specialists on site, including pathologists, dentists, radiologists, and fingerprint examiners.

Because each is unique, every disaster presents new challenges for the disaster response team. The flood at Hardin posed challenges that were unusual in a number of ways. The most remarkable of these, and the one that profoundly impacted the rest of the disaster response, was the simple fact that the "victims" of the cemetery flood were dead before the disaster occurred. This fact complicated the recovery, storage, identification, and return of the remains. It also deeply affected the living in the community of Hardin. The loss of the dead from the cemetery was a loss of history for Hardin, its ancestors washed away. Soon after the flood, *New York Times* reporter Isabel Wilkerson wrote of the disaster:

> Now people who lost everything else to the flood are left to weep for parents they mourned decades ago, the stillborn children they never saw grow up, the husbands taken away from them in farm accidents, the mothers who died in childbirth. It is as if the people have died all over again and the survivors must grieve anew.

The Disaster

Hardin, Missouri, is a farming community of 600, located six miles north of the Missouri River and fifty miles northeast of Kansas City. In many ways it is a typical small Midwestern town: a close-knit community with deep roots in its past. The cemetery lies just outside of town, bordered on the north and west by cornfields, on the south by a levee road, and on the east by Route 10, a local two-lane road. The cemetery started operations in 1810 and was still actively used at the time of the flood.

In July of 1993, heavy rainfall flooded 534 counties in nine midwestern states, encompassing an area extending from St. Louis, Missouri, to west Kansas and northwestern North Dakota. This "100-year flood" caused at least $15 billion in damage and killed 50 people.

On July 8, 1993, floodwaters crested a levee ten miles from Hardin and flooded tens of thousands of acres of farmland around the town. As the water level began to rise, the levee abutting the cemetery held back the water for a time. On July 10, the floodwater crested the levee and carved out streams along the cemetery roads (Figure 19.1). Soon these streams were powerful enough to scour away headstones, to lift two-ton burial vaults, and to empty caskets of bodies and bones, washing them out into thousands of acres of corn and soybean fields. Half of the cemetery became a lake, fifty feet deep.

FIGURE 19.1   THE HARDIN CEMETERY

This aerial photograph shows the Hardin cemetery during the flood. The water is moving from right to left. An unflooded portion of the cemetery (with several headstones) can be seen in the lower portion of the photograph.

Dean Snow, the county coroner, made his way to the cemetery to take in the watery resurrection of the town's ancestors. A local funeral director, Snow had embalmed and buried some of the dead, expecting never to see them after the soil was placed on the grave. But, as the county coroner, Snow now had the responsibility to recover, identify, and rebury these victims of the largest known cemetery flood.

Snow organized a local volunteer force of medical personnel, funeral directors, and equipment operators. In the days soon after the flood, while the waters were still high, the team used small boats to recover the caskets, vaults, and bodies that were entangled in trees and floating in the water. Once the water receded, more coffins, bodies, and bones were extracted from the mud and disentangled from fencerows. A temporary morgue was established at the county fairgrounds. Refrigerated trucks designated to store the remains arrived. Areas of the fairground were set aside to hold the hundreds of concrete and steel burial vaults and the new caskets to be used for the processing of the remains. Once the flood area was dry, two-person teams using all-terrain vehicles searched for bones and bodies, an effort that lasted until mid-October. The teams found remains scattered over twenty-five square miles of farmland. Comparing the eroded section of the cemetery to burial records revealed that 769 graves had been washed away.

The Response

The federal government takes disaster response seriously. A two-inch thick document called the Federal Response Plan details the responsibility of each federal agency during and after a disaster. When the president officially declares a jurisdiction a disaster area, the plan is immediately put into effect, and federal funds become available to pay for the response. The plan is well organized and thorough, but managing the dead had been just a footnote. Hardin changed that.

In 1992, a system of regional Disaster Mortuary Operational Response Teams (DMORT) was created to help overwhelmed local jurisdictions manage the dead following a mass disaster. DMORT was initially created within the National Funeral Directors Association. Shortly thereafter, it became a section of the U.S. Public Health Service's National Disaster Medical System (NDMS). The NDMS has the responsibility under the Federal Response Plan for providing medical support and victim identification and mortuary services in a disaster. The Hardin disaster was the first deployment of a DMORT team, and the NDMS was unaware of how integral DMORT would become in future disasters and of the important role DMORT would play at Hardin.

At the request of local officials, a DMORT assessment team arrived at Hardin in early August 1993. The team of four funeral directors and a forensic anthropologist (Sledzik) met with Dean Snow and Vernie Fountain, the regional DMORT commander who had been called in by Snow. As they walked the unflooded parts of the cemetery and examined the remains that had been recovered thus far, the team began to grasp the task ahead of them. Hundreds of burial vaults and coffins littered the roads and fields around Hardin. Individual bones could be seen amongst the debris at the cemetery, and many more had been carried far from the cemetery. The assessment team quickly recognized that the team of local volunteers organized by Snow and Fountain was now overwhelmed. They had done their best under the conditions of this unique event, but identification of the dead was beyond the expertise of the volunteers.

To gauge the feelings of the Hardin residents about what should be done with the remains, Snow organized several town meetings. The townspeople overwhelming wanted an effort made to identify the dead. They were aware that very few of the remains would be identified, but they felt that an effort should be made.

With this knowledge, the assessment team recommended activating a DMORT team consisting of forensic scientists and funeral workers. As the search and recovery operation continued through the late summer and early fall, the NDMS began to coordinate the personnel and equipment that would be needed when the DMORT team arrived. In mid-October, DMORT team members set up operations at the county fairgrounds. The team comprised anthropologists, radiologists, odontologists, fingerprint examiners, pathologists, and funeral service workers, numbering nearly fifty people at the peak of operations.

Identification Efforts

In typical mass fatality incidents, such as airplane and train crashes, the antemortem records needed to identify the deceased are available and relatively current. Although finding these records can prove problematic in some circumstances, the fact that the victim was alive until the time of the disaster allows disaster responders to locate the necessary information. This information includes dental charts and radiographs, medical records, fingerprints, sources for reference DNA, photographs, and other unique biological information. The ability to make a positive identification is based on the uniqueness of the victim's biology, the accuracy of the antemortem records, and the condition of the remains.

There are two levels of forensic identification. A presumptive identification is one that suggests who the person may be. In disaster situations, personal effects are often used to make this temporary assignment of identification. Because items such as wallets, clothing, jewelry, and legal documents are portable and easily disassociated from a body during a disaster, they can be used only for a presumptive identification. Presumptive identifications have no legal standing.

Positive identification, on the other hand, is accepted by the courts. Positive identifications require unique, or individualizing, personal biological traits. To positively identify a victim, unique biological information from the remains is compared to unique biological information extracted from the antemortem record. If either side of this identification equation is unavailable, identifications are extremely unlikely. The distinctive nature of dental fillings, old injuries, cancellous bone patterns in radiographs, surgical implants, fingerprints, and DNA make them ideal tools for positive identification.

The primary complicating factor in the Hardin disaster was that the "victims" were already dead, some for over one hundred years. The usual antemortem medical and dental records no longer existed. The forensic teams were able to distinguish hundreds of unique biological attributes in the remains, but without comparative antemortem data, this information was useless.

At Hardin, the family assistance center provided the living relatives of the deceased a place to obtain information about the progress of the operation. To help the forensic team, the relatives also brought information to the center in the form of photographs and recollections of the deceased. Family members were interviewed and asked to recall unique biological, medical, and burial features of the deceased. Recollections are a problematic source of information since memories can fade and family members often can't agree about certain details. Nonetheless, families documented unique identifiers such as healed fractures, diseases, unusual burial treatments, burial clothing, and cause of death. This information was entered into a computer database and served as the antemortem record for making identifications at Hardin.

Due to the concerns about inconsistent or unreliable antemortem information, the anthropologists at Hardin made identifications only when multiple unique biological features existed for an individual. In addition, personal effects found in sealed coffins were used to make positive identifications, an unusual practice in a forensic situation. The nontransferable nature of the personal effects interred with a body, the prevalence of sealed coffins, and the improbability that the dead would exchange jewelry allowed for personal items to be used when making a positive identification.

With this combination of biological and personal effects information, the DMORT team began the task of analyzing the hundreds of bodies and thousands of bones recovered earlier that summer.

Anthropological Work

The anthropology team consisted of four anthropologists with the occasional assistance of several graduate students. The work of the team varied depending on the condition of the remains: mummified, decomposed, or incomplete remains; complete skeletonized remains found inside a casket; and individual skeletal elements recovered from fields. Many caskets contained floodwater, which was drained before the remains were removed.

Preservation of the remains was remarkably inconsistent. The degree of preservation appeared to have no relationship to the length of interment. Well-preserved embalmed remains were seen in many cases that had been interred for over eighty years (Figure 19.2). In other cases, completely skeletonized individuals were found inside caskets that had been buried only twenty

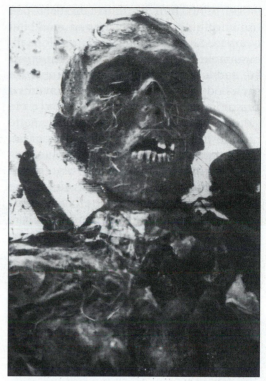

FIGURE 19.2   AN EMBALMED BODY

This photograph shows an embalmed body interred in the 1950s. Note the remarkable preservation of soft tissue and the funeral suit.

years earlier. Many bodies were mummified, the result of embalming. Some caskets were opened only to reveal a pile of jumbled bones. The varied preservation was surprising and provided an immediate lesson in the difficulty of estimating the time since death of human remains.

As each recovered coffin was opened, the condition of the remains determined whether a pathological or anthropological assessment was needed. The more well-preserved bodies warranted examination by a forensic pathologist. Remains that were less well preserved proceeded to the anthropology section for analysis. Thus, anthropologists analyzed remains that still had some soft tissue, such as mummified and decomposed remains, as well as fully skeletonized remains.

Thirty-two individuals still had some soft tissue (e.g., completely mummified, decomposed, or incompletely mummified remains). In these cases, the anthropologists created a biological and burial profile for each body. The biological profile included age at death, sex, stature, ancestry, antemortem trauma, taphonomic (postmortem) changes, and unique biological features, while the burial profile included data concerning artifacts, clothing, and burial position. In some cases, these analyses required dissecting soft tissue. To estimate age, for example, the pubic symphysis and sternal end of the right fourth rib were exposed by dissecting skin, muscle, and connective tissue in these areas of the body. Sex could be determined reliably in these cases by the external genitalia. Cemetery records indicated that all individuals in the cemetery were of European ancestry. Full body radiographs allowed for analysis of pathological features. Personal effects were catalogued, and any other unique burial features were noted. These included one body placed in the coffin facedown at the time of internment and newspapers found open to the obituary pages. In effect, the team analyzed both the body and the context of the burial, knowing that some of the more important clues for identification were going to be nonbiological.

Thirty-five caskets contained complete skeletons, allowing for a more thorough analysis, akin to a typical forensic anthropological case. The anthropologists collected similar biological information as that collected for the mummified and decomposed remains, but the examinations were more complete. Skeletonization allowed measurements of the crania and long bones and gross examination of the entire skeleton for pathology. Of the sixty-seven complete sets of remains, thirty-eight were males, twenty-seven were females, and two were infants.

In addition to the complete remains, the search teams also recovered thousands of isolated bones. For these individual skeletal elements, the anthropologists applied an approach similar to that used in an ossuary examination. The bones were first organized by element (e.g., cranium, humerus, femur, vertebrae), and then sided, if applicable. The remains were grouped according to age (infant, child, young adult, and old adult). Sex was assessed for each bone, when possible, in each element category. Each element was then examined for any features to help determine other biological and pathological information (Figure 19.3). In addition, an estimate of the minimum number of individuals represented by the thousands of skeletal elements was calculated. Not surprisingly,

FIGURE 19.3   ANTHROPOLOGISTS DAVID HUNT AND LAURIE CARROLL EXAMINE PELVES

skulls—the part of a human skeleton most easily recognizable to untrained people—were the most common element recovered. Over 3,400 isolated bones were analyzed, including 129 complete crania and 67 partial crania representing 99 males and 97 females. At least 145 individuals were represented by the noncranial skeletal elements.

In total, the anthropology team analyzed 408 "individuals" of varying completeness and preservation. Positive identifications were made on 119 remains: 93 from vaults or caskets that had a name on the vault or casket lid, 23 from personal effects, and 3 using anthropological methods. In one of the anthropological cases, a woman was identified because of a pelvic abnormality. The antemortem record also indicated that her infant was buried with her, a fact that was also confirmed by the anthropological analysis. Thus, her identification led to the identification of her infant. The third identification was based on the presence of a glass eye discovered during the analysis. The small number of positive identifications using anthropological methods was not surprising given the poor nature of the antemortem data.

The Final Arrangements

The identification process was completed by the end of October. The forensic teams completed their reports and departed for home, but the final disposition of the remains still needed to be settled. The townspeople approached Snow with their concern about the disposition of the still unidentified remains. During a town meeting, the residents reached a consensus that each skull should be considered an individual, and as such, each should be afforded a full casket burial. Snow agreed and approached the federal government with the request. The government agreed to cover the cost of

FIGURE 19.4   CASKETS AND VAULTS

Shown here are caskets and vaults containing identified and unidentified remains being arranged prior to reburial.

these burials. For the postcranial elements, the townspeople accepted Snow's suggestion that the remains be interred in separate coffins—one for male remains, one for female remains, and one for infant and child remains.

The people of Hardin were eager to have their cemetery returned to normal, but a large portion of the cemetery was gone. After the cornfield adjacent to the cemetery was purchased, a 24,000-square-foot area of the field was bulldozed. The vaults were arranged in rows, each with a unique number that would help to identify the vault and link it to the postmortem records for that burial (Figure 19.4). Identified individuals were placed in one section, unidentified remains in another. The area was covered with soil and a monument erected to the "victims" of the flood. The total cost of the Hardin cemetery project was estimated at $400,000, a small portion of the billions of dollars spent by the government for the entire flood relief effort that year.

Forensic Anthropology and the Aftermath of the Hardin Cemetery Flood

Managing the forensic specialties involved in mass disaster victim identification has undergone a dramatic change in the past decade. With the disciplines of forensic anthropology, odontology, and pathology sharing resources, information, and knowledge before, during, and after disasters, a new approach to managing mass fatality victim identification has emerged. Forensic anthropologists are a critical part of this new approach. Because of their training, forensic anthropologists are able to focus on human identification in its broadest sense. Human identification in mass disasters goes beyond skeletal identification. Among other skills, it involves a practical understanding of unique human anatomical structures (e.g., ear shape) that may be useful in identification, the ability to coordinate antemortem and postmortem biological data, and interpreting cultural aspects of body adornments and modifications (e.g., tattoos and body piercings). In addition, the anthropologist in a mass disaster setting must be able to assist with and oversee the recovery of fragmented and scattered remains, often under difficult conditions. To be truly effective, the forensic anthropologist working in mass disasters must think beyond the usual single skeletal case. The Hardin cemetery flood set the stage for anthropological involvement in these new areas of disaster response and victim identification.

Although forensic anthropologists have been part of disaster response teams for decades, their role in DMORT has allowed them to assist in developing disaster plans, guiding response policy, and conducting research into the effectiveness of disaster work. As of 2001, two of the ten national DMORT team commanders were forensic anthropologists. Additionally, forensic anthropologists have responded to every DMORT activation since Hardin (Table 19.1).

TABLE 19.1   U.S. MASS FATALITY INCIDENTS SINCE 1993 REQUIRING DMORT ANTHROPOLOGICAL INPUT

YEAR	EVENT	LOCATION	DEAD
1993	Cemetery flood	Hardin, MO	769
1994	Cemetery flood	Albany, GA	405
1995	Federal Building bombing	Oklahoma City, OK	168
1996	United Express 5925 crash	Quincy, IL	14
1997	Comair 3272 crash	Monroe, MI	29
1997	Korean Air 801 crash	Guam	228
1998	Amtrak crash	Bourbonnais, IL	11
1999	Tornadoes	Oklahoma City, OK	47
1999	Cemetery flood	Princeville, NC	230
1999	Egyptair 990 crash	Quonset, RI	219
2000	Alaska Air 261 crash	Ventura County, CA	88
2000	Executive Air crash	Wilkes-Barre, PA	19
2001	World Trade Center	New York, NY	~2,800
2001	United 93 crash	Shanksville, PA	44
2002	Crematorium event	Noble, GA	339

With this new expanded role in mass disasters, anthropologists have come to better understand the emotional toll that working with the dead on such a massive scale can have on responders. DMORT includes debriefing and counseling support for staff as a standard part of its operational plan.

In the end, forensic anthropologists provide a unique public service to the living by working with the dead. Although they are trained as scientists, they are not unaware of the deeply personal nature of their work. The needs of the next of kin and of society to identify those killed in disasters provides a focus to the work of the anthropologist; it gives it deeper meaning that is often missing in other scientific disciplines.

Oddly enough, Hardin was not the last cemetery flood to impact the living. The year after Hardin, a similar event befell the town of Albany, Georgia. Then, in 1999, Princeville, North Carolina, saw many of its ancestors wash into town on a wave of floodwaters. With a newfound expertise, DMORT responded to both of these disasters.

In December of 1998, a family member of a Hardin cemetery "fatality" contacted Dean Snow. They had located new antemortem information that might help to identify their loved one. Snow compared the information compiled by the anthropology team with the new records and determined that the remains could be identified. The remains were exhumed and reinterred in the identified section of the cemetery—a final reflection of the continued care and professionalism of the disaster responders.

Further Reading

Charney, Michael, and Charles G. Wilber. 1980. The Big Thompson flood. *American Journal of Forensic Medical Pathology* 1:139–144.

Gilliland, M. G. F., Edward T. McDonough, R. M. Fossum, Graeme P. Dowling, Patrick E. Bessant-Matthews, and Charles S. Petty. 1986. Disaster planning for air crashes: A retrospective analysis of Delta Airlines Flight 191. *American Journal of Forensic Medicine and Pathology* 7:308–316.

Hinkes, Madeleine J. 1989. The role of forensic anthropology in mass disaster resolution. *Aviation, Space, and Environmental Medicine* 60 (part 2):A60–A63.

Holland, Thomas D., Bruce E. Anderson, and Robert W. Mann. 1997. Human variables in the postmortem alteration of human bone: Examples from U.S. war casualties. Pp. 263–274 in *Forensic Taphonomy: The Postmortem Fate of Human Remains*, ed. William D. Haglund and Marcella H. Sorg. Boca Raton, FL: CRC Press.

Holland, Thomas D., and Robert W. Mann. 1996. Forensic aviation archaeology: Finding and recovering American MIA remains. *Cultural Resource Management* 19(10):29–31.

Kahana, Tzipi, Maya Fruend, and Jehuda Hiss. 1997. Suicidal terrorist bombings in Israel—identification of human remains. *Journal of Forensic Sciences* 42:260–264.

Randall, Brad. 1991. Body retrieval and morgue operations at the crash of United Flight 232. *Journal of Forensic Sciences* 36:403–409.

Saul, Frank P., and Julie M. Saul. 1999. The evolving role of the forensic anthropologist: As seen in the identification of the victims of the Comair 7232 (Michigan) and KAL 801 (Guam) aircrashes. *Proceedings of the American Academy of Forensic Sciences* 5:222.

Sledzik, Paul S., and David R. Hunt. 1997. Disaster and relief efforts at the Hardin cemetery. Pp. 185–198 in *In Remembrance: Archaeology and Death*, ed. David A. Poirier and Nicholas B. Bellantoni. Westport, CT: Bergin and Garvey.

Stewart, T. Dale, ed. 1970. *Personal Identification in Mass Disasters*. Washington, D.C.: Smithsonian Institution.

Thompson, Robert L., William W. Manders, and William R. Cowan. 1987. Postmortem findings of the victims of the Jonestown tragedy. *Journal of Forensic Sciences* 32:433–443.

Wagner, Glenn N., and Richard C. Froede. 1993. Medicolegal investigation of mass disasters. Pp. 567–584 in *Spitz and Fisher's Medicolegal Investigation of Death*, ed. Werner U. Spitz. Springfield, IL: Charles C. Thomas.

CHAPTER

20

PLANES, TRAINS, AND FIREWORKS

THE EVOLVING ROLE OF THE FORENSIC
ANTHROPOLOGIST IN MASS FATALITY INCIDENTS

Frank P. Saul and Julie Mather Saul

Public concern and expectations following recent mass fatality incidents (MFIs), whether due to accidents, natural disasters, or terrorist activity, have resulted in the increased application of forensically based multidisciplinary approaches to managing victim identification and other aspects of the incident, including evidence recovery.

This is perhaps best seen in the composition and organization of the ten regional U.S. Public Health Service Disaster Mortuary Operational Response Teams (DMORTs) that were created in 1992 to provide assistance, as needed, to local coroners/medical examiners (who, of course, remain in charge of the victims' remains). The working definition of a mass fatality incident is one more death than the local coroner/medical examiner can handle with local resources. Therefore, the actual number of deaths that will require federal support will vary from one jurisdiction to another. Teams are composed of forensic anthropologists, odontologists and

pathologists, fingerprint and computer specialists, law enforcement, and other support personnel, in addition to the morticians who first voiced concern about the proper care of victims and who remain the "backbone" of DMORT. All team members are volunteers who become temporary federal employees when activated during MFIs.

Activation and Deployment

Once local authorities make the determination that they need help, the request is forwarded to the U.S. Public Health Service, Office of Emergency Preparedness in Maryland, and the selection and notification of DMORT personnel begins. The types and numbers of personnel deployed to each MFI will vary with the availability of local resources and the number of victims. But the basic approach is likely to be similar.

At the scene of the incident, local law enforcement and emergency personnel will have begun to locate and remove survivors. At the same time, they will have controlled any access to the scene. The local coroner/medical examiner will have taken charge

---

Note: The opinions expressed in this chapter are those of the authors and are not necessarily endorsed by our sponsoring agencies.

of the dead, who are usually left in place so that they can be forensically documented before removal. Upon arrival, DMORT personnel (anthropologists, sometimes odontologists) will assist in the recognition, documentation, and recovery of each unit ("units" because bodies are often fragmented) of victim remains and associated evidence at the scene. Recently, the Federal Bureau of Investigation's Evidence Response Teams (ERT) have been assigned the primary responsibility for recovery at NTSB incidents and may or may not use DMORT personnel.

Morticians and other DMORT personnel will assist local authorities in the selection of a site for and establishment of a family assistance center (FAC), at which victims' families are interviewed to acquire antemortem information about the victims. The center also provides a place for the victims' families to gather to receive progress reports. The interviews yield information concerning victims' physicians and dentists (sources of antemortem radiographs), clothing, jewelry, and other identifiers. Morticians, who are often funeral directors, are especially valuable as interviewers because they are accustomed to interacting with bereaved families. The family assistance center is often located in a hotel where access can be controlled.

DMORT personnel will also assist local authorities in choosing and establishing a site for an incident morgue for the processing and identification of recovered remains. The incident morgue should be appropriately located for convenient and protected transfer of remains and should provide access to electricity, running water, and other needed utilities. It should be located within a building that will not become stigmatized in the future by such usage. Airplane hangers and warehouses are appropriate, but school buildings and churches are not. The incident morgue will be staffed with pathologists, anthropologists, odontologists, and fingerprint experts who gather

identifying characteristics from the remains while photographers and radiology personnel document the remains and morticians curate and preserve the remains.

Team members with computer and administrative skills will set up and staff an information resource center (IRC) to receive, process, and manage antemortem and postmortem victim data. Forensic specialists at the morgue obtain the postmortem data. A recently developed DMORT computer program (WIN ID/VIP) is used for data processing. The IRC may be located within or adjacent to the incident morgue.

The work at each of the above locations is facilitated with the aid of a federally sponsored DMORT Portable Morgue Unit (DPMU) containing equipment ranging from section partitions to gurneys and computers. The DPMU is palletized and ready for immediate deployment by air or overland to incident locations, along with personnel to set up and take down the DPMU. One DPMU is based in Maryland and another is located in California.

Incident Morgue Activities

After the remains are transported to the morgue, an escort person (often a local funeral director) is assigned to each numbered unit of remains to ensure continuity of the evidence chain, and the documentation of victim remains and personal effects continues as the victims move through the various morgue stations. The rescue of the living is, of course, a "round the clock" operation but morgue operation is usually limited to twelve hours per day every day until completion of the mission.

Photography and Personal Effects

This station is often staffed by law enforcement-related personnel, assisted by anthropologists who can recognize the type of remains present in the body bags even when fragmentary. Personal effects are photographed, removed, documented, and stored in a secure location.

Radiology

Immediate radiographic documentation is needed to locate plane parts, possible bomb parts, projectiles, and other foreign objects that may be a hazard to personnel and/or may be needed for analysis by the National Transportation Safety Board if it is a transportation accident. In addition, the radiographs record loose teeth, unusual or otherwise distinctive characteristics of the remains, medical/surgical devices, etc, that may aid in identification. Customary clinical views of the victims' remains are also needed—the type of views that might be taken during a person's lifetime (i.e., A-P and lateral radiographs of the chest, head/neck, ankle, wrist) in order to be available for comparison with any antemortem radiographs that may be obtained

(Figure 20.1). The identification process itself begins as each unit of remains passes through the pathology, anthropology, odontology, and fingerprint stations.

Pathology

As in their normal practice, pathologists attempt to determine cause and manner of death. The latter may seem simple in transportation and natural disaster incidents (i.e., accidental) but a homicide that may have caused a crash (Pacific Southwest Airlines, central California coast in 1987, see www.planecrashinfo.com) and a homicide that is unrelated to a flood (Del Rio, Texas, 1998, personal communication, H. Gill-King, 2001) have been found by careful examination of the remains. Also, improvements in safety have come about as a consequence of determining the actual cause of death. For instance, that death in some crashes was due to smoke inhalation rather than blunt force associated with impact has resulted in the use of fire resistant materials for seating and

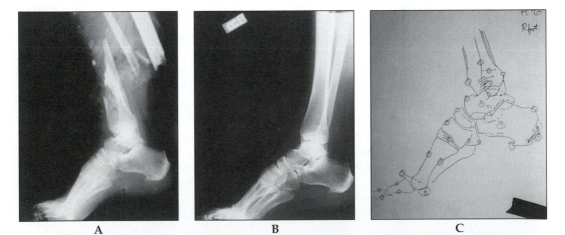

A   B   C

FIGURE 20.1   RADIOGRAPHS

(A) shows a postmortem radiograph of the badly damaged right leg and foot of an unknown victim (H-6). (B) shows an antemortem radiograph of the right leg and foot of a known individual. (C) shows a transparent plastic overlay tracing of postmortem radiograph (shown in A) used to positively identify the victim in (A) as the individual in (B). The circles on the overlay indicate matching features shown on both radiographs.

interiors. Notation of injury patterns can lead to other design changes that can reduce injuries and save lives. In addition, as presence of specific structures and condition of the remains allows, pathologists note sex (based on external and/or internal soft tissue), and even parity in females (based on the uterus), a rough estimate of age as suggested by the condition of the cardiovascular system, and potentially identifying characteristics such as the presence of moles, scars (and their significance), tattoos, and medical devices.

Anthropology

A basic contribution of the forensic anthropologist in the standard forensic setting (coroner/medical examiner office) is to help create a biological (or "biographic") profile by providing a skeletal assessment of sex, age, ancestry, stature, and so on for the otherwise "unidentifiable" individual so that appropriate antemortem dental and medical radiographs can be obtained from a variably sized pool of missing persons for comparison. These profiles may also include fleshed characteristics when available. It should be noted that "unidentifiable" in pathology usually refers to skeletonized, burned, decomposed, fragmented, or otherwise damaged remains. However, even relatively fresh and intact bodies require more accurate age estimates than can be provided by external visual inspection.

In a mass fatality incident, the process is similar to typical forensic cases but the timing is different. Antemortem radiographs can be sought for all members of the limited pool of potential victims (i.e., everyone believed to be aboard the plane). In the meantime, the anthropologists create a biological profile for each set of remains, whether an intact body or a body fragment. When (and if) antemortem radiographs arrive, these biological profiles will aid in locating potentially matching postmortem radiographs for comparisons that will hopefully result in positive identifications.

Commingling and Reassociation Prior to creating a biological profile, however, commingled remains must be separated. The forces inherent in explosions and impacts not only fragment the human body, but may also transport those fragments, throwing them together in deceptive relationships so that they may appear to be one individual while in actuality the parts represent several. Therefore, multiple units that are not connected through direct articulation or by a "soft tissue bridge" need to be disassociated and treated as separate units. Ideally, the "separateness" of these units is recognized on the scene during recovery and such units are bagged separately. Realistically, commingling within body bags often occurs, due in large part to the difficulties inherent in recovery at a disaster site. Anthropologists in the morgue then separate the commingled remains, and new (but related) numbers are given to each new unit.

The biological profile of a unit is primarily based on the anthropologist's assessment of the skeletal remains within the unit. Aside from visualization using radiography, anthropologists are likely to use appropriate dissection and cleaning of pubic symphyses, medial clavicles, rib ends, etc., to obtain the biological information stored in the bone.

In addition to profile characteristics, anthropologists record side and other descriptive information that may later be used to reassociate the unit with an incomplete set of remains that has a similar biological profile lacking that part.

Reassociation of units of fragmented remains may be based on the correct identification of each unit that is then linked to other possible units. DNA is of course useful for this purpose but is both expensive and relatively slow, and the results are not available in the field, so fingerprints and dental and medical radiographs are most commonly used for this purpose. In addition, a reassociation may be considered positive if fracture or joint articular surfaces match.

Strong presumptive reassociations may be based on surface morphology and radiographic comparisons (proportions, internal structure, unusual toenail shapes, etc.) as well as the process of elimination (sometimes based on well-defined age characteristics such as immaturity).

Antemortem and postmortem clinical view medical radiographs are compared in much the same way as dentists who use dental radiographs in order to obtain positive identifications. The antemortem possibilities are suggested by a combination of biological profiles and other individual characteristics produced by the VIP computer program. Anthropologists accustomed to using radiography to study growth and other variation usually do these comparisons. Anthropologists may also use antemortem photographs of distinctive body features (i.e., ears) in the same fashion.

Odontology

Dentists locate, chart, and radiographically record the teeth, restorations, and other dental characteristics present in the remains, including the dental ages of children. This information is then entered into the dental computer program WIN ID along with antemortem dental information. They will then compare the postmortem radiographs with the antemortem dental radiographs suggested for comparison by the computer program.

Fingerprinting

When possible, fingerprints and other dermatoglyphs are obtained by specialists from the FBI Disaster Squad. When reference prints are not on file, FBI agents or local law enforcement may obtain latent prints from personal belongings in a victim's home.

DNA

Meanwhile, a DMORT DNA team has been collecting DNA samples from appropriate tissues just in case positive identification cannot be obtained by the previously listed conventional means. When necessary, samples will be sent to the Armed Forces DNA Identification Laboratory (AFDIL) where DNA profile determinations and comparisons will be made. This is, unfortunately, a somewhat expensive and time-consuming process.

Returning the Remains

After passing through the above stations, the remains are usually stored in refrigerated trucks to await further developments. Once the forensic team has recommended a positive identification, the local coroner/medical examiner makes the final determination. The remains may then be embalmed by DMORT morticians prior to returning them to the next of kin or they may be embalmed by local funeral directors selected by the next of kin.

What Is a Positive Identification?

A positive identification may begin with a presumptive identification based on "portable" identifiers such as wallet or purse contents (including, but not limited to, drivers licenses and credit cards), clothing, and jewelry. Such items, as distinctive as they might be, are transferable and therefore cannot be used for a positive identification. There have been several aircraft accidents in which remains were identified on the basis of a wallet fused to the individual's thigh by fire. Unfortunately, in each of these cases, the wallet actually belonged to the adjacent passenger. However, a presumptive identification can be an important first step in acquiring the antemortem materials that are required for a positive identification. In the absence of a presumptive identification, a biological profile is used to narrow the field of "possibles."

Positive identifications require matching antemortem materials (DNA, fingerprints, radiographs, and occasionally photographs of distinctive physical characteristics such as ears or tattoos) of missing individuals with equivalent materials obtained from victim remains. The categories of positive identification (based on type of antemortem material available) are as follows:

1. Fingerprints (the traditional "gold" standard)
2. Radiographic
   a. Dental (a later "gold" standard)
   b. Medical radiographs (not as well known as dental but equally useful)
3. DNA (the new "platinum" standard)
4. Photographic (less used but goes back to the 1800s and Bertillon's studies of variation in physical characteristics, such as ears; may also be used with tattoos, scars, moles, etc.; photo must show specific characteristics clearly and *in situ*, showing surrounding characteristics, for direct comparison with remains)
5. Other (may include sufficiently distinctive and traceable—serial numbers, etc.—medical devices that have been permanently integrated with the individual's body)

Categories 1–3 are universally accepted as a basis for a positive identification. Categories 4 and 5 may be less familiar in some jurisdictions.

The number of match points required for positive identification will vary with the category, but basically the antemortem and postmortem materials must match in sufficient detail to indicate that they are derived from the same individual. There must be no differences that cannot be explained. Identification by exclusion, for instance, the only infant or the only edentulous individual or the only male or the only female on the passenger list, may also be accepted as the basis for a positive identification, but should perhaps be thought of as a very strong presumptive identification.

Visual identification, although accepted in many jurisdictions, should not be considered positive identification inasmuch as viewers may be lead astray by decomposition and/or

the circumstances, and personal gain may also influence the "identification." There are also circumstances (i.e., war crimes) in which appropriate antemortem materials are lacking and clothing and jewelry (plus a matching biological profile) may provide the only basis for victim identification, but such identifications should not be referred to as positive identifications. They are presumptive identifications.

Some Recent Mass Fatality Incidents

Two Airplane Crashes

Prior to 1997, we had never dealt with an airplane crash involving more than four victims (Burlington Air Freight crash, Toledo, Ohio, 1992). In January of 1997 we spent 5½ days as members of a DMORT team helping to sort and identify the remains of 29 passengers aboard Comair 7232, an Embraer commuter turboprop that plunged into the frozen ground near Monroe, Michigan, during a flight from Cincinnati to Detroit. In August of 1997, we were again called by DMORT to spend 24 days helping to sort and identify the remains of 226 passengers aboard Korean Airlines 801, a 747 jumbo jet that made a C.F.I.T., or "controlled flight into terrain" on its approach to Guam airport. Apart from the numbers of victims, the scene conditions were quite different. We will focus on some of the continuities and discontinuities involved in dealing with two crashes of such different magnitude, especially in regard to the condition of the remains.

Monroe, Michigan   The early evening Comair scene near Monroe, Michigan, was very cold (–48 degrees Fahrenheit wind chill) with snow and ice. As a consequence of in-flight icing conditions, the plane had impacted at a steep angle into the flat frozen ground with resultant fragmentation of the plane and its passengers, followed by integration of body fragments with plane parts

**FIGURE 20.2   THE COMAIR 3272 COMMUTER
AIRPLANE CRASH SCENE, MONROE, MICHIGAN**

The terrain was flat and the wreckage was confined to a small area.
The frozen ground required the use of jackhammers and other power
equipment to excavate engines and other plane parts.

(Figure 20.2). The cold made recovery difficult but at the same time limited decomposition and insect activity.

The human remains were severely fragmented and required thawing before examination. Refrigerated trucks actually
assisted in this process because they were
set at a temperature above freezing. The
morgue was a small, unheated, three-
walled hangar, requiring portable heaters
and the use of tarps to fill in gaps in walls.
Unfortunately, the hospital x-ray facilities
were located several miles away, thus slow-
ing down and limiting our radiologic
recording process.

Antemortem information from relatives
was excellent and dental and medical radiographs arrived in a timely fashion. Prior to
our arrival it had been decided that since
only twenty-nine victims were involved,
only the dental data, antemortem and postmortem, should be computerized. Therefore, other antemortem and postmortem
information were compared manually. Most
victims were identified by dental radiographs, a few by fingerprints, and two by
medical radiographs.

The Island of Guam in the Pacific   The Korean Airlines crash scene was very hot (100°)
and humid. It was the monsoon season and
we were soon to be hit by the outer portions
of two super typhoons. The Boeing 747 made
a gradual descent (a C.F.I.T.) a few miles short
of the runway during the dark and stormy
early morning hours. The terrain was tropical
mountain scrub with saw grass and was very
difficult to traverse. A very hot fire consumed
a portion of the fuselage (Figure 20.3).

Thanks to the relatively gentle descent of
the plane, 26 of the 254 passengers and crew
survived. The remains of the 228 victims included intact and fairly intact bodies, decomposed and decomposing bodies (and
body parts), burned and partially burned
bodies (and parts of bodies), and burned
bones that ranged from charred to black, gray
or white (calcined). Some units of remains
showed a combination of these conditions.

The morgue was a huge, nonaircondi-
tioned U.S. Navy warehouse "cooled" by
floor fans. We had outstanding portable x-
ray facilities and personnel supplied by the
U.S. Navy and Army. Excellent computer
support was also provided and utilized.

FIGURE 20.3   THE KOREAN AIRLINES 801 JUMBO
JET CRASH SCENE ON THE ISLAND OF GUAM IN THE PACIFIC

The terrain was very hilly and rugged. Some wreckage fell into adjacent valleys, but the main cabin burned in place.

The fact that the passengers were mostly foreign nationals (South Koreans) on an island thousands of miles from their homes (and ours) did of course create problems, especially in regard to interactions with families and obtaining the antemortem dental and medical radiographs needed for positive identification. These problems were further compounded by the terribly sad fact that entire families were lost and their relatives did not always know the name of the victim's physician or dentist. In addition, there were cultural differences ranging from surname similarities on through approaches to grieving that complicated matters further. On the positive side, South Koreans eighteen years of age or older are required to have their fingerprints on file and the FBI Disaster Squad obtained sixty positive identifications in a relatively short time.

At least twenty-seven individuals were identified by dental means, five by using medical radiographs, and two by using antemortem photographs that included distinctive physical characteristics. An additional seventy-two victims were identified by DNA. Fortunately, all data were computerized, making initial sorting for comparisons easier.

A Train Crash

The southbound Amtrak train "The City of New Orleans," which had left Chicago shortly after 8 P.M. CST on Monday, March 15, 1999, collided with a semi-trailer truck hauling steel at a Bourbonnais, Illinois, crossing grade at about 11:45 P.M (see Figure 20.4 on page 274).

The Illinois Funeral Directors Emergency Response Committee was notified at about 1 A.M. on Tuesday and DMORT was activated as of 8:30 A.M. Twenty DMORT members and eight Mission Support Unit administrative personnel from the National Disaster Medical System in Maryland responded.

One anthropologist and one dentist were sent to the crash scene to help emergency personnel recover remains from the burned and mangled sleeper car and other portions of the train until early Thursday. Joining emergency personnel, the anthropologist searched in, under, and around the mangled sleeper car, locating fragments that might otherwise have been unrecognized and therefore overlooked.

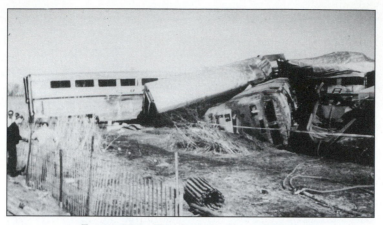

**FIGURE 20.4   THE AMTRAK TRAIN–TRUCK
CRASH SCENE IN BOURBONNAIS, ILLINOIS**

The sleeper car was draped over the burning engine, creating a blast
furnace-like draft.

Many of these fragments could be linked to remains already recovered, and some were the key to a positive identification.

The temporary morgue site, an unused lumber warehouse and yard, was cleaned and readied for the arrival of the new DPMU, which was deployed from Maryland by truck. It arrived during the early morning hours of Wednesday and the DPMU Team, with the assistance of others, had it fully operational by 1 P.M.

Morgue stations for Photography and Documentation (Illinois State Police), Fingerprinting (FBI Disaster Squad), Pathology (Cook County [Chicago] Medical Examiners), Anthropology, and Dental began processing the remains. The victim list was narrowed from thirteen (or more) to eleven definitely missing individuals, and the family assistance center (staffed with both local and DMORT personnel) started requesting the antemortem dental and medical radiographs needed for a positive identification. A new computer program (WIN ID/VIP), based in the information resource center, assisted in initial comparisons.

The antemortem dental and medical radiographs started arriving on Thursday and by the end of the day we had one positive medical (radiographic) and seven positive dental identifications, the former by Anthropology. Three others were uncertain because records for one were slow in arriving, another because the dentist was in jail (it was later learned that he was in a federal penitentiary for Medicare fraud) and the third because the dental records were in Japan. DMORT mortuary officers prepared bodies of those identified and the process of releasing them to local funeral homes began.

On Friday, Anthropology identified the person whose dentist was incarcerated by comparing an antemortem medical radiograph of the frontal sinuses to radiographs taken by Dental. The Japanese victim's dental radiographs arrived via e-mail (a first for us) resulting in a positive identification. Another set of dental films also arrived, so that all eleven victims were positively identified by noon.

After the remaining victims were processed for transfer to local funeral homes, the DPMU was taken down and repacked for shipment back to Maryland. All DMORT operations were completed by noon on Saturday.

A Fireworks Factory Explosion

Sometimes a multiple fatality incident can be handled without calling in DMORT if local personnel have appropriate experience, expertise, and adequate facilities. This was the case when a fireworks factory building exploded in Osseo, Michigan (near Hillsdale), on 11 December 1998. The building was destroyed, leaving only the foundation. Seven workers were in the building when the explosion occurred. Six "bodies" were said to have been recovered after the explosion, with a seventh individual unaccounted for. Remains recovered at the scene were brought to our facility at the Lucas County Coroner's Office in Toledo, Ohio, in twelve body bags.

The bag contents ranged from fairly intact bodies lacking some portions to torsos lacking major portions to bags containing only body parts. Dentitions provided the basis for positive identification of four victims by a local odontologist who compared antemortem and postmortem dental radiographs.

The anthropologists reassociated a number of body parts with specific individuals by matching fractures and joint surfaces. We were then able to identify the remaining three victims by comparing antemortem medical radiographs with equivalent postmortem radiographs of body parts. These activities enabled us to locate and reassociate parts from eleven separate body bags to "create" the previously unaccounted for seventh victim, whose family would now be able to bury their loved one.

Case Studies

We have selected the following actual cases to illustrate how forensic anthropology can be used to identify victims of multiple fatality incidents. These cases also demonstrate the kinds of individual variation involved as well as the importance of teamwork. Various descriptors have been changed or withheld in order to preserve the anonymity of the victims, but other circumstances are accurate.

Case One: The Two Mandibles

There was one incident in which extreme fragmentation had occurred and the only infant and the only individual with dentures on the passenger roster were still not accounted for. We learned that several bags of fragments, having been judged "unidentifiable" by the Pathology section, had not been sent to Anthropology for examination. Within those bags of fragmentary bone and flesh we found a portion of an infant's mandible and a portion of an edentulous, or toothless, mandible that had been overlooked.

This did not surprise us because we have frequently used a neonate (newborn) mandible as part of the tests that we administer to physicians, dentists, and others who attend the Forensic Anthropology courses that we help teach. It is rarely recognized as a mandible and when so recognized it is usually considered to be from a monkey. Most often it is identified as a hyoid bone. Edentulous mandibles may also confuse the nonspecialist inasmuch as, once the teeth are lost or extracted, the bone of the mandible undergoes considerable atrophy (bone loss) and changes form. For instance, the skeleton of an ancient Maya ruler from Belize, Central America, was thought to be lacking a mandible until we found it (edentulous and atrophied) in a packet labeled "clavicle."

Returning to our victims—we could not make the preferred positive identifications because we lacked the antemortem radiographs that the identification team would ordinarily use. However, as only one infant and one edentulous adult were among the victims, the identifications were considered to have been made by exclusion.

Case Two: The Survivor

We arrived at a crash scene and were asked to examine some remains that had been recovered to determine if they were human. The remains were human, and consisted of the lower end of a tibia. The foot had been separated at the ankle joint and was not present. The tibia fragment was that of a preteen child, judging by size and degree of maturation of the epiphysis. We later learned that a child of the right age had been rescued from the wreckage following a traumatic amputation of the foot. We requested that the hospital send us a radiograph of the affected limb made prior to performing a surgical amputation to prepare for fitting a prosthetic device. A few days later a shoe containing an immature foot was recovered from the wreckage. The foot articulated directly with the opposing ankle joint of the recovered tibia fragment. The fractured end of the tibia fragment fit perfectly into the fractured end of the tibia in the radiograph. We had found the child's missing foot and ankle.

We had not previously dealt with remains relating to a surviving victim, but we knew from media coverage that this survivor was a very courageous young person who, while still recovering from amputation surgery, insisted on returning to the crash site where several close relatives had died. We suspected that this youngster would ask questions about the lost foot and recommended that the family be notified and allowed to make the decision regarding its disposition. Incidentally, this valiant youngster has returned to full participation in school and sports.

Case Three: The Ear and the Mole

Although forensic anthropologists are best known for their work with the human skeleton, a well-trained physical anthropologist is likely to be knowledgeable about soft tissue variation as well.

In this case, a number of children had died in the crash and their "viewable" (fleshed, in relatively good condition) bodies were not identified until the mortuary affairs officers contacted the Anthropology section. At that point, an anthropologist created biological profiles for each child using soft tissue observations for sex and

radiographs of bony growth centers in the wrist and other joints for age range estimates. Stature and style of hair cut were also recorded.

As the identification possibilities were narrowed by the biological profiles, we sought antemortem dental or medical radiographs or fingerprint records of the appropriate missing children, and found that none were available. We did learn, however, that relatives had provided photographs of some of the children. Remembering that the configuration of the ear was a good identifier, according to the French anthropologist and forensic scientist Alphonse Bertillon (1853–1914), we checked this feature as shown in the photographs of two of the children.

The antemortem photograph of one child clearly showed the right ear in its entirety and provided so many match points (lobe and helix configuration, etc.) with one of the victims that, added to the matching biological profile, we felt justified in declaring it a positive identification. The antemortem views of the other child's ear were incomplete and we were on the verge of stating that we could not make a positive identification when one of our anthropologists realized that the re-occurring "dust fleck" shown in all the antemortem facial photographs was actually a small and distinctive mole that could be definitely matched in size, configuration, and exact location to the victim under consideration. This, plus the matching biological profile, enabled us to make a positive identification. The key to identification in both cases was the preliminary matching of biological profiles followed by the matching of sufficient points of comparison in the victim with antemortem visual records.

Case Four: The Unusual Crown

While reviewing postmortem radiographs of the victim remains, one of the DMORT odontologists noted a dental crown that he believed was associated with the type of dental work available in a certain country. Inasmuch as we had been looking for a specific victim from that country, we reviewed the morgue file for the remains in question and obtained the antemortem radiographs for the person we were searching for.

The morgue file for this severely burned partial torso contained a pathologist's assessment of sex based on burned soft tissue that was the opposite of that in the independent assessment based on skeletal pelvic morphology provided by an anthropologist. The biological profile produced by the anthropologist was consistent in sex and age with the missing person. It took quite a while and much effort to position the heat-distorted partial torso so as to obtain postmortem radiographic views that were equivalent to the antemortem radiographs. When this was finally accomplished, the antemortem radiographs matched the postmortem radiographs, producing a somewhat delayed positive identification.

Conclusions

All disasters have components that are different and the same, but our exposure to a variety of incidents within two years presented a unique opportunity to examine and contrast the roles of the forensic anthropologist and the forensic pathologist. Our main conclusion is that anthropologists have been under-utilized in the past. They have major roles to play throughout the operation, beginning with the recognition, recovery, and plotting in of remains at the scene, followed by interaction with the pathologists, odontologists, fingerprint specialists, and others as the remains are processed for identification. Although anthropologists are perhaps best known for their ability to elicit biological profiles from otherwise unidentifiable remains, they can also play an important role in determining the age of intact remains, linking disassociated remains and separating

commingled remains. Many forensic anthropologists are also experienced in making identifications through comparison of antemortem and postmortem radiographs and even antemortem photographs with distinctive body features, such as ears.

We are pleased to note that DMORT has recognized the value of anthropologists in a number of ways, including their utilization in various aspects of the recovery and identification process as well as the appointment of anthropologists as commanders of two of the ten Regional Teams. Finally, it is important to emphasize that all of our efforts are on behalf of the victims and their families.

Acknowledgments

Other DMORT anthropologists who were with us on parts of these missions included: R. Sundick and T. Simmons at Monroe, MI, and H. Gill-King, D. France, J. Williams, L. Fulginitti, F. Ciaccio, D. Dirkmaat, and N. Ross-Stallings on Guam. In addition, CILHI provided T. Holland, T. Woltanski, R. Mann, D. Rankin and H. Dockall. L. Eisenberg shared responsibilities with us at Bourbonnais, IL. We also thank C. S. Beisser, MD, who served as the forensic pathologist for the Hillsdale, MI, fireworks factory explosion.

Further Reading

Saul, Frank P., and Julie M. Saul. 1999. The evolving role of the forensic anthropologist: As seen in the identification of the victims of the Comair 7232 (Michigan) and the KAL 801 (Guam) Aircrashes. *Proceedings of the American Academy of Forensic Sciences*, 5, 222, Orlando, FL.

Saul, Frank P., and Julie M. Saul. 2000. The evolving role of the forensic anthropologist: As seen in the identification and reassociation of fragmented human remains. *Proceedings of the American Academy of Forensic Sciences*, 6, 223, Reno, NV.

Discovery Channel. 2000. On the Inside: Disaster Response Team.

SCIENCE CONTEXTUALIZED

THE IDENTIFICATION OF A U.S. MIA OF THE VIETNAM WAR FROM TWO PERSPECTIVES

Ann Webster Bunch and Colleen Carney Shine

Captain Anthony C. Shine, a U.S. Air Force fighter pilot (Figure 21.1), was listed as Missing in Action (M.I.A.) in Southeast Asia on December 2, 1972. For fourteen years his family heard nothing regarding his fate. In 1987, a refugee report associated with Lieutenant Colonel Shine* arrived, including photographic and identification information that indicated someone knew his fate.

In 1993, a joint U.S./Vietnamese team visited a crash site associated with Lt. Col. Shine. Three years later, with assistance from servicemen, civilians, and the Shine family, scientists—through a series of interviews, site surveys, investigations, excavations, and laboratory analysis of fragmentary remains—were able to conclusively determine that Lt. Col. Shine died on impact in 1972.

The invaluable, if slow and methodological, scientific investigative process that resolved Lt. Col. Shine's fate—carried out in jungles as well as laboratories—did not proceed in a vacuum. Instead, it was routinely

affected, for better and worse, by national and international politics, operational technology, resources, time, and the personal involvement of his family.

This chapter details a specific M.I.A. case from the distinct perspectives of its scientific and personal context. Dr. Bunch was an anthropologist at the Army's Central Identification Laboratory in Hawaii (CILHI); Ms. Shine is the daughter of Lt. Col. Shine and was integrally involved with the logistical aspects of the case for over a decade. The Shine case sheds light on the process of accounting for missing servicemen and civilians, and is a compelling example of the fact that scientists and investigators must remain neutral and unbiased, while never losing sight of the larger context in which they work.

Incident REFNO 1950: Two Perspectives

It was December 1972 when military representatives delivered the news to the Shine family. On December 2, Captain Anthony C. Shine, U.S.A.F., disappeared while on a reconnaissance mission over the border of

---

*Capt. Shine was posthumously promoted to Lieutenant Colonel.

FIGURE 21.1   CAPTAIN ANTHONY SHINE IN 1968

North Vietnam and Laos. After targeting a supply convoy on Route 7, Capt. Shine had radioed to his wingman that he was descending to visually reconnoiter the area. Due to heavy cloud cover, the wingman maintained only intermittent visual contact with Capt. Shine's A-7D *Corsair*. At 0950 hours the wingman notified the nearest Airborne Command and Control Center that he had lost all contact with Capt. Shine. No parachute was observed and no emergency beeper signals were received. Other aircraft searching in the area reported seeing evidence of ground fire near a possible crash site. A Search and Rescue (SAR) team arriving at approximately 1300 hours reported that the purported crash site appeared to be a brush fire and that they observed no evidence of aircraft wreckage. SAR efforts were

terminated the following day when no visual or radio contact had been made, and Capt. Shine was listed as Missing in Action (M.I.A.). At the time of the incident, Capt. Shine's case was assigned a reference number, "REFNO 1950," for official purposes.

At home in the United States, it was just days before Christmas, and only weeks before the signing of the Paris Peace Accords that would end official U.S. involvement in the long-fought Vietnam War. Capt. Shine's twenty-nine-year-old wife, Bonnie, was living in upstate New York raising their three children. Anthony, Colleen, and Shannon, were ten, eight, and three years old, respectively.

> A patriotic, military family, we were all-too-familiar with the costs of war. Dad's youngest brother Jonathan, an Army First Lieutenant fresh from West Point, had been Killed In Action in Vietnam in 1970. His brother, Alexander, was wounded on his second tour in Vietnam in 1969; and his sister Sarah had served there as a Red Cross nurse. Dad's father had served in WWII and in the Army Air Corps during Korea.
>
> We knew the risks involved—that Dad might be injured, killed or captured—just doing his job. Yet, as we took the Christmas presents out from under the tree that year, storing them in safekeeping for when Dad returned home, I don't think we could have ever fathomed the burden of uncertainty that would impact our family for years to come.
>
> Assuming the best, that Dad was alive, we each set out to do what we could. Hoping our messages might somehow reach him, we wrote Dad letters and mailed care packages of the precise size, shape and weight specified by the Vietnamese government. Visiting a giant warehouse of approved items, my brother Anthony selected an all-in-one compass-whistle-mirror gadget he hoped would help Dad escape captivity. I chose freeze-dried steak, because "Dad loves steak." By day, Mom fought against the anguish of not knowing, while juggling an ever-present barrage of logistics—calls to the government and

other POW/MIA families, letters, media inquiries and an endless array of questions from us kids. By night, she endured long hours of loneliness and fear, tormenting nightmares of worst-case scenarios, and the growth of a hope that would become our family's constant companion.

Political Barriers Prohibit Answers

The years immediately following Capt. Shine's disappearance were fraught with political tensions and constraints, both domestic and foreign. Following Operation Homecoming and the return of 570 prisoners in 1973, America was eager to put the war behind her. With the fall of Saigon in 1975, all official communication between the two nations ceased and the Vietnamese government failed to provide any information on the more than 2,500 Americans who had not returned, alive or dead, to U.S. soil. The possibility of any American investigative or search and recovery teams was indefinitely precluded by postwar politics (Mather 1994, 35).

Activists by necessity, the Shine family had immediately joined forces with the National League of POW/MIA Families, a nonprofit organization working to gain the release of U.S. prisoners, the fullest possible accounting for those listed as missing, and the repatriation of recoverable remains for those who died in service to their country. Despite countless efforts—speeches, lobbying, protesting, and trips to Southeast Asia—progress in accounting for America's missing was slow and answers were piecemeal. Successive U.S. administrations dealt with the POW/MIA issue with apparent falsity, inaction, and nonresponsiveness.

For more than a decade, the Socialist Republic of Vietnam (S.R.V.) and the Lao People's Democratic Republic (L.P.D.R.) failed to respond to requests for information on the Shine case, or that of other POW/MIAs. As time passed, frustration mounted among family members eager for an end to the uncertainty regarding the fate of their loved ones. A serious disconnect formed between the U.S. government and the families, and it became clear that achievable answers would be aided by the personal involvement of the families.

Relations between the United States and the Socialist Republic of Vietnam improved with regard to the POW/MIA issue during the Reagan administration. Through strategic and ongoing technical talks and government-to-government negotiations, some families began to receive answers. The Vietnamese government unilaterally accounted for scores of missing Americans through the turnover of stored remains and related documents. They also allowed the United States, on a limited basis, to conduct in-country investigations of last known alive and crash site locations. While the Defense Intelligence Agency maintained chief responsibility for pursuing the live prisoner issue, these in-country investigations, as well as interviews with villagers and refugees, were conducted by the newly formed unit represented by all military services, the Joint Task Force for Full Accounting (JTF-FA), in conjunction with the CILHI.

A Breakthrough on the Shine Case

Fourteen years after Lt. Col. Shine's disappearance, the Shine family finally heard some word regarding his fate. In 1987, a Laotian refugee in Thailand provided U.S. officials with identification, or "dog tag" data associated with REFNO 1950. The source enclosed a photograph of a dog tag bearing Lt. Col. Shine's identification information: name, serial number, religion, and blood type. Further interviews with this source proved fruitless in providing additional information. However, soon afterward a second source reported information related to a different dog tag. This report included a photograph of skeletal remains, allegedly associated with Lt. Col. Shine, which were said to be in the possession of a Laotian national living in Xiangkhoang Province, Laos. A cottage industry involving the sale and barter of information and remains of U.S. POW/MIAs made for difficult and tedious work as U.S. investigators pursued this and several successive reports, none of which provided any viable leads in determining Lt. Col. Shine's fate.

Since the end of the Vietnam War, a few indigenous Southeast Asians have attempted to utilize remains, identification tags, pieces of wreckage, and the like to their own personal advantage. Often these individuals are under the mistaken impression that they will either gain money or relocation to the United States if they provide evidence and/or information pertinent to an MIA case. In some instances, certain individuals repeatedly appear with "MIA remains" which turn out to be those of indigenous persons, sometimes recently deceased. Often these remains are "associated" with pieces of wreckage or an identification tag embossed with a fabricated name, social security number, etc., and long, detailed (and obviously false) stories are elaborated to support how the remains were found, recovered, and brought to the U.S. authorities (Mather 1994, 112–120).

For the Shine family, each legitimate lead brightened hopes that they might one day learn the fate of the man who was to them not just a tragic statistic of an unfinished war but someone who was missed and loved and remembered. They followed the reports closely, asking relevant questions and offering insights and information wherever possible.

By 1993, American investigation and recovery teams were regularly conducting joint investigations of last known alive locations of missing Americans with their host governments in Vietnam and Laos. In July of that year, a joint investigative team visited a remote location in Vietnam, about 15 kilometers from the Laotian border, tentatively associated with the Shine crash site. The team consisted of a U.S. Army officer serving as team leader, and enlisted members from various military branches providing linguistic, analytic, and medical support.

The team gathered evidence (e.g., aircraft wreckage fragments, pieces of material which might have been life support equipment), with as little disturbance to the area as possible, to determine whether a site existed that warranted recovery. The team also interviewed several villagers, one of whom imparted firsthand information about the crash. This elderly witness indicated that during a time frame that was later determined to correspond to late 1971, or early 1972, he saw two aircraft flying over the area. He claimed that one of the aircraft was flying very low, and that he later learned it had crashed into the mountains while attacking a Vietnamese supply convoy on Route 7. The witness reported that he had visited the crash site twice within a few weeks of the incident and that on his second trip he had encountered Vietnamese soldiers who told him they were burying the body of the deceased pilot. The witness claimed no knowledge of the exact burial location. However, he did indicate that approximately three years after the crash he had recovered a pilot's helmet from the vicinity, which he showed to the team. Following the interview, the villager led the team up a nearby mountain, where they discovered scattered shards of aircraft wreckage. This was the first physical evidence in the case to be found *in situ*.

Cooperation from this villager proved vital to the team's success. However, as is often the case when U.S. investigative and recovery teams in Southeast Asia pursue information from such sources, the reliability of the information received was affected by a variety of factors including the witness's age, integrity, and personal bias. Witnesses to incidents that occurred decades ago often have difficulty remembering the specific details and, in recounting the story, often change their facts. In addition, the witnesses are often peasant farmers who are intimidated by the interview process, which usually includes powerful individuals from their own national government as well as foreign U.S. representatives. This intimidation can lead to shortened versions of a recollection, as well as contradictions in response due to nervousness or fear of reprisals. Cultural and language differences can also have a major impact on witness interviews, as can the witnesses' expectation of rewards based on the information provided.

Pleased that there were viable leads to pursue, the Shine family continued to track progress on the various dog tag reports, some of which overlapped with the in-country investigations. They carefully considered each report issued by the JTF-FA following a phase of the crash site investigation, asking questions and offering insights gained through their own research and interviews with Lt. Col. Shine's fellow pilots and his wingman. In addition, the family actively monitored any legislation on Capitol Hill that would inevitably impact results in the POW/MIA issue.

Subsequent Visits Reveal a Burial Site

In May 1994, a second joint U.S./S.R.V. investigative team visited the village to re-interview the key witness. During this interview, the witness changed his story and gave new details about the incident, reporting that he had, in fact, viewed the pilot's body still in its ejection seat. He also led the team to a specific burial location in the garden area of one of the village huts that he believed contained the body of the pilot. The team probed the proposed burial site and recovered fragmentary human skeletal remains, deteriorated shreds of personal effects, and pieces of a pilot's personal gear and equipment. The team noted that the burial location appeared to have been

recently disturbed (green leaves were found beneath sterile soil), an indication that remains or other evidence may have been recently removed from the site.

Team members placed the recovered remains and personal effects in a sealed container, which they escorted to Hanoi for a joint forensic review, which was conducted by a forensic anthropologist from CILHI, in conjunction with his/her Vietnamese counterpart. Once evidence is recovered in a case, a stringent record of the chain of custody (i.e., the sequence of individuals/institutions that are safeguarding the evidence) must be maintained. This is accomplished with an official chain of custody document that accompanies the evidence within its sealed container. This important document is signed and dated by each individual who receives and releases the evidence.

Due to the results of the forensic review (which indicated a likelihood that the remains were indeed human and of European ancestry), they were selected for repatriation and released by Vietnamese officials to U.S. custody in June 1994. The remains were then flown to Hawaii, where they were received by an anthropologist at the U.S. Army Central Identification Laboratory, and assigned an accession number for tracking, prevention of bias, and maintenance of privacy during the analysis phase.

Initial Analysis and More Questions

At the CILHI, a forensic anthropologist, who had no previous knowledge of the case history, inventoried the skeletal elements and established an MNI (minimum number of individuals). In this instance the MNI was one. The anthropologist also assessed the condition and morphology of the elements in order to determine (a) the taphonomic processes that had affected the remains over time, (b) whether the remains were all human, and (c) the biological profile.

The forensic anthropologist performs his/her analysis blind; that is, without any knowledge of the case or information about the remains. The accession number assigned to the remains upon their arrival to the lab helps to ensure objectivity of the scientists working on the case. All remains are housed in a relatively cool and dry environment. When the remains are not being actively analyzed, they are kept within plastic bags, which in turn are contained in a labeled cardboard box. Each individual accession is maintained in an individual box to avoid any mixing of remains.

When a case is being analyzed, the remains are laid out in anatomical order on a large table inside the laboratory. Remains from specific cases are kept separate on individual tables, again, to avoid commingling. The accession number travels with the remains so that if the remains are being analyzed, the table upon which they are distributed will be labeled with the appropriate number to ensure the case is accurately tracked within the lab.

Since few skeletal elements were present for analysis in the Shine case, the lab conclusions that could be drawn were extremely limited. The remains were indeed human and appeared to be those of an adult. Brown staining on the surfaces of the bone fragments demonstrated that they had been in contact with soil for an extended period of time. No other determinations could be made.

The Next Step: Mitochondrial DNA Analysis

Since the anthropological information derived from the remains was not nearly specific enough to determine a personal identification, CILHI anthropologists turned to a different type of analysis. In November 1994, a bone sample taken from one of the bone fragments that had been excavated from the burial site was submitted to the Armed Forces DNA Identification Laboratory (AFDIL) for mitochondrial DNA (mtDNA) analysis.

Mitochondrial DNA analysis is a relatively new technology (Darley-Usmar 1993) that is now employed routinely as a tool to assist in the identification of MIAs. Bone samples are prepared at CILHI and sent to AFDIL for processing. CILHI anthropologists take a sample of the remains in a sterile "wet" lab, cleaning the entire lab with 10–20 percent bleach solution each time a new sample is cut. Samples of approximately 6–8 grams are ideal, and the harder, denser (cortical) bone is the target of sampling, since spongy (cancellous) bone does not contain as much bone material and thus does not produce results as frequently. CILHI's forensic odontologists can also submit dental (tooth-derived) samples to AFDIL; these samples are sent in a powdered state.

At AFDIL, a precise and sterile procedure is followed in extracting the mtDNA from the bone samples and tooth powder. The focus of the microbiologist's work are the tiny mitochondria, bodies that function in each and every cell in the body. If an mtDNA sequence is obtained from a bone/dental sample, and is able to be sequenced a second time, AFDIL will report this information to the CILHI. Eventually this mtDNA sequence will be compared by AFDIL to the blood-derived mtDNA sequence of known maternal relatives of the MIA. Maternal relatives of the MIA are the only individuals who can provide blood samples for reference since the mother passes on mtDNA to her children. Thus, an MIA's mother, maternal grandmother, maternal uncle, and siblings can be donors of reference samples used for comparison with an mtDNA sequence obtained from osseous/dental samples.

With regard to the specificity of mtDNA, sequences are common to families (since they are passed down along maternal lines), not individuals as is the case with nuclear DNA. When an mtDNA sequence is reported by

AFDIL, it is compared to a database of unrelated individuals to demonstrate its uniqueness. Some sequences are fairly common (for example, shared by roughly 2 percent of the individuals composing the database), whereas others are completely unique (shared by no others of the 1,660 individuals composing the database).

The mtDNA process can produce conclusive results, but mtDNA is not foolproof, nor is it as exacting an identification method as nuclear DNA. Technicians at AFDIL must produce repeatable results, and if bone/dental samples are degraded, small, or extremely fragmented, such repetition may be impossible. Thus, AFDIL reports may be "inconclusive" or provide "no sequence information."

Mitochondrial DNA is commonly used in identifying remains from the Vietnam War. When used in the identification process, the statistical probabilities involved in mtDNA analysis must be synthesized and understood by the family. Often, AFDIL's report comprises several pages of sequences (specific combinations of adenine, guanine, cytosine, and thymine), which appear as hundreds of four-letter combinations of A, G, C, and T. As the Shine family experienced, this evidence offers a striking juxtaposition between sterile scientific proof and the intangible, emotional truth it represents for a family searching for answers regarding the fate of a missing loved one.

Return to Vietnam for Excavation

While the forensic analysis continued in the United States, questions remained as to whether the crash site and burial site locations described by the witness might yield additional evidence. In May 1995, a recovery team was sent to systematically and thoroughly excavate both sites (see Mann et al., this volume, for more details on recovery teams). The team was composed of a forensic anthropologist, an Army officer, a life support technician (wreckage/equipment analyst), a linguist, a medic, a communication specialist (for high frequency radio communication in remote areas), an explosive ordnance disposal technician (to mitigate any possible live ordnance that still remained in the area), and mortuary affairs specialists. These individuals worked jointly with Vietnamese counterparts to excavate the crash and burial sites.

Living conditions for recovery teams are often exceedingly uncomfortable—the term *roughing it* would most certainly apply. The team usually constructs a small, simple base camp in the vicinity of the excavation site. This facilitates entrance to and egress from the site, which is often remotely located in a mountainous, triple canopy jungle environment that is difficult and/or dangerous to navigate (Figure 21.2). Weather conditions can be quite uncooperative—heavy rains often force teams to remain in a base camp until work on a project site can commence or resume. Severe heat can also impact the health and the stamina of team members during the course of a field activity.

Using standard forensic recovery methods, such as a grid system to document provenience of items recovered, photo documentation of all evidence, and screening all soil through quarter-inch wire mesh, the recovery team recovered additional human remains and personal effects, including an identification tag (Figures 21.3 and 21.4) bearing the name "SHINE, ANTHONY C." and pilot-related materials from the burial area (see Figures 21.5 and 21.6 on page 286). Furthermore, the crash site yielded aircraft wreckage (see Figure 21.7 on page 287) exclusive to Lt. Col. Shine's A-7D *Corsair*. These remains and personal effects were repatriated to the CILHI in June 1995.

Again, the skeletal elements were few and proved relatively undiagnostic for a refined age estimate or sex determination. Thus, in June 1995, two bone samples were taken from the accession and submitted to

FIGURE 21.2   AERIAL VIEW OF ONE OF THE EXCAVATION
SITES DUG BY THE RECOVERY TEAM (CENTER)

AFDIL for mtDNA analysis. In August 1995, at AFDIL's request, the CILHI submitted two additional bone samples for analysis since previous samples had produced inconclusive results.

Combined Analyses Provide Results

Scientists were able to sequence mtDNA from two of the five bone samples submitted to AFDIL. The two sequences were identical in their overlapping regions and match those obtained from three known maternal relatives of Lt. Col. Shine, namely his mother, brother, and sister. The longest sequence obtained from the bone samples was found to occur in less than 4 percent of the combined mtDNA database of 715 individuals used by AFDIL at that time. This was described by AFDIL as an mtDNA "match." However, since the sequence obtained was not unique to AFDIL's database, it was considered a relatively weak match.

Analysis of the material evidence in the case, such as the recovered aircraft wreckage with specific serial numbers, indicated

FIGURE 21.3   IDENTIFICATION TAG *IN SITU*

FIGURE 21.4   CLOSE-UP OF IDENTIFICATION TAG

FIGURE 21.5   BURIAL SITE PRIOR TO EXCAVATION BY RECOVERY TEAM

FIGURE 21.6   BURIAL SITE UPON COMPLETION OF EXCAVATION

that the crash site was specifically that of Lt. Col. Shine's A-7D *Corsair*. The identification dog tag found *in situ* at the burial location also supported the conclusion that the site was Lt. Col. Shine's. The provenience of these pieces of evidence was extremely important since they were found *in situ*, as opposed to when a local villager or refugee hands over any articles such that their original provenience can never be certified. Circumstantial evidence also corroborated the physical evidence, such as the witness's report, Lt. Col. Shine's last known alive location, and the fact that he was flying in a single-seat jet.

Since a complete skeleton with full dentition was not recovered, many pieces of evidence and types of analysis contributed to the final resolution of Lt. Col. Shine's case. The wreckage and life support recovered from the crash and burial sites was assessed at the Life Sciences Equipment Laboratory

FIGURE 21.7   AIRCRAFT WRECKAGE (ENGINE) OBSERVED ON SITE

(LSEL) in San Antonio, Texas. LSEL determined that thermal damage and dynamic loading had been some of the forces at work on the material recovered from the site. In addition, the flight helmet added supporting information, since Lt. Col. Shine's name was written on the inside. The handwriting was analyzed by the Federal Bureau of Investigation and was determined to "strongly correlate" to that of Lt. Col. Shine. Furthermore, the ink used to write the name within the helmet was dated by the U.S. Secret Service Laboratory, and was determined to be ink used by the U.S. Government in the 1960s to indelibly mark metal surfaces. Further, equipment personnel assigned to Lt. Col. Shine's Air Force Base at the time of issue confirmed that the helmet was of the type provided to pilots in his location at that time in the war.

All of the circumstantial evidence and analyses corroborated with the analysis of the remains. Thus, the CILHI moved forward with the case and assembled a lengthy identification report with the multidisciplinary contributions that tied all the pieces of evidence together. After internal review, the case file was sent to outside scientific consultants for peer review. At this point, consultants can either approve the case file with suggested recommendations (or simply approve it as it stands), or disapprove the case file. The CILHI anthropologists then make changes/edits (if deemed necessary) and the case file then is submitted for review by the Casualty Mortuary Affairs for the specific service, in this case Air Force, for final approval. The family must also approve the case file, and can request a review(s) by their own independent consultants as well.

File Review and Final Disposition

The case file was presented to the Shine family by a member of the Air Force Mortuary Affairs office. The family accepted the results, opting against an independent review. The now-identified remains of Lt. Col. Anthony C. Shine were inventoried as such by the CILHI and in October 1996 were officially transferred to Travis Air Force Base in California where Lt. Col. Shine's brother, Alexander, escorted them to Arlington National Cemetery where they were interred with full military honors.

Shine Family Involvement

Throughout the course of this case, which lasted more than twenty-four years, literally hundreds of communications occurred between the U.S. government and the Shine family. Initially, communications focused on the political process. However, once a crash site was located and evidence recovered, the Shine family became actively involved in the scientific investigative process as well. Each step taken by the U.S. government was conveyed in writing to the Shine family, who in turn maintained regular contact with each agency responsible for a given aspect of the investigation. The family carefully considered each report received, and responded with relevant questions and conveyance of pertinent insights and information. The family's involvement included trips to Vietnam, visits to the crash and burial sites, interviews with the key witness, and recovery of the flight helmet and pieces of aircraft wreckage.

On the home front, the Shine family worked to prompt responsible pursuit of the case and an honorable resolution to the POW/MIA issue via meetings with Defense Department analysts and senior level administration personnel, as well as contact with related agencies including AFDIL, CILHI, LSEL, JTF-FA, and the Air Force Casualty Office. The family also testified about the case before a military subcommittee of Congress and provided countless interviews with the local, national, and international press.

Long-Awaited Peace of Mind

After three generations of effort, our family finally had an end to uncertainty. Finally, we had a truth to face and to move forward from. The scientific evidence of these few fragmentary remains, coupled with the aircraft wreckage and circumstantial evidence, offered our family long-awaited peace of mind and heart. My

mother now knew that she was no longer a wife but a widow, and my brothers and I knew that our father was not being tortured, and that he would never walk back into our lives. Dad died doing something he loved, flying, and for a cause in which he believed.

Outstanding Questions

While the Shine family finally had an end to their uncertainty, many questions may remain unanswered. For example, how did Lt. Col. Shine actually die? The cause of death, which is a required finding on a medical examiner's autopsy report, was never determined in Lt. Col. Shine's case. Was he alive after impact? Was the villager's report that he was found dead in his ejection seat true? What happened to the majority of his remains? Were they intentionally removed, and would there be additional remains to deal with in the future? The fullest possible accounting for Americans missing from the Vietnam War is based on individual identifications, not answering all possible questions in a case. At the time of this writing (December 1999), more than 2,000 American servicemen and civilians remain unaccounted for from the Vietnam War. Politics, limited resources, and the death of family members in a position to prompt pursuit of individual cases continue to negatively impact results. Fortunately, a precedent has been set and procedures established—utilizing investigators and scientists from multiple disciplines—to prevent families in future wars from enduring a burden of uncertainty similar to that experienced by the Shine family.

Afterward

In February of 1997, just four months after Lt. Col. Shine's burial at Arlington, the Shine family heard word that additional remains had been submitted to the U.S. embassy in

Vientiane, Laos, with a direct association to Lt. Col. Shine. The remains comprised half of a mandible, with four teeth in place, each of which exhibited restorations. Through ante- and postmortem dental X-rays, CILHI odontologists were able to determine that the mandible was indeed that of Lt. Col. Shine; mtDNA analysis was unnecessary due to the exactitude of the odontological match. A new case file was assembled and reviewed and accepted by the Shine family. In July 1999, Lt. Col. Shine's son Shannon flew to Hawaii and escorted the additional remains back to upstate New York, where they were buried in a private family ceremony.

Note by Dr. Bunch

As a scientist, I recognize the importance of maintaining objectivity and "distance" from the cases on which I work—whether overseeing a recovery site in the field or analyzing remains in the laboratory. Still, scientific endeavors do not proceed in a vacuum. Applied science, such as forensic anthropology, is entrenched in politics and deeply impacts personal lives. In some instances, recognition of such outside factors can be a help rather than a hindrance to the applied anthropologist. While I did not perform work on the Shine case, my long-standing friendship with Colleen (we met as college classmates) and my knowledge of how her father's loss impacted their family, has inspired me to work diligently and conscientiously. Staying broadly abreast of the politics of the POW/MIA issue and knowing Colleen and her family has afforded me motivation and patience, and is a constant reminder of the larger context in which my work is applied.

References

Darley-Usmar, Victor M., ed. 1993. *Mitochondria: DNA, Proteins, and Diseases*, Monograph Series, No. 5, A. H. Schapira. Princeton, NJ: Princeton University Press.

Mather, Paul D. 1994. *M.I.A. Accounting for the Missing in Southeast Asia*. Washington, D.C.: National Defense University Press.

Further Reading

Fisher, Russell S. 1980. Aircraft crash investigation. Pp. 406–419 in *Medicolegal Investigation of Death*, ed. Werner U. Spitz and Russell S. Fisher. Springfield, IL: Charles C. Thomas.

France, D. L., T. J. Griffin, J. G. Swanburg, J. W. Lindemann, G. C. Davenport, and V. Trammel et al. 1992. A multidisciplinary approach to the detection of clandestine graves. *Journal of Forensic Sciences* (37):1445–1458.

Scott, Douglas D., and Melissa A. Connor. 1997. Context delecti: Archaeological context in forensic work. Pp. 27–38 in *Forensic Taphonomy: The Postmortem Fate of Human Remains*, ed. William D. Haglund and Marcella H. Sorg. Boca Raton, FL: CRC Press.

Stoutamire, James. 1983. Excavation and recovery. Pp. 20–47 in *Handbook of Forensic Archaeology and Anthropology*, ed. Dan Morse, Jack Duncan, and James Stoutamire. Tallahassee, FL: Florida State University.

Swegennis, Robert W. 1987. Impact angles and velocities. Pp. 1–16 in *Safety Investigation: Investigative Techniques*, ed. B. Carver. Washington, D.C.: Department of the Air Force.

CHAPTER

22

FORENSIC ANTHROPOLOGY AND HUMAN RIGHTS

THE ARGENTINE EXPERIENCE

Mercedes Doretti and Clyde C. Snow

During the 1970s, many South American countries were shaken by periods of intense violence and repression, including Argentina, Bolivia, Brazil, Chile, Uruguay and Paraguay. Severe human rights violations were committed, primarily by the state under the control of military government and, to a lesser extent, by guerrilla groups.

On March 24, 1976, the Argentine military, on the pretext of bringing order to civil society, deposed President Isabel Perón, dismissed the Congress, and took over the country. The new ruling body—the *Junta*—was a triumvirate composed of the military chiefs of the Army, Navy, and Air Force.

The Dirty War was a campaign of extermination against the *Junta*'s enemies, both real and perceived, and its tactics were kidnapping, torture, and extrajudicial execution. It was carried out by the Armed Forces and the police. Each group operated its own network of clandestine detention centers (CDCs) located in military bases and police stations throughout the country.

First to be targeted were the armed groups, the Marxist-Leninist Peoples Revolutionary Army and *Montoneros*, a left-wing

Peronist group. But the military extended its definition of "subversive" to include political liberals in all walks of life—students, professors, clergy, lawyers, labor leaders, journalists, and intellectuals. Typically, an abductee was taken to a CDC where he or she underwent interrogation under torture for several weeks or months before being released, becoming legal prisoners, or extrajudicially executed. According to more recently available accounts and information, some CDCs dumped their victims, bound and sedated, from military aircraft while flying over the Argentine Sea; others buried them in unmarked graves in municipal cemeteries. In cases of burials, shortly after the killings, the bodies were typically deposited in public places, and an "anonymous call" would be made to the local precinct. The police, sometimes accompanied by local judges, would go to the site and recover the bodies. Prior to burial, the bodies were often photographed, fingerprinted, and given a perfunctory examination by a police or judiciary forensic doctor, who issued a death certificate. These latter documents listed the victim as a *Ningun*

Nombre (*NN*), the term used to officially designate unidentified bodies in Argentina, despite the fact that the victims were known to the military and police. Judiciary and/or police files were opened but no further investigation ensued. Often, the discovery of the bodies was followed by a press communiqué issued by the regional military commanders, stating that "subversive individuals" had been killed in a shoot-out with security forces.

Late in 1983, democracy was restored, ending eight years of *Junta* rule. President Raúl Alfonsin promised the nation to investigate the disappearances and prosecute those responsible (Dworkin 1986). He created the National Commission on Disappeared People (CONADEP). The Commission took depositions from thousands of witnesses and collected an enormous amount of other documentary evidence chronicling the fate of the *desaparecidos*.* At the end of its nine-month tenure, the Commission issued a report entitled *Nunca Más* that, in chilling detail, described how the death squads abducted, tortured, and killed their victims. An appendix listed 8,961 *desaparecidos* by name, sex, age, date, and place of disappearance.

When families of the *desaparecidos* petitioned police or military authorities for information, they were routinely told that there was no record of them ever having been in custody, nor were the relatives ever notified of their ultimate fate. In short, almost literally, the *desaparecidos* vanished into thin air from the moment they were snatched off the street or from their workplaces, schoolrooms or homes by cruising death squads.

When democracy returned, some judges began to carry out exhumations in cemeteries thought to contain *desaparecidos*. Families of the victims sadly watched these proceedings with the hope of finding the remains of their relatives (see Figure 22.1 on page 292). These early exhumations were unsatisfactory in several ways. In the first place, the medical experts designated to perform the investigations had little experience in the exhumation and analysis of skeletal remains. As a consequence, they were carried out in an unscientific manner. For example, cemetery workers, and even bulldozers, were used to open the graves, and bones were broken, commingled, or left inside the grave. As a result, evidence necessary to identify the skeletons and determine the cause of death was lost or destroyed. Another problem related to the credibility of the medical experts. In Argentina, as in many other countries, forensic experts are part of the police or judicial system. Their findings are thus apt to be viewed suspiciously in nondemocratic periods or in cases in which the police or other governmental agencies are the alleged perpetrators. And, in fact, a number of forensic experts had been complicit in the crimes of the *Junta*. Some police forensic doctors, for example, disguised the real cause of death on death certificates to help cover up *desaparecido* executions. Such activities tainted the entire system of medicolegal death investigation.

The Founding of EAAF

In early 1984, concerned by these problems, CONADEP and the Grandmothers of Plaza de Mayo, a local human rights organization involved in searching for babies and children that disappeared with their parents, reached for aid outside Argentina by asking

---

*The closest English equivalent to the term *desaparecido* is the term *missing person*, which refers to those gone missing of their own volition as well as the criminally abducted. In Latin American countries, *desaparecido* has come to denote victims who have been secretly detained and executed by state-sponsored terrorists. It was first used in this sense in Guatemala in the 1960s.

FIGURE 22.1   PROVINCE OF BUENOS AIRES, 1984

Shown here are nonscientific exhumations conducted at the Avellaneda cemetery. Ms. Bonaparte, whose two daughters and one son "disappeared," observes the pile of bones lying on a white sheet resulting from these exhumations. (*Photo courtesy of Roberto Pera*)

for help from the American Association for the Advancement of Science (AAAS). Eric Stover, at the time director of the AAAS Committee on Scientific Freedom and Responsibility, took a delegation of U.S. scientists on a mission to provide advice to CONADEP. They found that several hundred skeletons had been exhumed but none had been identified. Most, stuffed into plastic bags often containing the commingled bones of several individuals, lay in dusty storerooms. Shocked by its findings, the delegation called for a halt to exhumations. Dr. Clyde Snow was asked by the CONADEP to help recruit a qualified forensic team. Snow's attempt to recruit a team of professional anthropologists and forensic specialists was disappointing: Some were simply not interested; others feared for themselves and their families should the military return to power; yet others were simply suspicious or unclear about the seriousness of the institutions involved. But, toward the end of his stay, he

was approached by a small group of anthropology students who, through the student "grapevine," had heard of his dilemma and volunteered to help. Concerned by their lack of experience but impressed with their enthusiasm, he agreed. Using techniques from traditional archaeology and forensic anthropology, Snow and the fledgling team conducted exhumations in which the evidence was properly recovered and analyzed at the laboratory.

Snow returned to Argentina many times to train and work with the team, spending over two years there between 1985 and 1990. A high point of this early period was when they were called upon to present their evidence in the trial that led to the conviction of the nine generals and admirals who ruled Argentina during the *Junta* years (Figure 22.2). More important, in cases where positive identifications were made, they were able to return the bones of *desaparecidos* to their families. Their work also marked the first use of forensic science in human

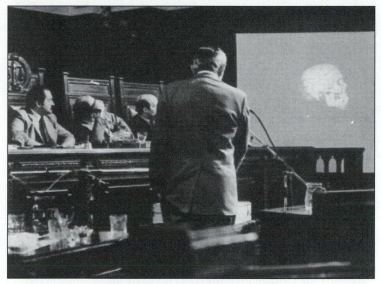

FIGURE 22.2   BUENOS AIRES, 1985

Forensic anthropologist Dr. Clyde C. Snow testifies before a panel of judges on the trials of the former members of the military Juntas. (*Photo courtesy of Daniel Muzio*)

rights investigations—a development of worldwide significance. In 1986, along with some new recruits, the team formally organized itself into the *Equipo Argentino Antropología Forense* (EAAF, Argentine Forensic Anthropology Team).

EAAF is a nonprofit organization dedicated to the application of forensic sciences to the investigation of human rights abuses. Today, our work entails a multidisciplinary approach that includes forensic anthropology, archaeology, odontology, human genetics, pathology, ballistics, cultural anthropology, and computer science.

Objectives of EAAF's Work

The mission of the EAAF includes the following six objectives:

1. We apply forensic scientific methodology to the investigation and documentation of human rights violations.
2. As expert witnesses, we give testimony of our findings in trials and other judicial inquiries in human rights cases.
3. Through the identification of the victims, we can provide some solace to their families who are at last able to properly mourn and bury their dead.
4. We help train new teams in other countries where investigations into human rights violations are necessary.
5. At the request of human rights organizations, judicial systems, and forensic institutes, we give seminars on the applications of forensic science to the investigation of human rights violations.
6. Finally, by providing scientific evidence of massive human rights violations, we provide evidence to reconstruct the often distorted or hidden histories of repressive regimes.

In 1986, EAAF expanded its activities beyond Argentina. Cases are now taken when judges, human rights groups, truth commissions, or the United Nations request its assistance. Our members are paid a regular salary from the team's general budget, allowing them to undertake foreign missions without relying on compensation from the inviting organization. This is very important, as human rights and judicial institutions in most of the countries where we work have few resources. Our institutional budget comes from the support of several European and American foundations. To date, EAAF members have worked in Bolivia, Bosnia, Brazil, Chile, Colombia, Cote d'Ivoire, Croatia, Democratic Republic of Congo, East Timor, El Salvador, Ethiopia, French Polynesia, Guatemala, Haiti, Honduras, Iraqi Kurdistan, Mexico, Panama, Paraguay, Peru, the Philippines, Romania, South Africa, Venezuela, Kosovo, and Zimbabwe. Dr. Snow is an honorary member of the EAAF and has worked with the team on many cases, including those discussed in this chapter.

Since EAAF was founded, other forensic anthropology teams have been established in Chile (1989), Guatemala (1991), and Peru (2001). Today, the Latin American teams regularly exchange members for cross-training and occasionally work together on foreign missions. Notable among the latter have been the United Nations War Crimes Tribunals in Former Yugoslavia.

An Epidemic of Homicide

Statistical analysis has also proven valuable in the search for the disappeared. In Argentina it helped us accomplish an obvious first step in any homicide investigation: finding the body.

When we began in 1984, the available data indicated that a large number of the disappeared had been buried as *Ningun Nombres* in municipal cemeteries. The problem was that the hundreds of such cemeteries in Argentina contain thousands of *NN* graves, not only of *desaparecidos*, but also of many ordinary people whose bodies, for one reason or another, go unidentified. Would every *NN* grave in every cemetery have to be opened in order to find

the *desaparecidos*? Or could statistics be used to help narrow our search? Could we treat the state-sponsored homicide in Argentina as epidemiologists study the outbreak and spread of a deadly disease?

Thinking about this, we reasoned that, in ordinary times, the "population" of persons who go to their graves unidentified in Argentina, as in many other countries, is largely composed of elderly indigents with no family ties. Within this group, men strongly outnumber women. Typically, they are the homeless and forgotten who die of natural causes related to neglect and old age—exposure, malnutrition and, frequently, alcohol abuse. Depending largely on the size of the overall population it serves, a municipal cemetery can expect a fairly constant annual number of *NN* burials. This number may show transitory peaks related to mass disasters and longer-term upward or downward trends related to population growth or economic factors influencing poverty rates and homelessness but, usually, it remains fairly stable for a given cemetery.

The *desaparecido* population was very different. Analyzing the data on 7,385 disappearances reported by June 1984, we found that, although they ranged in age from newborn infants to septuagenarians, nearly 70 percent were between sixteen and thirty-five years old at the time of disappearance and about one-third were female (Snow 1984). Furthermore, nearly all died violently, usually from gunshot wounds. For example, an examination of 124 cases from Boulogne Cemetery in the Buenos Aires suburb of San Isidro, showed that close to 90 percent had died of gunshot wounds to the back of the head.

With these differences between the ordinary *NN* and the *desaparecido* populations in mind, we gathered statistics on *NN* burials in municipal cemeteries of the Province of Buenos Aires. This province, about the size of Arizona, contained (in 1980) close to 40 percent of Argentina's total population. The survey was conducted through question-naires sent to the municipal cemetery directors of the provincial *departamentos* (counties). We asked them to provide the date of burial, sex, approximate age, cause of death, and grave location of all *NNs* buried in their cemeteries between 1970 and 1984.

The *departamentos* reported a total of 4,297 NN burials over the entire fifteen-year period. During seven of these years, 1970–75 and 1984, Argentina was under civil and other military governments; during the eight-year interval from 1976 to 1983, under *Junta* rule. We next compared the number of deaths reported for these sub-periods, "non-*Junta*" and "*Junta*" for each cemetery by Chi-square tests. In all, 25 (27.1 percent) of the 105 reporting *departamentos* showed a statistically significant increase in *NN* burials during the *Junta* years. This allowed us to considerably narrow the list of cemeteries to target for further investigation.

The data also revealed other clues that shed light on how the labyrinthine system of disappearance functioned. For instance, cemeteries statistically identified as harboring *desaparecido* graves could sometimes be linked to particular CDCs located in the same or adjacent *departamentos*. When we have information indicating that a particular *desaparecido* was seen in one of these CDCs, it makes it more likely that he or she was buried in the linked cemetery. Building on this kind of information enables us to reconstruct some of the many paths followed by the victims from their point of disappearance to their graves. Interested readers will find a more detailed treatment of our findings in a study published elsewhere (Snow and Bihurriet 1992).

This study also had an interesting legal ramification. When the *Junta* fell, General Carlos G. Suárez Mason, who commanded the military zone that included Buenos Aires Province, left the country and went into hiding. A few years later he was discovered living quietly in San Francisco and

the Argentine government petitioned the United States for his extradition. At the request of the U.S. federal prosecutor, who had entered the case as *amicus curae* (friend of the court), Snow sent a special report of the findings to the court for use as evidence in the extradition proceeding. It showed that General Suárez Mason, as commander of the 1st Army Corps, had overall command responsibility for the operation of the CDCs in the area where most of the cemeteries showing statistically significant increases in NN burials during *Junta* rule were located. The court ruled in favor of extradition. Upon his return to Argentina, he was tried and convicted.

Argentina: The Manfil Case

In 1992, after fifteen years of silence and anguish, Karina, Graciela, and Cristian Manfil finally learned what happened to their parents. One morning in January 1991, Karina walked to the huge municipal cemetery of Avellaneda, a Buenos Aires suburb. At the gate, she asked for directions to Sector 134, a small area separated from the main part of the cemetery by a high brick wall. She had heard that we were exhuming a mass grave there. When she found us, Karina said that she had turned eighteen and was now old enough to search for her disappeared family. Someone had told her that her parents and little brother were buried in Sector 134.

Sector 134

When Karina arrived, the EAAF had already been working in Sector 134 for three years. It is a rectangular area (12 x 24 meters) at the back of the cemetery, squeezed between the main graveyard and a city street. There was a small gate in the wall facing the cemetery. A gate in the street-side wall was wide enough to allow vehicles to enter. When the military took power in 1976, Sector 134 was placed under police guard.

The solid metal gates and high walls concealed it from the eyes of curious passersby. During the first three years of the dictatorship, when thousands of people disappeared, neighbors across the street observed military trucks and police vehicles entering Sector 134 through the street-side gate, day and night.

In 1982, the police guards left and ordered the cemetery workers to stay out of the sector. Isolated and abandoned for several years, it was gradually overgrown with weeds and small saplings. Although people suspected it concealed the bones of *desaparecidos*, Sector 134, like similar places throughout Argentina, could not be investigated until after 1983, when democracy returned.

As in most of our investigations, work on the case proceeded in four steps: (1) historical research, (2) collection of antemortem data, (3) archaeology, and (4) laboratory analysis. These are not always performed in strict sequence. For example, the collection of historical information and antemortem data in Argentina continues today.

Historical Research

The objective of this phase is to collect information shedding light on a case from surviving records and witnesses. From these sources, we try to answer such questions as: When was the grave made and how long was it used to bury bodies? Who made the grave? How was it made? How many people may be buried there? Who may we expect to find buried there? The answers to these and like questions enable us to develop strategies and hypotheses shaping our archaeological and analytic approaches to the case.

The cemetery registers, burial records, and death certificates showed that, despite secrecy surrounding the repression, at least 220 people had been buried in Sector 134 during the *Junta* years. Of these, 160 were unidentified young people killed by gunfire and brought there by police or military personnel. Most were buried between 1976 and 1978 during the period of the so-called First *Junta*, the most brutal years of the Dirty War. Afterwards, burials continued at a slower rate until 1982.

In many countries, human rights violations occur as village massacres and the victims are left for survivors or neighboring villagers to bury. Consequently, the locations of the graves are generally known to local inhabitants and, from survivor interviews, church or municipal records, and other sources, fairly accurate lists of the victims can be compiled prior to exhumation. This is not true in Argentina where the system of disappearance was more complex.

Prisoners could pass through several of the more than 350 CDCs identified throughout the country by the CONADEP. The possible combinations and permutations of this process are enormous, making the task of tracing the painful journey of a given *desaparecida* from her place of abduction to her grave a formidable problem. Fortunately, however, the paths were not completely random and, gradually, from painstaking study of the scanty documentary records and interviews of the few survivors, patterns began to emerge. In other words, the death squads—like common criminals—had a *modus operandi* that can be at least partially reconstructed to fill the information gap between disappearance and death. This allows us to trace the transfer of certain prisoners among the various CDCs and determine the possible local cemeteries used by a given CDC to dispose of the bodies. We also collect information about the members of union, political, student, and guerrilla groups who were primary targets during those years. When the kidnappers made "sweeps" targeting a particular group, their members were likely to wind up in the same CDCs and, eventually, the same graves. The same, unfortunately, is true of families. Such information allows us to build hypotheses about who might be in a given mass grave.

When such a hypothesis is confirmed through positive identification of one individual, it increases the probability that his or her disappeared associates or relatives may lie nearby. This analytical work continues and, in 1998, was tremendously advanced when EAAF was finally given access to hitherto nonpublic police records of the period.

Collection of Antemortem Data

Historical investigation also helps establish which families to contact. Antemortem data is then collected through interviews with relatives, medical doctors, and dentists of the victims. It includes physical variables that can be determined from the skeleton, such as age at death, sex, stature, and handedness, as well as dental information and any diseases or old injuries—particularly fractures—that might be visible on the bones. Today, genealogical information is especially important since family members may eventually be asked for samples for DNA identification.

Collecting such information may require several interviews with family members over a period of months or years. With patience and sensitivity, bonds of trust and understanding are built with the families, making it a little easier for them to dredge up old memories from a painful past.

Archaeology

Excavation of Sector 134 finished in March 1992 after the entire area (432 m^2) had been explored. We found a series of nineteen mass graves and eleven single burials (Figure 22.3). The mass graves were in the form of irregular ovals around three meters in diameter and extending to a depth of about two to three meters. At an average depth of about one to two meters, commingled skeletons were encountered (Figure 22.4, page 298). The number of skeletons per grave ranged from ten to twenty-eight.

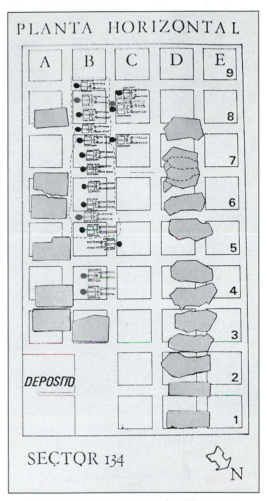

FIGURE 22.3 SECTOR 134 SITE DIAGRAM

This graphic shows the location of mass (gray) and individual graves found at this sector of the Avellaneda cemetery, Buenos Aires Province. (*Created by P. Bernardi/ EAAF*)

Nearly all were buried without clothing. Personal effects were rare. Wedding rings were found among the hand bones of two individuals and metal crosses associated with two others. Two coins, one dated 1958 and the other 1976, were recovered. Ballistic evidence consisted of more than 300 projectiles, many of which were fragmented or deformed. No cartridge cases were found.

FIGURE 22.4 EXCAVATION IN PROGRESS AT A MASS GRAVE IN SECTOR 134, AVELLANEDA CEMETERY

The use of archaeological techniques allows for the recovery and documentation of all the evidence on a site. (*Photo by M. Doretti/EAAF*)

Laboratory Analysis

The exhumed graves yielded a total of 324 skeletons—104 more than cemetery records indicated. Figure 22.5 shows the sex and age distribution of the series. Males comprise 77.8 percent of the skeletons. Most of the females fall into the younger age groups; thus they constitute about one-third of the twenty-one to forty-five year olds but only about one-tenth of the individuals over sixty. The overall pattern is a reflection of the fact that, during the six-year period (1976–1982) that Sector 134 was in use as a burial ground, the

bodies of "ordinary" people (mostly elderly male indigents) were buried in the same mass graves as the *desaparecidos*, who were predominately young and, often, female.

Evidence of gunshot wounds to the head and/or chest is found in 178 (55 percent) of the individuals, nearly all of whom were under fifty years of age at the time of death. On the other hand, such wounds are rare in the over-fifty age group. Some of the younger individuals displayed fresh or healing fractures from blunt force trauma most probably inflicted while they were in detention. Others showing no signs of gunshot wounds may have also died violently since it is known that a number of *desaparecidos* succumbed to the effects of physical torture (usually electrical) to which nearly all were subjected.

In short, the skeletons exhumed from Sector 134 fall into two groups. The first, smaller contingent consists of elderly individuals, mostly male, who had (as far as we could tell from their bones) died of natural causes. They, obviously, represent the "ordinary" *NN* population. The second, larger and much younger group, almost a fourth of whom are female, had died of gunshot

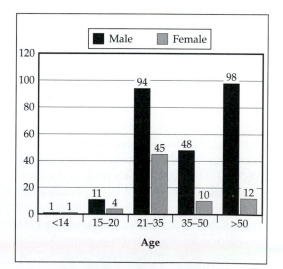

FIGURE 22.5 DISTRIBUTION OF SECTOR 134 SKELETONS BY SEX AND AGE

wounds. It was among them, obviously, that we had to search for Karina's long-lost father, mother, and little brother.

Resolution of the Manfil Case

In the early hours of October 27, 1976, a joint police-army death squad raided the third-floor apartment of the Manfil family in Avellaneda. The head of the family, thirty-year-old Carlos, was an employee of the Buenos Aires Botanical Garden. His wife, Angélica, aged twenty-eight, and three of their four children—nine-year-old Carlitos, four-year-old Karina, and Cristian, an infant of six months, were asleep. The oldest child, Graciela, aged twelve, was staying with her grandmother. Another family, temporary guests of the Manfils, were also in the apartment: Rosario Ramirez, her husband, Jose Vega, and their two children, Marcela and Adolfo, aged eleven and nine respectively. Carlos Manfil and Jose Vega were politically active Peronists, the political party that had been ousted by the military a few months earlier.

When the attack began, all of the children were sleeping in the same room. Alarmed by the shouts, Carlitos leaned out the window and received a gunshot wound to the forehead. He fell on Karina. Pushing his body aside, she hid under the bed with the other children. She heard her mother screaming in the next room, "Don't shoot, there are children inside!" Then, from beneath the bed, she saw military boots kicking the door open. A burst of bullets sprayed the room. Karina was wounded in the leg, Adolfo in his arm and leg, and Marcela in her chest. Cristian, who was with his mother, was not wounded.

Firemen took the three wounded children to a hospital, where they stayed for about a month. Adolfo and Marcela went to live with an aunt. Karina, Graciela, and Cristian Manfil were taken in by their grandparents. The children of the two families never saw each other again. Karina knew that her

brother had been killed, but she was never sure what had happened to her parents. Like many relatives of disappeared people, she thought there was some possibility that they might still be alive.

After hearing Karina's story, EAAF launched an investigation of the Manfil case. We learned that Karina's mother, Angélica, was killed inside the apartment. Carlos Manfil, Rosario Ramirez, and Jose Vega tried to escape by climbing down the drainpipes. Manfil and Ramirez fell, fracturing their legs. They were allegedly shot and killed immediately. Jose Vega escaped but about a year later was apprehended and disappeared. The bodies of Carlos, Angélica, and Carlitos Manfil, as well as that of Rosario Ramirez, were not returned to their families who were never officially notified of their deaths or told where they were buried. Later, some family members heard rumors that they were buried in Sector 134.

In several interviews with the two families, EAAF collected antemortem data on the missing persons. We then searched the available official records for clues to their fate. This hunt was rewarded by the discovery of their death certificates in a local vital statistics office. They showed that the bodies of the four had, indeed, been buried in Sector 134.

Among the skeletons from Sector 134 was that of a boy about ten years old. His skull had a single gunshot entrance wound in the frontal bone. No other boys were recovered in the entire excavation of Sector 134. The archaeological records showed that this skeleton had been recovered from Square B8. This square was part of a mass grave containing several adult skeletons. Among them were three that matched in sex, age, and stature to the scanty dental information recalled by the families and the antemortem profiles of Carlos and Angélica Manfil and Rosario Ramirez. The male and one of the females also displayed perimortem fractures of the long bones of the lower extremities.

In 1991, we found a file issued by a military court on the Manfil case, containing their autopsy reports. The type and location of the gunshot wounds described for the four individuals were fully consistent with the skeletons from Square B8. The report also described the leg fractures corresponding to those we had observed. On the basis of these consistencies, we could provisionally identify the four skeletons as those of the three Manfils and Rosario Ramirez but felt they fell short of positive identification.

We sent bone samples from the four skeletons to Dr. Erika Hagelberg at Oxford University. From them she was able to recover nuclear genetic material for DNA analysis. Teeth from each skull, along with blood samples from the families of the presumed victims, were submitted to Dr. Mary Claire King at the University of California at Berkeley. She was able to extract mitochondrial DNA (mtDNA) from the dental pulp to compare with mtDNA from the blood.

By August 1992, the studies were complete. Dr. Hagelberg established a filial relation between the two skeletons fitting the anthropological profiles of Angélica and Carlitos Manfil, mother and son. Meanwhile, Dr. King found an mtDNA match between teeth of the skeleton provisionally diagnosed as Angélica's and the blood of her daughter, Karina. She was also able to match the mtDNA from the teeth of the skeleton fitting the description of Carlos Manfil with blood from his mother (Karina's paternal grandmother).

The genetic analysis confirmed that the provisional identifications based on the historical and anthropological information were correct. The Federal Court of Appeals accepted the EAAF report on the Manfil case. Its favorable ruling allowed the remains to be returned to the Manfil family. In accepting the genetic findings, the Court also set an important precedent by paving the way for the acceptance of DNA evidence for skeletal identification in future cases.

While the fourth skeleton was consistent with our information on Rosario Ramirez, it took several years to track down her relatives. Once they were found, DNA analysis performed by Argentine biologist Ana Topft, University of Durham, UK, established a positive identification of the skeleton as that of Rosario.

In December 1992, Karina's sixteen-year quest finally ended when she was able to inter the long-lost bones of her father, mother, and little brother Carlitos, in a modest family crypt. Ironically, it stands in the cemetery of Avellaneda, not far from Sector 134.

El Salvador: The El Mozote Massacre

Historical Background

From the 6th to the 16th of December, 1981, the Salvadoran army conducted "Operation Rescue," in the northeastern province of Morazán. It had two objectives: first, to force guerrillas of the *Frente Farabundo Marti para la Liberacion Nacional* (FMLN) from the area and destroy their clandestine radio station, and second, to eliminate FMLN supporters in the civilian population. Spearheading the operation was the elite Atlacatl Battalion, a U.S. trained and equipped counter-insurgency unit.

After a few encounters and ambushes with the Army, the guerrillas left the area. On December 9th, the Army arrived in El Mozote. They killed the villagers, destroyed their houses, burned their fields, and slaughtered their livestock. They then used it as a base from which to launch daytime attacks on five other nearby villages where the troops massacred the residents they encountered, repeating the destruction of houses and fields. Many of the inhabitants of these outlying villages, alerted by the El Mozote massacre, managed to escape. Each night, survivors returned to their villages under the cover of darkness to inter as many victims as they could in common graves at the sites where they were found.

Most survivors escaped across the Honduran border to United Nations refugee camps; others joined the FMLN or took refuge in other regions of El Salvador.

Investigation of the Massacre

The villages remained largely abandoned until 1989, when many survivors began to return. El Mozote itself remained almost deserted until several years later. These events, known as the "Massacre of El Mozote," became the object of intense debate in both El Salvador and the United States. At the time, little information was available to the Salvadoran public regarding the nature of military operations in the countryside. There was no opposition press in the early 1980s, and such information that did exist was controlled by the armed forces. Only one local newspaper—*La Prensa Grafica*—reported on "Operation Rescue." In a story published on December 9th, shortly after the operation began, it noted that, according to military sources, the area was ". . . under strict control of the army to avoid whatever regrettable or unpleasant act," and that access was denied to journalists and the International Red Cross. The FMLN's *Radio Venceremos* reported the massacre toward the end of December 1981.

But the massacre became known to the international community on January 27, 1982, when three U.S. journalists, Alma Guillermoprieto of the *Washington Post*, Raymond Bonner of the *New York Times* and photojournalist Susan Meiselas walked into the area from Honduras. They interviewed survivors and took photographs. Their detailed accounts were published in both the *Times* (Bonner 1982) and the *Post* (Guillermoprieto 1982). Later, Bonner recalled,

> The fragrance of the tropical flowers was overwhelmed by the stench of decaying bodies. In one adobe hut after another charred skulls, leg bones, pelvises, femurs, rib cages, and spine columns protruded from the rubble of sewing machine parts,

children's toys, simple family belongings, smashed roofing tiles, and the charred beams that had held them. . . . On the walls of some houses, it was written: "We are the little angels from Hell—Atlacatl Battalion" (Bonner 1984)

Reports of the El Mozote incident sparked intense debate in the U.S. Congress, where the renewal of military aid to El Salvador was already the subject of controversy. Both the Salvadoran government and the U.S. State Department stated that there had been a military operation in the area, but that what had occurred in El Mozote had really been a battle between the Salvadoran army and the FMLN and that there was no evidence of a "massacre." Reports of a massacre were discounted as FMLN propaganda. Military aid was renewed.

The refusal of both governments to support further investigations into the incident succeeded in removing it from public attention in El Salvador and the United States for several years. Human rights groups, however, continued to press for an investigation. In 1989, at the request of organizations from Morazán, *Tutela Legal*, the Human Rights Legal Office of the Archbishop of San Salvador, launched an investigation of the massacre. It found that about 800 villagers had been killed and that over 40 percent of the victims were children under ten years of age. In October 1990, *Tutela Legal* helped several survivors of the massacre initiate a legal suit against the army. To help build their case, *Tutela Legal* planned to conduct exhumations in the El Mozote area and requested the assistance of the EAAF. In response, EAAF members made a preliminary trip to El Salvador in 1991 but the investigation was blocked when judicial officials refused to grant permission to exhume.

Investigations after the Civil War

In early 1992, shortly after the Salvadoran government and the guerrilla army had signed a peace agreement, *Tutela Legal* again invited EAAF to assist with its investigation. An EAAF team returned to El Salvador and spent three months making preparations and conducting preliminary investigations. With the help of survivors we were able to locate some of the graves, gain some idea of the number of bodies in each, and prepare lists of possible victims. We also encountered many bureaucratic obstacles used as delaying tactics by various officials opposed to the investigation. After these were overcome, we were finally officially named as expert witnesses in the El Mozote case. However, the Supreme Court and the local judge overseeing the case again denied permission to start exhumations and the EAAF team returned to Argentina. Finally, in the fall of 1992, the United Nations Truth Commission for El Salvador opened the way for exhumations and appointed EAAF anthropologists Luis Fondebrider, Patricia Bernardi, and Mercedes Doretti as technical consultants. They were directed to conduct

the excavation of Site 1 in the hamlet of El Mozote.

The site consisted of the ruins of a small (4.3 x 6.4 meter) one-room adobe building, *el convento*, which had stood next to the village church. Its walls had collapsed inward, leaving a meter-high mound of debris that included its charred roof timbers. Removal of this overburden revealed, lying on the floor, the commingled skeletons of 141 individuals, 134 of whom were under the age of twelve. The adults consisted of 6 women and 1 elderly man. Fetal bones were found within the pelvic basin of one of the women. Along with remnants of clothing were dolls, marbles, toy cars, religious medals and crosses, and a few small coins (Figures 22.6 and 22.7).

A total of 245 spent cartridge cases were recovered. Most were found in the southwest corner of the room, indicating that the shooters were most likely standing close to this area. They were submitted to

FIGURE 22.6 EL MOZOTE, EL SALVADOR, 1992

Site 1 consisted of the ruins of an adobe and stone one-room house adjacent to the church. Using traditional archaeological techniques, EAAF established a system of grids to register the findings according to their location. Individuals recovered at Site 1 numbered 141. (*Photo by M. Doretti/EAAF*)

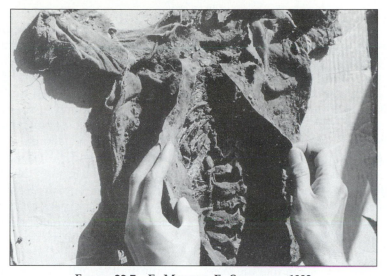

FIGURE 22.7   EL MOZOTE, EL SALVADOR, 1992

Of the 141 skeletons exhumed, 134 belonged to children under 12 years old, with an average age of 6. Among the adult remains, there was one woman in the last months of pregnancy. (*Photo courtesy of Stephen Ferry*)

U.S. archaeologist and ballistic expert Dr. Douglas Scott. All the cartridges, with the exception of one, were fired from 5.56 NATO caliber firearms. He found that they appeared to have been fired from U.S.-manufactured M-16 automatic rifles. All of the cartridge cases bore head stamps of the Lake City Arms Plant located near Independence, Missouri, a U.S. army provider. Firing pin impressions and ejection marks indicated that at least twenty-four firearms were represented among the recovered cartridge cases (Scott 1993). Various sources claim that the Atlacatl Batallion was the only Salvadoran army unit to use this type of rifle at the time of the massacre.

Two hundred sixty-three bullet fragments were recovered from within the building. Most were concentrated in the northeast side of the room, opposite the corner where the cartridges were found. Most were embedded in the bones of the victims or in close relationship to them. In nine cases, bullets had penetrated the floor directly under gunshot wounds of the skull or thorax, showing that these victims were lying on the floor and the shooter was standing more or less directly over them. (Fondebrider et al. 1993). While some of the children may have been shot outside and their bodies later dumped in the building, the recovered ballistic evidence shows that the number of rounds fired inside was sufficient to account for all of the deaths (Snow et al. 1993).

After exhumation, the skeletons were removed to a morgue in San Salvador for more detailed examination. At this stage, Dr. Snow and two other American forensic experts joined the team; forensic pathologist Dr. Robert Kirschner, and forensic radiologist Dr. John Fitzpatrick. Sex is difficult to determine in immature skeletons but, using the few clues available along with associated clothing and personal effects, we were able to conclude that about 55 percent of the 134 child skeletons were female. Osteological and dental age determination showed that these children ranged in age from birth to about twelve years, with a mean of 6.8 years. All of the victims, including the seven adults, exhibited perimortem trauma typical of high-velocity gunshot wounds, postmortem crushing injuries, and exposure to fire (Snow et al. 1993).

The findings at Site 1 were among the principal bases for the UN Truth Commission's conclusion that the Salvadoran Army had committed a massacre in El Mozote and five nearby villages, which resulted in the deaths of at least 500 persons and probably many more. The report also included the names of high-ranking officers in the armed forces of El Salvador who were responsible for the operation. The findings of the Commission prompted the Clinton administration to publicly rectify the U.S. State Department's former position that the massacre had never occurred. In El Salvador, the Atlacatl Battalion, which had committed the massacre, was officially disbanded, though its members were placed in other army units.

During the 1992 mission, EAAF exhumed only one site in El Mozote; many other clandestine graves still remain there, as well as in the other five villages. When it finished its work in March 1993, the UN Truth Commission strongly urged that the investigations into wartime human rights violations, including the El Mozote massacre, be continued. However, a few days after the UN report was released, the Salvadoran legislature passed an amnesty law that not only barred prosecution of persons who committed human rights violations during the war, but which was also interpreted at the time as closing any further investigations (and exhumations) of El Mozote and similar cases.

Despite the amnesty, relatives of the victims of the El Mozote massacre and other incidents of human rights violations around the country have consistently demanded further exhumations. Finally, in the past two years, several changes have created a political climate more conducive to such exhumations. As a result, *Tutela Legal* again petitioned the judiciary for further exhumations at El Mozote. The new president of the Supreme Court supported this request and ruled that the families of victims have the right to recover the remains of their relatives.

Since 2000, at the request of *Tutela Legal*, the EAAF has conducted further exhumations at El Mozote and surrounding villages. These missions have entailed a total of five months of field and laboratory work. We are working with and providing training for doctors and dentists from the Medical Legal Institute so that they can eventually do similar work in other cases related to the civil war. Our most immediate priority is to assist the relatives of the victims in their long search for the remains of their loved ones. But the findings of the investigation will help clarify the historical record concerning one of the most discussed and contested events in recent Salvadoran history. Moreover, by gaining acceptance into the Salvadoran courts, forensic anthropological evidence may also contribute to strengthening democratic and judicial institutions by providing new tools to uphold the rule of law.

Ethiopia: The Kotebe Case

Historical Background

During its seventeen years in power, the former Ethiopian regime, known as the Dergue, compiled one of the worst records of human rights abuses in recent history. According to Human Rights Watch reports, under the leadership of Colonel Mengistu Haile Mariam, state security forces tortured and executed thousands of persons suspected of belonging to urban opposition movements, while the military killed tens of thousands during indiscriminate campaigns against counterrevolutionary individuals and groups in rural areas. The Dergue also bore large responsibility for exacerbating and perpetuating the famine that killed an estimated one million persons during the mid-1980s.

In 1991, the Dergue was overthrown and a transitional government formed. As one of its first acts, it announced that it would formally prosecute members of the former regime who had committed human rights violations and hundreds of members of the former regime were arrested. To investigate and prosecute their alleged crimes, a Special Prosecutor's Office (SPO) was created. Since then, a new constitution established the country as a federal republic. Although there have been improvements, Ethiopia continues to have serious human rights problems. Nevertheless, the work of the SPO continues and, at their request, EAAF has conducted missions to Ethiopia in 1993, 1994, and 1996 to investigate mass graves containing the victims of the Dergue.

Case History

During our 1994 mission, we found ourselves inside a military intelligence compound in Kotebe, an Addis Ababa suburb, where the SPO asked us to investigate a clandestine grave where he suspected some Dergue victims were buried. The spot we were excavating was in a remote corner of the compound. Under two meters of heavy rocks, a layer of lime, and another of blankets, the first bones appeared. Over the next few days, the commingled skeletons of thirty individuals came to light. The skulls of many were broken by the huge stones used to close the grave. Even more curious was another finding: Encircling the disarticulated cervical vertebra of all but one of the skeletons was a lime-green nylon cord. The skeletons were brought to the morgue of the Black Lion Hospital in Addis Ababa. There, with the assistance of the morgue director, Mr. Ato Abebe Debosch and a group of doctors and archaeologists, the bones were examined in detail.

The SPO provided us with a list of thirty men thought to be in the grave. All had disappeared after being taken into custody by the Dergue. Through the SPO, we obtained antemortem information on fifteen of the victims after interviewing family members and/or former prisoners. Until they disappeared in 1979, the victims had been imprisoned for periods varying from several months to several years. Some had been held in Combolcha Prison in Wollo Province and the others in Makalewi Prison in Addis Ababa. During their imprisonment their relatives had been able to visit them frequently to bring them food and clean clothing. But toward the end of 1979, they were told that further visits were unnecessary since the prisoners were no longer there.

We were also able to interview several former prisoners of both prisons at the time of the disappearances. Those in Combolcha said that on October 7, 1979, an official from Addis Ababa arrived with a list of twenty-two prisoners to be transferred to Makalewi. They were loaded onto a truck but at the last moment two (including one of our interviewees) were ordered back to their cells. The truck left Combolcha with the remaining twenty men, none of whom ever returned.

The former Makalewi prisoners said that late on the night of October 7, a truck arrived in the prison compound and twenty prisoners were offloaded. The night was cold and many of the new prisoners had wrapped themselves in blankets. They were put in holding cells apart from the main cellblock. The next morning, at 10–20 minute intervals, the guards called out each of the twenty new prisoners by name and, one by one, they were marched away. Ten Makalewi prisoners were similarly called out and taken away. The thirty men never returned, and by late afternoon rumors began to circulate that they had all been executed.

Identification

At this point, aside from the October 7 date, we had no evidence that the men taken from Combolcha were the same as those brought to Makalewi. At the time, thousands of people were being held in prisons throughout Ethiopia. But we later found a clue that the men were indeed the Combolcha transferees when we compared the statements of the former Makalewi prisoners with those given by the relatives of the missing men. One of the Makalewi inmates, Lt. Colonel L. A. said that when the men who had arrived the night before were called out the next morning, he heard the name of a man he knew, Master Sergeant K. A. W. Shortly afterward, he saw the sergeant being brought along the corridor outside his cell. The sergeant's father stated that his son was arrested in 1977 and first detained in Makalewi. One of his fellow prisoners said that he and the sergeant were part of a group of twenty-six inmates transferred to Combolcha in December 1978. Taken together, these statements firmly linked the twenty Combolcha transferees with the ten from Makalewi who disappeared on October 8, 1979.

Eight individuals were positively identified based on antemortem data collected from families and fellow prisoners. These identifications made us fairly confident that the relatives of the seven families we had interviewed were very likely somewhere among the twenty-two unidentified skeletons. Once again, we asked Dr. Mary Claire King to perform DNA tests on the unidentified individuals.

However, before she could proceed, she needed control samples to determine the frequency of specific gene sequences in the population. From this, the probability of positive identification can be accurately estimated. The missing men belonged to four Ethiopian ethnic groups: Amharic, Tigrayan, Oromo, and Guragee. Blood samples were taken from thirty members of each group. These, along with blood from the maternal relatives of the seven families and two teeth from each unidentified skeleton were submitted to Dr. King.

At her laboratory, Dr. Michele Harvey was able to make five additional identifications, bringing the total to thirteen.

Cause of Death

Of the thirty Kotebe skeletons, twenty-nine were found with knotted ligatures encircling their cervical vertebrae. A single, loosened ligature was also found within the grave and it seems likely that it was used to strangle the thirtieth victim but, for some reason, was removed prior to burial. The ligatures were made from lime-green nylon rope 8 mm in diameter. Despite fifteen years of burial, this material showed few signs of deterioration due to soil moisture or chemicals. They had been cut to a near-uniform length of about 160 centimeters. After being cut from the parent stock, their ends had been heat-fused to prevent fraying. In twelve, simple overhand knots had been tied close to the ends, possibly to provide the executioner(s) with a better grip. The ligatures were applied by looping the cords around the neck and securing them with a square ("reef") knot.

The inside circumference of the ligature loops averaged 28.7 ± 1.6 centimeters. Some indication of the amount of cervical constriction this represents is gained by comparing it with the average neck circumference in the living. To do this, we measured the neck circumference of forty adult Ethiopian males between twenty and thirty years old. The mean neck circumference of this sample was 34.6 ± 1.90 centimeters. Thus, the circumferences of the loops averaged about 6 cm less than those of the necks in the living. This difference is statistically significant (Student's t = 13.737, 68df, p < .0001). To gain some idea of the constriction this entails, try buttoning a 14 1/2 shirt collar on a person who normally wears a size 17 collar.

Dried cutaneous tissue was tightly adherent to the inner margins of some of the ligature loops. When removed from the ligature, these skin fragments revealed deep impressions of the nylon cordage, providing evidence that great force was used in applying and knotting the ligatures. Twelve skeletons showed perimortem blunt force injuries ranging from simple nasal fractures to complete fractures of the bones of the extremities. Most likely, these were inflicted in attempts to subdue or restrain the victims at the time of execution.

Death from ligature strangulation is the result of pressure on the vascular and respiratory structures of the neck. The exact mechanism of death depends on the amount of force applied. The thin-walled jugular veins can be occluded with as little as 2 kg of force resulting in loss of consciousness in 1–3 minutes and death within 5–10 minutes. Forces in the range of 4–8 kg cause carotid artery compression, followed by loss of consciousness in less than a minute and death within 3–5 minutes. Obstruction of the airway, which requires about 15 kg of force in adults, is only rarely a factor in ligature strangulation.

The cords encircling the cervical vertebrae provided clear evidence that the men had been killed by strangulation. These nylon cords were remarkably well preserved after fifteen years in the grave. This was fortunate from a medicolegal standpoint, since, had the executioner(s) chosen to use ligatures made of natural fiber, it is likely that they would have disappeared, leaving no clue as to the cause of death.

DNA and Human Rights

Telling the family of a *desaparecido* that we have determined that a skeleton we have examined is indeed that of their loved one is never easy. But, at least, such an outcome offers some solace for both of us: We have solved another puzzle and the family can mark the end of a painful quest. Even in a case where the evidence excludes the victim, hope is not extinguished, for perhaps his or her bones will be revealed in the next grave we explore. So, in a way, the most difficult cases we have are those in which we must conclude that the evidence available is insufficient to give a firm answer one way or the other and, with this uncertainty, we must put the bones back in their box for storage. This was often the situation we faced in Argentina when we first began our work. Today we face it less frequently, thanks to DNA.

It began in 1984, when the Grandmothers of the Plaza de Mayo contacted AAAS and asked Eric Stover a single, stunningly simple question, but one that apparently had never been asked before: "If you can do paternity testing, why can't you do *grandpaternity* testing?" Stover contacted human geneticist Mary Claire King at the University of California and invited her to be part of the 1984 AAAS forensic science delegation to Argentina.

When she arrived, Dr. King found that the problem the grandmothers posed was another tragic legacy of the *Junta*. In some cases, older children were killed but many under two or three years of age were passed out to police or military families unable to have children to raise as their own. The same fate awaited the infants of female detainees who were found to be pregnant; these women were kept alive until their babies were delivered and then executed. By 1984, the Grandmothers had already located 172 children they suspected had been abducted (CONADEP 1986, 299) but were faced with the problem of how to prove it.

At that time, DNA identification methods had not been developed so Dr. King tackled the problem by using blood group antigens along with human lymphocyte antigen (HLA). Taken together, the genotypic combinations were sufficiently unique that children could be identified as descendents of a particular set of grandparents with a high degree of probability. The genetic evidence could also be used to show that the children could not be the natural offspring of the parents who harbored them.

Beginning around 1990, it was demonstrated that mitochondrial and nuclear DNA could be recovered from skeletal remains, providing another major breakthrough for human rights investigation (Boles et al. 1995; Hagelberg et al. 1989; Stoneking et al. 1991). This allowed identification of the dead through DNA comparisons with their living relatives. Dr. King performed these tests *pro bono* in cases involving human rights victims. In 1991, the Manfil case (see above) was the first in Argentina to be resolved with DNA, thanks to the joint efforts of Drs. King and Hagelberg. Since then we have been able to get positive identifications using DNA in more cases in Argentina, Guatemala, Ethiopia, and Haiti.

Unfortunately, DNA has not solved all of our problems. First, we must still track down relatives of victims to obtain blood samples. This is not always easy. The complexity of the system of repression in Argentina, for example, means we must do a great deal of historical research before we can form a hypothetical match between a particular skeleton and a given family. In some countries, we have found, families have become scattered and displaced—often as refugees in other countries. In others, notably El Salvador and Guatemala, the pattern of repression often involved the massacre of entire villages so that whole families were wiped out.

As a partial solution to this problem in Argentina, EAAF started collecting blood samples from the relatives of *desaparecidos* in 1998. With these samples, we have established a genetic database that we can use for identification. It enables us to conduct genetic analyses on unidentified skeletons already exhumed and it will be available in the future when, through emigration or death, relatives are no longer available.

Also, as DNA testing becomes less time consuming and expensive, we will be able to accelerate our efforts. This approach will be important in other countries as well. For example, in our ongoing investigations in Zimbabwe where, due to AIDS (current estimates are that about 25 percent of the adult population is HIV positive), the likelihood that relatives will be available to provide samples as remains are exhumed is smaller than in other places.

This brings us to a final problem: DNA analysis is still costly and time consuming. Presently, we must depend on services kindly donated by genetic laboratories in the United States and Great Britain and, unfortunately, can take only a few cases at a time. The lack of immediate access to DNA analysis and the length of time it requires can present dilemmas in human rights cases.

Sometimes, for example, there is important circumstantial evidence for identification. For example, in El Salvador, relatives were often able to bury their family members together in a single grave. Thus, these survivors not only knew the locations of these "family" mass graves but who was in them. In these cases, exhumation revealed, let us say, an adult male and a female skeleton corresponding in age, stature, and other characteristics to the father and mother, and the skeletons of several immature individuals matching in number, age, and sex to the family sibship. The relatives might also be able to identify the few personal effects, such as jewelry, clothing, or even children's toys found in the grave. Thus, while we might not be able to positively identify these victims or perhaps distinguish between two like-sex siblings close in age without DNA testing, we can say with confidence that we have identified the family.

Given the current state of resources in Argentina, if we use DNA testing, we can expect results in about a year. We face similar dilemmas in other countries—whether or not to encourage DNA testing, knowing that it might delay reburial for another year. Of course, in cases where our evidence may be used in court to prosecute the alleged perpetrators, we must insist that every forensic means available, including DNA, be used to establish positive identification. But in some countries, where immunity or amnesty laws protect the perpetrators and there is no judicial will to pursue the guilty, we must ask ourselves: Is genetic identification advisable?

Our approach, whenever possible, is to give the relatives the choice after explaining the delay and potential complications. In the El Mozote case, the relatives had no doubts: They didn't want to wait any longer because they knew where they themselves had buried their family members. They did not mind that we could not identify each of the skeletons in each grave, and they chose to rebury them all together.

The Role of Anthropologists in Human Rights Investigations

Forensic anthropologists have played an important role in human rights investigations during the last two decades. Prior to the *Junta* trials in Argentina, such investigations relied generally only on witness testimony and documentary evidence. The introduction of scientific evidence provided a new dimension. Since then, judicatory bodies ranging from national courts to the UN War Crime Tribunals have recognized and accepted forensic scientific evidence as a valuable tool in the pursuit of justice.

Although many forensic sciences (e.g., pathology, odontology, genetics, criminalistics) contribute to these investigations, forensic anthropology generally plays a central role. Forensic anthropology applies the physical anthropologist's knowledge of human skeletal biology to medicolegal problems. Beyond this specialized focus, however, most of us, particularly those schooled in the "four field" tradition, have had academic training, and, often, some fieldwork in archaeology and cultural anthropology. This enables us to bring a unique combination of skills and experience to cases involving human rights abuse. As we have seen, the victims of such abuses are often buried anonymously in common, and often clandestine, graves. Thus, a grounding in archaeology can be used in finding and excavating graves that may contain the commingled bones of many victims. Also, our training in cultural anthropology provides us with some insight and sensitivity in dealing with families and communities oppressed by the violence. This is especially valuable when those affected belong to non-Western societies.

Forensic investigations of human rights violations have several objectives. One is to collect, preserve, and objectively interpret physical evidence that might be used to bring the perpetrators to justice. This, of course, is not always possible, especially when the political and judicial will necessary to vigorously pursue such cases is lacking or when various forms of amnesty are implemented to protect the perpetrators. Yet, even in these situations, we are able to carry out a second objective by firmly documenting that the crimes were committed by entering the evidence into the historical record. Solidly based and objectively presented scientific evidence is difficult to refute. Confronted with such evidence, those who would like to "paper over" the crimes find it hard to do. For example, in Argentina, some apologists for the *Junta* claimed that most of the disappeared simply fled the country and were living anonymously elsewhere. But, when mass graves yielded positively identified *desaparecidos* with single gunshot wounds to the back of the head, it was no longer possible to argue that he or she was living comfortably in, say, Mexico City or Paris. Thus, by setting the record straight, science can serve history by protecting it from revisionists.

A third objective of our work is its potential deterrent effect. Forensic evidence strengthens legal cases and, as international human rights law is applied more broadly, repressive regimes may perhaps have second thoughts about committing human rights abuses.

Finally, and, in the long run, perhaps most important, we are often able to give some solace to the families by finding and returning the bones, thereby helping them to end their painful quests and heal the wounds caused by cruel uncertainty.

Acknowledgments

EAAF is currently made up of nine persons specializing in medicine, archaeology, physical and social anthropology, computers, and law. Current members are: Patricia Bernardi, Daniel Bustamante, Mercedes Doretti, Luis Fondebrider, Anahi Ginarte, Rafael Mazzella, Dario Olmo, Silvana Turner, and Carlos Somigliana. Board members (other than the members mentioned): Gustavo Politis and Sofia Tiscornia. Clyde Snow and Eric Stover are honorary members. Volunteers: Claudia Visso, Miguel Nievas, and Sofia Egaña. Consultants: Laura Roush, Pedro Linger, Elena Arengo, Elizabeth Ferry, Jennifer Burrell, and Robin LeBaron. Visit our website at <http://www.eaaf.org.ar>.

References

Boles, T. C., Clyde C. Snow, and Eric Stover. 1995. Forensic DNA testing on skeletal remains from mass graves: A pilot project in Guatemala. *Journal of Forensic Sciences* 40:349–356.

Bonner, Raymond. 1982. Massacre of hundreds reported in Salvador village. *New York Times*. January 27.

Bonner, Raymond. 1984. *Weakness and Deceit: U.S. Policy and El Salvador*. New York: New York Times Books.

Doretti, Mercedes, Luis Fondebrider, Patricia Bernardi, and Anahi Ginarte. 1994. *Kotebe Archaeological Report*. Special Prosecution Office of Addis Ababa, Ethiopia.

Dworkin, R. 1986. Introduction to *Nunca Más*. In *Nunca Más: The Report of the Argentine National Commission on the Disappeared*, ed. E. Sábato. New York: Farrar Straus Giroux.

Fondebrider, Luis, Patricia Bernardi, and Mercedes Doretti. 1993. *Archaeological Report on Site 1 of El Mozote*. New York: United Nations Truth Commission for El Salvador.

Guillermoprieto, Alma. 1982. Salvadoran peasants describe mass killing: Woman tells of children's death. *Washington Post*. January 27.

Hagelberg, E., B. Sykes, and R. Hedges. 1989. Ancient bone DNA amplified. *Nature* 342:485.

CONADEP, The National Commission on Disappeared People. 1986. *Nunca Mas*. London: Faber and Faber.

Scott, Douglas. 1993. *Firearm identification of the El Mozote execution site*. New York: United Nations Truth Commission for El Salvador.

Simpson, J., and J. Bennett. 1985. *The Disappeared and the Mothers of the Plaza*. New York: St. Martin's Press.

Snow, Clyde C. 1984. Sex, age, and other statistical characteristics of the *Desaparecidos*. Comisión Nacional sobre la Desaparición de Personas. Buenos Aires, Argentina.

Snow, Clyde C., and M. J. Bihurriet. 1992. The epidemiology of homicide: *Ningun Nombre* burials in the Province of Buenos Aires from 1970 to 1984. In *Human Rights and Statistics: Getting the Record Straight*, ed. T. B. Jabine and R. P. Claude. Philadelphia, PA: University of Pennsylvania Press.

Snow, Clyde C. 1994. *Observation on Human Skeletal remains excavated from Grave 1, Kotebe, Ethiopia. Part one: Identification. Part Two: Cause of Death*. Special Prosecutors Office of Addis Ababa, Ethiopia.

Snow, Clyde C., Robert H. Kirschner, and John H. Fitzpatrick. 1993. *Laboratory Report on Site 1 of El Mozote*. New York: United Nations Truth Commission on El Salvador.

Stoneking, Mark, D. Hedgecock, R. G. Higuchi, L. Vigilant, and H. A. Erlich. 1991. Population variation of human mtDNA control region sequences detected by enzymatic amplification and sequence-specific oligonucleotide probes. *American Journal of Human Genetics* 48:370–382.